David McGee

Go, Cat, Go!

THE LIFE AND TIMES

OF CARL PERKINS,

THE KING

OF ROCKABILLY

CARL PERKINS

AND DAVID McGEE

Go, Cat, Go!

HYPERION

New York

Song permissions and credits begin on p. 435.

Library of Congress Cataloging-in-Publication Data
McGee, David, 1948–
    Go, cat, go! : the life and times of Carl Perkins, the king of rockabilly / by David McGee with Carl Perkins. —1st ed.
      p.   cm.
    Includes discography and bibliographical references.
    ISBN 0-7868-6073-1 (alk. paper)
    1. Perkins, Carl, 1932—   . 2. Rock musicians—United States—Biography. 3. Rockabilly music—History and criticism.
    I. Perkins, Carl, 1932—   . II. Title.
    ML420.P453M34   1996
    782.42166'092—dc20
    [B]   95-31917
                                       CIP
                                     MN

Book design by Karolina Harris

FIRST EDITION
10 9 8 7 6 5 4 3 2 1

THIS BOOK IS DEDICATED TO THE TWO WOMEN
OF MY LIFE.
TO MY MOTHER, WHO DID WITHOUT TO FEED HER
KIDS AND WHO LOVED ME SO.
REST IN PEACE. I LOVE YOU, MOM.
TO MY WIFE, VAL, WHO HAS ALWAYS BELIEVED
IN ME AND HAS BEEN THE DRIVING FORCE
BEHIND WHATEVER IT IS THAT I AM.
MAY I ALWAYS HAVE YOU, VAL, AND OUR KIDS.
ALL MY LOVE, CARL.

FOR MY MOTHER,
OMA ELIZABETH NIX MCGEE
1911–1994
WITH ETERNAL LOVE

Here, gentle reader,
Make a moment's pause
Think how precious each life's joy
See Nature's bloom disrob'd by nature's cause
And death releasing what it can't destroy

—INSCRIPTION ON AN EIGHTEENTH-CENTURY TOMBSTONE
IN MILLERTON, NEW YORK

CONTENTS

ACKNOWLEDGMENTS

My old guitar has taken me to many places most folks only get to visit in their dreams. I've played my music everywhere from rural porches in west Tennessee all the way to the White House; before heads of state, inmates, truck drivers, doctors, factory workers, teachers, businessmen and -women, and people of all ages, color, and size. I've played my guitar and sung my song, anticipating the moment when I would see the first foot begin to pat in rhythm with my beat. My heart begins to race, and a thrill takes over my soul that ignites my very being—as much today as it did that day over fifty years ago when I sang "Home on the Range" for my first big audience, the kids at school. As great as the thrill is to be able to travel around the world doing what I love, I have to admit the greatest thrill in my life occurs every Thanksgiving Day at my home in Jackson, Tennessee.

Before the sun has had time to burn the clouds away, my wife, Val, and I are up to finish preparing the dinner she began two days before. Every year she says this will be the last time she cooks this much food, and every year she just keeps cooking more. There's not a lot she will let me do to help her, except for frying the country ham. Our only daughter, Debbie, arrives shortly. She and Val truly are best friends, who work so well together in the kitchen because they seem to be able to read each other's minds. And soon, Bart, Debbie's husband, is drawn from their home two doors down by the smell of the country ham cooking. I believe Bart Swift loves country ham better than anybody I know. They have one child, Suzy, who one day wants to be a lawyer, and possibly even a judge. Bart dreams of the day he can franchise Suede's Restaurant across the world, and I think Debbie would be content to dig in her flowers all day long. Their dreams are big, but not impossible. I'm living proof dreams can come true.

Our oldest son, Stan, his wife, Connie, and their three girls—Lesleigh, Carla, and Shannon—usually get here before Bart has sneaked too much of the country ham. (Stan also likes country ham!) Shannon and her husband, Chris, made Val and me great-grandparents with the birth of their son, Hayden. They are expecting another child in March. This is the second marriage for Stan and Connie, and they seem very happy. It is ironic that Connie was the first girl Stan ever went out with, and after many years they found each other again.

Greg, his wife, Dawn, and their seven-year-old son, Jay Paul, always come. Greg loves good food and enjoys Thanksgiving as much as anyone. (Thank goodness he likes all food and not just ham!) Jay always heads for the backyard looking for a baseball he can knock over the fence.

The gathering would not be complete without Steve, our middle son, his wife, Donna, and their four boys. Steve made a choice many years ago to leave the music business to me and his brothers. He chose to become a draftsman and has made me very proud to be his father. Donna is also a draftsperson, and she and Steve work together. They spend the rest of their time keeping up with Jonathon, Matthew, Cody, and Chase.

At straight up twelve o'clock Val calls us to dinner. We gather together around the table, joining hands. It is then I realize, as I look into the eyes of my family, the reality of my life. There is no thrill anywhere on this earth that compares to what I feel at that moment. I offer thanks to God for all this and more. Before I finish the prayer I can feel two big brown eyes staring at me. I open my eyes to find my youngest grandson, Chase, smiling mischievously at me. As I look around the table, I am always reminded by the faces I see that this is what life is all about. This is what Carl Perkins is all about. Family. My music will always be a part of my soul, but my love for my family is the foundation of my soul. There's no place like Thanksgiving Day at home in Jackson, Tennessee.

Carl Perkins
Thanksgiving 1995

Conventional wisdom holds that a biographer should never become friends with his or her subject. I thought this good advice, until I met Carl Perkins. Looking back, I wonder how we could have failed to forge a friendship.

From the moment of our first meeting, when I interviewed him for *Rolling Stone* in February of 1990, I felt an immediate connection to Carl. Even though we are of different generations, there is much common ground between us. We were both born of poor southern families that worked the land; both had strong mothers and sometimes irresponsible fathers (although Buck Perkins never hopped a freight out of town, abandoning his family, as did William McGee); both had older brothers who were the best sort of role models and died young; both are essentially loners who are most comfortable with longtime friends and disdainful of the public arena, although both of us must enter it from time to time to make our living. I could go on, but the telling fact is in the pages of Sam Phillips's Sun Records recording logs. In researching Carl's recording history, I discovered that he had recorded "Blue Suede Shoes" on December 19, 1955—my seventh birthday. Without even knowing that fact, Carl's wife, the ever-perceptive, always-blunt, uncommonly beautiful Valda, told Carl, after I had left their house following the *Rolling Stone* session, "You're going to see that writer again. God sent him here for a reason."

Carl did indeed see me again, perhaps, in retrospect, more than he had wished at the outset. In our interviews, I took him through his story chronologically, and as the years fell away amazing scenes were re-created in my mind's eye. The retelling of Carl's life brought countless moments of raucous, joyous laughter, as well as gut-wrenching ones that found us weeping openly. Whether we were laughing, crying, or merely straightening out the world's problems in deeply philosophical ruminations, we were sharing unabashedly our most fundamental beliefs. The man sitting across from me those one hundred hours spoke frankly of his alcoholism and the devastating effects it had had on his family and on his career; of opportunities he should have seized, but didn't, and for which failing he blames only himself; of his struggle to be a better husband and father to the people he loves most; of his troubled road to spiritual enlightenment. In other words, the man sitting across from me committing these thoughts to tape was on his way to being a fully realized human being, one not without flaws, but striving to grow every day.

A thousand miles of hard road now separates me from Carl and Valda, but they are always with me. To thank them seems inadequate to the task of expressing what's in my heart when I reflect on one of the most remarkable and soul-shaking journeys I have ever taken.

Along the way Carl and Valda's children and their spouses became part of this journey, and to them goes my heartfelt gratitude for extending to me the same courtesies as their parents did. They invited me into their homes, fed me, confided in me, and never failed to make me feel welcome.

This journey began in January of 1990 with a phone call from Fred Goodman, then an editor at *Rolling Stone,* who offered an assignment to interview Carl for a special issue on rock's first decade. When the interview grew into a book, Fred, who was a sensitive and sympathetic editor of the original, weighty transcript, maintained regular contact with me, even after he left *Rolling Stone.* He is an important part of this effort, and I am grateful for his friendship.

The suggestion that I would be the appropriate writer for the Carl Perkins piece came from Anthony DeCurtis, then *Rolling Stone*'s reviews editor and now editorial director at VH-1. There isn't space enough here to express my appreciation for all he has given me throughout our long friendship or for his note-perfect observations on this book's narrative line as it took shape.

While tendering thank you's to *Rolling Stone* colleagues, I would be remiss in ignoring *Rolling Stone* press editor Holly George-Warren. Every writer who is fortunate enough to meet Holly comes away with the same feeling: Her unbridled enthusiasm for rock 'n' roll—particularly the roots musics that are closest to my own heart—reminds us why we do what we do. In a sense, this book begins with my work on the third edition of the *Rolling Stone Album Guide*, for which she and Anthony DeCurtis served as my editors.

Much love and gratitude go to my agent, Sarah Lazin, yet another former *Rolling Stone* colleague, but one who was a friend years before I approached her about representing *Go, Cat, Go!* She was there every step of the way with her impeccable sense of when and how to push, when to criticize, and when to praise. This book would not be what it is without her steady hand guiding it along the way.

I cannot fail to thank *Rolling Stone* founder-publisher-editor Jann Wenner. His brainchild has given me a platform for my musings on music for the past twenty-one years, during which time his demand for excellence in the written (and edited) word has been a constant source of inspiration.

Paul Gallo, publisher of *Pro Sound News*, gave me a professional home in 1988 when I needed it most, and was patient with and supportive of me throughout this project. He has earned, in spades, the ultimate Carl Perkins accolade, "He's as good a man as ever put on a pair of shoes."

Also, my sincere appreciation of and admiration for the entire *Pro Sound News* staff, some of whom took on extra assignments when the book work became most demanding of my time. To Gina Costa, Tom DiNome, Erin Edman, Brian Merges, Andrea Rotondo, Joseph Spiegel, Tim Wetmore, Clive Young, and Joy Zaccaria, thank you for understanding.

My editors at Hyperion have been a blessing. First, Mary Anne Naples read the original manuscript and offered several suggestions for bringing an overlong tome into publishable length. Patricia Mulcahy become a tireless advocate for *Go, Cat, Go!* With clarity and sensitivity, she worked me through some difficult edits fairly painlessly, no mean feat given my sense of this as a cause mounted on behalf of an artist whose work had yet to be properly recognized.

I am indebted to Patricia Romanowski for her sure hand on the final, arduous edit—delicate surgery, to be sure. Every step of the way she demonstrated a keen concern for the integrity of the story as we compressed or deleted scenes to get the book down to size with the most salient points intact.

To all those who carved time out of their busy schedules in order to sit still for interviews goes my unending gratitude. Of these I must single out Johnny Cash, Naomi Judd, and Bill Denny for actions above and beyond the call of duty. Apart from out initial interviews, they were always available to me when I needed to check facts, track down photographs, or seek assistance in securing other important interviews.

A special thank you goes to Jim Bailey, one of Carl's best friends, who jumped into this project and became my right-hand man without portfolio. On three memorable occasions he invited me and my sons into his home, where he gave us food and shelter while we poured over his treasure trove of Perkins memorabilia. Many of the rarest photographs in this book come from his collection, and he proved indispensable in the research for an up-to-date Perkins discography. I'm right there with Carl in regarding him as one of the finest, most honorable men I've ever met.

Also, Pam Nash, executive director of the Exchange Club Carl Perkins Center for the Prevention of Child Abuse, graciously explained the Center's history, provided details of its fundraising activities, eloquently articulated its mandate, and outlined its plans for the future.

I might still be writing *Go, Cat, Go!* were it not for the diligent work done early on by my research assistant, Andrea Odintz, who uncovered some key articles and books I needed for background and helped expedite the organization of my interview files into a coherent directory. Later, Nancy Rosen came through with some eleventh-hour fact checking that proved critical to the accuracy of certain scenes early in Carl's career. Special thanks as well to Jack Darrel Wood of the Jackson Madison County Library, who came in on one of his days off and guided me through various reference materials relating to the remarkable history of Bemis, Tennessee.

Along the way many offered counsel, pep talks, and their unwavering belief in me and in the fruitful outcome of this project. I am blessed to call them friends: Mary Baruffi; Gary Belz of Kiva Recording Studio in Memphis; Rich Carpenter ("Hum-babe!") and family; Nikki and Art Collins; Riva Danzig; John Fry of Ardent Recording in Memphis; Renee Grant-Williams; Michael Grotticelli; Alan Jaffe; Howard Levitt of BMI; Susan Levy; Kathleen Mackay; Ira Mayer; Greg McCutcheon; Brian McKernan; Martin Porter; Willi Pittman of the Memphis Music and Blues Museum; Robert Rolontz; Lynn Rosen; Glenn Rosenstein; Mike Sigman, publisher of *L.A. Weekly;* Chip Stern; Bubba Sullivan of the Blues Corner in Helena, Arkansas; Carl ("What do I care? I'm gonna be outta this business in five years anyway") Tatz of Recording Arts in Nashville; and Stan Vincent. And always, Sally Nachamkin, my favorite country girl.

And where would I be without the Pros from Dover, who know how to crack a guy's chest and get out on the golf course before noon? To Jack Rosenberger, Michael MacAvennie, Brian Merges, and John Moore, I say, thank you, men. Thank you.

Every step of the way this journey has been shared by my oldest and dearest friends, the Tulsa crew: Gary Hamilton, Larry Gibson, Michael Rowley, and honorary Tulsan Jonathan Skiba. Thanks for the dreams, thanks for the laughs, thanks for the love, thanks for believing. It's been a hell of a party, hasn't it?

If there is anyone apart from Carl without whom this book would not exist, it is my mother. It had always been my dream that she would live to see my name on a book. Tragically, she died on September 9, 1994. However, her spirit informs much of the text, none moreso than part 1, "Cotton Patch Blues," for which she provided valuable background on the sharecropper's life and culture, gleaned from her own harsh childhood in the fields of Arkansas and Alabama. Alone among my friends, I was encouraged in my childhood passion for rock 'n' roll, thanks to her. As she put it in later years, "When you were listening to those records, I always knew where you were." Now that's sensible, loving parenting. Moreover, she espoused the principles of tolerance and compassion for others; raised in a violent, segregationist culture, she rose above that to teach in our home the lesson that a person's character, not color, is what counts, and then put this philosophy into practical application in her own life. I hope I am half as good as she was.

Finally, and most important, my sons Travis and Kieran shared this book as an idea and lived it with me as it became reality, as they do virtually every other aspect of my life. I am less of man without them, a better man because of them. I love you, guys. And that's forever.

David McGee

AUTHOR'S NOTE

I n large part *Go, Cat, Go!* is the result of some one hundred hours of interviews with Carl Perkins. Lest the reader be confused, Carl did not set pen to paper—or fingers to keyboard, as it were—but his active participation was so substantial as to warrant him being given a co-author credit. It was his and my intent from the start that this be a biography, rather than an as-told-to book, so that other interviews and my critical perspective on the body of his work would produce a broad, deep portrait of a rock 'n' roll pioneer's life, music, and times—hence the third-person narrative. However, Carl's reflections on the big themes in his life were so compelling that I constructed "The Voice of Carl Perkins" sections as a way for Carl, in the first person, to step out-side the linear chronology and address the impact specific events had ~ping the man described herein. These unexpurgated reflections ~elieve, to understand more fully the source of his resiliency ~rying times. What more to add, save Carl's own words: to think, when something's right it's just flat right?"

David McGee
Fall 1995

He really stood for freedom. That whole sound stood for all the degrees of freedom. It would just jump right off that turntable; live, it would create such a thump in your belly, you know. Everything—the vocabulary of the lyrics and the sound of the instruments. Where I particularly came from I don't know a lot of people who listened to it; I think myself and a few of my mates were definitely in the minority. But it made us feel less like wanderers around, that there was definitely a sun out there and a moon and there were celestial elements to life that were being expressed in just a small group of people, like Carl; I guess you could just about count 'em on one hand. It was everything. It was almost like another party in the room. It was coming from somewhere that we wanted to go; we wanted to go where that was happening. As opposed to a record on the radio where it might sound nice, but it doesn't give you any answers or make you think that there are any really. Or any other place to go besides the place you're perfectly adapted to.

—BOB DYLAN

1

COTTON PATCH BLUES

"Hello, my name is Carl Perkins. I am a sharecropper's son. I work very hard for what I have to eat, and a place to stay warm in the winter. My favorite fruit is the orange, although I don't get very many oranges. I love my Mama and Daddy, and my two brothers, Jay and Clayton. And I don't want to grow up to be a man like Hitler. Someday I want to be a big radio star. Thank you. Carl Perkins."

Lake County
1932–1946

"*the river's comin', Buck! Get your wife and them boys! The river's comin'!"* Jolted from the deep sleep he'd fallen into after retiring a bit past sundown, Buck Perkins leaped from under his covers, his gangly five-foot-ten, 150-pound frame landing on the cold floor of his three-room pine-board shack with a thud that rousted his sleeping wife, Louise. He slipped into his overalls while warning her of the oncoming flood. Their three boys, seven-year-old Jay, five-year-old Carl, and two-year-old Clayton (sandwiched between his brothers so he wouldn't roll off the bed), were asleep on the other side of the cotton sheet that served as the shack's sole partition dividing the adults' quarters from the children's.

Thin, plain-faced Louise threw a ragged dress over her diminutive frame, wrapped baby Clayton in a blanket, and pulled together some personal belongings. Proficient at performing several tasks simultaneously, she was also trying to awaken two children who, once asleep, were tough to rouse. "Boys!" she cried as Carl and Jay slowly opened their eyes. Carl was momentarily confused by the commotion; his sense of the moment, filtered through the narrow prism of five years' experience in the world, was that some terrible, incomprehensible trouble lay ahead.

"Get you some clothes!" Louise instructed in a strong but frantic tone. "Just put 'em in them pillowcases, just take the pillows out of them pillowcases and put you some clothes in them! The river's comin'!"

Suddenly wide-eyed, Jay and Carl hustled, slipping into their threadbare jeans and shirts while packing what little else they owned in the way of clothing. Buck was out firing up his wheezing old Ford; only minutes later Louise followed with Clayton in tow. Carl and Jay straggled behind, each toting a pillowcase lumpy with shirts and pants while balancing on their shoulders their rolled-up cotton mattress. Louise sat in the front passenger's seat with Clayton in her lap; Carl and Jay positioned the mattress between them in the back seat and rested their heads on it as Buck pulled out onto the muddy dirt road and headed for higher ground. As the Ford sputtered away and the Perkins shack receded in the distance, Carl raised his head to see the waters of the Mississippi lapping at the porch.

For Buck Perkins a flood was hardly an inconsequential matter, but natural disasters described the life he knew as a member of the only white sharecropping family in Tiptonville, Tennesssee. The Perkins family was born to the earth, their fate inextricably linked to the whims of nature, to the grace of the God they believed in so fervently. Floods came with the territory, literally, and Buck and Louise would survive this one and pick up again, as the family had in the aftermath of the terrible flood of 1927; they would survive and move on as they had during droughts, as they had when boll weevils ravaged the cotton. Whatever challenge God posed for them by way of His mysterious, awesome power, the Perkinses stayed close to the land and sought guidance and solace from the Holy Bible. In the evenings, gospel songs sung by the family comforted their souls and prepared them for the next day's work. What was a flood but another of God's tests of faith? Being tested was nothing new to Buck Perkins.

He was the fifth of seven children (five boys, two girls) born to James Washington Perkins and Bettye Azilee (Scott) Perkins. His mother was stout and severe, her weathered face showing the strain of the fields and of raising a large family on limited means. His father, the son of Mr. and Mrs. Davidson Franklin Perkins, defined toughness. Lean-muscled and standing slightly more than six feet tall, James Washington projected a menacing air. Heavy brows shaded dark, beady eyes, and a thick, drooping moustache hid his lips and set his face in a permanent frown. He is remembered as the absolute ruler of his domain, brooking no dissent from anyone in the household, including in-laws.

Stubborn and hardworking, J.W. possessed as well an inherent dignity that defined the Perkins family credo. Rather than accepting the built-in inequities of the sharecropper's life, J.W. fought the system every step of the way. Like most sharecroppers, his was a migratory existence that found him moving the entire clan from farm to farm. It was a point of pride with him that he never ran away from a debt. On the same note, he stood strong for himself and his family when it came time to settle the account after the cotton was in. If J.W.'s pay came in under what he knew he had earned, he broadcast it to the landowner loud and clear. Once, when a landowner who had cheated J.W. years earlier attempted to lure him back to bring in another crop, J.W. gave him a jut-jawed response: "You know you tried to cheat me. Let's start out by saying you cannot do that. I'll bring my bunch back and we'll make a crop for you. But if there's any attempt to cheat, it won't be as easy out for you as it was before."

Once his children had married and started families, J.W. gained leverage enough in numbers to survive these twists of fate. At one time he commanded a work force numbering some fifty men, women, and children. As the supplier of so many able, tenacious workers, J.W. would demand, and receive, a higher pay rate. He was a hard case who could labor a full day in the fields, come back for dinner, go out "night riding"—a tactic employed in dispensing vigilante justice in and around the Tiptonville area—into the early morning hours, and be the first one in the field at sunrise.

Like his brothers and sisters, Buck Perkins stayed rooted in Tiptonville and close to James Washington when he left home to marry Louise Brantley, the daughter of Clarence Edward and Martha Ann (Hood) Brantley and sister of Nell, who had married Buck's brother Ernest in 1929. Buck and Louise's first son, James Buck, was born in 1930; a third son, Lloyd Clayton, was born in 1935. No particular drama attended either birth.

Such was not the case with their second son, Carl Lee, born on April 9, 1932. At that time, the Perkinses' shack was shared with Ernest, Nell, and their only child, nine-month-old Martha Lee. Louise lay on one bed giving birth to Carl with a black midwife assisting. The closest doctor was twenty-five miles away in Dyersburg and wasn't due to make rounds in Tiptonville for another three days. On another bed, parallel to Louise, was Buck, failing fast with double pneumonia. When a friend came by to visit, Ernest urged him to find a doctor for Buck, and fast.

A doctor finally arrived and delivered a grim but not hopeless prognosis: "If he lives through this day and night, he might make it."

Buck lived through the night and gradually improved. The pneumonia left its mark, though: For the rest of his life he would be given to fits of hacking and coughing, from the combined effects of smoking and a lung-scarring bout with scarlet fever during his teenage years. Still, he was cut from the same rugged cloth as his father. Out in the fields, to the horror of the other hands around him, Buck would break into a coughing jag, spit gobs of bloody sputum onto the ground and then resume picking cotton. His only medication through the years was a self-administered spoonful of coal oil and sugar. "I figure it cleans out lead pipes, it can surely clean out my ol' lungs," he would say to Louise as he gulped down another dosage.

In 1938, when he turned six, Carl began his formal education, joined the family in working the Tiptonville cotton fields, and experienced the first stirrings of music's power to move his heart. His initiation into the sharecropper's workaday life began in April, the season of planting. As the new crop took root during summer's unrelenting heat and humidity, came the chopping—twelve to fourteen hours a day of working the rows with a hoe to weed out grass that threatened to strangle crops. Chopping assaulted each worker's physical well-being: The hoe's splintered wood handle blistered palms anew each day, back muscles strained and ached, and dehydration was an ever-present threat.

Though he had hit the fields with the enthusiasm of the unitiated, Carl learned early on that youth provided little immunity from the trials of those who would work the earth. His entire body ached too, from both his chores and the fatigue that overcame him during the spring and fall, when his school day would be followed by several hours' toil in the fields. During the summer he would work an adult's shift—"from can to can't," sunrise to sunset—and gained a small measure of pride in his efforts, knowing he and his older brother Jay were being paid. Together their output was regarded as equal to that of one adult and they were paid accordingly: fifty cents apiece per day for chopping, equaling the dollar apiece his mother and father earned. With this extra income, plus credit, Louise was able to keep beans and potatoes on the table and tobacco in Buck's pocket, and every so often she would allow the boys the luxury of a five-cent bag of hard candy.

In the fields Carl made an instant friend of a gaunt, gray-haired black man with deep-set eyes and the distant gaze of one whose troubles lay too deep for tears. John Westbrook, then in his sixties, talked sparingly of himself, refrained from criticizing others, and kept his own counsel. Pride radiated in his purposeful gait, his tender voice, and his work ethic. As productive as men less than half his age, he went about his thankless labor without complaint. When his work was done, he trudged across the field, his form outlined in the faint orange glow of a fading sunset, back to his ramshackle dwelling. There he ate his beans and potatoes, and relaxed with his battered acoustic guitar, working out on its frayed strings a slow, mournful blues instrumental or a gospel song. Carl called him "Uncle John," and came to regard him not only as a hero and mentor, but as a member of the family.

When it came time to pick the cotton in the fall, Carl's mother gave him a nine-pound burlap sack onto which she had sewn a padded shoulder strap. The bag would hold nearly sixty-five pounds of cotton, and even at age six Carl was expected to fill it at least once a day. The sun had hardened cotton's spring blooms into tough, thorny shells encasing the soft white bolls. For a picker, the trick was to snatch the bolls cleanly without raking fingers across the shells' razor-sharp points. However deep and painful a cut, there was no stopping for first aid; instead, the dirt served as a dry salve, rubbed into the wound as the picker pushed on down the row.

One day as Carl stopped to study his lacerated fingers, Uncle John shuffled by slowly, chuckling. His own hands bore the scars of too many encounters with cotton plants, but he had long since mastered his craft. Now he would pass on some hard-earned wisdom.

"Let me show you somethin'," Uncle John began. "You gettin' *over* your stalk with your little arms and your hands and blockin' the view. You gonna have to go to the bottom of the stalk anyway. Now think about it, little Carlie."

"Yes, sir, that's right, Uncle John," Carl agreed.

"So you go to the bottom first, and you'll be able to see every boll 'twixt the ground and the top of that stalk. Don't fight that stalk; just bend on down and get that part of it done and and make a fluid motion out of it. Keep one hand pickin' them bolls while the other one puts 'em in the sack."

Uncle John demonstrated in a move that was logical, clean, swift, and painless. Making his way through a sea of white stretching from one end of the fields to the far horizon, he expounded on his art. "You can relax knowin' you gonna straighten up. Eventually you gonna get that kink outcha back.

"Life's that way, little Carlie. You start on the bottom as a child, you work your way up as you get older. Yes sir, you do."

Idle conversation was a rarity in the fields. Once in a while Carl would hear someone speak of the world news—"I hear they're tryin' to start a war somewhere across the water. Arguing around." This would invariably inspire someone to break out in song—gospel, or hymns like the ones Carl heard in the Baptist church every Sunday

morning. Soon everyone was raising their voices in unison, or responding to the message. Carl felt chills when he heard the plaintive
voices cry:

I'm gonna lay down my burdens
(Uh-huh)
Down by the riverside
(Oh, yes!)
Down by the riverside
Down by the riverside
I'm gonna lay down my burdens
Down by the riverside
Study war no more
(No, no!)
I ain't a-gonna study war no more
I ain't a-gonna study war no more
I ain't a-gonna study war no more

Even the saddest refrains sung in the fields eased the burden of the
long, hot days. The more Carl listened, the more comfort he found.

Gripped by the gospel sound, Carl began to take more than a passing interest in his father's favorite Saturday night radio program, the
Grand Ole Opry, emanating from Nashville's WSM station. The Opry
had gone on the air in 1925 and by the year of Carl's birth, 1932, was
in a unique position to promote country music on a national level, having acquired a clear-channel frequency and increased its power from
5,000 to 50,000 watts. Between the Opry and the occasional country-
music shows Buck would tune in—for Buck was the undisputed ar-
biter of the airwaves in the Perkins household—Carl began absorbing
the sounds of the most important of modern country music's first-generation artists: From Meridian, Mississippi, came Jimmie Rodgers.
Being as conversant with blues and pop as he was with country,
Rodgers often fused what were then considered incompatible styles (he
became the first country artist to record with a black musician when
he used jazz visionary Louis Armstrong on "Blue Yodel No. 9" in 1930,
and he also recorded with Hawaiian musicians). From Clinch Moun-

tain, Virginia, came the Carter Family—A.P, his wife Sara, and Sara's cousin Maybelle Addington (later to marry A.P.'s brother and take the Carter surname)—who transformed the commercial country market with their graceful, haunting harmonies and yearning vocal solos, while Maybelle introduced an unusual strumming-and-fingerpicking style of playing that led to the guitar being widely adopted as a lead instrument. Maynardville, Tennessee, produced Roy Acuff, who had become the undisputed king of country music upon his Opry debut in 1938, when he performed "The Great Speckled Bird," an enigmatic song rooted in an Old Testament passage from Jeremiah 12:9: "Mine heritage is unto me as a speckled bird, the birds round about are against her; come ye, assemble all the beasts of the field, come to devour."

Hearing Acuff's music prompted Carl to ask for a guitar of his own. Having no money to spend on such luxuries, Buck instead fashioned an instrument from a broom handle with an empty cigar box nailed onto one end. When a neighbor in tough straits offered to sell his used instrument for a couple of dollars, Buck scraped together the funds and gave his son a rare present. The body was dented and scratched, but it was a Gene Autry signature model, and when Carl put his fingers on the worn-out strings, Buck and Louise saw only pure pleasure in the boy's eyes.

Carl demonstrated a good ear for music and was a quick study as a novice guitarist. The mystery of "The Great Speckled Bird" fascinated him, and once he had real strings to work with, he taught himself the first few notes of the song. As the weeks went by, he learned to make a C chord, a G chord; he learned how to tune the guitar. For a year he worshiped at the altar of Acuff, of "The Great Speckled Bird," of Acuff's roaring interpretation of A.P. Carter's "The Wabash Cannonball." Even as his repertoire grew, though, his technique remained rudimentary, his sense of rhythm predictably stiff. All that changed in 1939 when he heard yet another new Opry star, Kentucky-born Bill Monroe.

With his band, the Bluegrass Boys, Monroe shook up country music. He and his brother Charlie had worked together as the Monroe Brothers before splitting into separately led bands. Their music—

dubbed "bluegrass" by Bill in honor of his home state—was distinguished by spirited tempos, Bill's breathtaking, breakneck mandolin solos, and his open wound of a high-pitched, searching voice. Beyond his advocacy of a new style, Monroe elevated the mandolin from supporting role to star attraction, much as Maybelle Carter had done with the guitar. Like those who had come before him, Monroe drew from the deep well of country and folk influences in shaping his new sound.

"Charlie and I had a country beat, I suppose, but the beat in my music—bluegrass music—started when I ran across 'Muleskinner Blues' [Jimmie Rodgers's 'Blue Yodel No. 8'] and started playing that," Monroe told James Rooney, author of *Bossmen: Bill Monroe & Muddy Waters*. "We don't do it the way Jimmie Rodgers sung it. It's speeded up, and we moved it up to fit the fiddle, and we have that straight time with it, driving time. . . . It's wonderful time, and the reason a lot of people like bluegrass is because of the timing of it."

Monroe hit close to the feel Carl liked but couldn't yet execute. And the voice—Monroe's high lonesome sound—pierced Carl in a way no singer had ever done before. Acuff's big-hearted vocalizing had power, but Monroe's—detached but determined, wispy but challenging—told a story even young Carl could understand.

One evening as they wound up their work in the fields, Uncle John invited Carl to come over to his place and to bring his guitar with him. "I plays a little myself," Uncle John said.

Thus began a days-long ritual, commencing every evening after the family had finished supper. Carl would ask Buck's permission to go over to Uncle John's, and Buck would say no.

"Carl," Buck declared, "John's too tired to fool with you."

Carl was sure he knew otherwise. "But Daddy," he objected, "Uncle John told me to come!"

"It's too far and it's too late. You gotta hit them fields tomorrow."

Finally Louise stepped in. To Carl's amazement, she took up her son's cause. "It ain't gonna hurt nothing, Buck," she said in her commanding way. "Let him take his guitar over there." Louise prevailed, as was so often the case, and Carl took off across the field, his bare feet kicking up dirt behind him, one hand holding tight to the guitar neck.

Although the body of Uncle John's guitar bore the earmarks of a well-traveled instrument, its thick-wound strings were still in good shape. When Carl tried it out, he was surprised at how easily he could press the strings close to the frets and pick clean notes.

"Can you make E, little Carlie?" Uncle John asked.

"I don't know," Carl answered. His was an honest response, because he had yet to learn the names of the two chords he had already taught himself. "You make it, and I'll see."

Uncle John laid two long, bony fingers across the second and third strings, between the first and second frets—an E minor. He struck a hard chord, and as the notes rang, he took his index finger and pushed the third string rapidly up and down, making a trembling, dark sound.

"Don't hit your bass note, son," he instructed while playing the lick. "Just hit the bottom notes. Press down." Demonstrating, he cut loose with a stinging, raw riff that took his left hand the length of the neck and back, working from the lower, high-pitched strings to the top strings. Carl had never imagined such tones coming from a guitar. As Carl tried in vain night after night to duplicate Uncle John's technique, he began to believe that those notes were Uncle John's exclusive property and could be pulled out of one and only one guitar, and it wasn't his.

Seeing Carl's frustration mount, Uncle John counseled a gentler approach. "See, Carl, it ain't just in the guitar, it's in the fingers," Uncle John said. "And what I mean by that is *it's in the soul.*"

"Uncle John, *how can I get my soul in my fingers?* the befuddled six-year-old pupil queried.

"Well, chile, lean your head down on that guitar. Get down close to it. You can feel it travel down the strangs, come through your head and down to your soul where you live. You can feel it. Let it vib-a-rate."

These simple words—"Let it vib-a-rate"—had as much effect on Carl's playing as anything he would ever learn. Whenever he'd get flustered and start fighting the instrument, he'd hear Uncle John: *"Let it vib-a-rate."*

He wasn't sure how or why, but his playing improved markedly after only a few sessions with Uncle John. He was able to pick out songs as he listened to the Opry, and his chord vocabulary grew when he discovered how to turn a major into a seventh chord, and a major into a minor chord. Carl became relentless in his drive to master the instrument and undeterred by obstacles seeming to confront him at every turn. Broken strings were too expensive to replace, so Carl tied his together. But when he tried to slide down to another note, the knots cut into his fingertips. His solution was to bend the strings, pushing up or down behind the knots to create a crying effect that substituted for the desired note. What he had stumbled onto was a type of "blue note," the flatted third used by blues and jazz artists at the point where language is inadequate to the task of conveying the heart's deepest pains.

Carl quickly added every new technique to his limited repertoire. Between the ages of six and eight, he not only developed into a reliable rhythm player but also began shaping an individual instrumental voice out of the music he heard in the fields and on the radio. As stirring as he found Roy Acuff's "Great Speckled Bird," Carl heard it another way. In his mind he imagined its evocative lyrics joined to Bill Monroe's bluegrass tempo and the spirit of the field hands' gospel-blues shouts. Evenings he would take his guitar off its nail and go outside to practice, ever mindful of Uncle John's dictum: *Let it vib-a-rate.*

What a beautiful thought I am thinking

Dispensing with Acuff's stentorian style, Carl imbued the lyric with a strong rhythmic pulse, emphasizing the first and third beats. *Let it vib-a-rate.*

Concerning a great speckled bird

Here came a Perkins-style blue note, underscoring the singer's intensely emotional state. On he went, recasting the song to where it sounded like one he'd created out of whole cloth from no known source. It was a moment of great accomplishment for Carl, a moment when his pride was plain to all who saw him, a moment that lasted only long enough for Buck Perkins to declare Carl's version unfit for human ears.

"What are you singin'?" Buck demanded. "That's not the way Roy Acuff sings it, Carl."

"I don't know, Daddy," Carl said tentatively, not wanting to show his father—or Roy Acuff—any disrespect.

"It's terrible," Jay chimed in.

"That's right," Buck declared. "You just put that guitar back up on that nail. You're ruining Roy Acuff's music, and Bill Monroe's along with it. That ain't the way they play."

"Daddy, I—I don't think I'm messin' them songs up," Carl said in his defense. "I like the feel of 'em this way."

Again Louise came to her son's aid. "Buck! Why don't you leave him alone? Let the boy play it like he wants to."

As a student Carl was indifferent towards his lessons, despite applying himself well enough to earn mostly A's and B's, with an occasional C. Jay's grades corresponded to Carl's, but he stood apart from his brother in being a superior baseball player, who could hit, run, field, and throw as well as anyone his age. Carl's interest in athletics was minimal and largely confined to football, where his natural speed made him a scoring threat. In fact, his heart wasn't in anything relating to school, and he felt acutely self-conscious around the rich kids (even though he had a crush on Martha Faye Johnson, whose family was one of Lake County's most prosperous, a fact Carl knew consigned him to admiring her from afar); he wanted to be home, with his parents, with his guitar, and with Bildo, a hound dog he had adopted one rainy night after finding it curled up on his doorstep.

That Carl succeeded as a student was due more to his well-honed work ethic, his fear of failure, and his family's encouragement than it was to his being particularly brilliant. Neither he nor Jay needed advanced degrees to pursue the livelihoods they sought for themselves, but the more pragmatic Jay had a sense of mission about school, believing he could apply his classroom discipline in the workplace as well. To Carl, education was entirely secondary to the dream of playing on the Grand Ole Opry.

"Carl, why don't you wanna be a truck driver like me? You stand a chance to do that," Jay said as the brothers made their way to the cotton patch. "You will never be on the Grand Ole Opry. They make a lot of money. Roy Acuff, Bill Monroe—no telling how much money they make. They ain't gonna pay you. You'll never be like that."

"Well, you just drive your truck; I'm gonna be singing onstage," Carl answered with absolute certainty. "That's what I'm gonna do."

Apart from playing with his cousins and his brothers, Carl spent most of his limited leisure time with his black friend Charlie, whose parents and eight siblings were jammed into a tiny pine-board shack near the Perkinses and worked the same plantation. Charlie's clothes were even more threadbare than Carl's. In fact, everything about Charlie's appearance and home life suggested his family had far fewer resources than Carl's, and the boy's sad eyes betrayed the toll exacted by the drudgery and deprivations that were the sharecropper's lot.

Still, to Carl Charlie was good company, sympathetic company, and the boys enjoyed their time together to the extent society would allow. Charlie rode a different school bus, with the other black kids; couldn't drink out of the same water fountain in town as the Perkins brothers; couldn't sit in the same section of the movie theater with them for Saturday morning westerns. Yet he never complained to Carl about these restrictions. Occasionally they wandered over to a cemetery built in the middle of the 400-acre plantation where they worked. There they spoke of their dreams. Charlie's were always the smaller of the two.

"Carl, you say you ain't gonna stay down here?" Charlie queried one day as they reclined against adjoining tombstones.

"No, Charlie, I ain't gonna stay down here no longer than I have to," Carl replied, " 'cause I ain't never gonna have nothin' down here."

"But when you get bigger, you might be a tractor driver, or a foreman," Charlie averred. "See," he added, "I prob'ly won't ever be no foreman."

"Why?"

" 'Cause I ain't white."

Such inequities only strengthened Carl's resolve to be the best kind of friend to Charlie, and Charlie returned every loving gesture. If Carl had four marbles in his pocket, he gave two to Charlie. When Carl ate at Charlie's house, Charlie would break his bread in half and give some to Carl. As will happen with childhood friendships, theirs cooled when Buck took work at a new farm and moved the family to yet another dilapidated shack on the other side of Tiptonville. There were no good-byes when Carl's family moved, but the young friends, then nearing their eleventh birthdays, never played together again. But their friendship left its mark on Carl's heart. Charlie even liked Carl's music. It was as if Uncle John had been reborn a youth.

Apart from Charlie, Carl's social life centered on much-anticipated weekend sleepovers with his cousin Delmus, whose family lived near downtown Tiptonville in a house with electricity and indoor plumbing. Delmus's father, Luther (Doc) Burrus, had married Nell and Louise's oldest sister, Estelle. They had escaped the sharecropper's life by virtue of Doc finding employment with a highway department work crew and by Estelle being a skilled seamstress. At Delmus's Carl knew he'd be fed well—sausage and eggs for breakfast, some kind of meat for dinner. Estelle often came home from the store with a flavored powder mix to which she would add water to make a sweet drink or would pour it into molds, place a sucker stick in each one, and freeze. She called them "penny drinks," and Carl and Delmus would sometimes sneak out of bed in the dead of night to snatch one from the freezer, slowly licking it down to the stick, savoring every second of its brief existence. When there were no more penny drinks to be had, Carl would chip off a piece of ice to suck on. This was a luxury, something he could never get at home.

For Carl, these visits were bittersweet. Although he was treated with kindness in his cousin's home, its amenities underscored his own family's woeful state. There a coal stove provided abundant heat; at Carl's, an old oil drum mounted on bricks burned wood. But when the family went to sleep, the fire would die and the frigid winds would rush through the newsprint papering the walls, under the shack's foundation, and between the cracks in the floor. Morning would find icicles hanging from the ceiling and the water supply frozen solid in a bucket. Christmas at Delmus's house was a time of presents under a gaily decorated tree; at Carl's, it was a joyful occasion when Louise had enough popcorn and holly berries to string around a woebegone evergreen Buck and the boys had scavenged from the nearby woods. Presents of toys were things other kids received; the Perkins boys were happy to see oranges and peppermint sticks under their tree on Christmas morning. By age ten, Carl Perkins knew exactly how poor he was, even if he didn't understand why.

Visiting Delmus also meant Saturday night trips downtown to the Strand Theater. Carl's interest was solely in the westerns, unambiguous morality plays in which good always triumphed over evil, elders were respected, the hero rode off to connubial bliss with the most beautiful girl in town, and the world seemed a fair and orderly place. Carl related strongly to these ideals, so close were they to the lessons his mother had taught from the Bible.

Many nights Carl and Delmus were joined at the theater by Jay and Clayton, who came to town with their mother and father. Having no interest in westerns, Louise passed the time with Estelle. Buck would watch a movie if it featured Bill Elliott—he admired the way Elliott wore his double pistols butt-end out, and marveled at the fancy crossed-arm move Elliott had developed to be able to remove the weapon on his right hip with his left hand and vice versa. If Elliott wasn't on the bill, Buck repaired to the pool hall. Carl always noticed the difference in his father's demeanor before and after the movies.

Buck's drinking, self-restricted to weekends, worried Louise, because it hurt the family: He was spending money on alcohol that could be better spent on food, household items, or new shoes and pants for the boys. Always there was the concern Buck might be seriously injured or killed in a barroom fight—despite being of slight build, he had a reputation as a scrapper when pushed, and he reinforced it by carrying a curved blade (or "hawkbill") knife visible in his back pocket. But Buck always returned unscathed from his adventures, and Carl came to regard the knife as much a bluff as a threat.

Normally mild-mannered and soft-spoken, Buck loved a good joke and was a genial conversationalist despite having no education and being illiterate. But he became "aggravatin'," as Louise put it, when he started drinking. This mood expressed itself in loud, argumentative discourse and cursing jags. During the week his strongest epithet might be, "I don't give a damn"; but after a few drinks, he began taking God's name in vain, a violation of the Ten Commandments he and Louise had taught their sons to live by. Under the influence his temper turned hair-trigger quick, and the boys often felt the sting of Buck's leather belt on their behinds while he was high.

Come morning, Buck was sober, and once more the kind soul his boys revered. He was no different from most fathers—he made the rules and exacted punishment when the rules were broken. His was a black-and-white world, literally and figuratively, and there was no negotiating. When the boys stepped over the line, the belt came off, and it was always used. It was strict discipline, but more often than not Carl and Jay felt they deserved their whippings; and when they didn't—that is, when Buck had been drinking—Louise was there to console her children. To them she explained that their father, being sickly and weak, drank more than he should, trying to ease his pain, and that they should never forget how much their father loved his sons, even when he didn't seem to be himself. For all her goodness, Louise coddled her husband more than she reigned him in, and Buck seemed unable or unwilling to discipline himself as rigorously as he did his children.

When he looked around him and took the measure of his world, though, Carl recognized one immutable truth: Amid the poverty and abuse there was a bond of love among father, mother, and sons that was beautiful to be part of and to draw strength from. So blessed, he reached out for this love and bathed in its warmth.

by 1942, twelve-year-old Jay, two years Carl's senior and sturdier of frame, had worked up to picking 200 pounds of cotton a day on a fairly regular basis. Sometimes he could hit close to 250 pounds, a remarkable feat that became the talk of his fellow field hands. But to everyone's surprise, Carl caught up with and then passed his older brother, consistently producing the remarkable tally of 300 pounds in a single day.

The irony of Carl's ascendancy into the 300-pounds-per-day ranks was that it occurred at the moment the sharecroppers' way of life was ending, its death throes fueled by a series of government programs designed in theory to buttress the beleaguered King Cotton and by progressive advances in the mechanization of farming equipment. Irony on top of irony, the plight of the southern sharecropper might have remained unchanged for years had the bottom not dropped out of the stock market in October of 1929, plunging America into its Great Depression for the next decade-plus and consequently enabling the sweeping social agenda of President Franklin Delano Roosevelt's New Deal.

The Lake County of Carl's youth was a world in flux as New Deal programs lured good hands away from the fields to jobs offering better pay for shorter hours and less brutal work. The Perkinses, always following James Washington's lead, stayed with the land, which still offered them opportunity even as the cotton industry withered in the face of increased foreign production and a new domestic emphasis on synthetic materials. Farmers also began diversifying their crops: As cotton, tobacco, and corn acreage declined through the 1930s, soybeans, fruits, peanuts, rice, and sugar registered steady increases into the early forties. With new crops came new ideas, namely, the tractor and the mechanical cotton picker.

Mechanization was the last in a sequence of events marking the end of history. Increasing black migration to the north, relief projects, acreage reductions, and the shift from the labor-intensive staples (cotton, corn, and tobacco) to higher-yield, less labor-intensive crops (soybeans, among others) were reshaping the South well ahead of the first mechanically picked cotton bale.

As a ten-year-old boy Carl understood the fears people around him had of the oncoming mechanization, because it was a fear he and his family shared with everyone who worked the land. Yet there was no plan afoot in the Perkins house for the day when the mechanical picker would displace them. Cotton and corn were their sole livelihoods, and increasingly Jay and Carl came to be the family's primary sources of income. Buck's lungs were getting worse, and he had been told by the county doctor that he shouldn't be out in the fields at all. He continued to work, but only a few hours at a stretch on an irregular basis.

In fourth grade Carl came under the influence of a progressive teacher named Lee McCutcheon—"Miss Lee" to Carl—who had grown up in Lake County herself and understood the circumstances in which her students—wealthy and poor alike—lived. To these children she stressed the benefits of an education and encouraged reflection, making it a point to have them discuss their lives in a critical way.

Being in charge of the school band—the Lake County Fourth Grade Marching Band—Miss Lee was always on the lookout for new talent. It so happened that the very instrument the band was lacking was a guitar, or so she told Carl when she asked him to join the group. Aware of the Perkins family's limited finances, she presented Carl with a new white shirt and a new pair of white cotton pants, along with the official white band cap with red piping and a red cape with gold satin lining. To Carl, his first stage outfit looked as fine as any of the country singers' flashy sequined suits he'd seen in photographs. Louise kept it cleaned, starched, and ironed, and it was a proud boy that walked out of the Perkins shack on mornings when the band was scheduled to perform. One of the earliest photos remaining of Carl shows him in the band, on the back row, his hat tilted ever so slightly to his right, the cape barely visible on his shoulders, his guitar at the ready as if he's about to begin playing. His bandmates appear rigid in their posture, but Carl's is a bit casual, albeit straight. He looks like he's itching to step out for a solo—but it's not his turn yet. Through squinted eyes he stares directly into the camera, his grave mien radiating confidence.

One Friday afternoon Miss Lee assigned her students to take the weekend to "write some things you like about yourself," and turn their work in on Monday. After studying the finished papers, she read each one to the class.

Carl's was on the bottom of the stack. It stated:

Hello, my name is Carl Perkins. I am a sharecropper's son. I work very hard for what I have to eat, and a place to stay warm in the winter. My favorite fruit is the orange, although I don't get very many or-

*anges. I love my mama and daddy, and my two brothers, Jay and
Clayton. And I don't want to grow up and be a man like Hitler.
Someday I want to be a big radio star. Thank you. Carl Perkins.*

In eighty-two words Carl had captured the essence of who he was,
the values he held dear, the ambition driving him. For a ten-year-old,
it was a remarkable self-portrait.

Carl's curiosity was getting the best of him. Buck listened only to the
news and to country music, but Carl wondered what he might hear on
other stations. When Buck went into town to get groceries, or to the
pool hall, Carl's mother wouldn't object when he would sit by the
radio with his guitar and search for other music he could learn.

These odd forays to other frequencies found Carl settling on station KLCN in Blytheville, Arkansas. In 1942, at age ten, he was hearing his first recorded blues and beginning to put the Uncle John lick
in a wider context as he added his own style to it. His opportunities to
listen to KLCN were infrequent, and as a result no single artist made
a lasting impression, only their sounds. Given what the typical blues
station might be playing at this time, though, it's likely Carl heard Big
Bill Broonzy making effective use of silence as a dramatic element in
his music, sometimes using only a few strong angular retorts to punc-
tuate key lyrics; Lonnie Johnson fashioning exciting solos out of single-string runs; and T-Bone Walker blazing away on an electric guitar, searing the speakers with his fluid, unrelentingly rhythmic attack,
taking full advantage of the expanded sonic palette made possible by
the advent of electrified musical instruments.

Through the thirties country music embraced change and innovation as well, the introduction of electric instruments being only one
new step among many marking a decade of spectacular progress in
broadening the music's reach. The radio that linked the Perkins family to the outside world (even if it was never tuned any further east than
Nashville or further west than Blytheville) gave musicians greater exposure as well as the opportunity to hear and be influenced by artists
working in other genres. Also disseminating a wide variety of new
styles, the jukebox appeared in the mid-thirties and quickly became a

fixture in restaurants, beer joints, dance halls, and other public places. In essence programmed by the public via their coins, it became a barometer of popular taste in music.

One of the first important artists to take advantage of these changes to great and enduring effect—and to have a profound influence on Carl—was West Texas fiddler Bob Wills, who began his recording career in 1935. He brought to maturity a nascent offshoot of country called western swing—which in Wills's definition blended elements of country, jazz, blues, Dixieland, Mariachi, Cajun music, and the native dance music of the central European immigrants who had settled in the Lone Star state—and became its most popular figure.

As Wills was hitting his stride, another type of feel-good music was gaining popularity, especially among rural southerners, who were joining other Americans in finding themselves with more leisure time and a little bit of spare change, in part because of the Fair Labor Standards Act of 1938, which shortened the work week and provided for a higher minimum wage. Whereas western swing proffered a big-band sound, this new strain of country was rawer and stripped down to a basic ensemble of guitar, bass, a dobro or steel guitar or another guitar, and sometimes drums. Its lyrical content too was rawer and more direct than that of traditional country music or western swing—more kin to blues in its explicit descriptions of sexual longing, excessive drinking, marital infidelity, and bloody brawling. The rare love song even swung towards extreme emotions and veered into sentimentality and/or self-pity. Dubbed "honky-tonk," its variety of wild moods was the perfect evocation of the soul of the poverty-stricken white southerner.

History records the first public mention of honky-tonk as appearing in the February 24, 1894, issue of Ardmore, Oklahoma's *Daily Ardmoreite* newspaper, to wit: "The honk-a-tonk last night was well-attended by ball-heads, bachelors and leading citizens." Then as now, honky-tonks were racially segregated, peculiar institutions resistant to all manner of social reformation and cultural enlightenment. On the outside these were drab, forbidding structures made of wood or concrete blocks with few or, often, no identifying markings; the dimly lit interior housed a bar, a dance floor covered with sawdust, several wooden tables and chairs, and, in the more high-falutin' ones, a makeshift stage for a live band. Usually the band had no stage at all but was set up in the corner near the jukebox, in an area often barricaded floor to ceiling with chicken wire to protect the musicians when fights broke out.

Like western swing, honky-tonk music had its roots in Texas. Denton's Al Dexter, owner of an East Texas honky-tonk in the early thirties, brought pure honky-tonk music to public attention in 1936 with his hit "Honky Tonk Blues"; seven years later he wrote and recorded one of the genre's most revered and culturally revealing songs, "Pistol-Packin' Mama."

Apart from Dexter's contributions, honky-tonk's foremost early practitioners were steel guitarist Ted Daffan, guitarist Floyd Tillman, and piano player Moon Mullican. All three were alumnae of a popular western swing group, the Blue Ridge Playboys, and all were superior songwriters and instrumentalists whose work defined the parameters of honky-tonk's world view. Daffan, for instance, pinpointed the plight of the displaced in the too-true "Heading Down the Wrong Highway" and "Born to Lose," the latter's lyrics of lost love and wasted life taking on special meaning for people whose world was falling down all around them. His single-string solos modeled after Lonnie Johnson's, Tillman, while with the Playboys, helped popularize the use of the electric guitar in country music. He was also a prolific and literate writer whose lyrics spoke to the treacheries of love (1949's "Slippin' Around" being an oft-recorded—and once-banned—classic cheating song) and whose melodies and vocal style were pop-influenced. Mullican was a firestorm of a piano player who could move effortlessly from one genre to another, sometimes within the same song; his raucous style, well showcased in such entries as "Cherokee Boogie," represented the ferocity of the honky-tonk experience.

These formidable pioneering efforts aside, it was left to Ernest Tubb, a tall, gangly, sad-eyed, craggy-faced native of Crisp, Texas, to boost the music's popularity by quantum leaps. Beginning his career as a Jimmie Rodgers clone, Tubb even had his first recording sessions (1936) produced by Rodgers's widow. When those releases failed, he reverted to a more conversational singing style—in part, he claimed, because a tonsillectomy had changed his voice and made it impossible for him to yodel convincingly—and finally landed a recording contract with Decca in 1940. A year later he wrote and recorded his first million-selling single, "Walking the Floor Over You." Over a robust 4/4 beat driven by bass and Rodgers-style acoustic guitar, an electric-guitar solo set up Tubb's plainspoken rendering of heartbreak and anxiety over lost love. "Plainspoken" may be too generous a description of Tubb's singing. Although he bore some vocal resemblance to Floyd Tillman, unlike Tillman he was forever in search of the right note. But he put his songs across with such warmth and obvious sincerity as to render technical facility irrelevant. Everything about him—his shopworn features; his lived-in, bedraggled voice; his humility; his unflinching sentimentality (fully expressed in another hit from the April 26 session, "Our Baby's Book," inspired by the death of Tubb's infant son)—marked him as one of honky-tonk's own: Everybody in the joint could relate to Ernest Tubb.

In Jimmy Short and, later, Billy Byrd, Tubb's band had distinctive guitar stylists who favored single-string runs and made an ascending four-note fill a hallmark of Tubb's sound. Their playing intrigued Carl, who began incorporating some Byrd-style solos into his own playing. Jay, on the other hand, was completely possessed by Tubb's songs and voice. It was the first time Carl's older brother had shown anything more than a casual interest in music, leading Carl to use Jay as a sounding board for his musical experiments. On the surface nothing much had changed between the brothers when it came to issues relating to Jay's veneration of traditional country music versus Carl's more adventurous interpretations, except now the debate found Jay more engaged, more spirited in his putdown of, say, Carl's syncopated version of "Walking the Floor Over You." In Tubb Jay had found an artist who defined an aesthetic he could embrace, and he did so with vigor—or at least until Louise squelched his arguments with Carl by warning him, "Don't be messin' with the boy's music. *That's him!*"

Saved by his mother's support, Carl continued to follow his own muse. Blues and honky-tonk had fired his imagination. Now he needed someone to keep a rhythm going behind him as he worked out his solos. Using his thumb on the top two strings and his fingers on the other four, Carl had developed a variation on Maybelle Carter's technique that allowed him to play rhythm and single notes at the same time. But he wasn't yet as fluid a player as Carter or any of her acolytes, and the complex, percussive Delta-blues style of guitar that so transfixed him was way beyond his grasp. Having a ten-year-old's small hands and a thick-necked guitar, he couldn't make multiple-fret stretches or construct full bar chords. To compensate for his physical limitations, he played in open chordings and learned to establish a ringing rhythm on the top strings while soloing on the bottom strings.

It wasn't an easy sell, but Carl, seeing his brother's growing interest in country music, coaxed Jay into learning rhythm guitar. Eager to support Jay's budding musicianship, Buck—no doubt feeling the older boy could bring Carl back into the traditional country fold—bargained with a neighboring family for a used guitar. At first Jay was so completely befuddled by the instrument that Carl had literally to position his brother's fingers on the notes that made up a chord. Progress was slow, but with Carl's constant encouragement Jay stuck with it. In time he became a tireless rhythm player, using the tremendous strength he had built up in his wrists, while working the land and playing sports, to maintain a strumming motion as steady as a metronome.

As he gained more confidence, Jay liked to stick the needle into Carl a little bit. Although both boys were strong, their frames were all lean muscle; Jay stood a couple of inches taller than Carl, and he would use his physical advantage to try to intimidate his brother. Knowing Carl's love for Bill Monroe's soaring, ethereal singing style, Jay would come towering over his younger brother and tell him in no uncertain terms, "Man, those low notes that Ernest hits, that's a whole lot better than that ol' high stuff you do."

"I tell you one thing," Carl would counter, "Bill can whip Ernest."

"Well then," Jay would reply, bracing himself and raising clenched fists, "put your dukes up."

The boys might take half-hearted pokes at each other, but mostly they would wind up wrestling in the dirt until one of them surrendered. There was never anything less than unconditional love between Jay and Carl, despite the odd tussles. Jay could poke fun at Carl's heroes, but he would be the first one to come to his aid at school if one of the rich kids started picking on his brother. It was Jay who took Carl to the school bus in the mornings and afternoons and sat with him all the way to their destination; Jay whose discipline in the fields inspired Carl to reach down for a little more energy to pick a few more pounds of cotton; Jay whose humble, dignified manner, even as a young boy, was the best sort of example to Carl of the Golden Rule in action.

As the Perkins family slid deeper into poverty, Carl's questions about God's goodness and mercy grew more persistent. Questions became doubts, and had it not been for the strength of his mother's faith, Carl might have turned away from God at age ten. In all matters spiritual, Louise was the family backbone. Moreso than Buck she believed in the power of prayer and was persistent in her exhortations to "take it to God." When Carl remarked that God liked the rich more than the poor, Louise counseled, "Just keep prayin', son. God hears you. In time He'll answer, and we won't be so poor. Just keep prayin'."

After Carl became proficient on the guitar, she would ask him to lead the family in a gospel song. Her favorite, which she sang in a clear, piercing tenor with Carl while coaxing Jay into joining in on harmony, was "What a Friend We Have in Jesus." Buck wasn't big on vocalizing, but even he would get in the spirit after a while and underpin the whole thing with his bass hums. These family singalongs, regular Friday night occurrences once Carl had learned his first chords, released the tension of the week's toil and strengthened the family bond.

At night, long after Jay and Clayton had nodded off, Carl would lie awake, listening to the voices issuing from Buck's radio on the other side of the cotton sheet partition. With the melody echoing in his mind, his fingers formed chords on an imaginary fretboard—*if I go right here . . . no . . . here . . . finger there . . . got it! There it is!*—his heart pounding from the excitement of discovery.

All around Lake County the soothing chirp of crickets gently broke the night's quiet. Finally, Buck would douse the coal oil lamp, then click off the radio's fading signal. Only Carl would be stirring. Wide-eyed and restless, he would work out one song and then another, hearing sounds only he could hear, sounds echoing through the darkness into a distant but vividly imagined future.

By the time Carl was twelve, nine-year-old Clayton Perkins had made it clear that he was cut from different cloth from that of his brothers. Sometimes it was difficult for Carl to believe his younger brother was born of the same hardworking parents as he and Jay. He even looked a little different from the other Perkins boys. They were all skinny from lack of proper nutrition, but as they grew, Carl and Jay developed broad, sloping shoulders and solid chest and back musculature. Clayton, underweight at birth, was petite all through his childhood years, but strong. Carl and Jay had thin faces with high cheekbones, bright, welcoming eyes and high foreheads; Clayton's features, however, were more compressed on a rounded face, his eyes were mischievous slits, and his curly white hair fell over his forehead towards his eyebrows. About the only physical feature they had in common were their prominent noses and outsized ears.

If Clayton took after either of his parents, it was his father—or rather, the Buck Perkins who caroused a bit too much on Saturdays. Simply put, he would not work. After picking a few bolls, he would park his sack on the ground and lie down for a nap. Buck would find him, jerk him to his feet, and start whipping his bottom, telling him, "Now I mean you're gonna pick!" Clayton would take it, knowing his father was too weak to keep up the thrashing for very long. Finally Buck would run out of breath and energy, and as he stood there wheezing Clayton would meander back to the field as if nothing had happened. But his blue eyes would be full of fire. He'd pick a bit longer and then throw down his sack and start back towards the house. "It's too hot out here," he'd tell Carl and Jay. "I'm goin' home."

"You gonna get another whippin'," Carl would warn him. He and Jay would rather work seven days a week, fifty-two weeks a year in deadly heat than to take another of Buck's whippings. Not so Clayton. "Whippin' don't hurt but a little while," he'd tell his brothers. "This hurts all day. I ain't stayin' out here." Despite Clayton's disobedience, he was never subject to the same severe degree of discipline as Carl and Jay, and often found his worst behavior being excused. One day he was caught brandishing a hatchet in hands upraised over his cousin Martha's head; had Martha's mother not stumbled onto the scene and flown into hysterics, a tragedy surely would have ensued. Yet to Buck and Louise, this incident was dismissed as yet another of their high-strung baby boy's harmless childhood pranks.

When they weren't tending Clayton, Carl and Jay spent much of their spare time practicing guitar together, Carl teaching Jay new songs as he learned them. Jay was becoming the rhythm player Carl felt he needed to flesh out his own sound. And Jay was coming around to Carl's way of thinking when it came to arrangements and tempos. Strong and tireless, he would stay right on the beat, thrashing the strings, the chords ringing behind Carl's soloing. They had even begun working up some Ernest Tubb songs, and Jay would sing them in a strong, resonant tenor; he even had Tubb's inflections and phrasings down pretty well, and could deliver some on-key feeling to boot.

Having Jay behind him raised Carl's playing to a higher level. From once believing he looked right only when holding a guitar, he had embraced the instrument to such a degree that it had become a permanent part of his being. It was like a living thing—it would say "I love you" to Carl in the sweetest tones he had ever heard, as if it were an angel speaking. Sometimes, though, it would bow up and refuse his advances, holding out for days on end until Carl hit precisely the right lick, and then the instrument would submit totally to his touch.

"Sometimes it just gives it to me," he told Jay. "That sound I'm hearin' in my brain, sometimes it just all comes out like it's supposed to."

In 1944 Jay graduated from eighth grade and announced that his schooling was at an end. He had the size and strength to work full time in the fields, and the family's need was great for the income he could provide. Louise and Buck agreed, without argument.

By 1946 James Washington, his sons, and their families had all moved out of Lake County, Buck being the lone holdout. Their common destination had been Madison County, seventy miles southeast, via Highway 78. There at the turn of the century, Massachusetts businessman Judson Bemis had purchased 300 acres of land at twenty cents an acre, built a cotton mill and, around it, a self-contained community for the Bemis Bag Co.'s well-paid, well-kept work force. Olie Perkins was the first of the sons to move to the Bemis town, and the others followed in short order. Hearing of the mill's plans to add an extra shift, Buck decided it was time to pursue the possibility of a more prosperous, more stable life.

The men and women who had fought in World War II returned to a nation beginning to creak with change. Those who had left the cotton fields came back to the first confrontations of the civil rights movement and to growing anti-segregationist sentiment outside the South. Since 1940, southern blacks had been migrating north and west in an astonishing exodus that would reach 5 million over the next thirty years, their flight fueled by the more tolerant racial climate elsewhere and the undeniable specter of the mechanical cotton picker replacing human hands.

Sitting in the back seat of the family car as it backfired its way out of Tiptonville in January of 1946, Carl could see tractors' smokestacks off in the distance, even caught a glimpse of a mechanical picker or two on the way. While the magnitude of the sweeping change taking place in Lake County escaped him, he sensed the fading of the world he had known. His family, the near-palpable love they shared for one another, even the scars of their common struggle, were the treasures he was taking with him. In his heart he carried the unconditional friendship and love extended to him by Uncle John, Charlie, and Miss Lee. Bildo, honest and true companion, would live on in memory. Beyond this, he had one wish: "I hope," he said to himself as they crossed the Obion Bridge, Tiptonville fast vanishing behind him, "I never come back here."

Madison County

Jackson and Bemis, 1946–1954

Unlike his brothers, Buck Perkins was excluded from the promised land in Bemis, his application for employment having been rejected because of his poor health. It was back to the fields, back to a one-room shotgun shack of the sort they had left in Tiptonville. It had electricity, and a refrigerator (bought used by James Washington for twenty-five dollars), which meant Carl now had all the ice he wanted.

Buck and Louise offered no resistance when Carl decided to end his schooling with the eighth grade, as had Jay. He would now devote his days to chopping and picking full time, working alongside Jay, comforted by having a sense of contributing something vital to the family's cause—the cause being survival.

A better opportunity presented itself to the family when Fred Day, owner of Day's Dairy in the nearby community of Malesis, in Madison County, offered Carl a live-in job milking the cows and making deliveries early each morning. At the Days', Carl lived comfortably in a large, well-appointed frame house, and gained, through trial and error, some social graces along the way. His only humiliating moment came during dinner his first night, when Mrs. Day served him a T-bone steak, a cut of meat he had never seen before. He was so inept with a knife and fork that in trying to carve up the beef he mashed down on the bone at such an angle as to send the steak flying across the table and into Mrs. Day's lap.

Two and a half months after Carl's arrival, when the cotton crop was in, Buck and the rest of the family joined him in Malesis. Rather than work at the dairy, Jay took a well-paying job in Jackson at Bond's Mattress Factory; Buck then assumed the milking duties, freeing Carl to assist Mr. Day on the delivery route, where he proved to be speedy and efficient. The personal touch he added to the job would be to sing out "Mi-hilk!"—rising to falsetto on the second syllable—as he bounded onto each porch with his bottles. Within a year Carl and Buck were running the entire operation, Buck joining in whenever his health permitted. Carl vowed never again to pick another cotton boll unless it was on land he owned. He was out of the fields.

One day after work, Carl was sitting on the front porch alone, idly strumming his guitar. As he strummed, he began humming a melody. He strummed an A. Went to E. Broke into a 4/4 tempo and began developing the melody, chording E to A to B7—the standard I-IV-V progression common to country songs of the day. As he hummed and worked out the melody over the chord progression, he thought of Lake County, of Martha Faye Johnson, the rich girl he had adored during his elementary school years. And of all the comforts he had dreamed of for so long.

He sang, "Let me take you to the movie, Martha," but it didn't fit; the "th" in Martha's name threw the timing off.

Now let me take you to the movie . . .

E to A to B7 . . . *now let me take you to the movie . . . Maggie.* Maggie. *Now let me take you to the movie, Magg—* Movie. Magg. *Let me take you to the movie, Magg . . .*

So . . . *so I can hold your hand.*

And right out of Lake County came the rest of the verse:

> Oh, it ain't that I don't like your house
> It's just that doggone man
> And that double barrel behind the door
> It waits for Carl, I know

Flushed with excitement, Carl dug into his imagination and began constructing a world in verse. Those afternoons at the western movies had left him with a passion for sleek, fast, beautiful horses. All he had ever seen was a mule's rear end plowing up the cotton fields during planting season. At the movies he would sit transfixed as Roy Rogers galloped off on Trigger, the horse's lustrous white mane blowing in the wind. *Wouldn't that be the way to go,* he thought. *Man, I could jump on him and I'd ride out of Lake Country and go so far they'd never find me or my horse.*

Carl sang:

> So climb up on Becky's back
> And let's ride to the picture show
> I only see her once a week
> And that's when my work is through
> I break new ground the whole week long
> With my mind set straight on you
> And I polished up my old hoss' back
> And she looks good I know
> So climb up on ol' Becky's back
> And let's ride to the picture show

Here Carl took a solo break, coupling a single-string run of notes to a series of two-note chords winding back to the next verse:

> Oh, I slick myself for Saturday night
> 'Cause there's one thing I know
> I'm gonna take my Maggie dear
> To a western picture show

In only a few minutes of plumbing his past, Carl had produced a portrait of the Lake County life he knew: a poor boy's yearning for the girl of his dreams; the treachery of Tiptonville dating mores; a well-kept horse being regarded as more reliable and more attractive transportation than the rattletrap automobiles Carl knew; dressing up for a Saturday date, after the week's work was done; and most of all, taking the girl to a western movie. The romantic image in Carl's mind was of himself riding Martha Faye on a fine stallion, her arms holding tight to his waist as they galloped to the Tiptonville Theater.

Almost all of it was fiction. At age fourteen Carl had never been on a date, had only heard stories from friends about being out with girls and the sort of things that went on between males and females. He had never been on a horse, and he had never slicked himself up for Saturday night, only for Sunday morning church services. Yet he had captured in a few precise images the anticipation most of his peers (and many adults, to be sure) felt about their presumed weekend assignations.

Later that night he played the song for Jay, who had joined Carl on the porch after work so they could practice together.

"Where you get that name Becky?" Jay asked pointedly after Carl finished. "You ain't got no hoss. We ain't got no mules around here named Becky."

"But that's a good name for one," Carl answered.

"Well, why don't you call it ol' John?"

"I like Becky. It's my song and I'm gonna leave it like that."

Jay looked away and strummed a chord. "It ain't too bad," he admitted after a pause. "You sure you wrote it?"

"Yeah, I just wrote it. I'm gonna write the words down on paper here in a few minutes."

Jay nodded approval. "Well . . . that's alright. That's alright."

Carl then played it for his mother, who pronounced it "cute." She added that she thought Carl's father would like it too.

"You think he will?" Carl asked, fearing Buck's reaction, despite his mother's optimism.

When Buck came back from town, Louise requested Carl sing the song.

"What song is it?" Buck asked.

Carl hesitated, and finally said, "I wrote it."

"Well, sing it."

This would be the ultimate test. When Carl started in on his untitled composition, he could tell by the smile on his father's face that Buck appreciated the song's traditional strain. When Carl had finished, Buck nodded. "Pretty good song," he said serenely. "Pretty good song."

Carl wanted to shout. He had never had a bigger thrill than to hear his parents' approval of his self-composed ode to Martha Faye. Fired by this reception, he wrote constantly over the next few days, producing a batch of songs far less memorable than his first. Because it had come so quickly, Carl figured every song was complete in its initial form. Even without rewrites, Carl's original material indicated he had a way with lyrics. He could improvise a theme and develop it on demand. Listening carefully to and picking out tunes he heard on the radio had given him a sure sense of structure. Moreover, he wrote and sang with unusual feeling and perspective for one so young. A backwoods, underprivileged teenager bearing a man's burdens, Carl had missed the child's privilege of living in his head. But in writing a song he had found the exhilarating freedom of being able to reconsider his youth as it might have been.

Carl's first songwriting endeavor set a pattern from which he would rarely deviate, and then only with mixed results: His songs started not with a catchy phrase or interesting lick, but with an emotional flashpoint rooted in the personal. In Carl's case the threat of an irate father's shotgun and the yoke of a life so defined by work it allowed little in the way of social interaction were factual matters in Lake County; in his mind's eye Carl saw himself breaking the yoke and savoring a moment of independence wherein his own feelings and values counted for something meaningful in a hard world. This from a fourteen-year-old boy finding his wings.

In late 1946, Jay drove Carl some twelve miles south of Jackson on Highway 45 to a rather forbidding bare cinder-block structure with the words "Cotton Boll" painted on one side. Its green tin roof looked ready to collapse, and if it had, no one would have heard it, because the joint was completely isolated—it got its name from being situated in the middle of a cotton patch. A few old cars, some of them in worse shape than Buck's, were parked out front; a few yards from the back door sat a huge stack of empty beer bottles. Even though this was Buck's type of place, Carl knew little of the world he was preparing to enter.

His father never talked about it; Carl only saw the aftermath of those visits. Recalling Buck's ever-present hawkbill knife, Carl figured on encountering men with weapons inside. His apprehension on approaching the Cotton Boll's entrance was well founded: He was seven years below the legal age to enter such a place and had every reason to believe that behind closed doors lay absolute mayhem.

But the day was still young, and once inside Carl found the place eerily quiet. A few customers sat leisurely at utilitarian wooden tables, sucking from longneck bottles of beer, talking placidly among themselves, an occasional laugh spiking the calm ambience. As Carl walked towards the bar, his senses were jarred by the acrid scent of stale tobacco smoke mingling with the pungent odor of beer; the primitive bathroom emitted a smell all its own, familiar to anyone, such as Carl, who had been in an outhouse in stifling summer heat. His eyes immediately caught sight of a physically imposing middle-aged man with steely eyes and a heavy, stalking gait slowly approaching him from behind the bar.

"Yeah? What can I do for ya?" the man asked in a gruff tone.

"Well," Carl answered timidly, "me and my brother, we're the Perkins brothers."

"So?" the fellow growled, obviously unimpressed.

"We play music," Carl said.

"You do!" He stepped back and cast a baleful stare at Carl.

"Yes we do, sir," Carl responded quickly, "and we're lookin' for a place to play. And," he added, his nostrils flaring from the stench as he studied the room's rickety tables, broken chairs and well-trod wooden dance floor, "you got a good-lookin' place here."

The man behind the bar huffed, hitched up his pants, and Carl saw his mouth curl up a bit at one corner. Being snowed by a fourteen-year-old must have been a new experience for someone who seemed to have seen it all. "I don't have no use for you this weekend, because I'm pretty full." But as Carl turned towards the door, the man called to him. "I have big crowds on weekends. Wednesday's a pretty slow night. Y'all bring them guitars and come back down here on Wednesday an' we'll see how they like ya. I judge by how much beer they drink."

"We'll be here," Carl assured him.

"Well, I'm gonna tell everybody that comes through here that I'm gonna have . . . what'd you say your name was?"

"Perkins Brothers."

"I'm gonna tell 'em now. I'll be lookin' for ya."

"We'll be here," Carl pledged.

Arriving two hours ahead of schedule on Wednesday night, Carl and Jay were directed by the Cotton Boll's owner, Hubert Miller, to the corner of the tonk, where the duo could play by the dim yellow light of a Wurlitzer jukebox. There was no microphone. Carl stepped out to bid the audience—numbering around fifty customers—good evening. As he did, he placed an empty cigar box at his feet and announced that contributions were welcome, these being the band's sole source of pay for their night's work.

"We appreciate y'all comin' out to see us tonight," Carl said sincerely, directing a smile to no one in particular. "We're the Perkins Brothers. My name's Carl, and here's brother Jay to do an Ernest Tubb song for ya."

Jay stepped forward without expression as Carl kicked into his driving version of "Walkin' the Floor Over You," which succeeded in getting a few couples onto the dance floor. The repertoire for the next couple of hours was familiar contemporary country fare—some Bill Monroe (notably a new ballad Monroe had recorded that year, "Blue Moon of Kentucky," which Carl had reworked into an uptempo, country-blues shuffle), some Roy Acuff, a lot of Ernest Tubb, and a brisk take on Bill Carlisle's "Rattlesnake Daddy," featuring some new lyrics penned by Carl himself. Couples dancing and enjoying themselves made Carl feel good, because it was his type of music—country imbued with gospel fervor—that got their feet moving.

The boys played no more than three hours that first night, and Carl left feeling ecstatic. Even though the live music received only scattered applause, he had seen his style make a connection with complete strangers. No one—no one—had objected to his new interpretations of the country hits. Moreover, when Carl counted the change in the cigar box at the end of the night, he tallied nearly four dollars in coins, far more than he expected. At eleven o'clock, when the audience had dwindled to a few drunks slumped over at the tables, Miller fired up the jukebox again. "Boys, I don't believe there's gonna be nobody else here," he said. "Y'all can quit if ya want to." When he invited them to return the following Wednesday, Carl figured the beer must have been flowing.

During the evening Carl and Jay also had discovered one of the perks of being the evening's entertainment: free drinks. If Carl hadn't been feeling so energized by the mere fact of his first professional performance, he would have been flying high anyway behind the four beers he had consumed. It wasn't his first taste of alcohol: Two years earlier, Buck had given him, Jay, and nine-year-old Clayton each a sip out of a bottle of beer he had bought. Carl and Jay thought it was the foulest liquid they had ever had in their mouths; Clayton liked it ("It ain't too bad"). But at age fourteen, Carl took to the brew with more enthusiasm and drained each bottle he was offered. He liked the light-headed feeling he got from the alcohol and thought he played better as the night wore on, that he had more spirit to share with the audience. Jay drank some too, but not as much as Carl and certainly not enough to alter his cool, almost detached stage demeanor.

Wednesdays became the Perkins Brothers' night at the Boll, and after about a month of gigs there Carl and Jay were offered Friday and Saturday nights at the Sand Ditch, a tonk near the western boundary of Jackson, so named because of its location adjacent to a huge ditch running almost the entire length of the city limits. Carl accepted, but when he told his mother about their newest job, Louise cringed. "Boys," she implored Carl and Jay, "be careful. Please don't go playin' that ol' Sand Ditch."

"Momma, that's the only way we're ever gonna get anywhere," Carl insisted. "They ain't gonna pay us to sing in church. And we wanna do this!"

The boys went on and played the Sand Ditch, but Louise's fear proved well founded. Fights broke out repeatedly among the drunken customers, even more so than at the Cotton Boll, and Carl and Jay often found themselves ducking beer bottles aimed at someone on their side of the room. Carl and Jay came to expect several serious fights a night—serious being when one or the other or both fighters ended up spilling blood. No sooner would one fight finish than another would break out on the other side of the club. All the indignities and frustrations of the work week were taken out at the tonks, on the dance floor, out back, and by the side of the road next to the venue. The patrons ranged in age from late teens to late forties, few of them were much better off economically than the Perkins family, and most of them knew violence as a fact of life. In playing the popular honky-tonk songs of the day—tales of heartbreak and faithless love, senti-mental descriptions of hearth and home, lusty reflections on drinking and partying—the Perkins Brothers were telling the truth about the life these people knew intimately. Theirs was a curious bond, rooted in the grind of common poverty, observant of a code fashioned from biblical entreaties but recognized mostly at the moment of its being breached.

Oftentimes the fighting inside the Sand Ditch would spill out onto the road. Many was the night Carl and Jay saw someone hurled into the deep excavation, and kept down there by swift kicks to the side of the head as he tried to clamber back onto higher ground. The rarest sight of all was to see a police car pull up and send everyone scurry-ing for cover across the fields. Having no one to arrest, it was com-mon for the deputies on the scene to stop in and hobnob with the owner, who was quick to offer them a free beer.

The tonks had their own low culture—Darwinian to a fault—and the more nights the Perkins Brothers played, the quicker did they master the art of self-preservation. The first truth Carl learned was that almost all of the fights were over women. When one man thought his date was making eye contact with another man, be it real or imagined, his likely response would be to march over and take a swing at him. And be swung at in return. The dance floor would clear and the two would start flailing away, rolling around in the sawdust and oil cov-ering the dance floor, until the owner waded in to send the battle out-side.

Often the men fighting would pull hawkbills on each other, or blackjacks, but these were no match for the owner's weapon of choice: a leaded axe handle, the great leveler. Hubert Miller didn't want any trouble from the police. When he whomped a brawler on the skull with his leaded axe handle, the fighting ceased, usually because Miller's victim was unconscious and incapable of pressing his case. Earl Mills, who owned the Sand Ditch, was even rougher and more rugged than Miller, a real power hitter with the weighted lumber.

Rarely were the musicians drawn into physical confrontations. As skilled as Carl became in talking his way out of jams, his pride got ruffled (to a degree that correlated directly with the amount of alcohol he had consumed) when anyone suggested he was scared to step outside and get it on. Hardly one to let a personal attack go unanswered, Carl would then be drawn into battle, where he proved himself a savvy scrapper. Even in the early tonk days, he had been sharp enough to learn one critical strategy: Don't go outside to argue, go out to fight. Hit first, hit hard, hit often, don't negotiate. A couple of good licks would send a guy flying into the pile of beer bottles, and the fight would usually be over. In only a few months of playing the Sand Ditch and the Cotton Boll, the Perkins Brothers gained a reputation with their fists that was about equal to their growing popularity as musicians, to the point where many of the challenges issued to Carl and Jay were mere bluffs, designed to test their resolve. When the brothers would arrive outside, their opponents would have vanished into the night.

Jay was the reluctant warrior of the two, his involvement dictated primarily by his fear of Carl becoming the victim of a sneak attack by his opponent's friends. When he chose to step into the fray, he tended to be the human equivalent of a leaded axe handle. By his late teens he had grown to nearly six feet three inches in height, broad of chest and shoulders, thin but strong. His hands were large, with bony knuckles; whomever he hit he hurt, and his victims tended to be out for the count. Usually Jay wore a friendly, open expression, was quick with a toothy grin, and spoke softly and infrequently to others. But he went about the business of protecting his brother with the same sense of purpose he had about his work. Around the tonks, he was regarded as someone whose goodwill was to be cultivated.

As there was an unspoken bond among the patrons, so was there an emotional connection between tonk employees. Theirs, however, had nothing to do with shared lifestyles or economic status or blood sacraments, and everything to do with pure, raw greed—the lust for money. In fact, there was no bond, only a conspiracy between the bar girls and the Perkins Brothers to separate the customers from their cash as quickly as possible. In a nutshell, the girls tried to sell as much bootleg whiskey as they could without actually delivering it. A typical scene began with the waitress taking an order for a bottle from a single man sitting alone at a table: "Honey, gimme five dollars and I'll get us a bottle," came the offer through red, parted lips. Once she had the money in hand, she would get the customer onto the dance floor and keep him stepping while Carl and Jay pumped out their uptempo tunes. Her aim was to maneuver around to where the boys were standing, and while the man's back was to the band, hand Carl the money. When the man finally tired out and wanted to sit down and drink his moonshine, the girl would feign surprise.

"We done drank it!" she would insist.

"No, we didn't drink it!" came his protest. "You ain't brought it yet!"

"Yes I did! That was an hour ago! Oh honey, you just forgot." She would stroke his hair, kiss his cheek, brush her breasts against his body and . . . job done.

Sometimes the girl couldn't get her prey onto the floor until he had had a few nips from the bottle. Once they were dancing, another girl would sneak over to the table, swipe the bottle, and give it to Carl or Jay, who would sip from it for the rest of the night. Returning to the table sometime later, the man would find, to his astonishment, his bottle missing.

In this way was a single half-pint of whiskey sold four or five times before it was ever actually delivered, enriching the tonk owner manifold, endearing his employees to him, and, in the bargain, introducing Carl and Jay to the illicit pleasures of homemade liquor.

Madison County was rife with bootleggers supplying tonk owners, whose customers preferred the homemade brew to what they termed "government whiskey." Being illegal was the least of moonshine's calling cards; more to the point was the kick delivered by its 120-proof alcohol content. As Carl learned, the moonshine devotees were a breed apart, disdainful of beer drinkers, who sipped out of bottles. Theirs was an art meticulously practiced and perfected for maximum impact. The moonshine container, a quart fruit jar, offered a quick, almost debilitating high if the drinker's nostrils were inside the mouth of the jar during consumption. The key was to inhale the fumes while gulping the brew fast enough so that a bubble formed at the bottom of the jar and then burst, shooting alcohol fumes straight into the nostrils, as the liquid drained down the drinker's gullet. Moonshine so potent consumed so rapidly offered a devastating, immediate blotto effect, one cherished and sought after by the honky-tonk cognoscenti. Their use of beer was strategical, as support until they could get another swig of the 'shine, or as a mixer with the homemade brand.

(While most of the tonk owners were on friendly terms with the police department and could often buy immunity, raids remained a possibility, Madison being a dry county. Most tonk owners were alerted in advance of an impending raid. One of the first oddities Carl noticed at the Cotton Boll was a slab of concrete suspended directly over the bar by a thick rope that hooked onto the back wall behind the bartender. Once alerted that the cops were on their way, all the fruit jars and beer bottles were placed under the concrete, the rope was untied, and the slab came crashing down on the glass. The bartender then swept up and discarded the broken glass, wiped off the bar, and sat back looking innocent when the cops arrived and began searching for incriminating evidence.)

Carl liked the sizzle that ran up his spine and into his skull when he drank moonshine. He kept its effects at bay pretty well in the tonks by sipping it instead of guzzling, but when the evening was winding down he would always make certain he indulged in one long, uninterrupted drink before heading home. Jay was more partial to beer, but wasn't above nipping from the fruit jar himself either. In their first couple of years in the tonks, he exercised some restraint in his drinking so that he would be fit to drive home.

Once under the influence, Carl tended to get rowdy in his performances, kicking out a leg while he soloed at a breakneck pace, shouting and hollering at Jay during instrumentals, shaking his torso and leaping into the air between verses of a song. In no time his white shirt was completely soaked with sweat, and his black, curly hair, already thinning in his mid-teens, was plastered down on his head as if he had been standing in a shower. The furious pace of the Perkins Brothers' performance ignited the crowd; feeding off each other's energy, band

and audience had the inside of a tonk smelling like a locker room and feeling like a steam bath by early evening. Even Buck, present in his caretaker role, could be seen jitterbugging with one or another single woman while his boys blew the roof off the place.

Louise had other concerns once Carl and Jay began working regularly in the tonks. Having struggled with Buck's drinking during the Lake County years, she was now seeing her sons going down the same road. They were already smoking as much as he did, but this was less worrisome to her than when they came home smelling of moonshine.

"You know what it's done to your daddy," she began one of her lectures to Carl and Jay. "You can bet it's gonna do that to you boys. It'll ruin your music, and it'll ruin your lives! It's not good! Please don't do it."

Carl ignored his mother's warnings and drank whatever quantity and species of alcohol was placed in front of him. He did indeed know the effect it had on Buck, and he did indeed, deep down, feel tremendous guilt over disregarding Louise. But the Carl Perkins who picked 300 pounds of cotton as a boy, who taught himself "The Great Speckled Bird" and then juiced it up, was now a young man. He would drink and smoke more than he ought to, despite the dangers, because his was a way of extremes. The boy had some demon driving him to the edge of every experience. Away from the tonks he was as respectful and courteous and God-fearing and hardworking a young man as anyone knew. In the tonks, though, he became not only an eyewitness to but an active participant in this new world's mystery and allure. Women were plentiful and available, and he was taking advantage of every opportunity to savor the pleasures of the flesh; he had cigarettes, booze, all he could partake of; he had his fists with which to defend himself, and his punches carried the rage of all the deprivations and discriminations that had torn at him in Lake County. And with the music he played he had dominion over his audience's emotions.

Something was happening with the Perkins Brothers Band after their first couple of years in the tonks: They were becoming a big draw around the Bemis and Jackson areas, having branched out to play other tonks besides the Cotton Boll and the Sand Ditch (the Sand Ditch burned to the ground eventually, but Earl Mills was kind enough to call Carl beforehand so he could get his gear out ahead of the blaze). The Roadside Inn on Highway 70 heading towards Nashville was a lively spot that became part of the brothers' regular circuit, as did Mills's other rugged establishment, the Hilltop—where the chair backs were wired and nailed together because they had been broken over customers' bodies so often in fights—and, on Sunday nights, the Supper Club.

Where their competitors were offering straight country or western swing, Carl and Jay were taking the standard repertoire and injecting some bounce into it, reflecting Carl's continuing assimilation of gospel, country, blues, and Bill Monroe's bluegrass rhythms. From their earnings Carl made a down payment on a Harmony electric guitar (to be paid on the installment plan—one dollar a week—from Jackson's Hardeman Music) and concentrated exclusively on playing a style of lead guitar so deeply rooted in so many places that it seemed at once a summation of twentieth-century sound signatures and a wholly original voice. As a vocalist he had clearer influences, being beholden largely to the twin gods of Bill Monroe and Jimmie Rodgers.

A newer artist who had had an immediate effect on Carl as a singer was Kentucky-born Red Foley, who had joined the Grand Ole Opry in 1946 as host of the show's network coverage, replacing Roy Acuff. Foley's vocal style was the essence of smooth, and his material betrayed pop and rhythm and blues influences (the latter most prominent on a 1948 hit, "Tennessee Saturday Night"). Foley crawled under Carl's skin with a song he had written called "Old Shep," the story of a boy's love for his dog that had uncanny parallels to Carl's experience with Bildo, right down to the dog having to be destroyed when it got sick. Finally, in a nod to the impact of western swing on his sensibility, Carl appropriated Bob Wills's saucy exhortations to his band members and addressed them to himself and Jay during their solos.

Despite the band's growing popularity, Carl remained restless. Even with an amplified lead guitar, he felt their sound was thin. The Perkins Brothers were missing one of the key elements of the great honky-tonk bands they admired: a bass slapping out the rhythm. Noting that their friend Fred Jones, in Jackson, owned a homemade bass that was missing two strings and weighed about twice as much as a factory-made model, Carl broached an idea to Jay.

"Man, if we could just get Clayton to play," he said earnestly. "Jay, you talk to him. I'm gonna see if Fred'll loan us that bass and we'll keep it here at the house."

Jay wasn't opposed to having a bass player, but didn't see how Clayton could fit. Not only had he never professed interest in music, he hadn't the temperament to be a good musician. Like Carl and Jay, Clayton had dropped out of school after finishing eighth grade in 1948, when he was thirteen, but unlike them, he didn't go to work. His days were spent lolling around the house and hanging out with his friends when they got home from school. He didn't pick cotton, he didn't work at the dairy, he didn't help Carl with his deliveries—his was a life of leisure, made possible because Buck and Louise allowed it. They never pushed Clayton, and by his teens their youngest son was living life on his own terms, directionless and unambitious.

After rebuffing Jay's suggestion that he join the band on bass, Clayton then found himself facing Carl, who wouldn't retreat. Clayton kept saying no, Carl kept coaxing him to try it. "Naw, *I can't play!*" Clayton finally protested. "That bass fiddle's bigger than I am, man! I can't hold it up!"

But Carl's persistence paid off, and he finally persuaded Clayton to give it a try. After lugging the bass back from Jones's house, Carl demonstrated for Clayton some rudimentary chord positions on the two strings and explained to him as best he could the purpose of the instrument in the band context. He didn't want Clayton to play individual notes like he heard the bass players doing on the Opry, but to click the strings in time, to give him a sound like the one he heard when he tapped his foot on the rickety front porch of their shack while he practiced guitar alone. In short: "Get that slappin' thing goin', man, that slappin' sound from bouncin' them strings off the neck." The sessions with Clayton were tedious: His small fingers made some of the chordings difficult, and the instrument's tremendous weight further hindered his dexterity. After only minimal instruction, though, Carl added Clayton to the lineup, despite his technique bearing more kinship to wrestling than to music.

▶ THE VOICE OF CARL PERKINS

The minute Clayton started that clickin' behind Jay's rhythm, then it all exploded. I'm talkin' about when sounds first started coming into my brain, and, man, when I first heard what was happenin', and he'd learned him some chords—and we didn't play in that many chords—it came together. It doesn't take a great musician to play. It's a feel, and a sound, and that's what I heard. I heard this clickin' over here, and I heard this ringin' over here, and there was my two brothers. And I said, Oh Lord, we're gonna be somebody. I knew we had a different sound, and it was the same as I had heard in my head. I had heard it in the fields of Lake County. I didn't recognize it until it came to life. And I knew people would like it; they showed they liked it. We would fill up every club we'd play in.

I'm telling you there's times when us three boys sounded like five people. That bass sounded like two instruments—one clickin', one carrying that rhythm. Clayton attacked the bass; he had something to prove and he proved it. His attitude was, "Wait a minute, I'm part of this! I'm a big part of this and I'm gonna ride it to the hilt! I'm the best damn bass slapper ever come out of these parts, and I'm gonna make the girls look at me." And that was one of the reasons he pushed that bass hard and hit it hard. He blistered his hand but never backed off of it. The incentive for him was to show me and Jay that he could flat push us on out front with his playing. That big bass was louder than both of us could be together. Yes, he was a big part of it.

In addition to playing the tonks, Carl began appearing regularly on Jackson radio stations in the late forties. For a while he was a floating member of the Tennessee Ramblers, a band he had joined at the urging of his guitar-playing friend Ed Cisco, who sat in occasionally with the Perkins Brothers Band and had assembled the Ramblers around himself and his wife, who played mandolin. The Ramblers secured a Saturday morning show on WTJS when a local Buick dealer agreed to sponsor their thirty-minute segment. Carl drifted in and out of the Ramblers as they needed personnel, and also appeared solo on another 'TJS show, *Hayloft Frolic*, broadcast from Jackson's National Guard Armory and hosted by a local country bandleader who called himself Uncle Tom Williams. (Carl wanted Jay to appear with him, but his older brother declined—he needed time to chase girls.)

The show aired every Saturday night, and Carl was paid three dollars for two single-song turns over the course of four hours, slotted in between straight country bands, fiddle bands, string bands, and comedy acts. Although tempted to do his original songs, Carl took a different tack and mixed in talking blues numbers modeled on those he had heard delivered by the Grand Ole Opry's Robert Lunn (nicknamed "Talking Blues Boy"), whose songs were said to have so many verses it would have taken days to complete even one.

Uncle Tom also had a morning show on WTJS, *The Early Morning Farm and Home Hour*, and brought Carl on as a regular after he had proven his crowd appeal on the *Frolic*. His first appearances were as a solo act, but when he told Uncle Tom about the band he had with his brothers, they were invited on the show as well. Listener response to their performances was overwhelmingly positive—sometimes as many as eight fan letters a day, according to Carl—and the experience had the added benefit of making the band tighter. Playing in front of a cold microphone in a radio studio with no live audience was an entirely new discipline, and it took some adjusting for the boys to learn how to relate to their unseen listeners. But as they worked at polishing their radio shows, their music gained a professional sheen while its fire and fury remained undiminished. The biggest adjustment they had to make was in having crisp beginnings and endings to their songs. Denied the luxury of building to an explosive peak over the course of an hour's set, the band learned it had to hit cruising speed out of the gate.

Mother's Best Flour signed on to sponsor the Perkins Brothers in a fifteen-minute segment each morning, and the impact of this daily exposure showed in the larger crowds the band began drawing to its tonk dates. Most pleasing to Carl was the favorable reaction to his original songs, which he sprinkled into the sets among the usual country standards. For the year-plus of its duration, the Mother's Best segment of the *Early Morning Farm and Home Hour* found the brothers jelling as a trio; their limited time frame demanded cohesion and direction; it demanded more thought be put into song selection, into pacing, into mood; it demanded Carl, as the spokesman, let his convivial personality flower over the airwaves, that he see the microphone not as an unfeeling instrument of technology but as his entree into each listener's home, where he was a grateful and gracious guest. Uncle Tom died near the end of the decade, and the radio show with him. But by then, not only were the Perkins Brothers the best known band in the Jackson area, they were in their own league, with no competitors in sight.

Local success inspired Carl to test other waters. With the profusion of bands in the Jackson area came the advent of amateur contests held in high school auditoriums on a weekly or biweekly basis. Carl began entering the band in these, and the Perkins Brothers found themselves taking home first-prize money—five dollars—almost every time they participated. The competition was spirited, but Carl, Jay, and Clayton could bring the audience to its feet with their storming version of "Chew Tobacco Rag." More important to Carl was seeing a sober audience respond to the band with the same intensity as the beer-and-moonshine bunch in the tonks. He liked being able to look at the crowd and see clear-eyed smiles on the people's faces and their attention riveted on the band and the music.

Carl was branching out in other ways, too. At WTJS he took advantage of the technology at hand and of the station's generosity to tape-record the brothers singing some of his original songs. He then sent the tapes to Columbia and RCA Victor Records in New York in what were his first attempts to "get the music out of Jackson," as he said. But to no avail. Sometimes the packages were returned unopened, usually they weren't returned at all.

At the moment Carl was sending out his demo tapes, Hank Williams was making his commercial breakthrough with "Lovesick Blues" and exerting a substantial and dramatic influence on Carl and virtually every other aspiring and established country songwriter. In his self-penned songs he was chronicling his life and compiling an impressive catalogue comprised of good-time numbers (e.g., "Honky Tonkin'" and "Move It On Over"), heartbreak songs ("My Sweet Love Ain't Around," a precursor to "I'm So Lonesome I Could Cry," his 1949 masterpiece), and religious songs ("Mansion on the Hill").

A young man dedicated to exploring his feelings and life in song, and then sharing these with an audience, naturally would be drawn to Williams's work. So it was with Carl Perkins, who made careful study of the artist's self-penned lyrics, intrigued and bedazzled by his playful language.

Even Williams's band made an impact on Carl's music. The Drifting Cowboys had a redoubtable lead guitarist in Sammy Pruett, but among the top Nashville session players who sat in on the early sessions was electric guitarist Zeke Turner, who developed what was termed a "sock rhythm" technique by damping the strings with the back of his hand after playing them, resulting in a percussive effect. Carl had worked out a similar technique on his own, and hearing a variation of it in Williams's music further convinced him he was on the right track with his own style of country.

I t was only a moment, a few minutes together in the late summer of 1949. When it was over, the sharecropper's son had found the key. Still hellbent on making it to the Grand Ole Opry, Carl, through the good graces of his cousin Martha, fashioned a link with a kindred spirit whose unwavering faith gave buoyancy to his dream. This moment, like the trickle of water that begets a stream, which flows into the Mississippi River, was unremarkable in origin, but monumental in scope.

▶ THE VOICE OF CARL PERKINS

Martha was in a little ol' car with me, a little ol' one-seated Ford. It had to be about a '34 Ford and it was wore out. There was smoke comin' up through the dashboard. I don't know how a woman ever went with me; I didn't have no good car. They'd freeze to death in the wintertime, it didn't have no heater. I'd have flats and didn't have no spares. I'd take 'em home on a flat, man, whatever. Never could ride very far 'cause I didn't have no money to get gas. Fifty cents was pretty good. If I had a dollar I got fifty cents' worth of gas and I could ride 'em four or five miles and park. Had to make out like it quit, pull off somewhere.

Anyway, Valda was walkin' in front of that cotton mill, and I remember Martha sayin', "Well, there goes Valda!" I said, "Wow! She's pretty!" And I started stoppin', and Martha said, "Let's let her ride home with us." I said, "Sure." Martha got out of the car and hollered, and she ran across the street. Martha was out of the car, so that let Valda get in the center. She got in next to me and I remember smelling her perfume, and it smelled pretty good. And I told her, "Gosh, you smell good." And she said, "Why thank you." She had on a skirt and white socks, kinda rolled down. A sweater maybe. It was starting to get cool. Her and Martha was talkin' and chatterin' like girls do, y'know, and I didn't think I'd ever see her again. I let her out in front of her house and she said, "Thank you." I said, "Yeeeah." I thought, Wait a minute. She sure is a pretty girl. If I could just get her to stop laughin' so much . . . She's really pretty. I noticed she had beautiful teeth. 'Course I was havin' to drive that ol' car, which didn't have power steering. I couldn't look at her much. But when I let her out, it connected that that was who I'd seen standing in the door. I said, "Which one of these houses do you live in?" She said, "Right here. Right here." I said, "Well, I deliver milk here." She said, "I know." That stirred a little somethin' in me. I thought, Well, I'll be doggone. I didn't notice her being that pretty. So I got a little slower as I sat the milk down.

Born April 29, 1931, in Bemis, Tennessee, Valda Crider was the youngest of seven children of Bedford Cullie Crider and Lillie Matilda Laycook Crider, and the only one born in Bemis, where the Criders had migrated from Carroll County, near Huntingdon, Tennessee, about thirty-five miles east of Jackson. Before he got on at the Bemis mill, Bedford Cullie Crider had spent his whole life as a farmer and had struggled to support his family after the Depression. He was forty years old when he was hired by the Bemis Bag Company, and the job was a godsend. The twelve-hour workdays were grueling, but living in Bemis made it worthwhile. Their first home was in the Eastport section, but after a short time there they moved into a four-room house on Gregg Street in the newly opened New Town section. Valda was born there and never knew a day without electricity, indoor plumbing, and a coal stove, luxuries all.

Throughout her school years Valda was an honor roll student, mathematics being one of her strongest subjects (she had a ninety-eight average in a high school algebra course). She was salutatorian of her class at J.B. Young High School, an honor bestowed upon the second-ranking student. Against her mother's wishes, Valda declined a full academic scholarship tendered by Jackson's Lambuth University. Instead, she went from high school graduation to a full-time job in a five-and-dime store. Over the next few years she worked a succession of jobs—in a doctor's office, in a toy factory—before being hired in the early fifties by Central Service, a Jackson firm that computed and collected utility bills. It was the first job Valda found fulfilling, because it tapped her skill in mathematics. With something worthwhile taking up her days, and a budding romance with Carl to fill the evenings, Valda Crider felt her world was in order.

One of the common interests that had drawn Martha and Valda close was music. Martha knew and liked country music, but Valda's interest was strictly in pop. Gershwin, Berlin, Porter—these were songwriters whose sophisticated lyrics and haunting melodies moved Valda in ways three-chord country tunes couldn't. She didn't care for Roy Acuff's music; she liked Hank Williams's songs, but couldn't stand his voice; about the only country artists she found appealing were Eddy Arnold, and a newcomer on the scene, George Morgan, who'd had a big hit in 1948 with "Candy Kisses," and another strong entry the following year in "Room Full of Roses."

Martha and Valda's friendship extended to every aspect of their lives. It hadn't been unusual during their high school years to find one "meddling" (the term has a negative connotation that doesn't apply here) in the other's love life. Knowing Valda's family as decent and hardworking, Martha had an idea that Valda and Jay Perkins might hit it off, being from the same sort of stock, and Valda agreed to go out with him. Martha set up a triple date, with her and a companion, Carl and his girlfriend of the week, and Jay and Valda. They went to a movie in Bemis, and all through it Valda would sneak peaks at Carl and think to herself, *I wish I was with you.*

Valda had heard enough about Carl to know he was popular with all the girls around Bemis and that he played the field. He had no problem getting a good-looking female to go out with him. As Valda became more attracted to him, she began resenting the other girls, fearing Carl would fall in love with one before she ever got her chance.

After another uneventful date with Jay, Valda had to confide the truth to Martha. "Jay's a really nice boy, and I like him," she said, "but I'd prefer to go with Carl."

"You had?" Martha asked, both puzzled and surprised.

"Yes," Valda declared. "I don't know what it is, but I want to go with him."

Thus began a courtship that threatened to add new dimension to the adjective "rocky." Even though he was attracted to Valda, Carl was an elusive character who rebelled at the idea of "going steady," of dating one girl to the exclusion of all others. He would promise to go steady with Valda, and then she would hear about him being out with another girl. At one point Martha stepped in and upbraided Carl about his inconsiderate behavior. Her lecture registered, and he began devoting more time to Valda. Still, every once in a while he would slip and date someone else. Instead of putting up with it, though, Valda retaliated and started dating other boys, while making sure Carl got the word.

"He would get so mad," Valda recalls. "He'd be real upset. I never did understand why he did that way, but he did."

What Valda was observing was the red dog in Carl coming to the fore. He was jealous and quick-tempered, a dangerous combination, and a perfect product of his times in demanding Valda be faithful to him while he sewed his own wild oats. With the band's popularity gaining him a measure of fame around Jackson, Carl found the tonks drawing a larger and more enticing pool of young and beautiful women. His vow to be Valda's steady was nothing more than words, blown away in the first strong wind.

Carl's red-dog habits effectively shielded his real feelings. Despite his tendency to stray, he was, from the beginning, as drawn to Valda as she was to him. He thought she had a brilliant mind, that her ideas and intuitions about the way the world worked were those of a higher intellect. And she was fiesty, stood up for what she believed. Chivalry was not dead with Carl, who worked hard at being a gentleman when he was around females—opening doors for them, addressing them courteously, cleaning up his language. But the red dog occasionally slipped through, and out would come a four-letter word. Hard on its heels, from Valda, came a slap to Carl's jaw, earning her his immediate respect.

If that weren't enough, Carl also saw in her a teenage girl who was growing into a beautiful young woman. Her red hair, so silky it seemed to reflect the sun's rays, fell gracefully around her narrow face, framing its tender, straight lines in soft waves. Gentle hazel eyes radiated warmth and intelligence but would go steely and cold if anyone crossed her. When her thin lips parted in smiles or laughter, they revealed well-tended, straight white teeth. She was dazzling, a natural beauty. In short, she was everything Carl wanted in a woman but was sure he would never find. And having found her, wasn't sure what the future held.

Working long hours at the dairy and then spending evenings in the tonks was taxing Carl's stamina to the limit. Needing a steady nine-to-five work day, he left the dairy and hired on as an upholsterer at Bond's Mattress Factory, where Jay worked. From Day's the family moved as close to Bemis as it would ever get by renting another run-down dwelling—no indoor plumbing or running water—on a block known as Hickstown, named after the Jackson woman who owned all the houses. Standing parallel to the mill town proper, Hickstown was pure red-dog country, populated by desperate people permanently down on their luck, the cotton mill towering over them in the distance, a savior out of reach.

Jay didn't help matters any in 1949 by marrying a Bemis girl, Pauline Helton, and moving her into the already crowded Perkins family home. At best an uneasy truce existed between Carl, Clayton, and Pauline, with the brothers finding her personality off-putting. Carl in particular felt some jealousy towards her, because he didn't want anyone to supersede him in Jay's life. Jay remained the anchor for Carl, the one person who could keep him rooted on the occasions when he strayed from the course they were charting. As to that course, Carl was certain as well that Pauline was out to dash any ideas Jay harbored about making a living from playing music. In time this turned out not to be the case, but during the year the couple lived there, Carl and Pauline remained only distant friends at best.

With his family's move to Madison County in 1946, Memphis, seventy miles west in Shelby County, became a part of Carl's life, thanks to electricity. When Buck replaced his worn-out battery-operated radio with an electric model, Carl was free to explore the dial more than he had been in Lake County. Hearing so many artists and sounds he never knew existed opened up a new world of possibilities.

"My music started picking up steam," Carl says, "because I'd listen to blues, country, pop; I'd listen to the whole gamut. And a lot of those radio stations were coming out of Memphis."

Before he had ever seen it, then, Memphis meant music to Carl Perkins. He regarded it as a place of mystery and intrigue, where forbidden voices came to be heard, where the rules of the game were being rewritten with every new note sung and played. It was never what he expected, and more than he could imagine. Nashville was country music, but Memphis . . . Memphis was music, period.

A few names from those radio days still resonate with Carl. Bob McKnight and the Ranch Boys played rousing western swing, and all were blind; WMPS featured a popular country artist, Eddie Hill, on a live show, *High Noon Roundup*, which provided a showcase for the best local talent, in particular, an electric mandolin player named Paul Busker, who had only four strings on his short-necked instrument instead of the usual eight, and played it like a guitar. Whenever Hill was ready to give Busker a solo turn, he would cry out, "Awwright, Paul Busker!" and Busker would step in with a flurry of notes played at such lightning speed that Carl could not duplicate them on guitar. A female singer named Billie Walker was one of the few non-instrumentalists who caught Carl's attention in those days. The more he listened to Memphis stations, the more he realized that the town was full of stellar, unique musicians who approached their music in unexpected ways.

Memphis was typical of regional scenes throughout the country in the late forties and early fifties, when a boom arose in small, independent labels specializing in everything the majors left behind—gospel, some jazz, blues, fringe country (that is, country so raw it was deemed to have no commercial potential), and the newest kid on the block, rhythm and blues (part swing, part gospel, part blues)—in short, anything that smacked of ethnicity. Some of the most important artists of the time would be found on Savoy, Specialty, Chess, Atlantic, Duke/Peacock, and the like. Los Angeles–based Imperial Records had been releasing everything from blues to country to jazz to mariachi before mining New Orleans for talent and coming up with twenty-one-year-old Antoine "Fats" Domino. A Crescent City native, Domino had grown up absorbing all the richness of the New Orleans musical gumbo that blended Cuban, Cajun, zydeco, second-line brass, jazz, blues, and rhythm and blues into a singular sound and style.

Working with his producer–cowriter–musical mentor Dave Bartholomew, Domino fashioned an infectious, rocking sound made all the more compelling by the artist's ebullient personality. His first single, 1948's "The Fat Man," sold 800,000 copies. The major labels didn't rush to dig other Fats Dominos out of the woodwork, but "Fat Man" sales figures had served notice of something going on with which they had yet to reckon.

In Memphis, two years after "The Fat Man" broke through, Sam Phillips, a twenty-seven-year-old former radio announcer–engineer from Florence, Alabama, opened a recording studio, the Memphis Recording Service, at 706 Union Avenue, in an abandoned radiator shop measuring twenty by thirty-five feet. Its slogan was "We Record Anything—Anywhere—Anytime." And so it was—weddings and funerals paid the rent in the early days. An early label venture failed, and finally Phillips hit upon the idea of recording local and regional artists and leasing the masters to other labels. There was no shortage of distinctive artists in and around Memphis and the Mississippi Delta area and many of them passed through the doors of the Memphis Recording Service, including two who became towering figures in blues history, B.B. King and Howlin' Wolf.

As to his original goal, Phillips himself has muddied the water a bit—only a bit. In interviews he has cast himself variously as visionary, concerned folklorist, and opportunistic entrepreneur who got there first with the most. He was all of these at once: The Memphis Recording Service was a business, designed to allow Phillips to make a living doing what he liked best. That he recognized and supported music reflecting the human condition while offering something new is evident from his programming choices when he worked at Memphis's WREC. His playlist included any and every type of music he could find, with a special emphasis on blues and blues-influenced styles. That he thought there might be a larger audience for this type of music was only that—a thought, a hunch based on experience and taste.

"There were city markets to be reached," he told writers Martin Hawkins and Colin Escott, "and I knew that whites listened to blues surreptitiously."

A photograph of Sam Phillips from this time shows him in coat and tie, dark, shrewd eyes glaring defiantly at the camera, his mouth curling up slightly in one corner in a cocky smirk. His face is unlined, his square jaw firm, his shock of dark hair carefully trimmed, parted on his left and swept over into a neat pile on the right side of his forehead. There's nothing especially warm or friendly about his aspect, or threatening either. He is a man projecting the necessary attributes of confidence spiked with a touch of arrogance as he approaches the frontier, guided only by intuition.

When Valda came into his life, Carl's future rested not on his potential advancement in a nine-to-five job but on a long shot—that his music would be a passport out of poverty. This had been true since his childhood, but in Valda he had stumbled onto something he had not factored into the equation: a woman's devoted love for and belief in him. Of all the women he had been with, only this one did he take seriously; only this one had reached in and captured his soul with her strength and with the sincerity of her feelings for him. She was constantly telling him how attractive he was, even though the young man he saw in the mirror was a gangly country boy with curly, thinning hair, an oversized nose, teeth too far apart. And it was beyond his ability to understand when she insisted, "You're gonna sing on the Grand Ole Opry and anywhere else in the world you want to—if you want to, you can do it, Carl"—when he himself was ofttimes paralyzed with doubt.

In subtle ways, Valda—better educated, more self-assured, gracious and charming in public—was changing the man she loved. For all his kindness and genuine good-hearted nature, Carl was uneasy with the world, hostile and already set in his ways. Being sociable was part of the act he had developed as the band's spokesman on and off stage, but he carried considerable unexpressed anger over the conditions of his life, and towards a God who turned away when He was most needed. All he had to do was walk a block over to Bemis to feel the rage grow: *Who put me in this shack? Why couldn't I live uptown and get a good guitar? I could've had what I needed. I could've looked good.*

Playing in the tonks fueled this resentment, because he saw too much of himself in the red dogs who danced to his music. He didn't have to strain to be polite to his audience—he lived as they did, no better, no worse, and called many of them friend, and they he. But each night made him harder, quicker with his fists, and increasingly dependent on alcohol to soothe the ache in his soul. In the early-morning hours, when he and Jay and Clayton were clearing out of one tonk or another, Carl had to face the wrenching truth that he was on his way back to Hickstown, to a shack barely fit for human habitation, hardly better than what he had grown up with in Tiptonville. It was enough to make a man lash out and curse his very existence, and Carl did.

But Valda was showing him a place where he could learn to love unconditionally and in return be loved unconditionally. Learn to shuck the self-pity and believe, as she so fervently believed, in the future you saw in your dreams.

The purity of Valda's love shook him. So he tried to throw it all away.

Over the next two years, through 1951 and most of 1952, Carl was as unreliable and as untrustworthy a significant other as a woman could have imagined. And manipulative. He continued to insist on a double standard, and took it a step further by getting word out through his friends that he had fallen for somebody else—fallen so hard, in fact, that he was on the verge of getting married. These were all fabrications, designed to hurt Valda, for reasons unknown even to Carl.

Through part of '52 Carl had been seeing, on a regular basis, a fine-looking woman twelve years his senior, Betty Mayo, a divorcee with a young daughter. She too became the recipient of a ring from and a proposal of marriage to Carl Perkins, accepted, and began making her plans. They settled on a wedding date. Carl was to pick her up when she got off work at the grocery store and head for a Justice of the Peace.

As the hour neared, Carl sat fidgeting in his car, watching nervously as Betty checked out the last few customers lined up at her register. His clammy hands clutched the steering wheel; he watched the store clock creep towards seven, her shift's end; he saw some other girls in the store gather around Betty, each one giving her a congratulatory hug. Sweat poured off his forehead and down his face. Ten minutes to the hour.

If you gonna go, he thought, *you better go now.*

As Betty gathered her things to leave, she was surprised by a couple of her coworkers, who came over to present her with a corsage.

Five minutes to the hour.

As the corsage was being pinned on the misty-eyed future Mrs. Carl

Perkins, the bridegroom-to-be turned the ignition key and stomped on the accelerator. All he saw in his mirror was a huge plume of dust and rocks flying through the air as his tires spun, squealed, then gripped the road and shot him away from the store.

What he had been too stubborn to see before was now painfully obvious: His duplicity was going to cost him Valda's love. Thus chastened, he promised Valda—again—that he would be her steady. Despite temptations over the next few months, he was true to his word. In late '52 he asked Valda to marry him and move to Hickstown, where they would live with his parents. She accepted.

On January 24, 1953, Carl and Valda drove fifty miles to be wed in Corinth, Mississippi, with Martha and her husband, George Bain, themselves newly wed, along as witnesses. Jackson required couples to have a blood test before marrying, but in Corinth a five-dollar bill and the words "I do" got the job done quickly and far less invasively. They were escorted to and from Mississippi by the amiable tush hog Jackie Haskins, self-designated bodyguard for the Perkins Brothers Band and a licensed pilot with his own twin-engine Piper Cub. He buzzed Carl's car the length of the trip, flying low enough to the ground that they could see him grinning maniacally and waving. Every so often he had to ascend abruptly, to avoid crashing into a telephone pole or a barn. He was there to do what came naturally in the tonks—making sure no one jumped Carl. Other than Valda.

Clayton was coming into his own, in a manner of speaking, as one decade ended and another began. In 1949, shortly after his fourteenth birthday, he produced a phony birth certificate and enlisted in the Marines, telling his parents (who were unaware of the all-volunteer Corps's age restrictions) he had found his calling. Boot camp was at Parris Island, a living Hell populated by abusive drill instructors, according to his early letters. In one bit of correspondence, he begged to come home. His closing sentiments:

This is the last letter you'll get from your youngest son. I will be dead by the time you get this letter.

P.S.: Find my birth certificate and carry it over to the Marine office at the Post Office in Jackson. Tell the Sergeant who you are and show him my real birth certificate and they'll turn me out of this place. I got in here with a phony birth certificate and I can't stand it. They're killing me and I've got to get out.

Buck and Louise were frantic, especially Louise, who was in tears throughout her waking hours after receiving this correspondence. "Carl, he says here he's gonna kill himself!" she wailed.

"It's the best place for him" was Carl's response. "They'll make a man out of your little ol' mean boy now. They ain't gonna kill him. Anyway," Carl added, recalling some of the scrapes Clayton had been in at the tonks, "he liked to have got killed before he left here. Don't worry about him."

Less sanguine than Carl about Clayton's fate, Louise unearthed her last born's authentic birth certificate and ordered Carl to take her and Buck to the recruiting office. They stood in silence as Carl did all the talking.

"You remember a boy named Clayton Perkins?"

"Yes I do," the sergeant replied.

"You signed him and put him in the Marine Corps?"

"Yes I did."

"How old is he?"

"He's seventeen," the sergeant stated, his voice taking on a tense edge. "Had his momma and daddy's consent."

"He's fourteen and he ain't had no damn consent," Carl countered.

"Well, I got a copy of his birth certificate." The sergeant reached into his file drawer and shuffled through some papers without producing anything.

"You got a copy of a new one," Carl told him. "Mama, poke in your purse."

On the sergeant's desk Louise placed a wrinkled, fading document that showed Clayton's birth year as 1935. "The boy's fourteen years old," Carl reiterated, pointing out the date on the certificate. "This is his parents. I'm his brother, and I want him home immediately. I'll let you off the hook if you get him home immediately."

In the interim between receiving Clayton's cry for help and visiting the recruiting office, Carl had learned through friends that the sergeant was splitting fees with the counterfeiter who produced phony birth certificates for underage recruits.

"Your little racket's fixin' to come to an end unless you get my brother out," Carl warned. "If he ain't on the next damn bus from Parris Island, you're in trouble."

Less than a week later, Clayton was back in Jackson, chastened by his experience. Carl noticed a lingering melancholy in his brother, though. When he asked if there was a problem, Clayton admitted to having had some harsh words with one of the drill instructors as he was leaving. According to Clayton, the D.I. had threatened him, saying, "You've got about a year and a half of being out. We've got some money invested in you and we'll be calling you."

Despite Carl's assurances that he was beyond the Corps's reach, Clayton grew more despondent. One afternoon at the house, Buck and Carl heard a shot. Carl ran outside and found Clayton writhing on the ground and cursing, having been shot in the foot with a .22 rifle. Through gritted teeth he explained to Carl how he understood the service rejected anyone who had ever been shot. Pointing to his foot, he said, "That's the best place I knew to put the bullet."

Carl rushed Clayton to the hospital, where his wound was cleaned and his foot placed in a plaster cast. Finding the cast unwieldy, Clayton sawed it off. With the wound exposed and going untreated, the foot, then swollen to about twice its normal size, became infected and discolored. Carl thought it was going to rot off. Refusing to go back to the hospital, Clayton instead began treating it with a home remedy— whiskey. Poured over the foot. Gradually the wound healed, allowing

Clayton to return to the band and to his other passions—drinking, chasing women, and loafing around the house.

In the tonk culture, Clayton gained a distinction that escaped his brothers—he became a tush hog. More precisely, he was born a tush hog, but blossomed only after joining the band. Country folk know the tush hog in two forms: as a wild boar sporting long pointed teeth on either side of its jaw; and its human counterpart, a person, usually male, whose head, especially around the mouth, has been beat on so much that it has become calloused and set like iron. They tend to be brave beyond all reason in a fight, because they believe they are invulnerable. Hitting a tush hog in the mouth might break his opponent's hand, but won't hurt the tush hog.

The tush hog, then, is fearless. He is mean and he looks for trouble, especially in the tonks, where alcohol brings out the best in his personality. It was pretty well accepted in Carl's day that the only way to stop a tush hog's charge was either to hit him in the head with a leaded axe handle or to shoot him. As Carl notes, "When a tush hog gets hurt, he gets hurt bad. Usually somebody's trying to kill him, not just fight him. Because you can't win just fighting; it's too dangerous. The only way is to shoot. But you really don't wanna kill a tush hog, because he is popular. Everybody really would like him to be their friend, because there comes a time when you'd like him to be on your side.

"A tush hog's a type of guy, if you stopped on the side of the road, he'll help you change a flat and won't take a dime. He's good-hearted. He's not a guy who robs; that's not what he does. He takes advantage of you. If he got you knocked down and money fell outta your pocket, he'd probably pick it up and put it in his. But they're not thieves, per se, they're just toughs."

So Clayton Perkins adjusted to his celebrity standing in the tonks by being himself twice over. Carl and Jay would fight only as a last resort, but Clayton would talk back right away and be jaw-to-jaw with anyone who tried his hand. Women were drawn to him—even in his mid-teens he had a rugged, lived-in countenance—and a lot of the men were amused by his cocky, braggadocio bearing. He couldn't have escaped all the trouble he drew to himself, but those few times when he had the chance to walk away, he chose to stay and fight. It was Clayton's style.

As it happened, the Perkins Brothers weren't the Three Musketeers—all for one, one for all—at least not when Clayton and Carl got a little alcohol in them. One night at the Cotton Boll, Carl cut out on a guitar solo and broke into some dance steps as he played, sending the customers into a frenzy. Only Clayton wasn't amused.

"You're showin' out," he said during the next break. "Whatta you showin' out for?"

Carl was taken aback. "Noooo. No, I'm not," he said. But he couldn't let it lie. "Well, so what? Whatta you gonna do about it?"

"I might knock you down!"

"No you won't," Carl said. "Why don't we just go out and have some fun?"

"Well, we can have some fun without showin' out," Clayton replied.

Clayton continued to pick at Carl through the night about him "showin' out" during the sets, and finally Carl had had enough.

"Let's go out here in back," he said, pointing the way to the Cotton Boll's rear exit. "You been smartin' off all this time. Let's just get it over with."

No sooner had Carl stepped out the back door than did Clayton attack him without warning, popping him on the side of his head with his fist and pushing him to the ground. Carl clambered to his feet and tackled Clayton, as the tonk patrons gathered around and urged them on. They rolled around in the dirt, neither one having the advantage over the other, but when they got back to their feet, Clayton knocked Carl flying into the empty beer bottles piled high behind the tonk. Carl sprung back at Clayton and landed a hard blow to his head. Finally, Jay stepped in and, with help, halted the fisticuffs. It was time to start another set.

East of Jackson on Highway 70 sat the El Rancho, a club Jay and Carl had played when it was called the Roadside Inn. A wooden structure with white asbestos siding, it was by all indications a well-maintained establishment. True to its original name, it sat only a few feet off the road. Customers could park on each side of the building, but

on busy nights, automobiles lined the shoulders of Highway 70, sometimes for a quarter mile east and west. Once the Perkins Brothers became a steady attraction, the club, which would hold some four hundred patrons wall to wall, was always filled to capacity.

Under Truman Jones's ownership, the El Rancho had become a
classier breed of honky-tonk. Inside he had erected a small stage,
about a foot off the floor, placed two artificial palm trees at each end
of the stage, pinned a Mexican blanket on the wall behind the stage,
and even went so far as to put cloths on his tables. Any place that had
matching tables and chairs, *and* tablecloths to boot, was in its own
league. Jones also enforced a no-fighting policy within the club, which
over time attracted less combative types and gave the El Rancho at
least the veneer of civility.

So concerned was Jones about appearance that he decided the
Perkins Brothers band needed a makeover. The white cotton shirts and
threadbare black pants they had been sporting were hardly fit attire
for the club's star attraction. His solution was to take the brothers to
Nashville and buy them matching western outfits to wear onstage, a
sartorial touch Carl was convinced made the band play better. For lack
of funds, stage attire had been low on Carl's list of priorities to this
point, but with the new outfits had come both a greater sense of professionalism and a certain possessiveness he had not felt towards an
item of clothing since Lake County and his beloved secondhand knick-
ers. Even the El Rancho audiences seemed to regard the Perkins Brothers with more respect and courtesy, as if they had overnight risen to
a new plateau as entertainers merely on the strength of their
wardrobes. It both puzzled and delighted Carl, seeing so much fuss
being made out of fashion, particularly as it related to him.

Clayton provided the next bit of good fortune the brothers experienced in the form of an impulse he carried out extemporaneously in
midsong before a packed house at the El Rancho. Carl was working
out a sizzling solo when he felt something brush by him on the stage.
It was Clayton. He had jumped onto the dance floor and was riding
his bass sideways to the back of the room; on his return trip to the stage
he stopped, twirled the bass 360 degrees, mounted it sideways again,
and lay on it while balancing it on the floor, all the time never miss-

ing a beat. The crowd roared and cheered him on, and Carl collected himself quickly enough to signal Jay to shift the song into a higher gear. If it were possible for music to blow the roof off a building, the Perkins Brothers would have done it on this night.

Though he had had no warning of Clayton's antics, Carl encouraged his brother to keep it up. Jay didn't want any part of it. "I can't dance, and I *won't* dance," he informed Carl. "Don't even ask me." He was happy to play rhythm and be the still, quiet anchor onstage while Carl and Clayton cavorted around. For his part, Carl wanted him and Clayton to work out some pat routines to capitalize on Clayton's showmanship. Clayton, however, resisted all suggestions that they preplan something that had grown out of the spirit of the moment. His instinct served him well: Since nothing else about the show was regimented, not even the song list, it made more sense to move ahead on gut feelings and let the music take them where it would.

Clayton's act evolved. Where he had once lay prone on the bass while playing it, he started standing on it, balancing it with his feet, one foot in the curve of the body, the other at the top near the neck. As he did he would throw his hands up in the air and shout, "Yeeeaaahh!" He also found that if he put a rubber ball on the bass stand, he could ride it pogo stick–style out into the crowd. The only routine he would agree to with Carl was one in which Carl would casually walk behind him during a solo and make a motion as if he had kicked Clayton's derriere. Clayton timed it so he jumped when Carl swung his foot, and the boy could leap—a concert photo from the early fifties shows him jumping to the full height of the bass's body, Carl barely visible behind him.

Entertaining as they were, Clayton's routines were strictly self-serving. He hungered for the spotlight that was always Carl's, but the bass wasn't a solo instrument, and he was neither a singer nor a songwriter. Clowning around drew attention to him, even as it strengthened the band's reputation. This was the underside of his refusal to develop the routines into a planned act. There was something vital in their spontaneity, but more to the point, as Clayton saw it, it gave him some leverage—he was building a small following of his own, and giving Carl competition from within.

The most unsettling moment of the Perkins Brothers' early tonk years came at a time when Carl was beginning to question whether he and his brothers would ever make it to the Opry stage. By the early fifties he knew his kind of country was not Nashville's kind. Apart from lacking the proper equipment necessary to cash in on the schoolhouse circuit, he considered his style too raw and too wild for the young teens who filled the gymnasiums and auditoriums to dance to traditional country music. Unable to solve the mystery of where he belonged in the universe, he wondered if the Perkins Brothers were doing as well as they would ever do simply by being the top honky-tonk band around, while another part of him said to hold on to the dream.

As he conducted this internal dialogue regarding the future, he booked the band into Earl Mills's Hilltop Inn, a tonk notorious for its nightly mayhem. On a Saturday night, to a packed house, they opened their first set at the usual eight o'clock hour. Most of the customers knew Carl and his brothers from the other tonks, and he them; but through the early evening Carl took note of a new face in the crowd, a tall man who seemed infatuated with the Inn's voluptuous red-haired waitress. Time and again during the first few sets he coaxed her onto the dance floor with him, and ground his body against hers during the slow numbers. At a table to Carl's left, about twenty feet from the bandstand, sat the man's date, alone, nursing a long-neck bottle of beer, her eyes ablaze.

Between songs, Carl noticed the couple arguing. As he turned to count off a new song, he heard a loud crash, and looked back to see the woman on her feet, her chair overturned behind her. Glaring at her male companion, who stared back with a quizzical, frightened look, she jerked a pearl-handled .22 pistol out of her purse and shot him between the eyes. She pulled the trigger again while lowering the gun, and the bullet hit a concrete wall and started ricocheting around the room, sending the other customers diving for cover under the few tables on the sides of the dance floor. The man's head jerked back, and then his torso flopped forward, crashing on the tabletop, where he lay completely still.

In a split second Mills was wading through the crowd, leaded axe handle at the ready. The woman stood stock still, her face frozen in an expression of disbelief, a wisp of smoke trailing from the gun at her side. Without a word, Mills pulled her arm behind her back and snatched the weapon away. As his hogs came over to tend to the victim, Mills yelled to the bar girl to call an ambulance. As she dialed the number, one of the hogs turned to Mills and shook his head. "Ain't no need to hurry—he's dead."

The band returned the next Friday to find that Mills had installed a barrier of chicken wire from ceiling to floor in front of the stage.

"That chicken wire ain't gonna stop what happened here the other night," Carl told Mills.

"Why?" Mills asked.

"Because that was a damn bullet, man! If you're gonna protect us from that you're gonna have to put up a piece of solid steel!"

"Well, what's the crowd gonna do?"

"I guess they'll have to come behind the steel to listen to us," Carl said, laughing at the thought.

Chicken wire in front of the bandstand didn't bother Carl. But the endless violence and the mindless drunkenness tested his resolve. The tonk audience liked his original songs—"Let Me Take You to the Movie, Magg" had become a frequently requested number all over Jackson—but as each night wore on into the next day, it became apparent that the quality of the music, or the uniqueness of the band's sound and style, was of little concern. Drinking, dancing and fighting, fighting, dancing and drinking—there was little more to the tonk experience.

▶ THE VOICE OF CARL PERKINS

The tonks is where I got a reading on a lot of my stuff; I'd just try writin' it raw in the clubs, and if they jumped out there and kicked and got to rockin', I'd remember the titles and very little else. And that's the way I'd write my songs. But if they kept sittin' there I'd cut it pretty short. And later on, step out there on a limb and try something else with 'em. The more they got to drinkin' the less I paid attention to the reaction to 'em, 'cause once they get high they like everything.

I knew those people, knew when they had a new baby, knew their uncles and aunts. We were all family. I watched 'em grow up, I watched 'em sometimes get married in the tonk, have a tonk weddin', man. And we played. The Perkins brothers sang their love songs.

They kept us alive and kept us going in the same old places, 'cause you couldn't see the walls if you got a smiling face sittin' there. And that same ol' stinkin' cane-bottom chair, if it's got a soul in it that shows you love and compassion . . . they really cared about us. And they showed it. They fed us. It was their dollars we were livin' off of. It wasn't extra, it wasn't get-tin' us no fine cars and no pretty western clothes like we wanted, but we never got tired of playin' for those people, 'cause we had more of 'em than anybody else around here. I guess we showed 'em we cared about 'em and it became kind of a love affair with the Perkins brothers.

We never got down because of the years we spent in the tonks. We learned 'em well, we learned how to stay out of trouble, and we learned how to make the best life out of it that we could. It wasn't too bad being the best tonk players in the area. It's pretty good to work yourself; even though you're not on that big ladder of success, you are succeeding. And everybody's gotta be somewhere, and everybody can't be on the Grand Ole Opry stage. There were lots of times when I thought, "Well, I may never be there, but I'm a lot further than that Lake County cotton patch."

a f t e r Jay and Pauline moved out, financial pressures on Carl increased tremendously. Jay was now responsible for himself and his new bride, and it was left to Carl to support the rest of the family on his own. Clayton considered the band his work and didn't pursue other employment. Before 1950 was over, Carl left the mattress factory for a higher-paying job on the Ray-O-Vac battery plant's night shift. When lack of work forced the closing of his shift in 1951, he was hired as a pan greaser—the most menial and physically demanding task on the line—at Colonial Bakery, where he was teamed with his buddy Ed Cisco. Two years later that job petered out in the wake of a strike and the opening of a rival bakery, events to which Colonial reacted by trimming its staff. Although he was offered a chance to stay on in a part-time position on Fridays and Saturdays, Carl wasn't interested in any job that would interfere with his weekend tonk dates. In late January of 1953 he began working the tonks full time, a move Valda encouraged, saying, "It could be the best thing to ever happen. You'll start concentrating on your music now. I'm workin'. You don't worry."

Looking back on that moment, Valda says her decision was unremarkable, given her faith in Carl's ambition and ability: "It wasn't just a dream and that was it. He had the talent to follow up with what it takes to make a dream come true. We know it's hard for any entertainer to make it, that there's a lot of things that have to come together. But I knew they would with him. I just knew it. And I focused on the point of Carl making it, more for to prove that he could do it than what it meant in material goods. It did mean something with that, too, but I felt he had been denied so much. He was not allowed to be a child. How sad. I don't know of anything that's worse than not being allowed the freedom of being a child. So when it came time, I was going to do what a wife should do, and that is stand by her man."

In February, Valda learned she was pregnant, with the baby due in November. She continued working, Carl started playing six nights a week on the local circuit, and together they were making ends meet— nothing more, but at least that.

Late '53 saw Carl make another significant change on the professional front. For a weekend show at the El Rancho, Clayton had brought along one of his friends, a Bemis fellow he introduced as "Fluke" Holland. Tall, blonde, and sad-eyed, Fluke's given name was W.S. Holland. His nickname had been bestowed upon him by J.B. Nance, an employee of Tommy Newman's Pure Oil gas station and grocery mart near the Hollands' house. An admitted "smart aleck," Holland liked to pester the help by picking up items on the counter and asking, "What is that flukus you got? Lemme see that flukus." Nance soon began referring to him as "Fluke," and the name stuck.

After graduating from J.B. Young High School, Holland had gone to work installing awnings for the S.M. Lawrence Company. From his thirty-five-dollars-a-week pay he had saved enough to buy a used Cadillac. This luxury item made him the envy of his peers, especially the ambitious musicians he encountered in the Perkins brothers, who regarded his car as the ultimate status symbol.

Early into the band's first set that night, Carl was singing when he heard a new sound behind him, one that brought to mind "a freight train's wheels clattering on steel tracks." When he looked around, he saw Holland standing next to Clayton, beating out the rhythm on the side of the bass as Clayton slapped the strings. They were lost in their own world, cackling and cutting up as if they were alone on the stage. But Holland was right on the beat, and pushing it. Only when he looked over and saw Carl fixing a steady gaze on him did he let up on his attack.

"No, man!" Carl called out to him. "Hit that thing harder!"

"You don't care?" he asked.

"Man, hit it harder!" Carl implored again. "I like it!"

By sheer accident the Perkins Brothers Band became a quartet with the addition of Holland as a drummer. But Holland neither owned a set of drums nor had he even given a thought to playing in a band. As far as he knew, he possessed no musical talent, until Carl indicated otherwise.

While Carl respected Holland's musicianship, such as it was, initially he found him difficult on a personal level. W.S. tended to be quick to put down others and equally quick to praise himself, qualities disdained by the humble Carl and Jay, but fervently embraced by the upstart Clayton, hence the friendship. With his size—about six-feet-two, 200 pounds—he intimidated most anyone he met and could get away with being outspoken. Apart from his size, his appearance suggested a dandy with attitude: thick, curly blonde hair was carefully swept back from his forehead and pomaded into granitelike solidity; and he had a habit of wearing sunglasses, day and night, outdoors and in. In all respects but two he seemed the perfect companion for Clayton: Fluke Holland didn't drink or smoke.

After spending some time together, though, Carl not only found

Fluke's eccentricities amusing, but came to respect the man himself as a trustworthy, reliable addition to the group. He even defended Fluke when a tonk patron would object to the drummer's appearance, especially the sunglasses after dark, and in this way helped avert many physical confrontations.

The tactic worked well with the regular folk. But the tush hogs presented another problem entirely, one Carl could not negotiate. Between sets at the Cotton Boll, a hog approached Fluke at the bar and told him, "Man, you don't need them glasses on. Sun's down."

"I'm wearin' 'em 'cause I wanna wear 'em" came Fluke's in-your-face response.

"Well I don't like 'em," the hog shot back.

"Then why don't you take 'em off me," Fluke suggested, straightening up to his full height.

Undeterred, the hog not only knocked off Fluke's sunglasses but landed several hard blows to his face and body in rapid succession. Carl, standing nearby, watched the beating unfold. He made no move to aid Fluke, because he wanted to find out if his drummer was as tough as his talk; a part of him even felt Fluke needed a beating to help him grow out of his big-mouthed ways.

Not being a tush hog himself, Fluke offered little defense against his attacker. When the crowd saw the fight taking a one-sided course, several stepped in to pull the hog away from Fluke. Carl, Jay, and Clayton headed for their instruments and kicked off another set. The music had the desired effect of bringing people back to the dance floor, leaving Fluke to nurse his injuries and the hog to search out his next conquest. As it happened, Fluke had a couple more go-arounds with the hogs before he toned down his act; but tone it down he did finally, and looked more to Carl as a model for navigating the treacherous, tush-hog-infested waters of the Jackson honky-tonks.

On September 17, 1953, Valda awoke with the sharpest pains she had felt in her life. The baby wasn't due to be born for another two months, but it was on its way. Later that evening, after nine hours of excruciating labor, she gave birth to a six-pound baby boy, Carl Stanley

Perkins, who, despite his size, was still not fully developed and had to be sheltered in an incubator.

Carl had been waiting for the birth directly outside the delivery room's double doors, "just far enough away so that when they opened they wouldn't slap me in the nose," and before another half-hour passed a gowned nurse came through carrying a baby wrapped in a blue blanket, a boy's color. She saw Carl and stepped over to him, pulling the blanket back to show him the child's face.

"Isn't he a doll?" she asked.

He was anything but a doll. His eyes were puffy, his head elongated—Carl thought his first child the ugliest baby he had ever seen. His expression must have given him away, because the nurse was quick to assure him: "Oh, he's gonna be beautiful. He's not cleaned up, Mr. Perkins. You wait about an hour, then you come back. You'll see a doll; he's a pretty baby."

"Lord, I hope so," Carl said. "He's ruint right now. He sure is ugly, but I'm so proud he's here."

Carl was proud, and overwhelmed by the moment, the passage into parenthood, and the prospect of fulfilling his obligations as a father: "I was really so thankful that that boy was here. He was mine and I could talk to him about music, and I felt the responsibility of being a good daddy. I walked up to that window and I was waitin' to hear somebody say, 'Look at that little Perkins boy. Isn't he pretty?' They never said it, because he wasn't one of the prettiest ones in there. *But he was mine!* And boy, nobody had to tell me; I couldn't wait to get my hands on that little skinny-boned fella. They laid him in an incubator and rolled it up to the window for me to see. It was something. I just . . . I don't know . . . the love for Valda went to the bone *and through the bone.* Here was a woman who had given me a son. Those are magic moments in your life."

In addition to being premature, Stanley developed a problem keeping milk down. His weight began dropping, and there was concern that he might not survive. Finally a doctor tried goat's milk, and it took. But Valda and Carl were warned that their son's health was fragile, requiring that he be given careful tending.

Valda dreaded taking the infant back to the cold house in Hickstown. When Carl visited her one evening, she told him she would be moving back to her parents' house.

"I don't want to go back to Hickstown," Valda explained to a stunned Carl. "The baby's little, and Daddy keeps his house warm. It'll get sick down there at your house. And furthermore, I don't want to go back there! Not that I'm better than your Mama and Daddy, but they don't live like I was raised."

"I know," Carl said, and he did know. He had seen enough Bemis houses to know where he stood in the world. Valda's decision was like a great weight dropping out of nowhere and crushing his skull. But a part of him understood—the part that had seen all the good things in his life taken away. Rather than argue, he pled his case matter-of-factly. "I just want you livin' with me," he said.

"If you want me to live with you," Valda demanded, "get me a place to live."

In Jackson, a new government housing project, Parkview Courts, had been built. With rents keyed to income, it offered Carl the best option, given his fluctuating pay. Inquiring at the office, he was told one apartment was available, number 23D, a four-room split-level renting for thirty-two dollars a month for an occupant at Carl's income level. Handing over the money, Carl took the door key and headed for Tate Brothers Used Furniture in downtown Jackson. He paid fifty dollars for a bedroom suite, living-room suite, and a dinette—"used, very used."

Apartment 23D was the corner single unit adjoining a duplex book-ended by another single unit. A nondescript red-brick structure with a wooden overhang above the front door, its interior was fresh but drab—the floors were concrete. Downstairs were a living room and kitchen; upstairs, a bathroom and two bedrooms, the larger in the front of the apartment. Furnishings left little room for traffic or stretching out. Valda didn't care: It was home. "The happiest day of my life up to that time was the day I got to move to Parkview Courts. It was so wonderful," she recalls. "It saddened me because Carl was not happy. He felt when we moved that his parents could not make it without him, which was quite sad to me. But then we had not been living there a week until he told me, 'I did not know how unhappy you were in Hickstown. Now I understand.' "

"Movement was of the essence, and the faster the better." So wrote Theodore H. White, analyzing the 1950s in *In Search of History*. So it was in the boom time of postwar America, especially in regard to leisure-time pursuits. Sales of television sets doubled in the two years between 1950 and 1952; by 1952 the transistor was replacing the vacuum tube and with that came the introduction of the first pocket-size transistor radios from Sony. More powerful, more luxurious cars were taking over—General Motors had introduced a V-8 engine in 1949, requiring a new higher-octane gas; the advent of power steering, power brakes, and air conditioning followed close behind—and more Americans were buying them. To suit the quickening pace of daily life, other services began to appear, notably, fast food, for those on the go or too tired to cook after a long day on the job. In the late forties the McDonald brothers had perfected a mechanized kitchen, and, after some spectacular success in the early fifties, had begun franchising their operation throughout the United States to ever-growing profits.

Music too was starting to reflect—or anticipate—the changes going on in American society. In 1951, Sam Phillips cut a session with a band headed by Ike Turner, a disc jockey at WROX in Clarksdale, Mississippi. Jackie Brenston, Turner's underage, saxophone-playing cousin, sang lead on his self-penned "Rocket 88," a bristling bit of spitfire rhythm and blues inspired by a popular Oldsmobile coupe. Chess Records bought the dubs from Phillips, released the single in April, and had a number-one record in June.

A year after Brenston's hit, twenty-nine-year-old Cleveland disc jockey Alan Freed went on the air at WJW with a nightly show he called *Moondog Rock and Roll Party*. "Rock 'n' roll" was a term Freed claimed to have coined for the big-beat R&B he favored (he had been introduced to the music only a short time earlier by Leo Mintz, Cleveland's largest record dealer). In fact the term had been used in race records dating back to the early twenties, usually as a metaphor for sexual frolic. A 1934 film, *Transatlantic Merry-Go-Round*, featured the Boswell Sisters singing a song titled "Rock and Roll," written by a pair of pop composers, and variations of the term showed up frequently in the work of thirties' and forties' R&B artists and groups, among the most powerful of all of them being Roy Brown's explosive 1947 track, "Good Rockin' Tonight," which was also a hit a year later in a comparably incendiary cover by Wynonie Harris. In sound and style, Fats Domino's "The Fat Man" belonged under the rock 'n' roll rubric; Sam Phillips has even referred to "Rocket 88" as the first rock 'n' roll record.

So the term was hardly Freed's coinage—he usurped it and even applied for a copyright on it, hoping to get record companies to pay him a royalty for so designating their recordings. That aside, his show brought the music of black artists to his largely white listenership—a brave and almost singular move that earned him the immediate wrath of local segregationists, who denounced him as a "nigger lover." Compared to R&B, though, rock 'n' roll was a benign term to most white Americans, one free of racial overtones, further easing the music's entree into the mainstream of contemporary life. In March 1952 Freed mounted his first concert, the Moondog Ball, starring prominent black artists, at the 10,000-seat Cleveland Arena. Nine thousand tickets were sold in advance, but on the night of the show an estimated 25,000 kids showed up, forcing the show's cancellation. Again Freed was assailed by racist elements upset by the crowd's interracial makeup. By 1954 he had moved to New York's WINS, raised it to number one in its market, was making $75,000 a year and staging wildly popular concerts at the Brooklyn Paramount, again drawing sell-out, interracial crowds, minus the white enmity he had endured in Cleveland.

In the Northeast, integrated teenage audiences were packing theaters for shows featuring an electrifying potpourri of the new styles by both black and white artists. Rhythm and blues and rock 'n' roll dominated the bills, but doo-wop, another new style, began making its mark in the early fifties and it too had deep roots in the black experience, rooted as it was in gospel and early group harmony styles of the thirties.

Through the 1940s the black exodus from the southern states had wrought dramatic changes on the cultural landscape above the Mason-Dixon line, notably in Chicago, where the greatest concentration of black immigrants could be found. In the Windy City, where Big Bill Broonzy had reigned supreme among blues masters since the 1930s, the torch was being passed to a gifted singer-songwriter-guitarist from Rolling Fork, Mississippi.

Born McKinley Morganfield, the young man took his professional moniker from his grandmother, who called him Muddy, and from his playmates, who tacked on Waters. He had grown up studying and emulating the great Delta-blues artists of his youth. Charlie Patton, Son House, Robert Johnson, Blind Lemon Jefferson, and Lonnie Johnson were only the most prominent names whose work had shaped his musical vocabulary by the time he arrived in Chicago in 1943. A year later he had purchased his first electric guitar and by the end of the decade had developed the amplified, hard-driving sound of modern Chicago blues. Recording for Chess Records in 1950, Waters and the exemplary musicians in his band introduced rhythmic innovations such as stop-time patterns and driving backbeat that were quickly emulated by other artists, particularly those who played the earliest forms of rock 'n' roll.

That forces powerful and new were gathering strength became apparent on a grander scale in 1953 when Bill Haley, a struggling country-and-western singer from the Detroit suburbs (who had released his own cover version of "Rocket 88" on the small Holiday label out of Philadelphia), fronting a group he called the Comets, made it to the top 15 of the *Billboard* singles chart with "Crazy, Man, Crazy," a bopping blend of country and rhythm and blues written by Haley himself. It was the first rock 'n' roll single ever to make the *Billboard* top 100. Something happened. In 1954 Haley hit the top 30 with another single, "Rock Around the Clock," and later in the year the top 10 with a sanitized cover version of Joe Turner's lascivious "Shake, Rattle and

Roll." With the latter Haley became a national star, "the father of rock 'n' roll."

But the messenger of the covenant was in Memphis, with Sam Phillips and two country musicians, guitarist Scotty Moore and bassist Bill Black, getting ready to cut his first record at the Memphis Recording Service. In 1952 Phillips had formed his own label, Sun Records, and had had some success on the R&B charts a year later with his first release, "Bear Cat" by Memphis disc jockey Rufus Thomas (the song was an answer to Big Mama Thornton's "Hound Dog," which had entered the charts only two weeks prior to Thomas's response), and "Feelin' Good" by Little Junior Parker. He had also been signing some offbeat country artists, among these being Doug Poindexter's Starlite Wranglers, whose lineup included Moore and Black. In June of 1954 they were teamed in the studio with Phillips's newest discovery, nineteen-year-old Tupelo, Mississippi, native Elvis Presley, an aspiring singer with deep roots in country, gospel, blues, rhythm and blues, and pop music. The trio produced a startling cover version of "That's All Right," written and originally recorded by blues artist Arthur "Big Boy" Crudup in 1946. In Presley's hands the song became more than blues, more than the honky-tonk country suggested by Black's propulsive bass and Moore's full-bodied chording and crisp, minimal solos. The voice was defiant and independent, at once raging against a wayward woman and then challenging her to stay her heartless course. But as the song continued, Presley's attack softened slightly, enough to let in the hurt on the underside of his cocky declamations. The next day's session resulted in another wonder in a remarkable reworking of Bill Monroe's "Blue Moon of Kentucky."

Sun single #209, "That's All Right" b/w (backed with) "Blue Moon of Kentucky," was released July 19, 1954. *Billboard*'s review called the artist "a strong new talent" who could appeal to both the country and R&B markets.

In the interim between the July release of Elvis's first Sun single and the birth of Carl Stanley Perkins in September, Carl found reason to be upbeat. In his continuing effort to get his music "out of Jackson," he had received what he considered an encouraging sign from one of the New York record companies. The label had rejected his tape, of course, but this time someone enclosed a note with the return package. It read: "We think your music is interesting, but we don't know where it fits in with what we are promoting right now."

Carl took strength from the negative response, but Valda was curious as to how he regarded rejection as a positive event.

"That's what I want them to say, Valda!" Carl explained. "The music's not bad, but they don't know what it is! Someday somebody *will* know what it is!"

That day came before the summer was over. Valda was ironing clothes at the time, and had the radio on. A disc jockey announced the next record as being from a new singer out of Memphis, Elvis Presley. As "Blue Moon of Kentucky" began, Valda, stunned, stopped her work and listened to a sound she had heard before, when it had come from the Perkins brothers. She called out to Carl, who was in another room, relaxing after finishing his morning errands.

"Carl, listen to this!" Valda demanded. "Listen! They play like y'all! It sounds like *you!*"

It was close. The bass clicked and thumped like Clayton's, but the guitar had a full, thick sound, whereas Carl preferred his hard and trebly; and the expository solos were spare and linear, in contrast to the stinging, angular soloing Carl executed throughout a song to create something of an instrumental complement to his own lead vocals, almost a harmonizing voice. But the rambunctious, barrier-shattering energy was right in the pocket with the Perkins Brothers' rocking style.

The voice was something else, at once familiar and mysterious. Immediately Carl knew where Presley came from stylistically, because in this sense they were kindred spirits: Bill Monroe. He heard Monroe in Presley's upper register, in the inflection of certain lyrics, such as "Kentucky," with the emphasis on the second and third syllables ("Blue moon of Ken-*tucky* keep on shinin' "). Presley rolled off the lyrics with the grace and ease characteristic of Monroe, but with more tension in his young voice, and with his footloose spirit fired by the driving rhythm. It was in many respects similar to the arrangement Carl had worked up and used in the tonks since 1947.

"His style *is* a lot like mine," Carl agreed. When the song was over, he stood silently in the kitchen as Valda returned to her ironing. Eight long years in the tonks, chasing the dream he had brought with him from Lake County, had wound down to a single moment when he finally heard someone who wasn't merely hitting close to his sound, but was right on it. When later he heard the flip side, "That's All Right," he found even more common ground in the obvious influences Presley had picked up from black singers and incorporated into his up-tempo country music. All this time Carl thought his future lay in Nashville, only to find it beckoning from much closer to home.

"There's a man in Memphis who understands what we're doing," Carl said as "Blue Moon of Kentucky" faded out. "I need to go see him."

Before he made his first business trip to Memphis, Carl had a chance to see Presley perform, at a high school gymnasium in Bethel Springs, Tennessee, about fifteen miles from Jackson. At the gym, Carl, accompanied by Jay and Clayton, found only about a hundred people on hand in a place that could hold, by his estimate, nearly three hundred spectators. Still, Carl found it interesting that most of those present were young teens, as opposed to the older crowd he was used to seeing in the tonks. Until that moment it hadn't occurred to him that his style of music might appeal to this audience.

Shortly after Carl entered, Presley and his band came out and set up. While the bass player and guitar player were dressed in conservative sport coats and slacks, Presley was recognizable immediately as the star by his pink shirt, white sport coat, and black pegged-and-pleated slacks. With coat and shirt collars turned up, and thick, sandy hair slicked back, he looked like no singer Carl had ever seen before, either in person or in photos. His appearance had an electric effect on the audience, particularly the girls, who began screaming when they laid eyes on him. He played to them, especially, grinning as he stalked the floor, dark eyes searching out the prettiest ones in the crowd and fixing them with a playful but seductive stare. Experience had taught Carl that Presley's flirtatiousness and pantherlike pacing masked a bad case of nerves—he knew all the cover-ups too. But what Carl saw moved him. Presley wasn't wearing the sequined suits that had become so popular with country artists, and he wasn't going to be standing flat-footed in cowboy boots singing into the microphone. He was free to move around, as Carl was with his extra-long guitar cord. Only in his plain brown shoes did any aspect of Presley's appearance approach the conventional.

When they kicked off their show with "That's All Right," Carl was drawn to the front of the room. Standing off to the side, close to the band, he saw and heard an uncanny replication of the Perkins Brothers Band's sound: Elvis taking Jay's part and playing a solid, swinging rhythm; bassist Bill Black slapping the strings à la Clayton; and Scotty Moore picking lead lines. Unlike Carl and Jay, though, who harmonized and took turns singing solos, Moore and Black were strictly instrumentalists who stayed quietly and unobtrusively in the background. Black would occasionally swing his bass around and bop with it, Clayton style, but his routines were staid in comparison to those of the youngest Perkins brother.

Presley, like Carl, couldn't stand still while he sang. Carl had worked out his jitterbugging moves while still having to play lead guitar; Elvis slung his guitar behind his back and danced free, hips swiveling and legs shaking, his entire body convulsing in the grip of a kind of hysteria Carl had seen only in the most rabid churchgoers. When he moved, his hair flopped down into his face, partially obscuring his dark-eyed visage. When he sang he would sometimes hold the microphone tenderly and caress it, or tilt it towards the floor and lean into it, making over it as if it were his beloved. All the while, girls screamed and shouted, and the boys applauded and egged him on. Carl had seen similar responses to his music in the tonks, but he never knew if the tumult was more the product of genuine excitement over the sounds or the alcohol taking hold. Here there was no question—it was the music and it was the artist.

For all his apparent confidence, though, between songs Presley revealed his unease. In his patter he stuttered badly and tripped over himself, figuratively, trying to crack jokes. The entertainer in Carl, ever sympathetic, wanted to say, "Come on down, man. You're too scared." But in an odd way the stuttering worked to Presley's advantage. It might have made him even more endearing to the females, but it most certainly was of a piece with his singing style, in which he incorporated a stuttering technique that added extra tension to his material.

The set lasted only about half an hour, and in addition to "That's All Right" and "Blue Moon of Kentucky," Presley's repertoire included "Cotton Fields," and "I'm Movin' On," the latter a 1950 hit for Canadian-born country star Hank Snow, whose style had made its mark on Scotty Moore and kicked hard like Presley's and Perkins's music. In fact, Elvis didn't interpret the Snow song in his own style, but performed it in impersonation of Snow, and got close enough to the real thing to generate the wildest applause of the night apart from that greeting "That's All Right."

As Presley was taking his bow and backing away from the mic after his closing song, his feet got tangled in Moore's guitar cord and he fell square on his backside. With the applause rising, he jumped up and scooted out of sight, heading for the fire escape that would lead him to his car.

"I'm gonna say somethin' to him," Carl told Jay and Clayton as they exited and made their way towards the back of the building. When they turned the corner, Elvis, Scotty, and Bill were packing their gear into their car.

"Sure enjoyed the show, man," Carl said as he approached Elvis. Jay and Clayton lingered behind. "You sure can sing. Y'all are good, pickin' an' singin'."

"Well, thank you," Elvis said softly. He turned to look towards Scotty and Bill, and as he did, Carl saw what the upturned collar hid: a bad case of acne on Presley's neck. "Thank you," he said again.

"Reckon they takin' on anybody down there at Sun Records?" Carl asked.

"I don't really know." Elvis stared at Carl, and Carl stared back, figuring Elvis might have more to say. When he didn't, Carl pointed to Jay and Clayton.

"Well, this is my brothers there. We play about the same type thing you do."

"Well, good, man. Good," Elvis answered. Another pause. "I guess we better be goin'; we gotta get on back to Memphis."

Perfunct. Succinct. Matter of fact. Elvis had been polite and now was going on his way. Years later Sam Phillips would describe him as "probably innately the most introverted person that [ever] came into that studio." That's the Elvis Carl met in Bethel Springs, Tennessee. But Elvis had said enough; said it in the auditorium, with his music. Carl pulled out of the parking lot determined he would go through the same door Presley had kicked open, and soon.

Clayton didn't seem to care one way or the other about Presley, but Jay knew one fact to be true, and he told Carl straight out: "He's a sissy." Meaning homosexual.

"He ain't gonna last long," Jay announced. "They'll be some of them red dogs will tear him up, beat him to death."

"I don't know whether they will or not," Carl mused. "Why would they wanna whip him?"

" 'Cause he's sissy-lookin'."

"Well that don't mean you're gonna whip the son of a bitch because he looks sissy!" Carl replied.

"Well you know he's sissy!"

"I don't know he's sissy, Jay."

"Then what's he wanna wear pink for?"

Carl shrugged. "I don't know. He thinks he's pretty, maybe."

"He ain't near as pretty as he thinks he is," said Jay, the man's man.

"I think he's *very good looking*," Carl said, standing his ground as he prayed this wouldn't escalate into a fight. "You know he is too, Jay. We ought not to be talkin' about him. We oughta be pullin' for him, because he's sellin' records and we may have a chance down in Memphis."

▶ THE VOICE OF CARL PERKINS

By this time Jay and Clayton had pretty well settled in. There was not a lot of talk about the future; in fact, there was some statements being made like, "Ain't no need in us puttin' down no more of them sorry songs. Nobody gonna listen to 'em no way." I heard that, but I put a deaf ear to it. No, they weren't chasing the same dream I was. I don't know the difference it would have made. They might've got so good with their instruments that they might've started playing with somebody in Nashville and left me if they had had the same drive I did. I just wanted to learn more and more and get better and better. I always knew that some day I was gonna walk out on that Grand Ole Opry stage.

Nobody knew what this music was, and it's kind of hard for me to put it into the right perspective. Presley nailed it. He jumped right in the middle of what I was doing, and the minute I heard it I knew it. I started knowing that I had a shot then, because, you know, if you record "Blue Moon of Kentucky" by Elvis, you might record it by me too, because I sang it. I was a big enough fool to think if I'd go down there and sing it, he might like me singin' it too.

2

A SUMMONS

TO MEMPHIS

1954—1958

Memphis is something else. . . . Memphis is today.

—Peter Taylor, A Summons to Memphis

*I*n early October 1954, Carl loaded up his '41 Plymouth coupe for the trip to Memphis. Clayton and Jay held onto the guitars, and Carl wrapped the bass in a nine-foot tar-bottom cotton sack and tied it to the roof. Hardly a word was spoken among them on the way west. If Jay and Clayton didn't possess Carl's all-consuming drive to reach for bigger things in music, it wasn't apparent on this day.

Turning onto Union Avenue, Carl spotted a nondescript concrete building near the corner; in its window was a neon sign indicating this as the site of the Memphis Recording Service. Carl parked in front of the studio and told Jay and Clayton to wait while he went in to ask for an audition. Sitting at a desk in the outer office, slightly to the left of the entrance was a woman, identified by the nameplate on her desk as Marion Keisker. On the opposite side of the room stood a cardboard likeness of Elvis Presley, dressed much as he was the night Carl had encountered him in Bethel Springs a couple of weeks prior. No sooner had Carl stepped towards her, though, than did Keisker announce that Sun wasn't taking on any new artists. ("I guess," Carl said later, "you can always tell a hungry picker.")

"Well, ma'm," Carl began tentatively, "that's my brothers sittin' out there, and we sure did drive a pretty long ways to get here. We're from Jackson, and if somebody would just—"

"We have this boy Elvis Presley, and we aren't listening to anybody else right now," she snapped. "He's hot!"

"Yes ma'm, I know," Carl said politely. "I been hearin' him a lot. I sorta do that kinda music."

"Well, that won't help you," Keisker declared. "If you sound like Elvis, that won't help you."

"I don't sound like Elvis," Carl corrected her. "I said I do that kind of music."

"I can save you some time," Keisker advised. "Sam Phillips, the owner, isn't here. And he's not going to listen to you."

Carl thanked her and went back out to the car. As he was relating his experience to Jay and Clayton, a new Cadillac Coupe de Ville, with a dark-blue body and light-blue top, pulled in ahead of Carl's vehicle. When the driver emerged, he was dressed "like his car," as Carl remembers, in a light-blue sport coat and dark-blue slacks; he was well groomed and everything about his comportment bespoke to Carl a man of serious nature.

"Boys, that's got to be Sam Phillips," Carl said, rushing out of the car, angling towards the well-dressed stranger and blocking his path to the door. As Phillips tried to step around him, Carl introduced himself and asked for a tryout.

"Man, I'm too busy, I don't have time," Phillips said curtly, making another move for the door.

"Mr. Phillips, please," Carl pleaded. "Just listen to one or two songs, that's all. Man, you just don't know what it would mean to me."

Phillips knew what it meant to Carl, and later would tell him: "I couldn't say no; I couldn't turn you away. You looked like your world would have ended." So to Carl he said perfunctorily: "Okay, get set up. But I'm busy and can't listen long."

The Sun studio was slightly larger than those Carl had been in at Jackson radio stations, but still comfortably snug. In the control booth at the far end, where Phillips prepared to listen to the trio, Carl could see two tape recorders, Ampex 350 models. The out-of-view recording console was a rudimentary Presto five-input mixer with four microphone ports and one switch-operated multiselector port for microphone or playback. As Carl would learn, the echo he had heard on

Elvis's recorded voice—an echo reproduced live by Scotty Moore's amplifier—had been the product of Phillips manipulating the signal from one recorder to the other to create a split-second delay. Primitive but effective, it had given Sun Records a signature sound on the most meager of budgets.

When Phillips gave the signal, Jay stepped to the microphone and began one of his self-composed traditional country songs. Before he had completed the first verse, Phillips's stern drawl came over the studio speaker: "No. No. I don't like that. Got anything else?"

Again they tried one of Jay's songs. And again, Jay was nearly finished with the first verse when Phillips cut him off. "No. . . . No. There's already an Ernest Tubb out there."

Angry, Jay jerked loose his guitar strap and spun towards Carl. "Let's get outta here. I don't like that little son-of-a-bitch."

"Man, we can't go home!" Carl protested. "This is it! This is where Elvis is cuttin' his records! This is the very *room!*"

Jay and Clayton stared at their brother, who would not be moved. "I'm gonna play him one of my songs," Carl said.

"Let's get outta here," Jay insisted. "He's a smart aleck, and I don't like him. And he ain't gonna like your ol' song either."

Phillips emerged from the control room as if his work were done. Carl stopped him and suggested he listen to another song. Sam studied him for a split second. "Do it," he said.

With that, Carl began the first song he had ever written, his tale of young love in Lake County and the dream of riding into town on a beautiful stallion with his sweetheart, Maggie/Martha Faye, "to a western picture show." Losing himself in the performance, Carl danced around and belted out the lyrics as Phillips stood in front of the band, head down, listening intently, tapping one foot in time to the rhythm.

As he roared into his first guitar break, it suddenly hit Carl: *He hasn't stopped me yet.*

Sweat rolled down Carl's face as he deftly executed his guitar solo and tore through the song's final chorus. At the end of the song he cut loose with a flurry of notes, and Clayton tagged it with a triplet bass lick, an innovation new to this version and apparently thought of on the spur of the moment.

"Now that's original!" Phillips called out, a broad smile on his face. "That whole thing's original—the way you play it, the way you sing it, the way you wrote it. That's original! That's what we want. Do it again!

"But," he added, "can you stand still and sing?"

"Yes sir," Carl answered. "I just jump around a little in the clubs where we play."

"But they can't see you jumpin' in here," Phillips told him. "We're talking about records. Now stand in front of that microphone."

Struggling to stand still in one spot—not because he wasn't used to doing so but because his nerves were getting the best of him—Carl stumbled through a second version of the same song. When he was done, Phillips's mood was tamer. "That wasn't as good as the first time, but I like that song," he said. "It's country, but it's uptempo. It's a little different type of country. I want you to get some more songs like that. You come with another thing like that and we'll talk about a record deal. But right now, man, this new boy Elvis's got my hands tied."

Jay and Clayton were already heading for the studio door, with Carl straggling behind. A hand gripped his shoulder, and Carl turned to see Phillips trying to hold him back. "Now you're the one that needs to do the singin'," Phillips said in a near-whisper meant only for Carl's ears. "Your brother's a good ol' boy, but he sounds too much like Ernest Tubb," he continued. "You don't sound like anybody else; you may have a chance. Just keep writin' those uptempo things and stay in touch. There may be somethin' there."

What should have been a triumphant ride back to Jackson was instead bittersweet for Carl. Those few minutes in the studio had changed the Perkins Brothers Band irrevocably, as Jay, Clayton, and Carl knew. Jay might continue to split the lead-singer chores with Carl in the tonks, but the band's future now rested squarely on Carl's artistry—his songs, his guitar, his voice.

Carl had no problem coming up with another song for Sam Phillips. By this time he had written countless songs on the spot in the tonks, and a few had become favorites. Their lyrics changed with every performance, none had titles, none had been committed to paper or to any kind of formal arrangement. Some were extemporaneous observations-in-song about the goings-on Carl saw unfolding in front of him as he sang, others were sly commentaries on work and play, others were love ballads. The one he wanted to team with his first song had become a mainstay of the Perkins Brothers' sets to the point where it could be heard several times in various incarnations over the course of a Friday or Saturday night. Only the first verse remained unchanged from night to night:

> They took a light from a honky tonk
> Put the gleam in your eye
> They took a record from the jukebox
> And they bid my gal good-bye
> And now she's gone
> Ho-onky tonk babe

It was played in a jaunty 2/4 tempo, and Carl usually took a couple of guitar solos to break up the many verses he would improvise—"thousands and thousands" of verses over the years, he recalls. He sang it in a controlled tenor, cool, and almost detached until he got to "And now she's gone / Ho-onky tonk babe." Then he dipped into a bluesy vein and revealed the underlying hurt; the catch in his throat on "ho-onky tonk babe" sealed it with a tear, in a style identified with Hank Williams, although Carl had been employing such an approach long before he ever heard "Lovesick Blues." The song was only nominally about a honky-tonk gal; its real subject was the singer's determination to survive the gal's fecklessness and be strong enough to turn her away when she comes crawling back to her good thing.

A couple of weeks later, shortly before his next appointment with Phillips, Carl urged Fluke to buy a set of drums.

"What would I do if I had some drums?" asked the befuddled Holland.

"Well, you can play drums," Carl replied.

Fluke shook his head. "No, I can't play drums."

"Yeah, if you can keep time on that bass like that, you can play drums," Carl assured him.

For a date at the Cotton Boll, Holland borrowed a friend's drum kit.

Not knowing any better, he placed the high hat on his right, and played the bass drum with his left foot, the exact opposite of the standard setup. But it worked to Fluke's advantage by eliminating the crossover move from right to left to play the high hat, freeing his left hand to move around the other drums and cymbals. He wasn't smooth, but he was more than passable. From the Cotton Boll, he would sit behind the drum kit next, and for only the second time in his life, at the Sun studio.

Fluke drove the band to Memphis for the first session, in part because his Cadillac—which now had "Perkins Brothers Band" painted in script on one side—was the only vehicle any of them owned that was large enough to carry the brothers' instruments plus his drums. It was fairly quiet in the car, and Carl assumed everyone was nervous. He knew he was, and he had brought along a bottle of Early Times whiskey to ease the tension.

"Guys, if we get down here and get nervous, we're gonna blow this thing," Carl said between tastes. "Let's just make out like we're playing the El Rancho, that's all we gotta do." Swig. His body felt chilled, his stomach churned. "Let's just hook it together, because we're in this together, every one of us. Let's not be nervous."

"You're pretty damn nervous yourself right now," Clayton said when the pep talk ended. He took a long swig, but it was clear to Carl that Clayton was without fear. It was all so simple to him: Go to a studio, slap the bass, take a few nips from the bottle, come home. No big deal.

They arrived at Sun near one in the afternoon and started unloading.

"Whoa!" Sam Phillips commanded as Fluke lumbered by with part of his kit. "Whatta you need drums for?"

"They're part of the band," Carl told him.

"Well, what the hell do y'all play?" Phillips asked. "Whatta ya mean it's part of the band?"

"I mean it's part of it," Carl said. "You wait. It goes with it. Besides, that's his car settin' out there."

Accepting that the drummer and the car were a package deal, Sam repaired, without further comment, to the studio to set up for the session.

Carl's own memory is uncertain as to how his first composition came to be called "Movie Magg," but he admits that titling songs was his greatest weakness as a young writer. Phillips preferred shorter titles that could be set in large type on the small record labels, and he may have been the one to refer to Carl's song as "Movie Magg." At any rate, it was listed in the day's recording logs and thereafter referred to as such.

With Sam looking on from behind the control room window, Carl struck up the first notes of "Movie Magg"—three single notes leading into a brisk solo run before he began singing. While his vocal was assured and heartfelt, his guitar playing was tentative: the three-note lick that opened the song dragged, and he stumbled through his first guitar solo. Lyrically it was virtually the same song he had written at age fourteen, apart from a variation on one of the original verses:

> Well I slicked myself for Saturday night
> 'Cause there's one thing I know
> Now me and that little Maggie dear
> Are going to a picture show
> So look out, dad,
> Just back up, boy
> 'Cause you are in the way
> We'll see you down at the western show
> And we will watch the play

These lyrics showed a side of Carl he rarely revealed in public, that of the borderline tush hog who would be impudent enough to tell his girl's father, "Just back up boy / 'Cause you are in the way." It was an attitude he would never have expressed in Lake County, but it was reflective of one developed during the long, combative years in the tonks.

A second take of the song produced a version that pleased everyone. The guitar solos were smooth and fiery, the band fell in with an easy, swinging gait, and Carl's vocal was on the money—strong and determined, yet still suggesting the anxious feelings accompanying the plowhand's Saturday night date. Dropping the "So look out, dad" verse not only gave the song a consistent point of view, it also tightened the narrative line to a short, sweet portrait of backwoods dating mores.

"Yeah, man!" Sam exclaimed over the speaker after take two. "I really liked that song. It's a cute song—'Movie Magg.' And you've nailed it. We've got it."

"Movie Magg" was old hat to the band by 1954, but Sam's vote of confidence lifted the burden weighing on Carl's mind. The playback was exciting: He sounded good, the band sounded good, the arrangement was more polished than it had been in the tonks but no less spirited. When it was over, Carl was as anxious to play his new song for Sam as Sam was to hear it. Cutting out on the opening verse, he heard Phillips intone over the studio intercom, "Yep . . . yep . . . yep."

Sam then witnessed what Jay, Clayton, and Fluke had been seeing over the years: Carl gave them the signal and they were off, following his lead as he made up the next verses, some of the lyrics brand-new, some drawn from the many Carl had improvised in the tonks. His eye for the telling detail showed up in the first batch of lyrics, as did his skill for conjuring a real scene, introducing character and conflict, and dropping in some bits of hard-earned wisdom:

> Oh, she said she didn't love me
> And she didn't care no more
> She'd rather spend her life on
> A honky tonk hardwood floor
> But I'll be gone
> Ho-onky tonk gal
>
> Someday you'll come back crying
> Someday you will be blue
> That mean ol' honky tonkin' life
> Will grab the best of you
> And I'll be gone
> Ho-onky tonk babe
>
> (guitar solo)

Well she walked away and left me
She left me at the door
I know she'll come back crying
But I won't be here no more
And I'll be gone
Ho-onky tonk babe

They took the sand from the dance floor
And they made her slide away
But I know she'll come crying
But then I'm gonna have my day
And I'll be gone
Ho-onky tonk gal

La-di-da-da-da-da/la-da-di-da-da-di
You go on down and have your way
And just leave me be
'Cause I'll be gone
Ho-onky tonk babe

They took a light from a honky tonk
Put the gleam in your eye
They took a record from the jukebox
And they bid my blues good-bye
And I'll be gone
Ho-onky tonk babe

On his guitar solo, Carl spat out a series of two-note chords, struck full chords for two bars, and jumped to the top bass string for an ascending triplet that curled into a treble string run leading into the next verse.

A second take, indicated as "Honky Tonk Gal" on Phillips's logs, kicked off with a brief guitar solo. Carl's vocal presence was stronger this time, particularly in the spiteful tone he assumed in asserting, "I'll be gone / Ho-onky tonk gal." He revealed his feelings most dramatically on the lyric, "You'd rather spend your life on a honky tonk hardwood floor / But I'll be gone / Ho-onky tonk gal"—expressing disdain for anyone who would throw away another's true love for the honky-tonk life.

When it was over, Phillips said he liked "Honky Tonk Gal" but that the band hadn't "nailed it" as they had "Movie Magg." What he wanted was "a good, solid country song. I like this 'Movie Magg.' It's country; it's about the country. I wanna put it out as a record. But I want a good country ballad, man. Go write me a ballad."

Even though he liked his takes on "Honky Tonk Gal," Carl was prepared to do as Phillips suggested. For one, he had been quelling his inward shaking by sneaking nips of Early Times whiskey during breaks. By the time Phillips was ready to close up shop, Carl was feeling good—not drunk, but at least taxiing for a takeoff. For another, he had been chasing the dream too long to spoil it by being headstrong. Carl never went against his instincts, but he was trusting his fate to Sam Phillips's experience and judgment, completely. In bowing to authority the sharecropper's son was doing what came naturally.

The country ballad Sam requested took shape during a Perkins Brothers set at the El Rancho. Inspired and feeling blessed by Valda's love and support, Carl turned to the band and said, "Get in A, boys." Stepping up to the mic, he offered a heartfelt, improvised promise:

> When you're all alone and blue
> And the world looks down on you
> Turn around, I'll be following you

The band accompanied him in a straight 4/4, and Carl continued improvising verses to the langorous love ballad. His voice breaking on the phrase "turn around," he delivered an object lesson in unadulterated country soul, stylistically indebted to Hank Williams, but all Carl Perkins in sentiment and feeling.

Carl continued to sing the new ballad in the tonks for the next week, polishing the verses as he did. Less than two weeks after his first Sun session, he called Sam Phillips with news of "I'll Be Following You," and sang a few bars of it over the phone. Sam liked it, but told Carl, "The name of that song's gotta be 'Turn Around.'"

"If you like it," Carl answered, "I don't care what you call it."

Sam did indeed like the song and suggested Carl come back to the studio as soon as possible. When he heard the full song in rehearsal and realized Carl had written the prototypical country ballad, Phillips followed his instinct through its logical progression. He had recently hired two country-music veterans, Quentin Claunch and Bill Cantrell, native Alabamians who had worked in Muscle Shoals when Phillips was still in Florence. At Sun they were charged with rehearsing new country acts and were encouraged to bring new artists into the fold.

Phillips thought Claunch's electric guitar and Cantrell's fiddle might be the stylish, traditional touches "Turn Around" needed to crack the country charts. A run-through strengthened his opinion, and he added yet another musician, steel guitarist Stan Kesler, a song-writer-instrumentalist who had once been a member of West Memphis's Snearly Ranch Boys and was then on his way to becoming one of the Sun studio's most reliable session players.

With "Movie Magg" solidly in the uptempo country bag, Phillips sensed that with Carl's new song, a traditional ballad sung with uncommon commitment, he might have the ideal vehicle for launching the career of a unique artist: two good songs, one describing country life, the other a vow of devotion that skirted sentimentality but ultimately rang true and touched the heart. A comment made to authors Escott and Hawkins (authors of *Good Rockin' Tonight: Sun Records and the Birth of Rock 'n' Roll*), indicates Phillips well understood the scope of Carl's potential:

> *I knew that Carl could rock and in fact he told me right from the start that he had been playing that music before Elvis came out on record. I was so impressed with the pain and feeling in his country singing, though, that I wanted to see whether this was someone who could revolutionize the country end of the business. That didn't mean we weren't going to rock with Carl. That was inevitable because he had such rhythm in his natural style.*

Cantrell's fiddle turned out to be the star of the session. The song began with him striking two quicksilver chords, and then constructing a jittery solo line that added an unsettling counterpoint to Carl's deliberate, soul-wrenching vocal: Kesler weighed in with barely audible chiming notes at the end of the verses, and a delicate, mournful coda to bring the tearjerker home in heart-tugging fashion.

Between takes, Cantrell coached Carl on his vocal, which had been hurried on the first verse. A surviving tape of the session contains a revealing snippet of studio conversation in which a generation gap surfaces in Sam Phillips's own facility:

Cantrell: "Uh, right, right there on the first, you said, uh, 'When the world'—let's see—what's the words to the first line?"

Carl: (sings) "When you're all alone and blue—"

Cantrell: "Yeah. You didn't do it like that on, on that song that time. You said, 'When you're all alone and blue—' "

Carl: (sings) "When you're all alone and blue."

Cantrell: "Tha's right!"

Unidentified male (probably Claunch): "Whatta you boys think about Elvis Presley?"

Carl: "Man!"

Cantrell: "Good artist."

Unidentified male: "Huh?"

Cantrell: "Good artist. Yeah, I don't like that kind of stuff, I don't go for it, but it's great stuff."

Carl: "Boy it's somethin' isn't it?"

Cantrell: "It isn't my kind of stuff."

No, but it was Carl's kind of stuff, had been for years. He was itching to get it on record, but Phillips wasn't ready to abandon his adamant belief in Carl's potential to "revolutionize the country end of the business." Carl remembers Phillips telling him as well that having two artists on the same label cutting the same type of music was a commercial risk he couldn't afford. Elvis was selling a few records and drawing good crowds to his shows, and Sam worried that releasing Carl's uptempo music might result in the two artists canceling each other out in the marketplace.

That the first recordings of Carl's guitar playing find him assured and distinctive in his approach reflect not only the high caliber of his musicianship but also a newfound confidence stemming from his having acquired a big-league guitar in 1954. Since 1948 he had been listening to one of the most intriguing stylists he had ever heard in Les Paul, whose recordings with his wife Mary Ford demonstrated a visionary's command of studio technology. Paul, born near Milwaukee in 1915, had, as a teenager, devised a way to obtain a primitive stereo effect by wiring his guitar into a pair of radios placed on either side of him onstage. He also began experimenting with homegrown recording technology: At age fourteen he recorded himself on a homemade device fashioned from a weighted cutting lathe, a turntable made from a Cadillac flywheel, driven by a small motor and dental belts; at age nineteen, while tinkering with the idea of disc-to-disc multiple recordings, he found he could record duets with himself, or cut himself playing each of the instruments in the band.

The same year he cut his first disc multiples he also designed a solid-body electric guitar with two pickups, the latter a revolutionary innovation. Over the next few years he continued modifying and re-designing solid-bodies, and in 1952 signed a deal with Gibson for production of the Gibson Les Paul model, or the Les Paul Standard, with a gold top, two single-coil pickups, and what was called a "trapeze" tailpiece bar for muting the strings, a technique critical to Paul's unique sound, one he has steadfastly refused to dissect in public, save to describe it as "that big, fat, round, ballsy sound with the bright high end—nobody else has it."

This was the sound Carl was hearing on Paul and Ford's late forties–early fifties recordings for Capitol—"Lover," "What Is This Thing Called Love?" (a number-one single in '48), "Nola," "How High the Moon" (another number-one, from '51), and others. What Carl didn't know was that Paul was employing his entire battalion of forward-thinking techniques—"delay, echo, reverb, phasing, flanging, sped-up sounds, muted picking, and everything else," according to Paul—using multiple recording. Those impossible cascades of notes, so delicate and so dexterously executed, from one guitar! Carl was thunderstruck by the man's gift and, like most every other guitarist in America, tried to emulate Paul's style, but to no good effect on his cheap Harmony electric.

Shortly before he went to Memphis to audition for Sam, Carl saw a gold-top Gibson Les Paul in the Hardeman Music window. The owner, John Towater, a Perkins Brothers Band supporter, had sold Carl his Harmony electric. Spotting Carl gawking at the Les Paul display, he signaled him to come inside. He handed the guitar to Carl. "Take a look at this—it's new."

Carl cradled it gingerly, struck dumb by its heft and beauty. "Good God, that's heavy! But ain't it beautiful! Gold color! Lookee here, lookee here!"

Told it was a Les Paul model, Carl identified the artist as "the one that's making the guitar sound like four or five."

"That's him," Towater confirmed.

Carl plugged it in and hit some hot licks, working the full length of the instrument's neck. The other customers gathered around to listen, and soon people were coming in off the street to take in the guitarist's impromptu performance. All along Carl had been thinking that if he could get his hands on one of these instruments, he could play like Les Paul; when he did, he discovered he could play only like Carl Perkins. "Don't sound much like Les Paul, do I?" he said sheepishly when he finished his soloing.

"Well," Towater replied, "you know he does all that by multiple recordings."

"Oh sure," Carl said evenly, masking his complete ignorance of the term "multiple recordings." He was expecting Towater to place the guitar back on its stand in the showcase window; instead, Towater held it out to him, saying, "Carl, I want you to have this guitar."

"Mr. Towater," Carl stammered after collecting his senses, "I can't afford it."

"We haven't talked about that yet," Towater said. "I think you can. Can you pay five dollars a week?"

"Yes sir!" Carl answered. A few minutes later he walked out of Hardeman Music with his brand-new $600 Gibson Les Paul gold-top solid-body, "and I found my sound. When you changed tones on it, on a lot of them tone controls the variation was very minute. Didn't really do a lot. That guitar, when you went from one pickup to the other, its treble was treble, and you could get in between and you could get a sound of your own, or a tone of your own with 'em. That's what made 'em so popular; that pickup allowed for different tones and different qualities of tone, and individual guitar players got their identity with the sounds from that guitar."

The inventive guitar solos on "Movie Magg" and "Honky Tonk Gal" were indicative of Paul's influence on the still-developing Perkins style: the rapid two-note runs, quick hits on the bass strings, curling back into a flurry of single-string notes, returning to the tonic chord—it was one picker almost totally ignorant of technology's progress trying to achieve what another was doing with the aid of futuristic inventions and gear to give the effect of multiple instruments. This, on top of Carl's solid foundation of country, bluegrass, and blues, was as unique a voice in its own simple way as Paul's was in all its complexity. Sam Phillips acknowledged this when he told Carl after the "Movie Magg" session: "I'll say one thing for you—you got a good guitar and you know what to do with it. I really like the way you play that guitar."

The year ended on two notes that defined the extremes of Carl's life. During one of their tonk sets, Carl had noticed what looked like the butt end of a pistol in Clayton's back pocket.

"What's that in your pocket?" Carl demanded.

"That's none of your business," Clayton said contentiously. "Something I traded for."

Carl was both disappointed and angry at Clayton. Disappointed, because earlier in the year Clayton had met and soon married Ruby Sue Maness, a dark-haired beauty from Henderson, Tennessee, who had been more of a stabilizing influence on him than had anyone in his own family; so much so that Carl thought his brother might have turned a corner on his wild and rowdy ways. Angry, because of the threat the gun posed to everyone's safety if the tush hogs got hold of Clayton.

Returning to his mother and father's house after the tonk date (Valda was past her due date for their second child and Carl didn't want her staying at Parkview alone while he was working), Carl ordered Clayton to leave his gun at home the next time they played. "You can't ever go back on that stage with a pistol," Carl said. "You need to put it up and forget about it."

Clayton, who had been rocking baby Stan in his arms, whipped the gun out of his pocket and stuck the barrel in Carl's face. "I'll put it right between your eyes if you make one more move," he warned.

Carl moved towards Clayton, intending to disarm him. "Uh-uh, don't point that thing at me."

"I ain't jokin' with ya. You make one more step and you're a dead man."

Carl stopped. He knew Clayton would kill him, and might take his young son with him. Unaware of the unfolding drama, Valda casually strolled in from the bedroom and was quickly reduced to screams and tears by the sight she beheld.

Clayton kept Carl at bay while allowing Ruby Sue to take Stan without argument. From the rear, Jay approached stealthily. When he got close enough, he grabbed Clayton's outstretched arm and jerked it behind his back, wrenching it until Clayton was forced to drop the weapon. When he did, Jay threw Clayton down and stood over him, daring him to get on his feet and fight. Carl kicked the gun out of Clayton's reach and said to Jay, "Let him go." He wanted Clayton to get up so he could take a swing at him. Disarmed, Clayton wanted no part of Carl. The next day he acted like nothing had happened, and Carl went his own way too.

Valda didn't get over it so easily: "I think that brought my labor on, it scared me so badly. Clayton wanted his way with whatever it was and was willing to do anything to get it. And when he would indulge in drinking, he was even meaner. He was mean to Carl, he was mean to his own family, to his wife. He was just a mean person."

On November 9, 1954, Valda gave birth to a second child, Debra Joye Perkins, whose entrance into the world was smoother than her brother's: She was born full term and healthy and looked, to Carl, "absolutely beautiful." Having another mouth to feed, Carl stepped up the urgency of his entreaties to tonk patrons for their help in filling his tip kettle. The band's popularity was such that it commanded a higher percentage of the door, but on a good night the four-way split might amount to less than ten dollars per man.

After staring down the barrel of Clayton's pistol, Carl knew he was lucky to see the new year. Now he had to face the uncertainty that was his career. Once the emotional high of having recorded for Sam Phillips dissipated, the burdens of the real world quickly returned to prey on his emotions: He had no idea when his record would be released, had imposing financial responsibilities, and was dependent solely on the tonks for support. Alcohol obliterated some of his anxiety while he was playing, but at home and sober he saw little progress. All he could do was keep going to the tonks, keep hoping the record would come out soon and be successful so he could get some better-paying shows, like the ones Elvis was playing in schoolhouses.

The tonks were also losing some of their allure. No stranger to violence, Carl had had a narrow escape late in the year at the El Rancho. A fight broke out near the bandstand when one drunken man broke a full bottle of beer over another's skull. (Tonk customs dictated that a customer buy two bottles of beer at one time: one to drink, one to stay full in case it was needed as a weapon—empty bottles would bounce harmlessly off the head, full ones would break into pieces, slicing skin in the process.) At Carl's urging the band continued playing while the two men scuffled, but the one who had taken the hit was severely cut and had blood spurting out of the back of his head. He was rushed to the hospital via tush-hog transportation.

About an hour later the man returned with his head shaved and sewn up. He had a friend with him, and Carl saw the two of them sitting at a table, steely gazes scanning the crowd for the attacker. After the band concluded a set, Carl went outside to smoke a cigarette. Standing with one shoulder resting on the side of the building, he was knocked off balance by someone pushing him from behind. As he righted himself, he heard a click, then felt the cold steel of a switch-blade knife against his throat. On the other end was the man whose head had been split open earlier. Without saying a word, he jabbed the knife under one of Carl's ears, apparently intent on opening him up from one side to the other.

Oh, God, this is it, Carl thought.

Then a voice cried out, "That's the wrong one! Yonder he goes! Up the road!"

The man's buddy had spotted the person they were looking for running along Highway 70, heading for Jackson proper. Like Carl, he was dressed in a white shirt and dark slacks, and had about the same physical build. Drunk and wobbly, he was easy prey for his pursuer. A flying tackle brought him down, and the two rolled on the ground before dropping out of sight into a ditch. Minutes later the attacker scrambled back up to the road, bolted into a waiting car, and disappeared into the night. When Carl and the rest of the crowd arrived at the site, they saw the victim lying motionless in a gathering pool of blood; bloody bubbles percolated from his chest where one of his lungs had been punctured by a knife. Carl waited until an ambulance arrived.

Returning to the tonk shaken and disconsolate, he pondered whether a man with a wife and two children should carry on with this kind of life anymore. In an instant he had the answer: He plugged in his guitar, turned up the amplifier's volume, and rocked.

With that decision, Carl Perkins, dreaming of nothing more than singing on the stage of the Grand Ole Opry, stepped into the historical drama then beginning to unfold. The culture growing up around his style of music, a culture he had witnessed in his fleeting appearances at amateur shows and had observed most dramatically in force at Presley's Bethel Springs appearance, was itself hungering for a voice, a Prometheus around whom fashions, attitudes, language—indeed, fresh ideas about the way the world should work—would coalesce.

In the drift of time 1954 stands as a watershed, a year whose most important landmarks continue to affect lives four decades hence. Consider the events marking the midway point in President Dwight D. Eisenhower's first administration: After French forces had been defeated in Indochina (which was then partitioned into North and South Vietnam), U.S. Secretary of State John Foster Dulles vowed that America would not abandon the South to the victorious Communist forces now occupying the North; in *Brown v. Board of Education of Topeka*, the Supreme Court outlawed segregation by race in public schools; and Dr. Martin Luther King accepted an offer to be the pastor of Dexter Avenue Baptist Church in Montgomery, Alabama, a year before Rosa Parks defied city laws by refusing to relinquish her seat to a white passenger. Her action instigated a boycott of the public transportation system by the town's black citizens and thrust Dr. King into a leadership role in the budding civil rights movement.

Against this backdrop the release of a single record from a small, independent Memphis label seemed insignificant. Anyone who listened to the radio could recognize the dramatic change in American popular music without having to search for it on the dial, but the relevance of the new music as social phenomenon was yet to be revealed. Much of the excitement was coming from black artists, who had little or no access to mainstream American media and thus few opportunities to establish themselves as personalities in their fans' minds. Among the new white artists then making their mark, avuncular Bill Haley was hardly the type to stir youthful passion. Looking back on this time, Carl likens the young audiences at his and Presley's shows to "an idling engine waitin' for someone to put the gas to it." It would be a while before the pedal hit the metal, but the release of Presley's first single on July 19 revved up the engine a little bit.

O n a sunny afternoon in February of 1955, Carl drove to Jackson's Delmar honky-tonk and booked the band for a weekend gig. As he was about to pull out of the parking lot to go home, a country record playing on the car radio faded out, and a disc jockey came on the air to announce the next selection. Carl heard him say, "Listen to this Flip record by Carl Lee Perkins," followed by Bill Cantrell's opening fiddle licks on "Turn Around"; then his own voice came out of the speaker and filled the car. It was the first time he had ever heard himself on radio, and the sound paralyzed him for a moment.

Shortly after, Sam Phillips mailed him two copies of his first single, "Turn Around" b/w "Movie Magg," on the Flip label, a new subsidiary Phillips had formed. The 78 rpm discs were cracked, so Carl went to Hardeman Music and bought his own copy, then borrowed a friend's record player (Carl didn't own one) and headed for Martha's house. As "Turn Around" played, he listened intently to every note, again and again, sobbing softly, overcome by a moment so long in coming. When he got back to Parkview and handed the record to Valda, she broke down in tears.

"All the feelings were revealing inside of my soul and they really came to life when I got those first two records," Carl recalls. "I wanted to absorb every second of 'em. It was that dream I had chased all my life, and Valda shared that dream. She held that record like she held Stan when the nurse handed him to her. I'm a cryer—I get a soul-washing doing that—and Valda cried with me."

In Memphis, "Turn Around" caught the attention of disc jockey Dewey Phillips. Approaching music in an unexpected way was standard behavior for Phillips, another character who had come to public attention, like Sam Phillips (no relation), in 1948. His frantic, and wildly popular, *Red, Hot and Blue* show on WHBQ featured everything under the Memphis sun—the pop and country otherwise heard on WERC and the blues common to WDIA. Most of all, it featured Dewey Phillips unchained; a man who, according to writer Stanley Booth in his book *Rhythm Oil,* had been fired from the Taystee Bread Bakery for "causing/inspiring the entire workforce . . . to stop making loaves of bread and make little men, like gingerbread men."

With "Turn Around" getting good airplay on WHBQ, other country stations across Tennessee began airing it regularly, and soon it was showing up on local charts around the South and Southwest, Texas being one of the states where the single was especially well received. Carl became a celebrity around Jackson; whichever tonk had the band for a night or two did turn-away business, and the band members were always assured a good payday. With the single clicking a little bit, Carl received an offer from Bob Neal to go out on the road with Presley, playing schoolhouses and theaters on a circuit that would take them to Arkansas, Texas, Mississippi, and Louisiana.

Neal, a former Memphis disc jockey who was moving into the booking-agency business, had taken over from Scotty Moore as Presley's manager in November 1954, after landing the artist a contract to appear as a regular on *The Louisiana Hayride.* By the time Carl had made his debut on disc, Presley had two more singles out and was busy touring the South and Southwest, building his audience on the road. Wherever he appeared, he brought out a youthful, vociferous crowd of teenagers and young adults; a healthy contingent of females was always on hand, screaming until they were hoarse, bopping in their chairs and chewing their nails down to the quick, their pent-up sexuality about to boil over at the sight of the young Adonis beckoning them with every leg shake and pelvic thrust. To the males, Elvis was either a threat or a fellow traveler, more the latter than the former, as evidenced by the widespread adoption of Elvis's long, greased hair and sideburns. The look wasn't all that uncommon around the South at the time of Elvis's emergence, but his popularity had given it the cachet of a fashion statement singular to his generation, a slap in the face to the older crowd's crew cuts, brush cuts, and close-trimmed businessman's coifs.

Such was the scene Carl walked into when he was booked for his first two dates with Presley, at theaters in Mariana and West Memphis, Arkansas. As the opening act with a country record to his name, he received a polite reception and no more. Presley was the attraction.

The nervousness Carl thought he had detected in Presley at Bethel Springs turned out to be the real thing. He and Presley had spent a little time together at Sun, and Carl had come to know him as polite, sincere, ambitious, and completely devoted to his music career. He envied Presley's seeming self-confidence only to learn it was an illusion, like his own. Backstage before their first shows together, Presley paced the dressing room, unable to sit still. Carl, who had braced himself with a few slugs of Early Times before his opening set, stared in curiosity at what appeared to be a breakdown in the making.

"Man, why are you nervous?" Carl asked following his set in Mariana. "They're gonna love you."

"Oh, God, they may not," Elvis said, his voice trailing off weakly.

"Aw, get outta here. You're scared and they ain't never booed you off."

"Now you're through and if I'd of went on first I'd be through—oh my God!" Elvis clutched his head and moaned, "Man, you done got yours over with!"

"But they're ready for *you*, son!"

Elvis fell silent, listening to the emcee on stage talking to the audience. "Oh Lord," he moaned. "They're announcing me." In an instant he was up and out the door, sprinting for the stage. When he came off, after raising the usual tumult, Carl was there to get on him. "You can't tell me you were scared," he said to Elvis. "You started rippin' 'em."

"I wasn't rippin' 'em," Elvis corrected him. "I—I was just movin' around a little. They did it. I didn't do anything."

"Well, you don't have nothin' to worry about," Carl assured Elvis. "Tomorrow night'll be the same thing you did tonight. Yeah, they're doin' it themselves, but you're causin' it."

All the wild goings-on Carl had been party to in the tonks couldn't compare to the energy generated by Presley and his adoring audience. "He bowed up as if to explode, but he never exploded," Carl recalls. "It's like his clothes were gonna—whap!—fly off into space, but they never left his body. The audience anticipated the whole stage end of the building to blow out. But that didn't happen. The storms would settle back down and you could feel it brewing again. It was like a little tornado coming; you could feel a little vibration and they'd get together and all of a sudden, man, he'd throw out a finger, or he'd kick that leg out, and they all together would just scream. And they didn't plan it—they didn't say, 'One-two-three scream.' It was an impulse thing that happened.

"It was all brand-new. I'd watch it from the side of the stage and I'd stick my head out and see when they'd scream so loud and just be crying. Tears rolling down their beautiful faces. Girls lost, just totally out of it, falling with their head back against another's face; they'd be stacked against the stage so much they didn't know. And to be near it happening, and to have been out there just a few seconds before that yourself and feel that wind gathering, knowing where it was heading . . . When I'd jump around they'd scream some, but they were gettin' ready for him. I think if he had been an ordinary-lookin' guy like me, it wouldn't have happened as wild and big as it did and as quick as it did. It was like TNT, man, it just exploded. All of a sudden the world was wrapped up in rock."

Presley stood apart in many ways, and though Carl was by far the more experienced of the two musical artists, watching Elvis helped him refine his stage persona. Despite his nervousness, Elvis had a native instinct for performing that belied his inexperience at it, and he had an infallible sense of style, of what looked good on him, from the way he slicked his hair back to the length of his sideburns to his unusual choices in clothing. The latter he bought almost exclusively at Lansky Brothers (owned by Guy and Bernard Lansky) on Beale Street, "the Main Street of Negro America," as it was called by black business leader George W. Lee. As "Negro America" had produced the music that was the bedrock of rock 'n' roll, so was its primary commercial and cultural center in the South the home of rock 'n' roll fashion.

Well ahead of his arrival at Sun, Presley had discovered Beale Street. It was where he could hear—and according to some accounts, sing—the blues he loved, and where his fashion sense was formed. Sam Phillips was fond of telling his artists, "If you're gonna be on that stage, you need to have on something that the fan sittin' out in the front row ain't got. He don't want to be sittin' out there and have on the same shirt that you got. Now your music's different, you look a little different, your clothes gotta be different."

Carl was amenable to Phillips's suggestion but had a problem in having to support two children, a wife, and his mother and father. Sam suggested he follow Elvis's example and shop at Lansky's, "a black store, down on Beale Street. Let him take you down there and try on some stuff. He goes down there all the time."

When Elvis wasn't touring, he liked to hang around the studio or its adjoining restaurant ("That's where he learned to like cheeseburgers," Carl asserts), the latter being where Carl found him lounging one day, conspicuous in a yellow silk shirt with billowing sleeves. It looked good on Elvis—everything looked good on Elvis—and had a flair in its design that Carl found appealing: the bright color, the big upturned collar, the slight V neck, and the outsized sleeves cuffed around the wrist, cried out to be noticed. When he queried Elvis about their making a joint trip to Lansky's, it was as good as done. Elvis always seemed ready to check out new clothes.

In the middle of the store sat a long, rectangular table piled high with factory-fresh, wildly patterned, boldly colored synthetic silk shirts, most of which could be had for less than two dollars apiece. No more perfect a statement could be found for Elvis Presley than Lansky's clothing—it was colorful, it was outlandish, it was strange, it was original. And no one could match Elvis's radar for locating the spot-on, drop-dead shirt.

"Man, they had a blue one that'd look great on you," Elvis told Carl anxiously as they approached the table. "If I can find it, if they ain't sold it." He started digging through the shirts, tossing the rejects to the far end of the table. Finally he pulled out a shiny blue shirt, silk-looking if not the real thing. "Here it is, here it is, Carl," he said, handing the shirt over. Carl tried it on and showed Elvis, who approved. "Man, that'd look good with some black pants," he said, and back he came with a pair of new slacks, which Carl tried on and bought, along with the shirt.

After taking care of Carl, Elvis tended to his own needs. Picking carefully through the entire table of shirts, he settled on one that had the most bizarre multicolor design and tried it on. Emerging from the dressing room bold and vibrant, he adjusted the fit in the mirror as one of the Lansky brothers looked on approvingly.

"Man, it looks good don't it, Mr. Lansky?"

"Yes, it does, Elvis," Lansky answered.

Then Elvis turned up the collar, and Carl saw him transformed into the Hillbilly Cat in front of his eyes. "Yeah, it looks right," Elvis said softly, as much to himself as to anyone else, while preening over the image looking back at him.

For his part, Carl had become enamored of the silk stripe adorning each leg of a pair of tuxedo slacks. Unable to afford a tuxedo, he had asked Valda to sew a pink ribbon the length of each leg of his Lansky's slacks, then completed the ensemble with a pink shirt and a pink sport coat. The first time Carl donned the slacks for a show, Elvis took notice. Eyes widening and jaw dropping, he pointed at Carl's outfit. "Whoa!" he exclaimed in the voice of a man who has been both one-upped and impressed at the same time. "Them pants!"

"That ain't nothin' but a piece of ribbon, man," Carl told him. "Valda sewed it on there for me."

Shortly thereafter, Elvis, whose passion was for the sequined suits worn by many country acts but who was a few thousand dollars shy of being able to purchase one, showed up with a stripe running down each leg of his slacks. The final, classy touch was a pair of white buck shoes: the Hillbilly Cat in full regalia.

"That piece of ribbon was a brand-new accident," Carl says. "It looked so good and different. It made you forget that the idea was stolen off a tuxedo, 'cause that is black on black and it shines. But pink on black—back off! I didn't know what it was gonna look like; I just knew it was gonna be different. And I thought it was gonna look good to match the pink shirt I had, and man it looked great. I was the first person at Sun to wear 'em, and pretty soon some of the other guys started doing it. Elvis had every color in the rainbow. The one thing I never saw Elvis wear was blue jeans. He didn't like blue jeans. When he was offstage, he looked neat. He had a thing about looking different. He really wanted to be noticed and knew that loud clothes and those sideburns were a way to get noticed. They were gonna notice him anyway for the way he looked. He was just a hell of a good-lookin' guy. But his clothes made him look even better. He looked casual and he wore coats that were too big, and pants legs that were too big, but that was cool, man. He invented cool."

By the end of 1955 the music industry's artifically constructed racial barriers, which had been gradually crumbling in the fifties, were close to toppling completely. In 1954 the Chords' "Sh-Boom" became the first interracial pop hit, crossing over from the R&B chart to hit the top 10 early in the year. In late '54 and into early '55 the Charms were in the top 20 with a group harmony rouser, "Hearts of Stone," and without much fanfare, Fats Domino had made the pop charts' top 30 in '52 and '53 before hitting the top 10 in '55 with "Ain't That a Shame," another in what was becoming a steady flow of stellar recordings from the New Orleans artist. Concurrently a new Chess Records artist, St. Louis–born Chuck Berry, a distinctive guitarist and droll, perceptive writer, made a grand debut with a number-one R&B hit, "Maybellene" (a song modeled on an old country number, "Ida Red"), and saw it cross over and rise to number five on the pop chart.

As rock 'n' roll entered the mainstream, the "idling engine" that was young America began to rev up. There had always been alternatives to pop, and there had always been teenagers. The difference in America in 1955 was money and time. The younger generation's access to disposable income fueled the growing subculture and its symbols—transistor radios, flashy clothing, fast cars, and, most of all, rock 'n' roll. By the spring, Presley's records were selling at a pace that outstripped the capacity of Sun's manufacturer, Plastic Products of Memphis, to meet the public demand. Carl, eager to showcase his own rocking style on record but respecting Sam Phillips's insistence that he stick with country, bided his time in Jackson as a new era dawned in popular music.

In mid-June Carl arrived at the studio with four songs in various states of completion. Once again Cantrell, Claunch, and Kesler joined the sessions, which produced an August release, "Let the Jukebox Keep On Playing" b/w "Gone Gone Gone," on the Sun label, Flip having been disposed of after a like-named West Coast label threatened legal action against Phillips.

"Let the Jukebox Keep On Playing" was another country ballad in the "Turn Around" vein, inspired by an El Rancho patron who had objected to Carl pulling the plug on the jukebox when the band started its set. "Let the jukebox keep on playin'," the customer protested to no avail, but the phrase caught Carl's attention.

Cantrell's double-time fiddle lick kicked off the song before settling into a straight 2/4 solo line; Kesler topped off the intro with four crying quarter notes. As Cantrell continued soloing (much the same lines he played on "Turn Around") and Kesler added crystalline fills, Carl delivered his strongest studio vocal to date, sincere, heartfelt, and bluesy. He phrased each word precisely and deliberately, his voice cracking with emotion on key lyrics, most effectively on the sentiment following the title phrase—"till I'm ho-holding you." Kesler and Cantrell took the instrumental break, Kesler's in particular heightening the heartache and longing the singer describes. Two takes were virtually identical, save for minor lyric changes; at their completion Phillips declared the song "a masterpiece." Apart from this debatable judgment, "Let the Jukebox Keep On Playing" was a model country ballad, with a story the country audience could relate to, sung with deep feeling, and featuring exquisite instrumental solos.

Staying in the country-ballad mode, Carl then cut another original song, "What You Doin' When You're Cryin'," again featuring Cantrell sawing away on fiddle, and Kesler's evocative steel guitar, plus a tasty, minimal solo from Carl. Having no memory of ever recording the song, Carl believes he wrote it as the tape rolled, and that the surviving version is a first and only take. It was followed by an uptempo shuffle, "You Can't Make Love to Somebody," which had some instrumental similarity to "Movie Magg" but moved along at a brisker pace, with Carl's vocal loose and carefree, pushed by a forceful beat laid down by W.S. and Clayton, who were fast becoming a formidable rhythm section. The lyrics, constructed at the moment Carl sang them, detailed the travails of two-timing, and were given an hilarious "Who me?" reading by Carl.

"Loose and carefree" also describes the mood in the studio. During breaks most of the musicians would partake of their share of Early Times or anything else that would burn, and the effects started to show on tape. Before his solo break in "You Can't Make Love to Somebody," Carl shouted, "Yeeeah!" and cut out on flurry of double- and single-note runs; his voice rose frequently into the upper register and back to its normal tenor, always cocksure tone, as if daring the listener to challenge the essential truth of his statements.

In between cuts, Sam would beseech the band to "do me a show! Show me what y'all are playin' on the shows now!" Off they'd go into the Perkins Brothers repertoire, rekindling their stamina with liberal swigs from the Early Times bottle, feeling no pain. This day's long session set the pattern for what was to come. Over the course of the afternoon, other musicians would wander into the studio. It was common, Carl recalls, to get drunk "two or three times a day. We'd sober up and say, 'Well, we better be going on back toward Jackson. Who's that out there that pulled up?' And here comes another musician, and maybe he'd have a bottle. 'Boy, he can slap an ol' bass. Get him in here!' First thing you know he's back playing with you, and drinkin' and havin' a good time, so I thought."

By the time he was ready to cut another new song, Carl was the living epitome of its title: "Gone Gone Gone." The first take found him stumbling through the lyrics, forgetting a word here, mumbling incoherently there, but it had the spirit in its rocking 4/4 beat, in Clayton's slapping bass goosing it forward, and in Carl's outlandish lyrics and loose, comic vocal. Cantrell's fiddle was inaudible in the background; Kesler didn't bother to get in on the action. Compared to the other songs Carl had cut, "Gone Gone Gone" blew in from nowhere: It was a rowdy, crude, swaggering bit of tush-hog posturing, hillbilly-fired R&B, pockmarked by Carl's scatted nonsense lyrics, drunken exhortations, and a couple of preternatural guitar solos for good measure. He made it up as he went along, working variations on lyrics he had been writing and rewriting for years "every Saturday night" in the tonks. The first take:

Weeeell, it must be jelly
'Cause jam don't shake like that
Well, it must be ja——
Jam don't shake like that
I love my baby
She's a real cool cat

(chorus:) Well, Hi'm gone, gone, gone
Well, I'm GONE! Gone, gone
Yeah I'm gone, gone, gone
Yeah I'm gone, gone, gone
Well I'm gone, gone, gone
Well I'm gone in New Orleans

I'm gonna round dance, square dance
'Cause everybody's jumpin' tonight
I'm gonna round dance, square dance
'Cause everybody's jumpin' tonight
Well I love my baby
With all my lovin' might

Well I'm gone, gone, gone

I'm gone, gone, gone

I'm gone, gone, gone

I'm gone, gone, gone

Well I'm gone, gone, gone

And I'm gone from New Orleans

Ah do-ba, do-ba, doodley-bop a do-ba

(solo)

It must be jelly

'Cause jam don't shake like that

It must be jelly

'Cause Perkins don't shake like that

I love my baby

She's so big and fat

We-we-hell we're gone, gone, gone

Well I'm GONE, gone, gone

Well I'm gone, gone, gone

Well gone gone gone

Well I'm gone, gone

Gone from Bowling Green

(solo)

Oh, I wanna round dance, square dance

'Cause everybody's jumpin' tonight

Oh, I wanna round dance, square dance

'Cause everybody's jumpin' tonight

I love my baby

With all my lovin' might

Ahoo, ahoo, gone, gone, gone

Gone, gone, gone

Gone, gone, gone

I'm gone, gone, gone

(Let's go, cats!)

Gone, gone, gone
Well I'm gone from Bowling Green

With his "Let's go, cats!" charge to the band, Carl employed the language he had been hearing used by some of younger tonk-goers. It captured the spirit of the music, that word "cats," by evoking the feral quality of Carl's sound: beautiful and alluring in its mystery, sleek, at root unknowable, untamed, threatening, intractable.

As amazing as the first performance was in all its primitive simplicity, the second, more refined take better indicated Carl's artistic discipline. Even under the influence, he massaged the lyrics into something approaching sense, barely, without losing any of Take 1's abandon. His first guitar break was extraordinary, a firestorm of bent notes, and double- and single-string runs that exploded upon Carl's savage cry of "Yeah, cats!!" At the end of the song, he cut loose with a deft, ascending solo run and Clayton, just so you'd know he was there, tagged it with a bass lick.

Weeeelll, that must be my gal
Yours don't look like that
Well that must be my gal
Yours don't look like that
I know my baby,
She's so round and fat

Well, well, gone, gone, gone
Ah-oh, gone, gone, gone
I'm gone, gone, gone
Well gone, gone, gone
And I'm gone now,
Gone on down the line

Well I'm gonna round dance, square dance
Everybody jumpin' tonight

Yeah, I'm gonna round dance, square dance

Everybody jumpin' tonight

I love my baby

With all my lovin' might

Well-a-well-a, gone, gone, gone

Bopa, bopa, well gone, gone, gone

And I'm gone, gone, gone

I'm GONE! Gone, gone

I'm gone, gone

Gone on down the line

"Yeah, cats!!" (solo)

Yeah, that must be my gal

Yours don't look like that

I said it must be my gal

Yours don't look like that

I know my baby

She's so big and fat

Well-a, well-a, gone, gone, gone

Gone, gone, gone—aaaahh

Now gone, gone, gone

Well I'm gone, gone, gone

Well I'm gone, gone

Gone from Bowling Green

"Let's go, git it now!"

Do-ba, do-ba, do-ba (solo)

"Yeah, let's get gone, watch it!"

Oooohhh!

Gone, gone, gone

Gone, gone, gone

Well I'm gone, gone, gone

And I'm gone, gone, gone

And I'm gone, gone

Gone from Bowling Green

When it was over, Sam had only one remark: "I like 'Gone, Gone, Gone.' It's awful close to some of the stuff we're doin' on Elvis, but I'm gonna put it out."

▶ THE VOICE OF CARL PERKINS

We were all nervous when we went in for sessions. Pressure's part of every record. That don't go away. Well, it does for some artists. I see guys that are cool all the way through. Eddy Arnold was one; his records were so good and his voice was so clean and clear, uncluttered by alcohol. I can tell you them dudes that's on [alcohol] a lot of times by listening to their records, and I could back then. There's a looseness about a singer that's had too much to drink that you can't cover up. Now the world may not know it, but he does. The public don't know exactly what it is that's making him sing so happy on record. I was bad to holler on record, and scream out things, 'cause, man, I was rockin'. And the jug wasn't empty and I knew it. It quieted down on over in the night, but sometimes it'd get louder 'cause you'd get too much to drink and you'd have to shut it down. Just have to quit, go on and get drunk and lay in the floor. Wake up and pick again. It really never got that loose at Sun Records. It's been said, but I'm telling you, we drank to celebrate after we got that record cut and Sam said, "Boy, we got somethin'." Then he'd join. For the most part he never drank when we was cuttin'. If he did he hid it back there and I didn't know about it.

But I found him to be strictly business in cutting records. Letting you do your thing. He'd just sit back there, and when you'd hit something he'd punch a button and say, "You're gettin' close." He had a knack of knowing when we had it pretty well together, and he'd say, "We oughta start taping some of them now." And that's how he'd do it. But he'd let you take all the time you wanted. Let the bass player try different things, guitar player, singer, he never rushed us. That was one cool, good thing about Sun Records. That clock wasn't on that wall and there wasn't no red light that come on and scared you.

It was always dark when we got through. I don't ever remember going in there and not doing from six to sixteen hours. I have been in there all day and all night and half the next day. Yes, sir. And got some good stuff at two or three o'clock in the morning. In fact, after about the second record, Sam found out that along about dark is when artists come alive simply because that's the way we'd always done it. Playing in the tonks, you don't go in at one o'clock in the afternoon. So the afternoon parts didn't have that edge on it. He'd say, "Boys, it's good but it ain't got that edge." I wondered what he was talking about, "edge." And one day I asked him. I said, "Mr. Phillips, what is a 'edge'?"

He said, "Carl, I knew you was gonna ask me that and I've been trying to think of the right phrase to tell you what it is. It's raw and the bottle is spilling over your soul. If you channel it out your mouth, then that's what you've got. But when you put that edge on it, it's coming out your mouth and spilling out both sides," which was a great analysis of it. He said, "You're puttin' it out your mouth into the microphone and it's still spilling out both sides of your mouth. You're just singing your heart out or you're playing your heart out. You're doing things on that guitar you know you've never done before. That's the edge. And I want every one of you to give me that edge."

Prior to the "Gone Gone Gone" session Sam had introduced Carl to Johnny Cash, the newest addition to the Sun roster. "Is that your real name? Johnny Cash?" Carl asked, shaking the newcomer's hand.

"Well, it's John," Cash drawled. "Sam put the Johnny on there."

"That sure is a pretty name—Johnny Cash," Carl said. "Like *cash.*"

Sam had told Carl he would get along with Cash, and Carl did. The two had much in common. Only six weeks older than Carl, Cash had grown up in Dyess, Arkansas, about twenty miles south of and across the Mississippi River from the Perkins family in Tiptonville, Tennessee. The Cashes had worked the land as tenant farmers; Cash, like

Carl, bore the scars of his days in the cotton fields. As a child his passion was music, especially the gospel and country he heard all around him. Each man had an X-shaped scar on the forefinger of his left hand from his whittling days as a boy. Each one's right leg was scarred in the same place from having been caught on a barbed-wire fence. Each was married, and Cash had one child, a daughter. Both had dreamed of a life in music, and both had arrived at Sun within months of each other.

All Cash knew of Carl at that time was "Movie Magg," a song he liked. But after chatting with Carl for a few minutes, he felt a strong connection to his labelmate.

"I felt like I'd run into a brother, you know, that I hadn't seen in a while," Cash says. "It was like we'd known each other all our lives and all we had to do was catch up on things. I mean I connected with him like nobody ever did before in the music business. We played our first show together at Parkin, Arkansas, at a theater. There was no toilet in the place and Carl and I, before the show, went around the back of the theater, on the ground, like country boys do, and we talked about it then. We were still country boys, playing the big theater in Parkin—I don't know but it would seat two hundred people, but it was a big deal for us."

Although Sam heard some commercial potential in Carl's original music, he heard none in Cash's, whose self-composed songs were of a religious nature. Sam wanted these even less than he wanted an Ernest Tubb soundalike. Like Carl, Cash had been turned away by Marion Keisker and had had to pester Phillips for an audition, but repeatedly— so much so that he told an interviewer, "I don't feel like anybody discovered me, because I had to fight so hard to get heard."

Favorably impressed with Cash's singing voice, Sam asked to hear the full band. Cash returned apologetic over the group's lack of polish, but Phillips found something interesting in their sound. Marshall Grant was barely proficient on the bass, and Luther Perkins's (no relation to Carl) limitations as a guitarist were extraordinary for one aspiring to professional status. He rarely ventured below the top three strings, and when he did solo on the bottom strings, he kept it as succinct as possible. Even Cash himself was little more than a functional guitarist, whose saving grace was that he could keep a decent rhythm going. Steel guitarist Red Kernodle, the most experienced of the lot, was no Stan Kesler. Despite their shortcomings, the quartet clicked even as it stumbled, and Phillips was impressed enough to start working with them, on the assumption that Cash would deliver more commercial fare.

Cash came in for his third session with Phillips with a couple of new songs he hoped would fit the bill. One, a homesick southerner's lament titled "Hey! Porter," was originally a poem he had written while serving in the Air Force (between 1950 and 1954) and had published in the Armed Forces magazine *Stars & Stripes;* another was a prison song, "Folsom Prison Blues," a rewrite of Gordon Jenkins's 1954 pop entry, "Crescent City Blues." Phillips liked the former, passed on the latter, and again told Cash to bring him something new, "an uptempo weeper." A few days later Cash returned with "Cry! Cry! Cry!" ready to bake.

With Cash and his band (dubbed the Tennessee Two by Phillips in the wake of Kernodle's departure following the first session), Phillips further defined the Sun sound. Placing Cash's rugged, ragged baritone voice up front in the mix, he used tape delay to create a slapback echo on both the voice and Luther Perkins's "boom-chicka" guitar stylings; minimal though they were, two rousing Perkins solos on "Hey! Porter" helped drive the track. Behind him Cash and Grant flailed and slapped an unwavering, lumbering rhythm support, evoking the unrelenting trundle of a locomotive burning down the rails.

Phillips was making the most out of low-tech gear; sheer ingenuity; and necessity, the mother of invention. While he preferred to cut Carl clear and clean, with little or no echo, Elvis's vocals were heavily echoed and atmospheric. Carl witnessed some of Sam's tinkering during his second session. Sam placed cardboard boxes over the amplifiers, turned them toward the corner where two walls met and miked them from the rear. He cut a hole in one of the boxes and got a crude fuzz effect from the rattling sound. The mic placement, as Phillips explained to Carl, brought sound in from the back and from the waves bouncing off the wall.

"He was right," Carl says. "It was a little hesitation, coming out of that speaker back through the amp, and the speaker was throwing the sound out against the walls. It was hittin' between those walls. He said, 'It won't do it if you just put it against a flat wall. It won't sound the same.' It was picking up a little rumble sound as it made its way out. Sam was a good sound man. He'd fooled with it for a good while before he started making records with us, fooled with it with blues people, and he knew about recording. Sun Records had a little different sound to 'em. And it wasn't the room, it was the players and the equipment he had. It wasn't high-priced equipment, but there was always a little roar about the records. It's not a real noticeable roar, but it's a little roar. I've always heard it in Sun records. Those cheap microphones were being overworked probably."

Back on the road after completing his "Gone, Gone, Gone" session, Carl played a few dates with Cash and Presley, giving Carl a chance to see Sun's latest acquisition up close. The Tennessee Two were no match for the Perkins Brothers Band as musicians, but their stark, no-frills approach created dramatic ambience well suited to Cash's commanding baritone and simply constructed, folk-influenced material. Theirs was not a show of instrumental flash, only support in the truest sense of the word.

Tall and thin—again like Carl—Cash possessed Presley-like dark good looks ("He had some charisma going for him," Carl says). He wore his black hair swept back, with the requisite long sideburns; his brooding eyes seemed both forbidding and friendly, and he was given to furtive glances that sent the females in his audience into a swoon. A hint of an overbite and an easy, crooked grin suggested a man of common country stock, which he was, albeit one with star quality. Even his most noticeable imperfection, a small crater of a scar on his lower right cheek, was of a piece with his rugged bearing (as a teenager he had lanced a pimple with the sharp end of a buck knife that he had heated over a match flame). Audiences and his fellow musicians took to him; he was one of them and they were all together.

Carl, Cash, and Presley went out on the road together several times over the summer of '55, short jaunts into Arkansas and Mississippi, through Little Rock, Forrest City, Corinth, Tupelo. Most of these were hit-and-run dates that would find the musicians returning to Memphis after the shows—Cash and his band were still working day jobs and couldn't stay out for multidate engagements. Whenever a break in bookings occurred, Carl and his band headed back to the tonks, where they could make better money than they could on the road. On the tours with Elvis, Carl and the band's single largest pay night, for a show in Parkin, Arkansas, netted each member fourteen dollars. To celebrate that occasion, Elvis, Carl, and all the band members repaired to a local truck stop for food. Flush with cash, Elvis ordered three cheeseburgers with tomatoes, onions, lettuce, and mustard. "Boys, I'm gonna eat all I can hold," he announced. "I'm gonna show you somethin'. Watch this one disappear." Three or four bites later, the burger was gone. Then another. Then another.

Among those on tour, only Jay remained unsettled by Elvis's appearance and manner. He thought Elvis a "smart aleck," and, still, a "sissy." To this Carl responded that maybe Jay simply didn't want to like Elvis, with whom no one else seemed to have a problem.

"No I don't," Jay agreed. "He's *sissy*. He's sissy and you know he is. Look at his fingernails."

"They're just clean."

"No they're *filed!*" Jay said of the damning evidence.

"They look good," Carl replied.

"No they don't; look like a girl's."

Carl's contention is that "Elvis meant to be striking on and off the stage." In complaining about Elvis's immaculate fingernails, the country boy in Jay sensed and resented someone straying far from his humble roots. Even though he defended Elvis, Carl was sometimes surprised by the Hillbilly Cat's attention to the most minute details of his stage appearance. Backstage before a show, Carl came into the dressing room to find Elvis picking at his eyes, or so it appeared. When he got closer, he saw Elvis working on his lower line of eyelashes with a Maybelline eyeliner stick.

"Whatta ya doin' with that on your eyes?" Carl asked.

"It makes your eyes look bigger," Elvis told him as he dabbed carefully at his lashes.

"Look around here," Carl ordered. Elvis turned his head so Carl could peer at his handiwork. "Damn! They do look big!"

"Go ahead, man. Try it." Elvis handed the eyeliner to Carl. Bending down towards the mirror, he aimed for his upper eyelid. Being a bit wobbly from having had a few slugs of Early Times, he missed his target and poked himself in the eye.

"Damn!" He dropped the eyeliner and began checking his eyeball for damage, as Elvis convulsed in laughter. It was the end of Carl's experiment with eyeliner.

Apart from Carl, one of the strongest friendships Johnny Cash formed at Sun was with Clayton. Cash had enough tush hog in him to recognize and appreciate a fellow traveler. By this time Carl had already been advised by Sam Phillips that he "better watch that boy," meaning Clayton, who had precipitated the comment by biting Phillips's ear during a break in the second session. According to Carl, Cash encouraged this behavior in "Floyce"—Cash's pet name for the youngest Perkins brother—by being diligent in his quest to point out "a good-lookin' ear" on various unsuspecting souls. Seconds later Clayton would be sampling same. Everyone, Cash says, was fair game.

After watching Clayton's antics onstage, Cash sought him out and the two found common ground, their bond almost as unfathomable as that between Clayton and the teetotaling Fluke Holland. At the truck stop with Elvis, Cash discovered another of Clayton's talents. "Here, Floyce," Cash said, "open my Coke." Whereupon Clayton placed the bottle cap under his upper front teeth, gave it a quick, downward pull, and off it popped. Everyone was impressed, the conventional wisdom being, according to Carl, "Guy walks around opening Cokes with his teeth, you say, 'Ain't no need of me hittin' him, 'cause I ain't gonna hurt him anyway.' "

Cash wasn't around for one of Clayton's finest hours. The band was booked for a weekend show at the El Rancho, and between sets Carl and Jay were sitting together having a beer and amusing themselves watching the mating dances going on around them. Suddenly, a friend of theirs, Pat Durbin, rushed over, screaming that Clayton had swallowed a straight pin.

Carl followed Durbin over to a table where Clayton sat nodding off, having had one too many shots of moonshine.

"Clayton!" Carl shouted, startling his brother into semi-consciousness. "Clayton! Did you swallow a straight pin?"

"Yep," Clayton mumbled, resting his head on the table.

"Well then, let's go! We gotta get to the hospital! This can kill you!"

Clayton didn't budge, so Carl and Jay dragged him outside to Durbin's car. Jay stayed behind as Carl joined Durbin for the trip into Jackson Hospital. At the wheel, Durbin was mashing the accelerator, driving wide open. In the back seat, Clayton was passed out. Speeding into the city limits, Durbin lost control on an S curve. The car flipped, skidded into a concrete embankment, ricocheted off a telephone pole, and began spinning on its top, glass flying, steel grinding against concrete. Finally it came to a rest upside down in the middle of the street.

When he got his bearings again, Carl saw that Durbin was still alive, but was pinned to his seat by the steering wheel, which had been pushed against his chest. He craned his head, trying to check Clayton's condition in the back seat, but couldn't see anything. Then he realized to his horror that Clayton had been thrown from the car.

Smoke billowed from the engine as Carl crawled from the wreckage. Apart from a few cuts, he seemed to be in good shape, miraculously. He ran around to Durbin's side and got down on all fours so he could get in close to check on the driver.

"Carl," Durbin gasped, "you better get away. This car's gonna blow up. It's fixin' to catch fire."

Bracing his feet against the windshield frame—the glass had been completely shattered—Carl reached in and tried to pull Durbin out. He couldn't get any leverage with the car overturned, and Durbin was in tight. Overcome by smoke, Carl, coughing violently, backed away from the car.

I can't let him die.

Crawling back to Durbin, Carl braced himself and "put the death jerk on him." Out came Durbin, lacerated but alive. Carl dragged him safely away from the wreckage and went searching for Clayton. He found him lying beneath some shrubbery almost a block away, moaning "Waaaah" and complaining that he felt sick. An ambulance arrived and rushed everyone to Jackson Hospital. Durbin and Clayton, Carl was told, would be fine, although Durbin would have to stay overnight. After a couple of hours in the emergency room, Clayton, a broad smile on his face, came sauntering out to meet Carl.

"What's so funny?" Carl demanded.

"I never swallowed no damn pin," Clayton answered, breaking into a hearty laugh. "I don't know how come me to think of that," he added, proud of his achievement. "But it worked out pretty good, didn't it?"

In Clayton's world, tomorrow was always another day.

a u g u s t 1955 was notable for Carl on a couple of fronts. For one, he learned Valda was pregnant again, with their third baby due in April. Of more immediate significance, the first day of the month had seen the simultaneous release of "Let the Jukebox Keep on Playing" b/w "Gone Gone Gone" and Elvis's "Mystery Train"/"I Forgot to Remember to Forget." Although Sam was sure he had a country hit in "Jukebox," Carl was hearing more about the flip side when he visited area radio stations to promote his new recording. At almost every stop he was told by the resident disc jockey that "Gone Gone Gone" was "the kind of music the younger people are eatin' up," and it was soon showing up on regional charts as the favored cut.

At the same time, Carl's music, along with Elvis's, finally found a name. Its origin is uncertain, but over the course of the early fifties the style combining blues with country, honky-tonk, and/or bluegrass had evolved from "hillbilly blues" to "hillbilly bop" to, finally, "rockabilly." It wasn't all coming from Sun. Lew Chudd's Imperial label, which had been doing fine with Fats Domino, was building a sizable roster of country performers whose music swung towards rockabilly, Bill Mack's 1953 single, "Play My Boogie," being one early example. On Decca in early '55, Roy Hall cut a rousing track in tune with the times, "See You Later Alligator," which Bill Haley would cover a year later as a top-10 pop hit. From Capitol's country roster in '55 came a wild, odd bit of borderline rockabilly from country artist Jimmy Heap in "Sebbin Come Eleven." Independent labels throughout the South were assembling rosters of rockabilly artists in response to Elvis's widening popularity. Still, the finest and purest rockabilly came from Sun; Elvis, Scotty, and Bill had pioneered it on record, and, now, with "Gone Gone Gone," Carl had brought its rawest form out of the tonks. Other than being different, though, he still wasn't sure how to classify the music to which he gave definition.

"I knew I was some form of country, but not Hank Snow and not Ernest Tubb and not Roy Acuff," Carl says. "I heard something else in that music and worked all my life to find what it was. It's the way it's chopped that makes a difference. And the rhythm, the beat, the mixture that's in it. It's two or three kinds of music together is what rockabilly is. And there's a spirit roaming around in it that keeps it all tied together. Don't ask me what that is. But you can feel it."

Even with "Gone Gone Gone" becoming the radio side of choice, "Jukebox" managed to make a ripple. Shortly after its release, Sam received an inquiry from Webb Pierce's management concerning Pierce's interest in covering the song. Pierce was as hot an artist as country music had seen in years. Through the early and mid-fifties he had racked up a staggering twenty-one number-one records, many of which wound up in the Perkins Brothers' repertoire, most notably the tonk favorite, "There Stands the Glass." Pierce wanted to cut "Jukebox" and "Turn Around," according to Carl, if he could get a share of the publishing credit on both. Sam refused to yield, despite Carl's willingness to "give half my writer's credit to Webb to hear him sing it." Even though he had signed publishing contracts with Sam's Hi-Lo Music after each of his sessions, Carl, without the benefit of legal counsel, had no clue as to what he was offering to relinquish or even much of an idea about the nature of publishing and his rights as a performer and writer. All he knew he had learned from Sam. In the end Sam held firm on his offer, Pierce's people did the same, and nothing happened—no Webb Pierce cover, no hit for Carl after a promising start.

With the release of "Jukebox," Carl was booked for some regional shows with Presley and Cash. Their bands met in Parkin, Arkansas. Cash strode into the small dressing-room area behind the stage and greeted Carl with a firm handshake and a toothy, crooked grin. The two men, now staunch friends, hadn't seen each other in a couple of weeks. Cash immediately asked Carl if he'd been doing any writing.

"Ain't nothing worth writin' home about, John," Carl replied with a slight laugh.

"Tell you what," Cash said. "I had an idea you oughta write you a song about blue suede shoes."

Carl had noticed shoes of blue suede showing up in some of the stores around Jackson and Memphis, but writing about them seemed silly. "I don't know nothin' about them shoes, John," he said.

Cash began relating an experience he'd had in the Air Force with a smart-dressing bootblack named C.V. White, who told Cash his initials stood for Champagne Velvet. Cash's recollection: "Of course we wore our fatigues when we worked our job in the Air Force, but when we got a three-day pass everybody would dress up in Air Force blues and black shoes. I told Carl C.V. White was a friend of mine. And before he'd go on his pass to go to town, he'd always come by and get me to inspect him, because he wanted to look the best he could look for those women in Munich. I'd look him up and down and say, 'You sharp, C.V. You got your shoes shined up really good.' And he said, 'Those are not Air Force black. Those are *blue suede* shoes tonight.' And he said, 'Don't step on my blue suede shoes.' "

With diminishing interest, Carl shrugged off Cash's idea. "Well, I've never owned a pair of 'em, so I don't know anything about those shoes."

It was time for the show to start, so Carl headed for the wings of the stage, where he would stand and watch Cash, giving him and the band a thumbs-up sign to signal his approval of what they were laying down. As an idea, blue suede shoes seemed to have had its day.

In early October, Jackson's Union University asked the Perkins Brothers Band to play a school dance at the Supper Club, an upscale night club, which Union had rented for the evening. Carl accepted, eager to play for the same type of audience he had been enjoying on his shows with Cash and Presley.

On October 21, a lively group of well-dressed, fresh-scrubbed college students packed the Supper Club, with many mingling around outside waiting for an opportunity to get through the front door when space permitted—it was a tonk crowd, but a sober one. At the appointed starting hour of nine o'clock, Carl and the band began blazing away on some rockabilly and got the room shaking. From his vantage point on the tiny bandstand Carl could see everyone in attendance. The energy coming off the dance floor to the stage was, as Carl recalls, "electrifying," teenage voices laughing and shouting their approval, young bodies bopping in time to infectious rhythm. Scanning the crowd, he picked out a handsome couple near the front of the stage and in effect began playing to them, watching in delight as they responded physically to quirks in his playing by kicking a leg out, or jerking a foot in a different direction, giving physical expression to the guitar licks.

Carl had finished singing a song and was regrouping for the next number when he heard a harsh-sounding male voice near the front of the stage. Turning, he saw it was the male half of the couple that had been bopping to the music only seconds ago, suddenly angry at his date, who was standing there silent but visibly distraught.

"Uh-uh," the boy said in a stern, forceful voice. "Don't step on my suedes!"

"I'm sorry," the girl said, her voice trembling. "I'm really sorry."

When he looked down, Carl could see that the boy was indeed wearing blue suede shoes, one of which now had a white scuff mark on the toe.

The Perkins Brothers played on, and the dance ended uneventfully and on time at one a.m. Although the young couple had continued dancing together, Carl could see that the boy never forgave his date her unfortunate faux pas.

Good gracious, Carl thought, *a pretty little thing like that and all he can think about is his blue suede shoes.*

When Carl came home after the dance, everyone was asleep, and as usual he took a few minutes alone to relax before going upstairs. But he couldn't unwind: Even after settling in next to Valda, he lay wide awake as the clock moved on towards three a.m. In his mind's eye he saw a boy and a girl dancing, he heard the boy issuing his warning, "Don't step on my suedes!" and recalled the girl's frightened look as she acknowledged her mistake. Images and more images, an endless loop: the couple gyrating on the dance floor; Carl spotting them and giving his solos a little extra twist to energize their dance; the girl's pleated dress billowing up when her boyfriend twirled her, showing off a fine pair of legs and flash of panties. Always, always he came back to the boy: "Don't step on my suedes!"

In an instant Carl recalled Johnny Cash's notion that in blue suede shoes lay a story. But how does it start? Carl's first thought was to frame it with a nursery rhyme:

"Little Jack Horner sat in a corner . . . "

No.

"See a spider going up the wall / To get his ashes hauled."

Stupid.

"One for the money / Two for the show / Three to get ready / Four to go."

"One for the money, two for the show . . .

Carl "felt a song writing itself," he would say later. He eased out of the bed, crept down the cold, concrete stairs to the living room, and picked up his Les Paul (he didn't have his amp at home, so he played it acoustic). Strumming an A chord, he hummed the melody he had been hearing and then added a lyric:

> Well, it's one for the money—

He hit a two-chord lick and stopped the music:

> Two for the show—

Another two-chord lick, and another pause:

> Three to get ready
> Now go, man, go!

He broke into a boogie-woogie rhythm, and in an instant he had a song. Rushing into the kitchen, he emptied a paper bag of its Irish

potatoes, grabbed a pencil, and began writing as fast as lyrics were
coming to mind:

> But don't you
> Step on my blue swade shoes

Lyrically and musically the basic structure of the song was there.
Another verse suggested itself:

> Well, you can knock me down
> Step in my face

What now? "Disgrace my name"? No . . . had to be a better word.
"Slander." Now that had some impact, generated a gut reaction.

> Slander my name all over the place

Then back to the key sentiment:

> Do anything that you wanna do
> But uh-uh, honey, lay off my shoes
> Now don't you
> Step on my blue swade shoes

The third verse came easy:

> You can burn my house
> Steal my car
> Drink my liquor from an old fruit jar
> Do anything that you wanna do
> But uh-uh honey, lay off my shoes

As he played, Carl heard the arrangement coming together in his
head, particularly the slapping bass line of Clayton's that would pro-
pel the boogie feel. He toyed with a couple of guitar solos to break up
the verses, and then sat there playing the song over and over, trying

out different lyrics, working on solos. As the sun was rising, he went
to bed. When he awoke later, Valda was in the kitchen fixing breakfast. Carl got dressed and, without acknowledging his wife's presence,
headed for his guitar and started playing the song again.

Valda turned to Carl, intrigued by what she had heard. "Carl, I like
that," she said enthusiastically. "I really *like* that."

"Do you?" Carl asked with a certain diffidence that masked his pleasure at Valda's reaction. Still strumming, he was playing it cool.

"I think it's real good," Valda added before turning back to the task
at hand.

"Well, if you like it now," Carl told her, "wait'll you hear it when
Jay, Clayton, and W.S. join in. If we get it done like I hear it . . . " His
voice trailed off. *If we get it done like I hear it.* Deep down he knew the
song he referred to as "Don't Step on My Blue Suede Shoes" (Valda
had corrected Carl on the spelling of "suede") was big-league, one that
could boost the band up to the next plateau, maybe get them out of
the honky-tonks for good.

After a hurried breakfast, Carl ran across the street and came back
with Jay and Jay's guitar in tow. Jay listened patiently as Carl played
his new song. "I hear what you're gettin' at, Carl," Jay responded, as
he strummed the rhythm.

Carl nodded. "You just play that rhythm, man. But remember"—
Carl hit the opening stop-time licks—"you got to hit them stop places
like that."

The brothers started again, but Jay continually missed the two-beat
stop-time effect. He may have been in mind of the one-beat break in
Bill Haley's "Rock Around the Clock," but whatever the reason, he
struggled with the extra pause Carl wanted. The afternoon passed, the
complaints mounted, but eventually Jay got it down.

On Saturday morning Carl walked to the pay phone on the corner
and called Sam Phillips to tell him about "Don't Step on My Blue
Suede Shoes."

"Is that like 'O, Dem Golden Slippers'?" Phillips queried, his voice
deep and gruff.

"Nooo," Carl answered, irritated that Phillips wasn't more enthusiastic. "This cat don't want nobody steppin' on his shoes. Goes like this—" and Carl sang the opening and the first verse.

"Sounds good," Phillips replied matter-of-factly. "But the title's too long; it'll take up the whole label. We'll call it 'Blue Suede Shoes.'"

Carl was ready to record, but Phillips wanted to let "Gone Gone Gone / Let the Jukebox Keep On Playing" run its course. He told Carl to keep on working and be patient.

Over the course of that Saturday's gig, the Perkins Brothers Band played "Blue Suede Shoes" some eight times, by Carl's recollection. Not only did the response assure Carl he had written a hit, but it also afforded the band a chance to smooth out the arrangement. When Carl packed up his gear to head for home early Sunday morning after the last drunk had left the El Rancho, all he could think about was getting to Memphis, to the Sun studio, and committing "Blue Suede Shoes" to tape. All the questions had been answered now.

This was his moment.

I n the late fall of '55, Carl, Elvis, and Cash played two more dates together, the first in Amory, Mississippi, followed by a show in Helena, Arkansas. During one stretch of the brief trip from Memphis to Amory, Carl rode with Elvis ("a good driver, especially compared to Cash, the worst driver in the world"), and they had their longest conversation to date about their personal tastes in music. Elvis asked Carl to guess his favorite song, and when Carl drew a blank, Elvis gave him a clue: "It's about a dog."

"About a dog! Mine's about a dog too. What's your dog's name?"

"This song's 'Old Shep,' by Red Foley," Elvis answered.

"You gotta be kiddin' me," Carl said.

"I know every word," Elvis told him.

"Okay, you sing it, and I'll sing harmony," Carl suggested. They did a note-for-note duet of the Foley version until Carl worked in his own variation on the final verse, replacing Old Shep's name with Bildo's.

Carl explained the song's parallels to the life and death of his lamented canine. Elvis listened without comment, then went off on a different tangent. "Man, I love them black-gospel quartets; they tear me apart. That rhythm!" Changing course again, he asked if Carl had heard of a group called the Platters: "Y-y-you heard their song?" The song he was referring to was "Only You," which was on its way to being a major crossover hit after being released as an R&B single the previous May. The quintet's defining voice was that of lead singer Tony Williams, whose melodramatic, soaring tenor (octave leaps were commonplace) was stylistically beholden to the Ink Spots' Bill Kenny and to the Ravens' two outstanding tenors, Maithe Marshall and Joe Van Loan. Carl heard something else in Williams's attack that hooked him: a similarity to Eddy Arnold's smooth, pop-country, control-and-release style. Arnold, says Carl, "had that bubble in his voice, and he burst it." Incorporated into his stage show, Carl's countrified version of "Only You" generated good audience response as a change of pace from the burning rockabilly—in fact, Carl had sung the song during a solo date in Amory only a month before this engagement with Elvis.

"Yeah, I know the song," Carl said without elaboration.

"Man, I do too," Elvis said as they pulled into town and headed for the National Guard Armory, where a sellout crowd was gathering.

When Carl came onstage, he was greeted by rowdy applause from the packed house; having Elvis on the bill had brought out the entire town, apparently. Between songs in their twenty-minute set, someone in the crowd shouted, " 'Only You,' Carl!"

"You got it, hoss!" Carl shouted back, gliding into the opening chords. As he sang the final notes—"only you-who-who"—rising to a falsetto—the crowd rose to its feet and thundered approval. Carl finished up with a couple of his own songs, including "Gone Gone Gone," took his bow, and retreated to the dressing room. There, sitting in front of a row of lockers, sat Elvis, head down, oblivious to everyone around him. Elvis was always the first to congratulate him after a set, so Carl knew something was amiss. To the question of whether he was feeling okay, Elvis replied: "Aw, ain't no need in me goin' on."

Nerves again, Carl thought. *The usual.* "What?" he asked incredulously. "They're gonna tear your clothes off you, boy! That crowd is ready."

"They're ready for *you!*" Elvis said, his voice rising in anger. "What'd you do 'Only You' for?"

Taken aback, Carl tried to collect his thoughts. Elvis hadn't told him he would be singing the song, and it had been in Carl's act for a month. Carl staked his claim: " 'Cause I wanted to! 'Cause I can sing it. There's two reasons. You want another one?"

"Well I was gonna do it!" Elvis blurted.

"Well go on out there and do it!" Carl shot back. "Hell, the Platters are singin' it somewhere tonight."

"I ain't that big a damn fool," Elvis countered. "I ain't goin' out there and sing something you done sung. You done tore 'em all to pieces. I might as well quit! Might as well go on to the car."

Instead of leaving, though, Elvis hit the stage dancing. Midway through his first song a call started building from the crowd, and soon engulfed the entire building: "We want Carl! We want Carl!" Standing in the wings, Carl became unnerved. He knew he had given a strong performance, but felt bad that Elvis was being treated so rudely as a result.

It didn't take long for Elvis to find his groove, however, and leave Carl with little reason to feel sorry for him. Whatever emotion Elvis was feeling, he channeled it into a performance to rival the best Carl had ever seen from anyone. Over the next half hour he watched awestruck as Elvis "just poured it on. Sweat popped out on him and was drippin' to the floor and he had that hair flyin' and them legs movin'. He dug deep. He pulled it off—he *rocked*. They wasn't hollerin' 'Perkins' at the end. They only did that for a little bit after he came out. That really embarrassed me."

After the show, Elvis and his band headed quickly to the car instead of hanging around and signing autographs for the fans, as was the custom. Carl knew Elvis's feelings had been hurt, but thought, *He'll get over it.*

On the ride back to Memphis, Clayton was ecstatic. "We burned him!" he cackled. "He got mad. He pulled every move he had in his soul; he did everything but do a flip out in the audience!"

Cash, who had opened the show, retains vivid memories of the Amory date, because Carl did a number on him as well: "I opened, then Carl went on, *destroyed* 'em, then Elvis went on. And I mean it was Carl's show. It was unbelievable how during Elvis's show they kept yelling for Carl Perkins. It made an impression on me and I know it made an impression on Elvis. He said, 'It's the last time I'll ever work with Carl Perkins.' I guess I couldn't blame him, because Elvis was really hot, and there comes Carl Perkins stealing his thunder. No, he didn't steal Elvis's thunder; he had his own. Didn't leave any for Elvis, or for me either. Carl was just doing what Carl does. He was at his best. Elvis loved Carl, thought Carl was really good. He loved Carl's work. Except that one night in Amory."

After a night off, the Perkins and Presley troupes reassembled in Helena, Arkansas, for a double bill. Carl didn't sing "Only You"—"I knew Elvis liked it and wanted to sing it, so I didn't"—but he was on his game again onstage. Elvis came out to an instant repeat of the Amory show, and again had to jack up his own performance a few notches to quell the audience's chant for Carl.

On the way back to Memphis, Elvis, who had brought his mother, his father, and a girlfriend, Barbara Hearn, to the show, stopped for gas. Carl pulled up behind him and waited as the attendant serviced Elvis's car. After paying, Elvis trotted back to Carl. "Man, you were rockin' tonight," he said with lukewarm enthusiasm.

"Boy, you were too!" Carl responded cheerily. "You really done good."

"You did too." Elvis paused. "We gonna stop and eat after while. Y'all wanna stop and get some cheeseburgers?"

"Elvis, we got a pretty good ways to drive; we're gonna head on back to Jackson," Carl said. "I'll see you in a few days."

Elvis nodded, bid good night to Jay, Clayton, and W.S., and took off. The strained collegiality of the farewell made an impression on Carl: "I knew [Elvis] didn't like that night either. I never really cooked him but twice onstage and it happened back to back. And I never played another show with him after that."

It was an interesting turn of events, because it was the first, slight breach in the genuine camaraderie binding these Sun artists together. Having been there first, Elvis had assumed a mantle of leadership in the eyes of Carl and Cash, but Elvis would not lord it over them. They all had egos and dreams, but the long nights on the road, driving 100 miles per hour on two-lane highways, all the cheeseburgers and Cokes, all the comparing and contrasting of individual styles and preferences in everything from fashion to music to cars to girls, had cemented their friendship in a deep and meaningful way. After all, they were, as Scotty Moore recounts, living on a precipice, or so they thought: "I think all of us felt like heck, tomorrow might be our last one. The next record, if it flops, we could be history. Sam got Elvis on the Grand Ole Opry in 1954, and he had to do some heavy pleadin' to get us on there. After it was over we were thinking, *Where do we go from here? We're done for! There's nowhere else to go!*"

In Memphis Sam Phillips was having problems. What appeared on the outside to be a thriving little record business was in fact in shambles. Sam owed money to pressing plants, to Chess Records, even to his own brother Jud, whose share of Sun Sam had agreed to purchase in 1954 but had yet to pay in full. He owed artist royalties, publishing royalties, and his assets were so scant that the Memphis banks refused to lend him any more money. Despite Sun's low overhead—rent on the 706 Union Avenue building was less than $200 a month, and he paid Marion Keisker around $25 a week—Phillips had serious, potentially devastating, business crises looming. In January he had detailed his precarious position in a letter to Jud, wherein he revealed that "the Sun liabilities are three times the assets and I have been making every effort possible to keep out of bankruptcy . . . Surely you see the precarious position of the company and know that we are making every effort to salvage the company and pay off all its obligations and avoid the embarrassment of bankruptcy. Anyone less interested in saving face would have given it up long ago, but I intend to pay every dollar the company owes—including you—even while I know there is no possible way to ever get out with a dollar."

In February Presley's manager Bob Neal, eager to expand his client's audience beyond the South, had signed a booking agreement with Jamboree Attractions, a Nashville concern owned and operated by country singing star Hank Snow and a former carnival barker turned artist manager (for Snow and Eddy Arnold, most notably) who went by the self-designated honorarium "Colonel" Tom Parker. Jamboree got to work and before the month was out Presley had played dates in Carlsbad, New Mexico, and in Cleveland, Ohio. Word of the young artist's dynamic stage shows had spread beyond the South and Southwest, and by the beginning of the summer Phillips was receiving inquiries from major labels interested in signing Presley when his Sun contract was up.

Presley was Sun's only significant asset at that point, though, and Phillips wasn't interested in losing him, secure in the belief that Presley would be successful enough to bolster the label's sagging fortunes and establish Sun on a national level. In July Presley broke into the national country charts for the first time with "Baby Let's Play House" b/w "I'm Left, You're Right, She's Gone," and this glimmer of widespread recognition served to buttress Phillips's unswerving faith in Presley's potential.

Parker, however, had designs of his own. He knew of Sun's shaky status, of Phillips's inability to put much money towards promoting Presley, and that Presley's Sun contract had only two years to run. Maneuvering to become Presley's manager, Parker cut a deal in November with Phillips, Hill and Range music publishing, and RCA Records, whereby the agent, the publisher, and the label would jointly purchase Presley's contract. Hill and Range was to front $15,000 in exchange for the publishing rights on at least one side of every Presley record and a copublishing deal on the Hi-Lo Music catalogue owned by Phillips. In all, Phillips received $35,000 from Parker, RCA, and Hill

"The Perkins family was born to the earth": The indomitable James Washington Perkins and Bettye Azilee Scott Perkins (seated front, second and third from left), surrounded by their sons and daughters, date unknown. In the front row, kneeling, are Dea Perkins (left) and Earnest J. Perkins. Back row, from left: Buck Perkins (Carl's father), Hattie Gertrude Perkins, Eula Mar-Virginia Perkins, Hubert Perkins, Olie V. Perkins.

The Martha Perkins Bain Collection

Buck and Louise Perkins's home in Tiptonville, Lake County, Tennessee. Carl was born here on April 9, 1932.

The Jim Bailey Collection

Best friends Martha Lee Perkins (left) and Valda Crider together in 1949, during their high school days. Valda remembers this photo as having been taken shortly before her introduction to Martha's cousin, Carl Perkins.

The Carl Perkins Collection

Sixteen-year-old Valda Crider in a portrait from 1947.

The Carl Perkins Collection

Carl working out at Jackson's Chatterbox honky tonk in 1954. Clayton's bass is unattended behind Carl. Where was Clayton? "He was drunk," Carl says, "dancing with some redhead right in front of where I was standin' there playin'."

J. Frank Johnson/The Carl Perkins Collection

Carl (front) plays at the opening of a Jackson hardware store in the early '50s. Jay is behind him on rhythm guitar.

THE JACKSON SUN/The Jim Bailey Collection

▌ackson, Tennessee,'s hottest honky tonk
band, The Perkins Brothers—Jay, Carl, Clayton—in a
1954 photo.

The Jim Bailey Collection

Jay, Carl, and Clayton on their way to work as the Perkins Brothers Band. Carl identifies this photo as having been taken in 1954 on the day after the band's second audition for Sam Phillips at Sun Records.

The Jim Bailey Collection

Carl, Jay, and Clayton between sets at the El Rancho in 1955, with their friend Pat Durbin, who bore an uncanny resemblance to Fluke Holland, the band's drummer. A few hours after this photo was taken, Clayton told Durbin he had swallowed a straight pin and needed to be rushed to the hospital. On the wild ride into Jackson, Durbin's car flipped over going around a curve. Upon being treated and released, Clayton revealed to Carl that the straight pin story was pure fiction.

The Jim Bailey Collection

Carl in an early Sun publicity shot, 1954 or 1955.

The Jim Bailey Collection

Apartment 23D, Parkview Courts, Jackson, Tennessee. Carl and Valda's first "home" after moving out of Carl's parents' house in Bemis. It was here that Carl wrote "Blue Suede Shoes." Today, the building looks almost as it did in this photograph from the mid-'50s.

The Jim Bailey Collection

Sun Records owner Sam Phillips presents Carl with a gold record for "Blue Suede Shoes" in April 1956. Carl was to have received the award during his appearance on *The Perry Como Show* in March, but was seriously injured, along with Jay, in a car wreck on the way to the show, forcing cancellation of his first booking on national television.

Courtesy: C. Escott/Showtime Archive, Toronto

Sam Phillips hands over the keys to a new Cadillac to Carl in 1956 on the occasion of "Blue Suede Shoes" being a certified million seller. Carl was the first Sun artist to achieve that distinction.

Courtesy: C. Escott/Showtime Archive, Toronto

The original cat dusts off his blue suede shoes backstage before a show with Johnny Cash in 1956.

Courtesy: C. Escott/Showtime Archive, Toronto

Valda in the hospital with baby Steve Perkins, April 1956.

Courtesy: C. Escott/Showtime Archive, Toronto

and Range, and Presley was paid $5,000 due him in back royalties. The final tally also showed that Parker was the sole manager of Elvis Presley, much to the chagrin of Neal and Snow, who were removed from the picture altogether without further compensation.

Long ago Carl had vowed that he would give his children the Christmases poverty had denied him. But with the holiday season approaching in 1955, he and Valda were spending everything they made (Valda had been ironing clothes for pay) to take care of their family and Carl's parents. Although his first two singles had not been national hits, they had been popular in the South, enough so that Carl thought he must be due some money from Sam. But when asked, Sam revealed that Carl owed money to Sun for his recording costs.

With their finances ebbing, Carl went back to the one place where he knew he could hire on for a few days' work and then take his wages and walk away. As he drove towards the city limits, he hated himself, hated his life, hated what he was having to do, hated that all his years of hard work had brought him back to a cotton field. About ten miles out of town, he parked, took a sack off the wagon, and headed out to pick "from can to can't."

As he made his way down a row, an elderly man on the next row straightened up and stared at him. "You look like that sanger," he drawled, as Carl made a slight gesture of acknowledgment. At the end of the day he collected fifteen dollars and walked off humiliated and bitter.

"I worked on that froze ground and my hands bled. If that don't callous you; if that don't hurt about as bad as anything, to have some ol' farmer recognize you out there. Course I'd been singin' around here for years. I'd been in these tonks, everybody around here had seen

Carl Perkins, everybody around here was proud Carl Perkins had a record called 'Turn Around.' Every disc jockey around here played it. And when I pulled cotton before Christmas 1955 I had *two records!* As far as the cotton pickers in this part of the country was concerned, I was a big shot. And it was embarrassing for me to hear them say, 'You just out here for the exercise?' I pulled cotton for my kids' Christmas."

On December 19, Phillips summoned Carl to the studio. Behind the board, Phillips uttered the words Carl had been waiting to hear: "Do me that 'Shoes' song."

The first take was tentative, stiff. Carl changed his original lyric of "Go, man, go" to "Go, boy, go," and added "I don't care, baby, just what you do" before he sang "but uh-uh, honey, lay offa my shoes." His initial guitar solo was tepid and sloppy; he was searching for some fire but managing only faint sparks. After the second verse he shouted to the band, "Go now!" and cut out on a solo that blended chordings and single-string runs. It sizzled and moved the song forward.

Phillips kept the tape rolling. On Take 2 Carl altered the lyrics again; where he had been singing "Go, man, go" or "Go, boy, go," he cried "Go, cat, go!" and eliminated the superfluous words from the end of the first verse to make it "do anything that you wanna do, but uh-uh . . . ," and hit a tough solo during the first break that moved him to exclaim, "Aaah, go cat!" in the middle of his playing. Before he went into orbit on a second solo that was almost a mirror image but hotter than his second solo on the first take, he barked out a command for the band to "Rock!" Carl was cutting loose on his vocal too, singing with an easy but driving swing in his voice, and an ingratiating ebullience. The lyrics were tighter, the instrumentalists better locked into each other, and the feel was fresh and lively; it had the abandoned quality of "Gone, Gone, Gone," but it also had a vitality quite distinct from any other of the Perkins brothers' records. Jay, Clayton, and W.S. backed Carl with a bedrock rockabilly attack, but Carl's solos were coming from somewhere else—from country, from blues, from R&B, from all the sources Carl had absorbed over the years. A third take was mediocre, closer in feel and attack to the first than the second. Carl picked a rousing second solo, as he had done on the previous takes, and shouted out, "Yeeeah, them blue suede shoes!" but then he got carried away at the end of the song. Instead of repeating "blue, blue, blue suede shoes," hammering home the image as he had been doing all along, he varied the lines: "I said my blue suede shoes / Don't you step on my blue suede shoes / I said my blue suede shoes." He was trying too hard, adding filigree where none was needed.

When Phillips left the control booth, Carl called out: "I gotta do it again!"

Phillips turned, a quizzical look on his face. "Why?"

"I made a mistake," Carl answered sheepishly. "I said 'Go, cat, go.' "

"I heard it," Phillips replied, "and you ain't changin' nothin'."

Phillips's intransigence startled Carl. Surely Sam could recognize how important this moment, Carl's moment, was; surely. "But Mr. Phillips," Carl implored. "I made some bad guitar mistakes in there."

"Listen to it," Sam said, returning to the tape machine and playing back the tape.

"Mr. Phillips, that's wrong," Carl said after listening to the three takes. "I can beat any of that with the guitar."

"You just listen to this break," Sam answered, cueing up one of Carl's solos. "Did you hear that? You *burnt* it! We're not changin' anything. Smash, smash, smash—this record's a smash!"

Carl had never seen Phillips so excited, so carried away by a song. The more they talked about "Blue Suede Shoes," the more Phillips's eyes grew wide and wild in anticipation of loosing the record on an unsuspecting public. He even called Dewey Phillips to hype him on the day's events. "Man, you ain't gonna believe it! You ain't gonna believe it!" he shouted in the disc jockey's ear, working himself into a lather like the Baptist preacher whose earnestness had frightened Carl during his churchgoing days in Lake County. "Carl Perkins has got a smash. *Do you hear me, Phillips!?*" Sam exclaimed, gesticulating with his hands, his hair falling uncharacteristically out of place onto his forehead. *"Do you hear me!?"*

Hearing the playback of Take 2, Carl, who had not regarded the song as his best effort when compared to "Turn Around" and "Let the Jukebox Keep on Playing," sensed the magic that had so captivated Phillips. Take 2 was beautiful: "I felt I had the best rockabilly song I had ever written. I liked the beginning and I liked the way I sang, 'Blue,

blue, blue suede shoes, mm-hmm, blue, blue, blue suede shoes.' That was jive; that was in the pocket, shakin' 'em loose, gettin 'em ready to play it again. I felt really good when it was played back through those cheap speakers at Sun. I had a tingle that had never been there before. I looked at Jay and Clayton and W.S. with, I know, a different look. I had to. That was the moment I had really searched for all my life. We pulled away from the studio that night aching to hear that song again. We talked about it all the way home. Jay said, 'That one might do it. You may have cut something that's gonna get someplace, Carl.' "

More significant for Carl, seventeen years of his life, from the time he had first strummed a guitar at age six, had spiraled down to a precious few seconds in the Sun studio. The wisdom that had guided his young life—"Let it vib-a-rate"—"Keep prayin', Carl, God will hear you"— the distant dreams, the hand-to-mouth life of the tonk player, the pursuit of an elusive grail—all of it poured out onto the fretboard of the Gibson Les Paul as Carl's fingers found each note that would tell his story, make his statement in the most personal and most dramatic terms: "I went off into deep water on the neck of that guitar on the second solo. Way over my head. I only knew, Here's my shot. This is my song. It's cookin'. Get somethin' outta this box you ain't never got before. And I did. I never had played what I played in the studio that day. Never. I know God said, 'I've held it back, but this is it. Now you get down and get it.' I felt all kinds of things going on in me, and I tore into brand-new territory. I was so nervous when it was over . . . When Sam played it back, it just made my fingers tingle. I'd done pulled my guitar off and was standin' there leanin' against a chair. I looked down at it, much to say, 'I thank my own guitar for what it did.' I felt that: 'Thank you, boy. We connected.' I knew it."

As a potential B side, Carl offered "Honey Don't," another song developed in the tonks. Its public debut had come the preceding summer at a combination club-restaurant in Jackson called Tommy's Drive-In. In warm weather bands played on the roof, where the manager had constructed a dance floor and bandstand, with protective railing around the sides. Tommy's was a far cry from the surrounding honky-tonks: It had a friendlier ambience and fewer tush hogs, featured barbecue chicken on its menu, and drew large contingents of high school- and college-age youths on weekends. The Perkins Brothers rarely played Tommy's, because the money was so slight (stingy management and no cover), but Carl tried to work every night and would go there when other places were unavailable.

Deep in the throes of an Early Times–induced fog, Carl struck up the song on a whim without telling the band, singing:

Well how come you say you will when you won't
You tell me you do, baby, when you don't
Put your arms around me, let me know how it feels
Now come on tell me, is love real?
But uh-uh, honey don't

He started playing in E, and Jay was following along until Carl shifted to a C chord, stopping Jay cold. "Where you goin'?" he whispered anxiously to Carl. On the bass, Clayton was working out as if he had heard the song a million times, he and W.S. maintaining a chugging rhythm ("He didn't hear a damn bit of difference," Carl says of Clayton. "It sounded the same wherever he was.")

"I'm goin' from E to C!" Carl told Jay.

"That won't work!" Jay complained.

"Just go!" Carl urged.

Jay picked up the chord progression as Carl improvised some more verses. But during a break, he confronted Carl. "I know where you're trying to go with that new song of yours, *but it won't work! It ain't right!*"

"It *will* work," Carl insisted. "I put a C in there, come back to E, go back to C, come back to E, then next go to B. It'll work."

"That's the craziest mess I ever heard," Jay said, disgusted. "Whatta you drinkin' tonight?"

"Just do it," Carl replied. "Let's just do it."

Jay did it, but he was never comfortable with the song. Carl says the song upset Jay "because he thought something had happened to my mind. He looked at me real curious and said, 'It's not only that the melody is not right, but what are you sayin'? Honey don't? Honey don't? What are you trying to say?' He said, 'I won't have nothin' to do with it.' And he didn't. He never sang on that song. He thought it was the nuttiest thing. And he was right—it was."

On the other hand, Sam Phillips thought its unlikely chord progression inspired and its lyrics strong. "Good God, yeah, man!" he shouted after the band had completed a run-through in the studio. "Oh, yeah, man! What a thing! Do it again!"

The band cut three versions of "Honey Don't" at the session, the third being released on the flip side of "Shoes." Of all the Sun tapes extant the variations heard on "Honey Don't" provide the best glimpse into how Carl shaped his art, from the song's stream-of-consciousness origin at Tommy's Drive-In to the refinements of those ideas into a commercial work. On the roof of Tommy's that summer night in 1955 Carl sang something nearly identical to Take 1 of "Honey Don't":

How come you say you will, baby, when you won't

You tell me that you love me, baby, but you don't

Let me know how you feel about me

Tell the truth, baby, please, please, please

But uh-uh, oh, honey don't

(chorus:) Well, honey don't

Honey don't

Well, honey don't

Yeah, honey don't

Say you will when you won't

Huh-uh, honey don't

Well I love you baby, and you oughta know

I like the way that you wear your clothes

Everything about you is so sweet

Tell the truth, now, please, please, please

But uh-uh, oh, honey don't!

(chorus)

Here, Carl cut out on a guitar solo that wound down into a boogie-woogie riff before a stop-time measure kicked off the next verse:

> Sometimes you say you will when you don't
> Tell me baby, now, do you or won't
> Put your arms around me, honey, and tease
> Don't tell a lie, no, please, please, please
> Huh-uh, no, honey don't
>
> (chorus)

On Take 2 the narrative had evolved. Both versions are about sex. The first, however, found the singer fearing he's being led to the throne only to be turned away at the critical moment. On Take 2 the singer was either entangled with a champion tease or a faithless lover, or both; either way, the end result was the same.

> How come you will you say when you don't
> Tell me baby don't you know you won't
> Please, baby, honey don't you tease
> Look out, gal, now please, please, please
> Uh-uh, well honey don't
>
> Sometimes I love you every Saturday night
> Sunday morning you don't look right
> You've been out a-paintin' the town
> Look out gal you been slippin' around
> But huh-uh, oh, honey don't

As he started his guitar solo, Carl shouted, "Let's go now, chillun!" and in midsolo exhorted the band: "Let's rock it!"

> Sometimes you will, baby, when you won't
> I know you can even if you don't
> Tell me baby that you sho' love me
> Uh-uh, oh, honey please
> Uh-uh, oh, honey don't

("Hang on, chillun, let's rock!")

Say you will when you won't
Uh-uh, honey don't

Everyone was dissatisfied with the first two versions. Carl was rushing his vocal to fit too many words into too few measures, bogging down the momentum. Sam stopped the tape and the band tried several revised versions of "Honey Don't" before Carl came up with a streamlined model that better captured the sexual anxiety expressed in the narrative line. Take 3 opened with solo guitar line, then Clayton kicked in behind with the clicking bass as Carl sang:

Well how come you say you will when you won't
You tell me you do, baby, when you don't
Let me know honey how you feel
Tell the truth now is love real
But uh-uh, oh, honey don't

(chorus)

Well I love you baby and you oughta know
I like the way that you wear your clothes
Everything about you is so doggone sweet
You got that sand all over your feet
So uh-uh, hey, honey don't

(chorus)

("Hang on, chillun, let's rock now!")

Sometimes I love you on Saturday night
Sunday morning you don't look right
You been out a-paintin' the town
Uh-huh, babe, you been slippin' around
So huh-uh, hey, honey don't
Say you will when you won't
Huh-uh, honey don't

("Get it, cats, let's go now!")

Well, well, honey don't
Oh, honey don't
Honey don't, bop-bop-bop-ba
Honey don't
Say you will when you won't
Huh-uh, honey don't

At the end of the song Carl hit a descending riff that curled back in on itself. He and Clayton meshed on the coda, and Clayton, as he did on the first two versions, tagged it with his identifying bass lick, "for meanness," Carl asserts: "It was like he was sayin', 'If they don't hear me all the way through there, they're gonna hear me on the end.' And it didn't make no difference—Sam had to leave him on there. He didn't have no splicing gear to take him out. He'd say, 'There's ol' Clayton's signature.' Listen to the Sun records—you don't hear him too well, but he's there at the end. Sam liked him very much because he quickly turned into a hoss of a bass player. I'd go over to Mama and Daddy's and catch him practicing over there, and pretty soon he could take as good a bass break as you ever heard."

The long session wound up with two more cuts, "Sure to Fall" and "Tennessee," the latter being another that came together as it was being recorded. "Sure to Fall" featured Jay trading verses and harmonizing with Carl. It was a straight country weeper, partially credited by Carl to Claunch and Cantrell, who had smoothed out some of the lyrics. Jay's vocal was straightforward and solidly masculine, without much inflection or deep feeling, but he came to life on the harmonies, when his and Carl's voices blended together beautifully in plaintive declaration of unending fidelity. In contrast to Jay, Carl's solo turns were inspired and moving affairs, soulful and emotional.

By far the weirdest song Carl had ever recorded, "Tennessee" was nothing more than a tribute in country-shuffle form to things wondrous in the Volunteer State, from Eddy Arnold to the atomic bomb, the uranium for which had been separated at a plant in Oak Ridge. As Carl wrote it:

They make bombs they say can blow up our world, dear

Well a country boy like me, I will agree

But if all you folks out there will remember

They made the first atomic bomb in Tennessee

Sam paired the last take of "Honey Don't" with Take 2 of "Blue Suede Shoes," paired "Tennessee" with "Sure to Fall," cut the masters on his Presto lathe, and shipped acetates to Superior Records in Los Angeles. He enclosed instructions for Superior to ship sets of 45 rpm and 78 rpm stampers to Plastic Products and requested a rush on "Blue Suede Shoes / Honey Don't." By the end of December the first commercial copies were ready for release, but Phillips had already sent some test pressings to radio stations, where the reaction to "Blue Suede Shoes" marked it as a potential hit.

The special feeling Carl felt during the playback of "Blue Suede Shoes" stayed with him the rest of the night. Early the next morning he walked into apartment 23D at Parkview Courts, and the woman he loved was there with their children, all asleep. As Carl rested on the side of the bed, Valda woke up. "Carl, did it come out good?" she asked in a groggy whisper.

Carl hesitated, still hearing the song in his mind. "Valda," he said calmly, "I've done it. I wish you could hear it."

They embraced, and waited.

A few days later the band played the El Rancho, and had a special guest in Scotty Moore, who sat in on guitar for the entire evening. At the end of the night, about two a.m., Carl invited Moore and his wife over to the apartment. He wanted Scotty to hear "Blue Suede Shoes" and to "taste some of Valda's homemade biscuits."

Valda was asleep when Carl and Scotty arrived, but she was soon up and fixing an early-morning breakfast of scrambled eggs and biscuits for everyone (this was fairly routine for Valda, because Carl was always famished when he came home from the tonks). After eating, she visited with Scotty's wife while Carl and Scotty sat on the kitchen floor with their guitars and a bottle of Early Times, playing, according to Scotty, "a little bit of everything—blues, some of Carl's own songs, everything. We would sit there and amaze each other, just stretchin'.

Never played the same thing twice. Just whatever felt good at the time. We didn't use amplifiers, but I remember Valda would come in there and say, 'Don't make too much racket! Don't wake up them kids!' "

With Christmas then only a few days away, Carl drove into town to the John A. Parker Seed Company. He had ten dollars with him, all the money he and Valda had left in the world, and they were going to use it to buy Stan and Debbie each a Christmas present and some stocking stuffers; he and Valda would go without. Carl had spotted a red wagon made of wood at the Parker company, retailing for nearly three dollars. Holding Stan on his hip, Carl pointed out the wagon to Parker as the one he wanted.

"Is this for that boy?" Parker asked as he brought the wagon down from its wall perch.

"Yes, sir."

"This wagon's too little," Parker warned.

"Well he'll just pull it," Carl said. "He can't ride in it." Parker couldn't see Carl's insides knotting up anymore than he could know the shame Carl felt.

On Christmas morning he placed Stan, then a year-and-a-half old, in the wagon. Immediately the child's weight caused it to tip over backward, depositing him head first on the concrete floor. Valda cradled Stan in her arms as he screamed. Carl saw a sizable knot welling up on Stan's skull. Abruptly he turned and stormed out the back door and stood crying on the stoop outside, humiliated by the thought of his best efforts to do right by his family yielding so little reward and causing such great pain for those he loved most.

Valda saw their standing in a different light: The wagon was a wagon. It wasn't big enough, but it was still a wagon. And Debbie had her doll, a little doll for a little girl. On balance, as Valda emphasizes, things could have been bleaker: "It did hurt me and I had tears in my eyes. The way I looked at it, we could've not had the money even to buy those things. There was times that our groceries were very slim; we didn't have all that much to eat. Carl would go to Mr. Yates's grocery store, and Mr. Yates would give him the ham hocks. I would cut all the meat off and there would be little pieces I could fry. They were small pieces, but they didn't taste any different than big pieces."

Carl was humbled by Mr. Yates's gift of ham hocks, telling himself, "Boy, it sure is good to have friends to let me have this." On each occasion when he returned home with a handout, he would pick up his guitar and urge himself: *Come on, Carl, write you a song! Don't be a charity case! You can do it, you can write, come on! Dig! Dig!*

"Hour after hour I forced myself, but you can't force a song out," Carl says. "I'd almost go crazy trying to. I was some kind of artist wantin' to be born. It was in me and I was tryin' to force it out. I'd set in Parkview tryin' so hard. I was depressed. We were dirt poor, it would be snowin' and I knew there wasn't gonna be nobody at the club that night. I'd make just two or three dollars, and it was tough. It was tough."

Never tougher, though, than it was on that Christmas Day. Tears streaming down his face, Carl looked heavenward. Quietly he spoke, as Stan's crying rang in his ears.

"My momma raised me to go to church," he said in beseeching his God. "I know I haven't been living as good as I should, I know I could do better, but I'm not a mean man. I never robbed, I never stole nothing. I was taught better than that. But Lord, this is it. If by next Christmas I can't get that big wagon for my boy, if I can't buy my girl as pretty a doll as the other girls have in this town, I'm tellin' you, Lord, you're gonna have a thief on your hands to deal with. I'll take my shotgun and rob a service station to get it.

"I need Your help."

S h o r t l y after the end of World War II, CBS laboratories engineer Peter Goldmark developed the first long-playing record made of polyvinyl chloride (PVC). Introduced to meager sales, it gained converts each year and by 1955 occupied a fairly solid market niche alongside 78s. A more immediate threat to the 78's preeminence came by way of another postwar innovation. In the wake of Goldmark's 33⅓ record came an announcement from RCA Victor's engineers of a seven-inch, large-holed microgroove version of the single disc that played at forty-five revolutions per minute and required a special adapter for standard phonographs. Priced comparably to—and often less than—the 78, the 45 made an immediate impact on the retail marketplace. It was more durable than its more cumbersome, fragile counterpart, was easier to transport, easier to store (and several astute manufacturers rushed out compact carrying cases for single records, creating an entirely new branch of the record accessories market)—it was an altogether sleeker product, well suited to an American public that had shaken free of the strictures of war and was exulting in an atmosphere of unprecedented prosperity.

Change and revolution were the orders of the day, in science, medicine, politics, the arts, sports. New frontiers were being opened at an astonishing clip in a society where this sense of forward momentum could be heard and felt on a daily basis in the big beat of the younger generation's music. As rhythm-oriented music was consigning the Hit Parade to the history books, so was the 45—new, light, resilient, compact—a "sexy" product in a time of heightened passions—displacing the stodgy 78 as the recording medium of choice.

So preoccupied was Carl with keeping his family fed, clothed, and sheltered that he had completely missed the introduction of the 45 rpm single record. In the tonks he studied the songs, not the spinning discs, on the jukeboxes; and being unable to afford a record player, he visited music stores only to buy new guitar strings. At any rate, he was less interested in format changes than he was in hearing his new single on the radio, as he did often in Jackson, where "Honey Don't" was more frequently being programmed than "Blue Suede Shoes." He describes the two-week interim between the recording of "Shoes" and its initial airplay (on the day of its release, January 1, 1956) as "the longest wait in the world." But even coming over tiny, crackling speakers, the song had undeniable power, so much so it was almost palpable to Carl: "The day I heard it I had the same feeling I had had at the studio. It was there. I knew if it did go, then I was the one that sold it. Me, Jay,

Clayton, and Fluke. Our playing, my song, and my guitar would be what sold that record. And I knew it would do a lot for me as a guitarist, as a singer, and as a songwriter."

Sam mailed Carl two 78 copies of "Blue Suede Shoes" and, as had been the case with his first single, both arrived broken. Too impatient to wait for another mailing, Carl drove downtown to Hardeman Music, where John Towater had sold him his first Les Paul two years earlier and had boosted his confidence along the way by asserting, "It's gonna happen, Carl. You're gonna have a big record."

Carl rushed in and asked Towater for a copy of "Blue Suede Shoes." Reaching under the counter, Towater said he'd had a shipment come in the day before. He pulled out a 45 and laid it on the counter in front of Carl.

Carl smiled and pushed the record back toward Towater. "No, sir," Carl said gently, not wanting to be overbearing when the man had made an honest mistake, "that ain't my record. See, my record's a great big one with a little bitty hole in it." As he studied the 45, Carl wondered how something so strange would fit on a record player's spindle.

"This is what they've gone to, Carl," Towater reported to his befuddled customer. "They aren't going to make any more 78s. Even the jukeboxes are going to this."

Carl felt his body go limp. In disbelief he complained to Towater that the 45 "won't sell! That big ol' hole, little bitty record . . . nobody's gonna buy that! I don't want it."

Carl knew Valda was waiting, eager to hear "Blue Suede Shoes" on record; when he walked in, he tried to avoid her. Finally he said, "It's over, Valda. It looks like I might have a hit record, but I ain't gonna have one. They've messed it up."

Seeing Valda's shock, Carl launched into a lament over the record being the wrong size—"It ain't as big as a saucer, and it's all hole!"—and expressed profound puzzlement about the ways of a business that would destroy itself by changing its product so drastically and apparently without warning.

Ever positive, Valda assured her husband that there must be some logic behind the change. "It's got to work or they wouldn't be changing them. *It's got to work!* Those big records, they break!"

"Valda, these are like paper! They bend!"

"Well that's why they did it—to keep them from breaking," Valda surmised.

Momentarily comforted by Valda's common sense, Carl nonetheless remained suspicious that he was being punished even as he had tried to do right. After some dogged research—that is, paying more attention to the world around him—he discovered that kids indeed were buying 45s and that jukeboxes had gone over to the new format as well. Thanks to the installment plan at the Tate Brothers store, he purchased a used record player complete with a 45 adapter, and at long last cued up his "Blue Suede Shoes" single. To his relief, it was the same song he had recorded in December.

Like the Jackson station, Memphis radio was programming "Honey Don't" as the A side and receiving good response. In Cleveland, though, disc jockey Bill Randle was featuring "Blue Suede Shoes" prominently on his nightly show; overwhelming listener response was translating into brisk sales, and before the month was out Sam Phillips had a request from the Cleveland distributor for another 25,000 copies. Even Elvis hadn't caused such a stir, and for Phillips solvency was in the offing.

He phoned Carl to inform him of the Cleveland breakout. Stunned, Carl could not believe the number Sam quoted him.

"Cat, I said *twenty-five thousand*," Phillips repeated. "I told you it was a smash!"

"But they ain't playin' 'Blue Suede Shoes' up around Jackson," Carl noted.

"Well, we don't care if they play the hole in the middle of the record," Phillips retorted. "It's happenin', and it's 'Blue Suede Shoes.' "

After talking to Phillips, Carl wandered around the apartment in a daze, trying to grasp what was happening. His first thought was that it was in fact not happening at all; that come morning Phillips would be back on the phone telling him, "Naw, they didn't want 'em. They made a mistake." It was too good to be true.

Almost immediately Carl had reason to wish it all were a fantasy. A reporter for the *Memphis Press-Scimitar* heard about the early demand for "Blue Suede Shoes" and contacted Phillips for a story that was published a few days later. In it the reporter claimed that in one week Carl had made $20,000 from his new recording. This was big news to Carl, who had hardly any money to his name when the story ran. The following day Carl was visited by one of the directors of Parkview Courts, informing him that his income, as reported in the Memphis paper, exceeded the maximum allowable for tenants residing in the government-subsidized complex. The Perkinses would have to move immediately from their $32-a-month apartment.

Four blocks from Parkview, on Camden Street, Carl rented a three-room apartment, but at a slightly higher rate than he had been paying. It had no appliances, so back he went to Tate Brothers for a used stove and refrigerator. After these purchases, Carl was "flat broke."

Carl's fortunes, literally and figuratively, picked up in the following weeks as "Blue Suede Shoes" became the side of choice at most radio stations throughout the South and Southwest. On February 11 the single entered the Memphis country charts at number two, and the following week it topped the chart, where it would remain for three months. Sales throughout the South were strong, and requests for personal appearances were coming in faster than Bob Neal could respond. Booked on Sun package tours with Cash and as a solo act, Carl and his brothers saw their going price rise from $100 a night to $250 a night. One of the plum bookings Neal arranged for Carl was an appearance on Dallas's *Big D Jamboree* radio show—sort of a Grand Ole Opry of the Southwest—that in turn generated a string of one-nighters in West Texas and on into Albuquerque, New Mexico. The acclaim and the money were on a scale previously unimagined by Carl, but the most satisfying aspect of his newfound success was his status as a headliner. Elvis wasn't on the bill anymore, and Carl finally knew, without doubt, that the rousing reception greeting his appearance was solely for him. Carl Perkins's music had become a defining element in these fans' lives. When they sang along with him, Carl's spirits soared, because the kids knew every lyric as if they'd written it; these weren't a bunch of drunks back at the El Rancho. Every time Carl played for the teenagers, he knew that he and "Blue Suede Shoes" mattered in some important and perhaps undefinable way; he knew the feeling from his own youth, from the first time he heard the field hands' gospel raveups, and Bill

Monroe's "Blue Moon of Kentucky" on the Grand Ole Opry. What was unusual, what neither Carl nor anyone else had seen before, was a song of such ample dimension. Carl's exhortation to "Go, cat, go!" was at once an astute summation of America's new spirit and an entire generation's *cri de coeur*. "Blue Suede Shoes" evoked a phenomenon bigger than, but inseparable from, the music itself.

Carl had given voice to his young audience's growing fascination with fashion as personal statement, as metaphor even, much like James Dean's omnipresent red jacket in *Rebel Without a Cause*. Symbols and attitudes of a new sensibility were encoded in the lyrics. And however simple, the choice of words was complex in subtle ways. Drinking liquor from a fruit jar was an image straight out of the rural Tennessee of Carl's youth, while the proper use of slander in describing oral defamation was fairly highbrow for a rockabilly lyric.

And it was more. In celebrating the simple pride in ownership of a single item of clothing, the song spoke the language of the working-class poor, irrespective of race, of anyone who had struggled and kicked and clawed and scratched to have a single good thing, a solitary shard of beautiful light cutting through poverty's degrading, suffocating darkness. The singer drinks moonshine, not the choice beverage of the privileged, and indicates by subtext that his house and car aren't worth burning or stealing, so go ahead, knock yourself out. But the shoes, not leather but *suede*, fine, soft, elegant suede, make the man one to be reckoned with, if for no other reason than right here, right now, they are his: See and believe. Go, cat, go!

Bob Neal booked Carl and Cash on the usual southern circuit to take advantage of both artists' new country hits—Cash's "So Doggone Lonesome" b/w "Folsom Prison Blues" had been released in mid-December and was going strong by the new year. The first show was in a high school gymnasium in Gladewater, Texas, a regular stop for Carl, a place where he had played shows with Elvis.

In Gladewater the young audience responded wildly to Carl's performance of "Blue Suede Shoes," screaming, shouting, dancing frantically as soon as he belted out, "Well it's one for the money!" The Texas teens were the first to hear the song in its final form, as it was on record, and their enthusiasm for it startled Carl. As much as he believed he had hit on something unique, he was unprepared for the forcefield of energy the kids released when he shouted "Go, cat, go!" The whoops, the screams, the sensual charge of the moment jolted him, unsettled him a bit, so close was it to being out of control.

The scene in Gladewater was replayed at every stop. By late January the scope of what was developing in the wake of "Shoes" 's release became clearer to Carl with his first of several regular appearances on the *Big D Jamboree*. Like the Opry, the *Jamboree* asked its featured acts to commit to one appearance a month; unlike the Opry, its lineup represented a wide variety of country-music styles, in keeping with Texas's rich history as a fertile breeding ground for both traditional country music and its renegade offshoots such as country and western and honky-tonk. Rockabilly, the wildest mutant of country music, was embraced by Texas like a prodigal son.

"Rockabilly was *loved* in Texas," says Carl. "At first we played more in Texas than anywhere else. It was so big, and the music just flat took off out there. Texas is very big for western and rockabilly music, 'cause they're the type of people that like to have a good time. I'd see cowboys and cowgirls come in and dance and never sit down. Stand up for three or four hours and dance. We'd take fifteen-, twenty-minute breaks every hour, and they'd just stand around waitin' to dance again."

The show emanated from the Dallas Sportatorium, a warehouse-sized steel building with a seating capacity of approximately four thousand, with performers playing in the round in a wrestling ring stripped of its ropes, with plywood boards placed over the mat itself. Ed McLemore, who ran the *Jamboree*, liked to have artists perform twice over the course of a four-hour show (eight p.m. until midnight). He changed the policy for Carl. As his turn to perform arrived, the young audience surged towards the stage, where Jay, Clayton, and W.S. had already set up and were playing an introductory instrumental. As Carl wound his way from the dressing room area to the stage, he had to duck to avoid hands reaching out to touch him or to grab at his clothing. The largely teenage audience was screaming, their voices resonating off the concrete and steel to such a painful degree that the crowd sounded about twice its actual size. By the same token, the cavernous venue served as a huge echo chamber, perfect for adding a bit of sizzle to the rockabilly sound.

Carl made four appearances on the regionally broadcast *Jamboree* in early '56, and these led to a string of dates to the furthest regions of southern and western Texas—Houston, Port Arthur, San Antonio, Amarillo, Odessa, El Paso—"good rockabilly towns," as Carl recalls. And all-night drives. The world was opening up for Carl. The *Jamboree* sold out for each of his appearances, and it was after a huge order came in from Dallas music shops for "Blue Suede Shoes" that Sam Phillips predicted to Carl, "Man, this is gonna be a million-sellin' record. I can't believe it."

Carl and Cash aided their causes while on the road by serving as their own promotion men. As Carl remembers it, Sam advised: "When you boys are going down the road, don't wait until you get to the town you're playin' in. Put them records in the back of your car and you listen to that radio all the time. Find a country station and the louder it gets, the closer you gonna be to it. Whip that car in there and go in and just shake hands. Don't worry 'em; they're busy now. Them disc jockeys can't talk to you all the time."

Looking back on Phillips's tutelage—counseling the artists on every aspect of their careers, from appearance to self-promotion—Carl sees how "little bitty things helped the label. Sam didn't miss very many turns. Little things like us goin' to the radio stations and lettin' 'em know. He'd say, 'Right after you say hello, let your second line be, 'Man, I sure appreciate you playin' my record.' That's gonna set him up. He likes to hear that. Don't go in there cocky; don't be no smart aleck. That ain't what this is about. You guys are passing through and you stop to thank 'em.' I probably thanked a lot of 'em that didn't even have the record. I never had one to tell me he didn't have the record, but I'm sure there were some of those little stations that didn't have it. We did that before 'Blue Suede Shoes' came out and after it came out. But then things started changing and you couldn't do it very much. Everything changed after the record."

In its first two months of release "Blue Suede Shoes" climbed rapidly in local and regional charts, hit number one on many country charts, ascended to the upper regions of pop charts, and even drew airplay on R&B charts, a reverse crossover rarity. A *Song Hits* review of the single, published February 18, offered a portent of things to come: "Difficult as the country field is for a newcomer to 'crack' these days, Perkins has come up with some wax here that has hit the national retail chart in almost record time. New Orleans, Memphis, Nashville, Richmond, Durham, and other areas report it a leading seller. Interestingly enough, the disk has a large measure of appeal for pop and r.&b. customers."

Carl stood onstage and saw bright, smiling faces yelling out his name, kids kicking up their heels and immersing themselves in a moment he was creating. If there had ever been a point of turning back, it had passed forever by the end of January 1956. Carl's memory of this time indicates his sense of being swept up by events he had helped set in motion but seemed powerless to control, as well as a certain incredulity over having attained such acclaim: "The last part of January, the whole month of February, and up until March, it was changing so drastically. The places I was playin' were bigger, and I didn't need Elvis to be on the show. I was drawing 'em myself good. That song was carrying its weight out there and they were coming to see the guy who did the record. It was my name that was on those marquees that was drawing those kids in there, and they was hollerin' and screamin' and jumpin' up for me, just like they had been for Elvis. It was *me*."

fo u r unreconstructed rockabillies, at least two of them—Carl and Clayton—tush hogs to greater or lesser degrees, were bound to find ways to amuse themselves on the road, none more so than Clayton. "Cash put Clayton up to most of his stuff," Carl insists, and Cash himself owns up with, "I would admit to part of it. Not all of it, though." It's also true that Clayton brought considerable personal history to bear on his antics: He had a track record. Once at a motel in West Texas, Clayton went out in the morning and returned before checkout time with a dead fish. As the band members were packing to leave— they slept four to a room, two on beds, two on the floor—Clayton slipped the fish deep under the mattress.

"Clayton!" Carl barked. "They'll never get the scent out of that mattress. Throw that fish out!"

Clayton, his features scrunching into a sly grin, refused, but amiably so. "They got more mattresses; don't worry about it, Carl. Just think how funny that'll be when some ol' guy lays down with his wife and says, 'You gotta take a bath!'"

"Cash saw some intelligence in a guy who could see further than puttin' a fish under the mattress," Carl says. "Clayton could see the results three or four days later, with this dude and his wife checkin' in that room and him being mad at her because he kept smelling fish. John was fascinated with this fella who would go out and buy a fish and just leave it under a mattress. It was hilarious stuff for John."

Offstage pranks aside, an early 1956 jaunt into West Texas underscored the extent to which Carl and Cash had clicked with the public. In its February 18 edition, *Country Song Roundup* reported: "Despite the worst snowstorm in 50 years, which hit the area the day before, Carl Perkins and Johnny Cash and their aids and Jimmy and Johnny, Helen Hall and the Belew Twins, of 'Big D Jamboree,' Dallas, pulled an S.R.O. house of 1,600 at San Angelo, Tex., February 3, with another crowd of 1,600 nearly filling the field house at Odessa, Tex., the following night."

Often the band's schedule was so tight that they had to drive through the night and the following day to get to their next date on time. Carl came up with his own solution to the problem of getting a restful sleep: crickets. Being away from his family was a great sacrifice for Carl, who always cried when he left, no matter how brief or lengthy the road trip. In the immediate aftermath of "Shoes"'s fast start, he felt an aching loneliness he had not known before stardom beckoned. Jay, Clayton, and Fluke were of some comfort by their presence, but the car, the dressing room, the stage, the motel rooms—these places weren't home.

On one of their long drives, inspiration struck when Carl spotted a bait shop. There he bought a box of crickets and an aluminum carrying container, which he outfitted with fresh leaves for the crickets' dining pleasure and suspended under the dash. When he was ready to go to sleep, he placed his rock-hard travel pillow on the floor, swung his body around to where he could lay his head and shoulders on it— his face only inches from the chirping crickets—and rested his feet on the back of the seat. "I'd hear them crickets and think about fishing at Reelfoot Lake in Tiptonville," Carl explains. "I'd drift on off to sleep. They're quiet in the daytime; they don't raise much Cain. But they were *right* at night; that's when a cricket comes alive. It was just the tranquil thing that would put me on out."

A bizarre footnote to the "Blue Suede Shoes" saga occurred in mid-February. Sam Phillips received a letter, dated February 11, from one Curt Peeples of Peeples Music Publishing Co. in Pasadena, Texas, asserting that "Blue Suede Shoes" had been published by his company and "cleared through BMI on the date of August 22, 1955.

"At present time I hold the copyright to said song," Peeples's letter continued, "and the one of the same title, theme, and tune which you just recently released is so similar in every detail, that I could not possibly release the one I have in my catalogue.

"The writers [whom Peeples does not name in his letter] feel that the song belongs to them and I am sure that if you knew the reasons why they make their claims, that you would be interested.

"We would prefer to make an amicable settlement regarding the publishing rights to this song; but we do feel that the song belongs to us."

However fanciful Peeples's claim, Phillips's response, dated February 15, offered an equally skewed interpretation of the song's origin. Wrote Phillips:

The song recorded and released on Sun record #234 is a joint work of two of our artists, Johnny Cash and Carl Perkins, and was virtually composed, over a period of several months, in our studios . . . We have no desire to intrude on anyone's rights and interests, and if you wish to furnish us with a lead sheet of the composition that you have copy-

righted, we shall be glad to have an impartial professional lead-sheet man run a comparison of the melodies. Again we say, however, that should any appreciable similarity be shown, it would be a surprising coincidence, as we know under what circumstances the Sun recorded song 'BLUE SUEDE SHOES' was composed and written.

Curt Peeples was never heard from again; Johnny Cash has claimed no connection to "Blue Suede Shoes" beyond suggesting the idea to Perkins backstage at the Parkin, Arkansas, show; and Carl, who has no memory of Peeples's claim, stands by his account of the song's origin, writing, and recording, which has otherwise remained unassailed.

With his income rising, Carl made two big-ticket purchases in early '56 by way of upgrading his equipment. From Hardeman Music he ordered an $800 Gibson ES-5 Switchmaster hollow-body, maple-top electric that had three pickups and separate tone and volume controls for each. At the top of the neck, near the tuning pegs, Carl rigged up a crude vibrato bar. By adjusting the tone and volume controls Carl could get the stinging Les Paul sound he liked, albeit fatter, as can be heard on his Sun recordings from 1956 onward.

At the same time he purchased the Switchmaster, Carl contacted Ray Butts, an electronics wizard living in Cairo, Illinois, who had developed an amp he called the Echoplex. Nashville guitar virtuoso Chet Atkins, who had become one of Carl's favorites, along with Les Paul, had been the first to own a Ray Butts amp; Scotty Moore was the second. Moore had used it on Elvis's recording sessions, most prominently on "Mystery Train." By way of a tape loop installed in its guts the amp gave off a slapback sound, much like what Sam Phillips achieved by creating a split-second tape delay with two recorders. With the tape loop, the original sound was fed back on itself to create a delay; Record-Erase-Playback controls, as would be found on a regular tape recorder, were provided as well. The user had the option of choosing the delayed sound or one Moore terms "tick-tack."

Carl believes his was the third Ray Butts amp in existence, and he paid according to Butts's terms: $250 down, $250 cash on delivery. The amp allowed Carl to duplicate his Sun sound onstage, so the money was freely given: "It had pickup and two playback heads on this little piece of tape that was about twelve inches and continuously went around," Carl remembers. "And as you hit a note you could speed that tape up; turn a little knob on front and click-click-click-click-click, it sounded the same note you hit. If you got it just right you get any amount of echo on it that you wanted."

By early March "Shoes" was starting to catch on nationally in a major way. It entered *Billboard*'s Hot 100 singles charts on March 3, as did Presley's first RCA single, "Heartbreak Hotel," and a week later Carl became the first country artist to appear on the national R&B chart. On local and regional pop charts throughout the country, "Blue Suede Shoes" and "Heartbreak Hotel" were swapping the number-one spot; Carl was, as he said, "standing toe to toe with that pretty Elvis."

Cover versions of "Shoes" began appearing, from artists as disparate as western swing's Pee Wee King, honky-tonker Roy Hall, pop singer Jim Lowe, and the king of "champagne music," Lawrence Welk. Presley had spent his first couple of months at RCA in sessions for his debut album, and among the tracks he cut was "Blue Suede Shoes." Seeing Carl's version take off as it did, Presley's producer, Steve Sholes, had placed a panic call to Sam Phillips, wondering if the label had signed the wrong artist—Perkins, after all, was a writer as well as a singer and instrumentalist. Phillips counseled patience with Presley, and assured Sholes that he would, in time, see satisfying results. It has also been reported, and confirmed by Phillips, that Sholes agreed not to release Presley's version of "Blue Suede Shoes" as a single while Carl's was still hot, and, indeed, it was released initially on a four-song EP (extended-play record) in March and, later that month, on his self-titled debut album.

Scotty Moore discounts other published reports in recalling how Presley's decision to cut Carl's song was made for personal reasons stemming from the friendship born at Sun and on the road: "It's been claimed that RCA and Col. Parker were trying to get Elvis to do the song, but he did it more as a tribute thing than anything else. He had been talking to the band about it, and then he just decided he wanted to do it."

The beauty of Presley's unrestrained performance on "Shoes"—he eliminated the stop-time break and instead tore through the opening, barely taking a breath—was its link to the Sun style. As they had when working with Phillips, Moore, Bill Black, and Presley's new drummer, D.J. Fontana (who had been working with the house band on *The Louisiana Hayride* when Presley hired him), set up and blew, according to Moore: "We just went in there and started playing, just winged it. Just following however Elvis felt."

The track had all the fire and roar of something that could have come out of the studio at 706 Union in Memphis.

On March 17, Presley introduced the song to a national television audience when he performed it, along with "Heartbreak Hotel," on *The Dorsey Brothers Stage Show* in New York. His first television appearance had been on the same show the preceding month, on February 18, when he performed Little Richard's "Tutti Frutti" and the flip side of "Heartbreak Hotel," a wrenching tale of lost love and self-recrimination titled "I Was the One," sung in a melodramatic but deeply felt style that suggested remarkable development of his interpretive artistry in the two short years since his Sun debut.

With "Shoes" breaking out nationally, requests for personal appearances by Carl poured in. In demand coast to coast, he had accepted offers to appear on Red Foley's *Ozark Jubilee* on March 17, followed by a March 24 date in New York on *The Perry Como Show*, these shows bookending a string of concert dates that would take Carl and the band into northeastern cities for the first time.

With Carl having a big hit on the charts and scheduled to be on the road for a while, Sam decided to have him record some songs for a follow-up single before the band went on tour. Carl remembers the session beginning mid-afternoon and ending at daylight the next morning, although exactly how much work was done in the final hours is questionable: Carl says the alcohol was "flowing pretty good" after ten p.m.—"There was some drinkin' that took place to stay awake and keep the energy up." Eight songs came out of the session, with "All Mama's Children" and "Boppin' the Blues" released as a single in May 1956.

Both songs were collaborations, the former between Carl and Cash, the latter between Carl and a Jackson friend from Parkview Courts,

Howard "Curly" Griffin, whose tape recorder Carl had used in some of his ill-fated efforts to gain the attention of Nashville and New York labels. "All Mama's Children" had been composed largely in the car on one of Carl's trips with Cash, and like "Shoes" it drew on a children's rhyme for its opening lyrics and went on to invoke blue suede shoes as a symbol of high living, a conceit he emphasized better in a second take of the song. The song was marked by high spirits, a jaunty rhythm, and a mock-serious vocal by Carl that put a humorous spin on his tale. Take 1:

Well there was an old woman who lived in a shoe
Had so many children she didn't know what to do
They was doin' alright till she took 'em to town
Children started pickin' 'em up
And puttin' 'em down

(chorus:) All your chillun wanna rock, mama!
All them chillun wanna roll
Wanna roll, wanna rock, wanna bop till they pop
All them chillun wanna rock

Well they're not tryin' to live too fast
We might as well try to live in class
We better move out 'fore the rent comes due
Cause we wanna live in a blue suede shoe!

(chorus)

"Now go, cats!" (guitar solo)

Now every night when it's quiet and still
You can hear it echo through the hills
From a blue suede shoe on a mountaintop
All mama's children are doin' the bop

(chorus)

"Rock!" (guitar solo)

(Back to verse 1)

On Take 2 Carl made minor lyric changes, most of which underscored the idea of the blue suede shoe as the best kind of shelter for a poor family. Relative to Carl's own situation at home, it speaks a truth he knew well. Seen in this light, "All Mama's Children" can be viewed as another of Carl's insightful statements of his own condition at the time of the song's recording. Was anyone else in America better qualified to extol the sheltering virtues of a pair of blue suede shoes?

A third take of the song was nearly identical to Take 2, save for a better executed guitar solo, one heavily reliant on single-string runs and cascades of double notes. According to Carl, the lyric "She was doin' all right until she took 'em to town / Children started pickin' 'em up and puttin' 'em down" was Cash's contribution to the song's opening verse after Carl had come up with a melody. From that point they traded lines as quickly as they came to mind, Cash printing everything on a piece of paper ("John never writes—he prints. But he can print as fast as I can write.") Later that night Carl wrote down the lyrics as he remembered them, and had a completed version of the song ready when he came to Sun for his first March session. Cash later told Carl he had completed his own version of "All Mama's Children," but he never played it for Carl, nor did he ever record it.

Curly Griffin, who is credited as cowriter on "Boppin' the Blues," could have been the male counterpart to the old woman who lived in a shoe. According to Carl, Griffin was nearly blind and had "five or six" children to support, all of them crammed into his tiny Parkview apartment. He was a rockabilly fanatic, though, and often dropped in at Carl's Parkview place with poems he had written, hoping Carl could set his words to music. One of these about which Griffin was most enthusiastic bore the title "Rhythm and Blues." Carl's response: "Curly, that ain't no good. Everybody says rhythm and blues." It was the wrong time to dismiss Griffin's effort out of hand, though, Carl recalls, because "on that day Curly was lookin' for a lift. He looked sad, man. He could hardly see, was real skinny—and countreeee—boy, he was *country*. I loved him 'cause he was really kind, but he got on my nerves knockin' on my door with old ideas. And I only used two out of all of 'em that he offered me. I had to do somethin' for him, so I sat down that night and wrote 'Boppin' the Blues' out of 'Rhythm and Blues.'"

Of those he had taken time to compose on paper, it was one of Carl's quickest compositions: He borrowed his stop-time trick from the "Blue Suede Shoes" opening, but for a single beat instead of two beats—"one hard lick," as he says—built a simple, plain melody over a three-chord progression, and extended Griffin's idea about rhythm music's healing powers:

> Well all my friends are boppin' the blues
> It must be goin' 'round
> All them cats are boppin' the blues
> It must be goin' 'round
> I love you baby
> But I must be rhythm bound
>
> Well the doctor told me
> Carl, you don't need no pills
> The doctor told me
> Man, you don't need no pills
> Just a handful of nickels
> A jukebox will cure your ills
>
> (chorus:) Oh, all my friends are boppin' the blues
> It must be goin' 'round
> All them cats are boppin' the blues
> It must be goin' 'round
> I love you, baby
> I must be rhythm bound
> ("Aw, cats, rock!")

(chorus)

Well, my grandpa done got rhythm
And he threw his crutches down
Well the old man's done got rhythm and blues
He threw his crutches down
Grandma, he ain't triflin'
The ol' boy's rhythm bound

(chorus)

("Aw, get it!")

A second take, the one issued as a single, was more forceful and equally wacky in its declaration of the music's obvious benefits to one's physical well-being:

Well, the ol' cat bug bit me
Man, I don't feel no pain
Yeah, that jitterbug caught me
Man, I don't feel no pain
I still love you baby
But I'll never be the same

(chorus)

"Git it, cat! Let's rock!"

(guitar solo)

(chorus)

Well, grandpa's done got rhythm
And he threw his crutches down
Oh, the ol' boy's done got rhythm and blues

> And he threw that crutches down
> Grandma, he ain't triflin'
> Well the ol' boy's rhythm bound
>
> (chorus)

"Man, you've cut your next record right there!" Carl heard Sam cry out over the intercom after the second take. "That's it," he continued. "You took one of the beats outta 'Blue Suede Shoes,' and you gotta stay in this vein. This is the song; this is it!"

During a break in the recording Carl was idly strumming the guitar and singing variations on some lyrics he had worked up in the tonks. Sam heard him singing, "Everybody's tryin' to be my baby / Everybody's tryin' to be my baby / Everybody's tryin' to be my baby now" and stopped him.

"Wait a minute—did you say, 'Everybody's tryin' to be my baby'?" Sam asked.

"Yes sir," Carl replied.

"Man, I like that!"

"Well, I guess I better write it down," Carl said casually.

"Oh, here we go again!" Sam complained, shaking his head. "You mean you haven't written down what you just sang?"

Carl's penchant for making up songs on the spot was starting to irritate Sam, who thought Carl was losing many of his best ideas. After one session he had told him, "You never got back there. You got a pretty good song, but you never said what you originally said."

"Everybody's Trying to Be My Baby" was born at the El Rancho, when a pair of attractive women approached Carl at the bandstand and began flirting with him. Winking and leering, they requested a song. Carl laughed, nodded agreement, and turned to Jay, saying, "Man, everybody's tryin' to be my baby tonight."

"Sounds like a song to me," Jay muttered as he waited for Carl to kick off another tune.

When Jay's comment registered, Carl stepped away from the microphone, gave his brother a thoughtful stare, and bobbed his head towards Jay's guitar neck. "Get in E," he said, swinging his guitar around to where Jay could follow the chord changes—A to B to E; over the next three or four minutes, Carl improvised lyrics and added "Everybody's Trying to Be My Baby" to the band's repertoire. Like "Gone Gone Gone," the song had been through many incarnations by the time Carl offhandedly doodled with it in the Sun studio.

("Everybody's Trying to Be My Baby" had a history before Carl's version was recorded. In 1938 a group out of Dallas headed by Roy Newman cut a like-titled song in a version that combined elements of western swing and Dixieland. Lyrically the songs share some similarities in their first verses but are otherwise different in every respect. Carl has no recollection of ever hearing Newman's recording—he was six years old when it was released—and his best guess is that somewhere along the honky-tonk trail someone must have been playing the song when he was around and what little memory he had of it was triggered by the El Rancho's flirtatious females.)

But Sam's initial enthusiasm wasn't borne out by the lackluster performance the band committed to tape. Clayton and Fluke gave the rhythm everything they had, but the arrangement lacked oomph. Even an urgent vocal by Carl failed to bring it to life. Similarly, a cover of "Only You," the Platters song Carl had angered Elvis by performing, arrived stillborn on a dirgelike rhythm and a well-meaning vocal by Carl that was too pop to be country, too country to be pop.

Clayton and Fluke had their day elsewhere, on Carl's rollicking country shuffle, "You Can't Make Love to Somebody" (another of his on-the-spot writing jobs) and a cover version of Willie Perryman's 1951 R&B hit, "Right String, Wrong Yo-Yo." Considering how hard he tried to be noticed at the end of every song, it's hardly surprising that Clayton starred on two songs tailor-made for the bass to play a featured role. "You Can't Make Love to Somebody" gained its undeniable energy from him whacking away at the strings so hard as to be the most prominent sound in the mix; it was a first-rate comic instrumental performance by a player who was seizing his moment in the spotlight. Fluke was right there with him, too, forceful and swinging mightily in service to the song's driving rhythm.

As wonderful as he was on "You Can't Make Love to Somebody," Clayton topped himself on the rousing "Right String, Wrong Yo-Yo."

Slapping, clicking, working his way up and down the length of the bass neck on two solo turns, he played the role of an instrumental, comedic Greek chorus to the woebegone soul expressed in Carl's steely, minimal guitar solos. It was all played for laughs—right down to Carl's voice cracking in fright on the word "wrong" when he sang the title sentiment—and the chief clowns were Clayton and Fluke, coming through like a runaway freight train of a rhythm section, hard on Carl's fleet heels all the way.

These two cuts illustrated the astounding dynamic among the quartet of musicians. That someone as rowdy and undisciplined in every other aspect of his life as Clayton could step up after several hours of playing and deliver a performance as note-perfect and personable as his was remarkable testimony to the focus he had gained on the road. Playing with feeling was easy for the Perkins Brothers Band, but the rigors of recording and of performing before young audiences in sober environments had pushed the musicians to raise their games to a level that would have never been required of a tonk band. In the studio Carl saw his cohorts become models of professionalism playing a style of music that demanded a free-spirited approach: "Everybody in there looked to me," Carl says. "Sometimes on some of the songs, Fluke would try a little drum lick and me or Sam would say, 'That don't sound as good as the other did. Go back to where you was.' And he'd jump back to where he was. Jay figured I could handle it. If I wrote the song and I wanted it played faster or slower, it was fine with him. And that was alright with Clayton—never had a problem with him in the studio. No sir, never. We had some arguments on the way back home, but never in the Sun studio."

Recording at a time when "Blue Suede Shoes" was without question a hit record had further bolstered the band's confidence, especially Carl's. Despite his tendency to create songs extemporaneously, he was as ready for this session as Sam Phillips ever could have hoped: "When you've got a hit record out there playing, going in the studio is just reinforcing your feelings about what that next record's gonna do and how big you're gonna be. It was very uplifting to go in there. I guess it happens to everybody. You get the feeling you ain't gonna miss now. And it used to be that if you had a monster record you hung around for several years. So I knew I had found the niche, that I could make a good living. And making records was fun. I lost the tension and the time just flew by. It was a good time; a very upbeat, happy time. You walked in there somebody and you knew it."

A few days after the session, Carl and the band headed to Springfield, Missouri, for a February 17 appearance on Red Foley's *Ozark Jubilee* In 1953, after a long association with the Grand Ole Opry, Foley relinquished his role as host of the Prince Albert portion of the show and moved his business to Springfield the following year. There he hosted several popular syndicated radio shows and brought country music into the nation's living rooms every Saturday night with his widely watched TV program. His standard closing hit the country audience where it lived: Sitting in a rocking chair onstage, he would wave and offer in sing-song tones the salutation, "Good night, Mama; good night, Papa," before strolling casually through the audience and out the back of the studio—sort of the rural version of Jimmy Durante's "Good night, Mrs. Calabash, wherever you are."

In short order Foley had became a beloved national figure. As the composer of "Old Shep," he seemed heroic to Carl, whose music had been touched by Foley's assimilation of black musical styles and by the conviction with which he rendered gospel songs. It was almost more than Carl could handle, being on national television and standing side by side with Red Foley.

Arriving for afternoon rehearsal, Carl was directed to Foley's office off the side of the stage. Creeping up to the open door, he stared around it and saw Foley standing sideways in front of a mirror, sipping from a bottle of whiskey. This was the first shock, "because he had such a big following in the religious field. Don't get me wrong. If a man can handle his liquor, I don't know what damage it does to his relationship with God. I know it'd make me mean, or other times I'd be drunk and crying and I would pray myself to sleep. I don't know whether those prayers got through or not."

Having taken a few slugs of Early Times himself before leaving the hotel, Carl would not judge Foley harshly, but he wouldn't knock on his door either. Instead, he backed off and stood alone in the dim light of the hallway. A few minutes passed before Foley came out of the office and was startled to find someone standing right outside.

"You gotta be Carl Perkins," Foley said, smiling and offering his hand.

"Yes sir!" Carl replied hastily. "How you doin', Mr. Foley?" He took Foley's hand in his. "Now don't pay no attention to my hand shakin', sir. I'm nervous."

"Whatta you nervous about, son?" Foley asked in his warm, folksy tone.

"Gosh, this *Ozark Jubilee*, I've watched it so many times. I sure hope I do good."

"Aw, you'll do great," Foley assured Carl, throwing a hand over the young singer's shoulder and walking him out to the stage for a run-through. When Carl had finished, Foley invited him back to the office and gave him a drink of whiskey. Carl threw it down and got up to leave. "I'm gonna go back to the hotel and get my pickin' clothes on now, Mr. Foley," he said, shaking the star's hand again.

"When you get back, come on in the office here," Foley offered, "and we'll see if we can do something about them nerves."

"Well, I don't know," Carl replied. "I may have to have me a little toddy."

"That'll be alright. That'll be alright. Little toddy's good for the body." Carl thought: *I love this joker. I love him.*

As they imbibed in Foley's office ahead of the show's start—"How do you like your toddy?" Foley asked. "Right straight outta that bottle," Carl replied—Foley found himself constantly having to reassure Carl that he would go over well. He was right: A mildly buzzed Perkins got the audience moving with "Blue Suede Shoes" and generated strong applause for his efforts. Foley chatted with Carl afterwards onstage, Carl stumbling his way woodenly through the lines written for him on cue cards: "Yes, Mr. Foley, I am twenty-four years old. Yes sir, I did write 'Blue Suede Shoes.'"

At the end of the show, sitting in his rocking chair, Foley shocked Carl by offering an unprepared statement to his viewers. He announced Carl's appearance the following Saturday on *The Perry Como Show*, opposite *Ozark Jubilee*, and suggested everyone tune in to see

Carl's portion of the show. Carl's memory of Foley's directive: "If you want to watch this boy, you can leave my show and switch back and watch him do 'Blue Suede Shoes' again. Then turn back over to *Ozark Jubilee*. It'll be alright with me." (Unbeknownst to Carl, "Blue Suede Shoes" had already sold more than 500,000 copies, prompting Sam Phillips to opt for the grand gesture: He would surprise his star artist by appearing on the Como show and presenting him with a gold record in honor of his achievement.)

Foley in fact was one of the first Nashville establishment country artists to endorse the new music of the day. Moreover, he saw the bigger picture of technology's impact on society in concert with the music's appeal.

Writing in the *Memphis Press-Scimitar* of April 10, 1956, entertainment reporter Robert Johnson observed:

> *Red Foley makes an interesting point on the strange wedding today of country, blues, and pop music. Country music as we knew it is gone, he said. "Presley and Perkins, why they're basically more rock 'n' roll than country, but they're making the kind of records the juke boxes want. And as they say—if you can't fight 'em, jine 'em. There'll be no turning back. What has happened is that things like TV and radio have brought the country closer together. The fellow in the hill country sees the same program as the man in the city."*

A March 21 show in Norfolk, Virginia, would be the band's last stop before proceeding on to New York. Telling Carl, "If you're going to New York, you gotta go in style," Sam Phillips rented a Chrysler limousine from Southern Motors and hired Memphis disc jockey Stuart Pinkham (variously known as Dick Stuart and, on the air, as Poor Richard; along with Bob Neal he had booked some of Carl's and Cash's first shows, and he was married to Sun artist Charlie Feathers's sister) to drive the band from Memphis to Norfolk and then on to New York City. Leaving Memphis, Carl was grateful to Phillips for this unusual accommodation because he was exhausted, and with good reason: The pace he had been keeping since the single broke was making it difficult for him to remember fundamental facts, such as the exact day and date, which town he was in, which town came next on the itinerary . . . But when he rolled into Norfolk, Carl's mind was clear and his adrenalin was flowing. The Como show, he was certain, would break his career open to a degree he found tantalizing but unsettling: the Lake County sharecropper's son singing his own song and playing the guitar in forbidding New York City with the whole nation watching. It was a thought that shook Carl to his core, because it sent him back to the fields, where his journey had begun at age six with the simple lessons taught by Uncle John: Life's that way, little Carlie. You start on the bottom as a child, you work your way up as you get older. Yes sir, you do.

In Norfolk, on March 21, 1956, Carl Perkins understood better than anyone around him that the past eighteen years of his life were leading him to New York City, where one month prior the spark of Elvis's career had exploded into a supernova. On the outside, Carl stood tall and proud, a stone rockabilly forging his own trail against all the odds; inside he carried the burden of his history, from the abject poverty of Lake County to the long march through the tonks to the echoing plaint of Elvis's voice summoning him to his destiny in Memphis. Getting to New York would not be enough; he would have to leave there with his name writ large, larger than Elvis's perhaps, to convince himself and the rest of the world that he belonged not merely "toe to toe with that pretty Elvis," but on a different plane, where his worth would be measured not by the standards of the day or by comparison to his peers, but singularly, by virtue of his own merits as a musical artist with something to say and a distinctive way of saying it: Carl Perkins, *rara avis*.

The Norfolk promoter was Bill Davis, better known as "Sheriff Tex," a disc jockey on the local country station, WCMS. A month before Carl arrived in town, Davis, fellow disc jockey Joe Hoppell and WCMS station manager Roy Lamear had sat as judges in a contest held to find talent for a new Norfolk TV show, *Country Showtime*. Out of the 100 entrants, 10 finalists had been selected. One of these was Gene Craddock, a twenty-one-year-old native son newly discharged from the Navy following a motorcycle accident that had crushed his left leg. Despite suffering an injury that limited his mobility, Craddock cut loose like Presley when he hit the stage, and immediately became *Country*

Showtime's most popular attraction, especially among the females. A year earlier he had been in the audience when Hank Snow's *All Star Jamboree* came to the Norfolk Municipal Auditorium. There he had seen Presley perform for the first time, and began modeling his own style after that of the rising Sun star and generating the same kind of frenetic response.

Craddock also was a writer, and Davis noticed that the artist's original songs were being as well received as his cover versions of current hits. Sensing an opportunity to capitalize on Craddock's appeal to the rock 'n' roll audience, Davis threw in with Lamear and Sy Blumenthal, partners in L&B Talent Management. They signed Craddock and began grooming him for the national arena. Needing a band for his young charge, who had been playing with the WCMS house band up to that point, Davis brought in some of the best musicians in Norfolk: drummer Dickie Harrell; rhythm guitarist Willie Williams; bassist Jack Neal; and an extraordinary, inventive lead guitarist named Cliff Gallup. Craddock and the quartet meshed beautifully in their first session at the WCMS studio, and Davis sensed that his gut instinct about Craddock's potential was on the mark.

Backstage at the Norfolk Auditorium, preparing to play for two thousand paying customers, Carl was dressing for the show when Davis approached and introduced himself. "Carl, I got this boy I'm fixin' to manage and I want you to come here and watch him," Davis requested. "He's gonna sing a song I'm gonna cut on him. I wanna know what you think of it."

Carl stood in the wings as the band went on. A couple of facts were apparent right away: None of these boys would give Elvis a run for the money in the looks department, and the blue newsboy's caps being sported by the backing band set them apart from the young groups coming up. The lead singer, though, was something else entirely.

He was skinny and raw-boned, physically not unlike Carl, with a thin face that seemed forever contorted into a painful grimace. Dressed in black leather from head to toe, he had a shock of curly jet-black hair on his head that held maximum grease and tumbled forward into his eyes as he rocked in wild abandon, dropping to his knees, twirling his guitar around like it was a dimestore toy, and treating the microphone and microphone stand with utter disdain, even contempt. Legs shaking and body trembling, the singer affected a Presley-style catch in his vocalizing; his performance was all base, raw sexuality, and he had the females in the audience crying and screaming for him almost from the moment he started singing the song about which Davis had sought Carl's opinion. Lyrically and structurally it was fairly straightforward, but the singer's lubricious delivery invested it with darker import. His plaintive tenor communicated both barely controlled passion and unbridled longing, and the band's instrumental work behind the vocal created a wild scene Carl knew well from working the southern states with Presley and on his own in the wake of "Blue Suede" 's explosive start. All in all, Carl thought, it was an impressive performance.

"It's kinda like my 'Blue Suede Shoes,' " Carl said, turning to Davis, who had been keeping a silent but concerned vigil alongside him. "There ain't a lot to it, but it's an effective ol' song."

Davis nodded and smiled. "That's all I wanted to hear. That's good enough for me."

Before Carl went on, Davis brought the musicians to the dressing room and introduced them around. "Carl, I want you to meet Gene Craddock," he said as the lead singer, wide-eyed and awestruck, extended his hand to Carl.

"Man, I hope I can do what you're doin'," Craddock said, speaking in a hushed but excited tone. "I won't ever be like you are, but that's what I wanna do. This here Davis is gonna be my manager, and we're gonna make a record."

Assuring Craddock that his original song had something going for it, Carl wished the young rocker good luck. Less than four months later the band, renamed Gene Vincent and the Blue Caps, had been signed to Capitol Records and was in the top ten of the pop, R&B, and country and western charts with "Be-Bop-a-Lula," confirming Carl's assessment that it was "an effective ol' song."

Departing Norfolk after another well-received show, Carl, Jay, Clayton, and W.S. engaged in easy banter about their prospects for stardom in New York. Once out on the highway, fatigue settled in. W.S. was driving, with Clayton slipping down in the front seat between him and Stuart Pinkham. In the back, Jay stretched out on the seat, curling around Clayton's bass fiddle, the neck of which extended towards the windshield, close by W.S.'s head. Carl relaxed on the floorboard, eyes closed, body going limp, as the car tooled across Chesapeake Bay. As he was nodding off, he remarked to Jay that this was indeed one beautiful car Sam had picked out for their grand entrance into New York City.

On a flat stretch of highway in an unpopulated area outside Dover, Delaware, shortly before sunup on March 22, W.S. pulled into a gas station and bought a bottle of Coca-Cola from a machine. He liked to have cold Cokes in hand while he drove, so he could rub the bottle against this face to keep him awake on the long drives. As he walked back to the car, Pinkham stepped out and offered to drive.

"Sure," W.S. said, "if you're not sleepy."

Pinkham took the wheel, Holland rested on the passenger's side in the front, and Clayton dozed on unaware. When Holland awoke, he was sitting on the white line in the middle of the road. He heard voices crying out, and struggled to his feet, disoriented but uninjured save for some minor cuts on his forehead. He couldn't believe the scene he saw around him: "I didn't feel a thing, didn't ever hear a thing. The side I was against, the right front fender, the doors, the whole side was gone. Car flipped over and landed in kind of a ditch of water about a foot deep. Clayton cut his forearm really bad, Stuart Pinkham cut one of his legs really bad. Broke Carl's collarbone. I go down and the back seat of the car is still in the car, but it's loose. So I pulled it out and Carl's laying under water. Under water. So I lay the seat beside of him and pull him up on the seat, and that gets him out of the water. The guy in the pickup was hollering for help, and I go up and help him.

"The ambulance comes, we get everybody in the ambulance, and everybody gets in the back of the ambulance but me and J.B. He's sittin' in the grass, I get him up, set him in the car between me and the driver in the ambulance. We get to the hospital, the guy in the truck died. Everybody was examined. Carl's collarbone was broke, Clayton cut.

"Now, J.B., of all things, broke his neck. The doctors said there was no way anybody could live walking up that bank, sittin' in that ambulance, that far with a broke neck. But he did. They put him in traction."

The band's Chrysler had plowed into the back of the truck, sending its driver, Thomas Phillips, a forty-four-year-old farmer from Paradise Valley, Delaware, full force into the steering wheel. The Chrysler had then lurched out of control, rolled four times down the road, demolishing a guard rail along the way, then plunged over a bridge, coming to rest right side up on the banks of a stream. Jay was knocked unconscious, but came to with half his body inside the car, the other half hanging out a window. Despite having fractured vertebrae in his neck and suffering from severe internal injuries, he managed to climb out of the car and up the bank, where he was sitting when W.S. found him. Other than their cuts, Clayton and Pinkham were in good condition; Holland's cuts were mere scratches. Thanks to W.S.'s quick action, Carl, who had been lying face down in the water, was saved from a certain drowning. His numerous injuries included a broken collarbone, a severe concussion, and lacerations all over his body. At Dover Hospital, X rays revealed the extent of Jay's injuries and he was then transported to the hospital in Wilmington, Delaware, which had a better facility for treating serious head and neck injuries. Fluke and Clayton were treated and released.

f i r s t he saw light, bright white light. Then there was sound, muffled, as if in the distance, or imagined by a fevered mind. Finally, a recognition of voices, human voices. *Children's voices.* Distinct and clear, from the other side of the room, came words he understood: "That's him. That's the one wrote the 'Blue Suede Shoes.' One of 'em was killed, but that's the one wrote the 'Blue Suede Shoes.' That's Carl Perkins lying right over there."

Groggy and disoriented, Carl struggled to locate the source of the sound. A brace around his neck and a strap around his skull prevented him from turning his head. He knew he must be in a hospital, but he didn't know where, or how he got there, or what day it was. He could cut his glance enough to see young faces peeping around the curtain circling his bed. Then came an older man's voice.

"One or two of 'em died, but that's the one that wrote the song layin' right there."

One or two had died? Who had died? Clayton? Jay? Fluke? Who had died!?

Panic-stricken, Carl shouted, "Somebody, come! Come! Come!"

A nurse hurried to his bedside. "Mr. Perkins, you have to calm down," she said. "You're disturbing the other patients. Now calm down!"

"Who was killed in an accident?! What happened?"

"Calm down, Mr. Perkins," the nurse insisted. "Your friends are fine, and you will be too, if you remain quiet." She handed Carl a cup of water.

"But I heard them say one of the people in the accident was killed! Who was it? Are my brothers alright?"

Again the nurse urged Carl to relax, at the same time telling him it was the other driver who had been killed. "Now please try to keep quiet," she pleaded.

Carl went limp at the news of the death. Did the dead man have a wife and children? Who's going to pay their bills, feed the kids? Tears welled in his eyes. He fought to control his emotions, trying to maintain his composure as he replayed the trip from Norfolk over again in his mind. The nurse returned with a syringe, and jabbed the needle into his hip. Above his bed, Carl saw the white lights begin spinning, and heard voices fading away as he drifted into unconsciousness.

Several hours later, Carl awoke to see Fluke sitting beside the bed. Solid, sturdy, sober Fluke, the drummer more valued for his car than for his musicianship, at that moment was the greatest comfort in Carl's world. Fluke was alive. Which meant . . .

"Fluke," Carl whispered, "where's Jay and Clayton?"

"Well, Carl, now just . . ." Fluke stammered, "uh, everybody's fine."

"They said two was killed, Fluke," Carl said, growing agitated. "What happened? Did we have a wreck?"

"Yeah, we had a wreck," Fluke answered. "But none of us was killed."

"Where's Jay? Where's Clayton?"

"Clayton's up in Wilmington, Delaware, with Jay."

"What's he doing in Wilmington, Delaware?" Carl asked warily, needing an answer, not wanting to hear what he felt in his gut. "Where am *I?*"

"You're in Dover, Delaware, sixty or seventy miles from where Jay is."

"Fluke, don't lie to me, man," Carl demanded. "I gotta face it. And how bad am I hurt?"

From Fluke Carl learned that he had been unconscious for a day after the wreck, but that his prognosis was good for a complete recovery—"Just a broken collarbone and few other things, Carl"—and that while Clayton had come out with only some bruises and scratches, Jay was more seriously injured. Fluke knew little more about Jay's condition, and Carl, sensing this to be the truth, backed off.

Later that afternoon, Clayton came to visit Carl, told him the particulars of the crash, and about the other driver that had been killed. Of Jay's condition, Clayton reported: "He's alive, but now I tell you, Carl, Jay's unconscious, like you used to be."

"Are you hurt?" asked Carl.

"Just a few skin't places," Clayton answered. He leaned towards Carl and smiled. "Carl, boy, it's good to hear you talkin'." It was a rare show of tenderness on Clayton's part.

"Why is Jay so far away?" Carl asked.

"You know your neck, the traction you're in, he's in the same thing," Clayton said. "He's about got the same thing you have. Only you fractured three of your vertebrae. That's what's happened to you. Jay's got a total broken neck. It's broke."

"He's paralyzed."

"No. He hasn't woke up so they don't know. But the doctors, they're tracing the spinal fluid and it's still connected. He's gettin' a flow of spinal fluid all the way down his spine."

To Carl the turn of events was unbelievable: On the eve of the band's most important night, the culmination of years of work, everything had fallen apart. More than fame and fortune, though, what he saw going up in smoke was the good life he wanted for Valda, Stan, Debbie, and their third child, then a month away from its birth. Tears streaming down his face, Carl lay immobilized, fearful for Valda, back home in Jackson, alone, pregnant, and probably frightened out of her wits.

On March 23, Valda spent the day leisurely cleaning house and ironing clothes, anxious for Carl to do well on the Como show but at the same time wishing he were there with her and the children. Occasionally the thought crossed her mind that the simplicity of life at Parkview Courts had some advantages over a schedule that took Carl so far away from his family for such long periods of time: "I was very excited about Carl's success. I was very proud of him and of course I didn't want him to have to be gone from home, but I knew he had to be. So I did accept that. That was a change for both of us. You know, you learn to deal with any kind of problem. Something you want to achieve as badly as he wanted to achieve his goal, you learn to deal with the problems it creates."

Thus her thoughts when the phone rang that morning. On the other end of the line was Marion Keisker, calling from Sun Records. Asked how she was doing, Valda replied, "Well, I'm doing fine," and didn't suspect anything out of the ordinary. Then Keisker said she had something to tell Valda, and her voice took on a somber tone.

"Carl has been in an accident," said Keisker. "They've all been in a pretty serious wreck. You're probably going to hear about it on the news on television. A man was killed, but not in Carl's car."

Sheer terror swept over Valda, and she began to feel weak and nauseous. "Oh, me!" she cried. "Oh, me!"

Keisker tried to calm her down. "He's going to be alright, Valda. Jay was hurt worse than Carl."

Valda knew there had to be more. Mustering her strength, she steeled herself to ask Keisker for the truth. Told again that Carl had been injured but would recover, Valda remained in disbelief.

Two days after Carl came out of the coma, he was able to call Valda. His voice was still weak, but he assured her he was doing fine. Valda, relieved to hear his voice, thought otherwise.

"Carl," she implored, "please tell me the truth."

"I'm telling you the truth," Carl answered. "I'll be okay. And I'll be home soon, Valda."

The staff at Dover Hospital would have welcomed Carl being able to go home immediately. Getting confirmation of Jay's condition only made him more irascible, forever demanding someone attend to his needs—most of which boiled down to being told the truth—and flouting the rules at will.

On the evening of March 23, after the lights were out, Carl was about to doze off when he sensed someone standing near him. The room was dark and he could barely make out a male figure at his bedside. Then he heard a familiar voice whisper, "He's asleep," followed by footsteps creeping slowly away.

"I ain't asleep," Carl called out. "Who is that?"

"Hey Carl!" came the excited reply from Bill Black. "Hey, man, Elvis sends his love," Carl heard Black say as his voice drew nearer.

With Black were Scotty Moore and D.J. Fontana. They were on their way to New York to back Presley on the Dorsey Brothers show the next night. Presley had flown and was already in Manhattan awaiting the trio's arrival by car from Memphis. Emboldened by his Sun buddies' appearance, Carl set out to take care of business right away.

"Bill, I need a cigarette, man. Get me a cigarette," he implored Black.

Demurring, Black pointing out to Carl that the patient in the next bed was under an oxygen tent. Lighting a cigarette, Black said, "will blow him up."

"Then blow him up, man," he ordered. "I gotta have a cigarette."

Black lit a cigarette in the hallway and brought it back to Carl. "All right, you're on your own," he said, placing the butt end between Carl's lips. "If you blow yourself up, I done what you asked me to."

"I love you, Bill," Carl said sincerely. "Tell Elvis I said hello."

After Scotty, Bill, and D.J. had left, Carl took a long, deep draw of the cigarette, reducing half of its length to ash ("That cigarette was so nice"). Within seconds a rotund nurse came marching into the room, yanked the cigarette out of his mouth, and crushed it underfoot.

"Whoa!" Carl cried. "Don't be so rough!"

"Do you realize what you're doing?" she screeched. "I don't care if you are a star! You're gonna behave yourself! You have done nothing but raise Cain and just drive me crazy! You're just gonna have to get settled down! Where'd you get that cigarette?"

"I ain't tellin' you!" Carl snapped. The nurse jerked the sheet off Carl's body, then started poking under his pillow. Carl laughed. "I got my sources," he needled her.

"You and your sources are fixin' to get outta here. You're driving us crazy!"

Early the next morning the hospital's chief administrator came to Carl's room. Carl looked up from his pillow to see a rumpled, gray-haired figure staring back at him in ill humor. "Perkins," the man said slowly, "got to talk to you."

"You're the very cat I been waitin' to talk to," Carl replied sternly.

"Now look here," he admonished Carl, "we're doing everything we can. You're giving the nurses and the staff a hard time, and we are not going to put up with it."

"Well there ain't but one thing you can do," Carl snapped, "and that's load me up in an ambulance and take me to where my brother is. Then I'll shut up. That's it; that's all I'm askin'."

"You can't be moved while you're in all this traction," the administrator replied.

"I can and I will," Carl countered. "I'll get up and tote this bed, man, you don't know this ol' redneck Tennessee boy. I mean business with you. I want to see my brother, and I *will* get up there. Look, they can take this bed and put it in the back of a truck. I'll pay for it. I just want to see my brother. If he's up in Wilmington, I want to see that he's there."

The administrator turned to leave, and as he neared the door Carl heard him say, to no one in particular, "We have to get this crazy bastard outta here."

On the evening of March 24 Carl watched Elvis on TV performing "Heartbreak Hotel" and the Drifters' R&B hit, "Money Honey." Reports since then that a bedridden and banged-up Carl sat in Dover watching with withering countenance as Elvis sang "Blue Suede Shoes" are off by nearly two weeks: Carl saw Elvis sing "Shoes" on television, but it was during an April 3 appearance on Milton Berle's show from San Diego, by which time Carl was back in Jackson.

Nearly a week after the wreck, the get-well cards and letters of sympathy were piling up. Pointing to a yellow envelope marked "Western Union," a nurse told Carl it had arrived earlier in the week but had been misplaced. Dated March 23, it read:

> *We were all shocked and very sorry to hear of the accident. I know what it is for I had a few bad ones myself. If I can help you in any way please call me. I will be at the Warwick Hotel in New York City. Our wishes are for a speedy recovery for you and the other boys. Sincerely, Alvis Presley, Bill Black, Scotty Moore and DJ Fontana.*

No matter that the name had been misspelled, the greeting from Presley boosted Carl's spirits immeasurably. Even as their paths diverged with Carl out of commission, his friendship with Elvis remained true and strong, in and of itself a source of strength.

He was sifting through his mail when two ambulance attendants arrived and began preparing to move him out of the room. When they strapped him down on a gurney, he panicked.

"Whatta y'all doin'! What's up!?" Carl demanded, fearing he was being carted off to the psycho ward.

"All we know is this is our orders. We're just doing our job," an attendant answered, then asked: "What you so ill about?"

"That's my business!" Carl snapped. "I'm not ill with y'all. Just don't say nothin' to me. I got something else on my mind. I don't wanna talk about it."

As they wheeled him down the hall and out into the open air, Carl realized he was going to Wilmington. After being deposited in the back of the ambulance, he heard a car pull up. A door slammed, and a moment later the ambulance doors were flung open. In leaped Clayton.

"Ya pulled 'er off, didn't ya!" he said cheerfully as he caught his breath.

After the first good laugh Carl had had since the accident, he issued a warning to Clayton, but couldn't suppress a smile as he did. "Yep," he said, "I'm gonna see if you're lyin'. I'm gonna know in less than an hour."

At the Wilmington hospital, Carl, still in traction, had the head of his bed placed at the foot of Jay's, so he could see his brother.

Jay lay still, completely still, with his eyes closed. His neck had been stabilized by a halolike metal brace that was bolted to his skull. His breathing was steady, but shallow.

The next morning he stirred. As he moistened his dry lips with his tongue, his eyelids fluttered open briefly. Then a loving voice called his name.

Directing a sleepy-eyed gaze toward the foot of his bed, he caught sight of Carl's beaming mug.

"Gawd, you look beautiful," said Jay softly.

"You don't look too bad yourself," replied Carl.

Carl reached over and took Jay's hand. The brothers wept in the quiet of their room, taking strength from each other's presence: "It was wonderful, such a wonderful feeling," Carl remembers. "That cotton-field love just poured right through me. He had suffered; his eyes were sunk in and dark. My eyes were dark too because of the lick I had took on my head. We just looked at each other. He didn't really feel like talking. I was a little ahead of him, I wasn't hurt as bad, but I sensed he just wanted to look at me. And every time, for about three or four days, I'd reach my hand through my bed, and if he was awake he'd reach his through his bed."

Within forty-eight hours of his own arrival in Wilmington, Carl had been taken out of traction and placed in an upper-body cast. His recuperation was progressing on schedule. Clayton and Fluke were on their way back to Jackson, Jay's wife was on her way to Wilmington, and Carl was beginning to see a time when he would be reunited with Valda and the kids.

When Jay was alert again, Carl began telling him what he knew of the wreck. While speaking, he became aware of some activity in the hall outside the room. An orderly, who was supposed to be mopping the floor, was instead bopping and singing, "Blue, blue, blue suede shoes / Blue, blue, blue suede shoes / Well, it's one for the money," with the same vocal inflections Carl had used on the record.

"Hey!" Carl called out. "Hey, you! Come in here!"

The janitor entered sheepishly, carrying his mop in one hand. He looked frightened.

"What do you do here?" Carl asked gently.

"I clean up this place." He paused and looked warily at Carl. "That's your song, ain't it?"

"Yeah."

"Well, you doin' fine."

Striking up a conversation, Carl found out the janitor was learning to play the guitar and had one of his own at home. "Bring it in, man," Carl urged him. "I'm wantin' to pick."

Obliging the request, the janitor showed up with an old F-hole Gibson with frayed strings. No matter—Carl cut out on some blues runs as the janitor looked on. After a few minutes of hot licks came a request: "Let me hear you do some of that 'Blue Suede Shoes.' "

Carl started in on the song, but before he was finished a nurse came running in, upbraiding Carl for being so loud. Hers was a timid tongue-lashing, because this particular nurse was young, and a fan. "If you're gonna disturb the people around here, sing the whole thing and we'll open up the intercom and everybody that wants to can hear you," she suggested with a smile.

When the intercom had been turned on above his bed, Carl sat up in bed and greeted his audience: "I don't know who's listening," he began, "but I hope everybody's feeling better and is getting well." He launched into "Blue Suede Shoes," much to the delight of the janitor, who demonstrated some fancy footwork while Carl performed.

Finishing "Shoes," Carl announced "Honey Don't" as his next number—"Now here's the flip side of that record, in case anyone out there has heard it."

> Well, how come you say you will when you won't
> You tell me you do, baby, when you don't
> Let me know, honey, how you feel

Tell me the truth now, is love real

But, uh-uh, honey don't . . .

As he completed "Honey Don't" another nurse came in and said, "Some fella down the hall wants to know if you'd sing 'Turn Around.'" Carl was happy to oblige. For him, this was therapy of the highest caliber—a real healing session.

As Jay's condition improved, Carl yearned more for home and for Valda. After speaking to the hospital director in Wilmington, he was given the go-ahead to finish his recuperation at the Jackson hospital. Home beckoned.

When he got off the plane in Memphis, Carl found his father and Clayton waiting to drive him to the Jackson hospital. Instead, as Carl recalls, they "came up to and drove right on by the Jackson hospital and went home." When he walked into his apartment, still in his upper-body cast, he and Valda locked eyes. No words were spoken. She embraced him as best she could and held him as close as the cast would allow. They kissed as they cried. When he came up for air, Carl declared that he would not return to the hospital, doctors' instructions be damned. "I got a bed right here that's more comfortable than theirs, and I ain't sick," he told Valda. "I'm just waiting to heal."

While "waiting to heal," Carl saw "Blue Suede Shoes" rise to number one on most regional charts—pop, R&B, and country—throughout the nation, making him the first artist to top all three with the same record. "Heartbreak Hotel" had a choke hold atop the *Billboard* Hot 100 and country charts, but "Blue Suede Shoes" spent four weeks at number two before beginning a slow descent. On the R&B chart, however, "Shoes" performed slightly better than Presley's single, peaking at number two, while the latter dropped after reaching number three. By mid-April, "Shoes" had surpassed the one-million sales mark.

Though he wasn't due a royalty payment from "Shoes" till later in the year, the single's astonishing sales augured well for the Perkins family's long-term financial prospects. Moreover, Carl's success, along with Cash's, proved instrumental in saving the floundering Sun label and benefited Sam Phillips, who bought a new house with his share of the publisher's commission (he retained the rights to "Blue Suede Shoes" even though it was now represented by the New York house of Hill and Range as part of the Presley buyout).

Despite an inopportune setback, Carl felt better about the future upon pondering it from the sanctity of home. Jay would be released in April. Offers were still pouring in for concerts and TV appearances. Not even Elvis could take "Blue Suede Shoes" away from him: It had become part of the national consciousness. Shortly after returning to Jackson he accepted an offer to go out in the early summer, at the un-heard-of sum of $1,000 a day, on an extended tour billed as "Top Stars of '56," a package headlining Carl, Al Hibbler, and Frankie Lymon and the Teenagers, with eight other acts rounding out the show, including Cathy Carr, Shirley & Lee, Chuck Berry, Bobby Charles, Della Reese, the Cleftones, and the Spaniels, with Illinois Jacquet's "Big Rockin' Rhythm Band" providing instrumental support. Having a million-sell-ing single fueled Carl's drive to write and perform again. In less than a year and a half he had come out of the dark, tumbled back into it at the moment he was in the brightest light, and was emerging with new confidence. From where he stood, "Blue Suede Shoes" was far from being the only aspect of his life blessed with a golden hue. Still, in his quiet hours, he was haunted by the thought that he had been denied.

During his recuperation, Carl received three visitors from the east; Nashville, that is. The trio's leader was Jim Denny, one of the most powerful men in the Nashville music industry by dint of having been manager of the Grand Ole Opry. With responsibility for booking tal-ent, he had recast the Opry from a barn-dance type of show to one fea-turing the top country stars of the day, a move that increased its stature and its popularity substantially. When he arrived at Carl's Camden Street address in 1956, Denny had left the Opry to form his own publishing company, Cedarwood, with his partners Webb Pierce, the dominant country vocalist at the time, and businessman Troy Mar-tin; with country singer Carl Smith he had formed a second publish-ing concern, Driftwood.

As he had changed the Opry's focus with an eye towards the future, so was Denny setting out to alter the landscape of Nashville's music publishing business—heretofore dominated by Roy Acuff and Fred Rose's joint venture, Acuff-Rose—by assembling what would become one of the most prolific and important staff of house songwriters the city would ever see (Acuff-Rose had staff writers and gets credit for the idea, but Cedarwood exploited it to its fullest potential, which led to a publishing boom in Nashville). With Denny on his trip to Jackson were booking agent Oscar Davis, and artist manager Dub Allbritton. All three had something to offer Carl Perkins, then one of the two biggest stars in rock 'n' roll and completely without management or independent business counsel.

Carl invited them in, and as they took seats, Denny asked Carl if he wrote a lot of songs like "Blue Suede Shoes." Carl shrugged and picked up his guitar. He had played a couple of new songs he was working on when Denny cut him off. "I've heard enough," Denny said, nodding. "I've heard some good stuff.

"We're here for one reason: We want to make the star out of you that you potentially are," Denny told Carl. "The three of us are willing to take you on and try to take you to the top. That's where we think you belong, that's where you are at this moment, but a lot more has to be created for you for this success to hold up. We'd like to see that you make the right decisions. If it's Hollywood where you want to go, we're familiar with those people. We'd make our suggestions to you, but it would ultimately have to include what you want to do too.

"Think about what we've offered you," Denny concluded. "We're offering our services because we believe in you. I spearhead this operation, but you'll have the best booking agent in Oscar Davis, and the best manager in Dub Allbritton. Think it over and let me know what you'd like to do."

Early the next morning Carl called Sam and told him about Denny's visit. "They're wantin' to sign me, Mr. Phillips," Carl said. "Wanna make a star outta me."

"Can't nobody make a star outta you—you're already a star!"

Phillips told Carl. "What they're wantin' is twenty percent of your money. Just like that Colonel is diggin' into Elvis. I've told y'all about them shysters out there."

"Well these fellas don't seem that way. Now Jim Denny isn't no shyster."

"They are, Carl," Phillips insisted. "If they wasn't thinkin' that you was gonna make a lotta money, they wouldn't of been down there."

"They're only wantin' twenty percent," Carl said. "That leaves me eighty, the way I figure."

Sam corrected Carl's math. "It don't work that way. That twenty, they're just wantin' to get you on a contract. Now they'll start addin' the bookers and all that stuff on there. You better watch out. You gotta hit record and you don't need nobody. I'll help you with your career. We've got the setup down here to take care of you and any of the rest of the artists. You know that. We've done mighty well. I got you on the Como show before you had that wreck. You missed it, but you're gonna get all that stuff. We can get anything they can."

When Carl took stock, he had to agree with Sam. Bob Neal's Stars Incorporated was doing the job for him, as far as Carl was concerned, and there was no reason to believe he would be hurt by staying put: "Bob Neal worked us all. We didn't get top money, and he wasn't nationally known, but who's to say he wouldn't have been? Till he lost Elvis he was gonna get nationally known."

Denny accepted Carl's decision to stay put without argument. But he added before signing off: "My offer's still here, and don't wait too long to change your mind. If you don't, I'll understand. But if you want to go, now's the time to do it. You can't wait till your record starts going downhill and you miss all the opportunities that we can get for you right now. You're a hot item and need to be treated as such."

As far as Carl was concerned, he was being treated as a hot item at Sun. Sam was calling nearly every day, telling him of "Shoes" 's staying power and urging him to get back on the road as soon as possible to capitalize on the demand for his public appearances. Before the start of the "Top Stars" tour, Sam flew him to New York to be fitted for a toupee that would cover his head where it had been shaved and stitched up after the wreck. With his own hair thinning anyway, the hairpiece, a conservative pompadour, sliced a few years off his appearance and was from thereafter rarely seen off his head in public. Carl was ready to rock again.

Carl Perkins is sufficiently recovered from injuries sustained in an auto crash in Maryland to permit him to make the "Big D Jamboree" tour opening at Beaumont, Tex., April 21 and following with Galveston, San Antonio, Wichita Falls and other Texas spots. Others injured in the same crash with Perkins are also reported on the mend. On May 5, Perkins returns to Dallas for an appearance with "Big D Jamboree" at the Sportatorium.—Song Hits, April 21, 1956

at each stop of the tour, Carl had requested in advance that a telephone be placed near the stage. With Valda's due date approaching, Carl wanted to hear the news at the earliest opportunity. On April 23, as he was preparing to walk out to start his show, the phone rang. Carl took the call. When he had finished talking, he handed the phone to the stage manager and strolled to the microphone.

"Good evening, ladies and gentlemen," Carl said as the crowd roared its welcome. "It's a boy." Another roar went up from the audience, followed by sustained applause and whistles. "I wanted to be here so bad in San Antonio, Texas, that my wife just gave birth to a baby boy in Jackson, Tennessee. Again the applause broke out and mutated into rhythmic clapping as Carl began rocking with "Well, how come you say you will when you won't . . . " on the day of Stephen Allen Perkins's birth.

As Carl was preparing for his tour, he received a call from Sam asking him to be at the studio the next morning. On April 10, he pulled up in his '50 Chrysler; Sam, waiting outside, climbed in and directed Carl to drive on down Union to the Southern Motors Cadillac dealership.

At the lot, Sam escorted Carl to a new two-tone Cadillac, with a blue body and a white top. A photographer emerged from the office and captured the moment when the Sun owner presented the label's reigning star with a set of car keys.

Carl stood there in abject shock as Sam began orating as if he were running for office. "I said when I entered the recording business that the first artist to sell one million copies of any record, I would give him a brand-new Cadillac. It looks as if Carl Perkins is that lucky man. We're here this morning to present Carl Perkins with Sun Records' first Cadillac."

"Tell me you're kiddin' me, man," Carl stammered. "Or hit me and tell me I'm dreamin' and wake me up."

"Naw, it's yours," Sam assured Carl. "I'm glad it happened to you. I always knew it would, and I'm so proud for you. Got you a hit record and a new Cadillac."

From his Chrysler Carl unloaded a couple of spare tires, a jack, and a chain that belonged to his uncle Ernest, gave the old rattletrap a swift, hard kick to its driver's side door, and never looked back as he maneuvered the Cadillac out of the lot and towards Jackson. Attempting to operate the car's electric seat adjustments, he managed to work himself into such an awkward position that his vision was partially blocked by his knees—"I was just about in the back seat." He had to pull over and readjust the seat to the proper position; when he got back on Highway 70, he proceeded to take his time rolling into Jackson, making the hour-plus trip in nearly four hours, stopping at service stations along the way, treating customers and help alike to cold bottles of Coke, and showing off his new jewel.

When he finally got home, he found the car was longer than the apartment. He could stand in the front door and see the tail fins, go to the back door and see the hood. Getting the kids together, he took the family for a drive, a long drive, visiting all the relatives and tooling around town aimlessly. It was nearly midnight when they returned home.

Sam didn't let up, booking Carl for another recording session ahead of his busy spring and summer concert schedule. With Jay out of commission, Ed Cisco filled in on rhythm guitar, and session pianist Jimmy Smith was in for part of the evening. The main order of business was to find another single. Sam persisted in believing "Everybody's Trying to Be My Baby" could be a strong entry with some minor adjustments in arrangement. A new take of the song found the band making a change in key and discarding a stop-time figure it had employed at the beginning of each verse in the song's original version. Breaking into a loose, loping swing, Cisco, Clayton, and Holland offered steady if unspectacular support behind Carl's easygoing vocal. Carl made one minor lyric alteration, rewriting the second verse but stumbling vocally when the tape rolled:

> Well I don't guess Daddy to move his star
> They wanna ride in my big blue car
> Everybody's tryin' to be my baby . . .

On Take 3 the stop-time figure appeared again, along with another key change, and the rhythm section pounded out the beat more forcefully behind Carl's devil-may-care, swaggering vocal. He became less popular in this version, too. His original lyric had him coming home at half-past four in the morning to find nineteen women knocking on his door; the number was reduced to fifteen in the song's third incarnation. A fourth take combined elements of all three previous versions with minor lyrical adjustments:

> Well they took some honey from a tree
> Dressed it up and they called it me
> Everybody's tryin' to be my baby
> Everybody's tryin' to be my baby
> Everybody's tryin' to be my baby now
>
> I woke up this mornin', half-past four
> Fifteen women knockin' at my door
> Everybody's tryin' to be my baby
> Everybody's tryin' to be my baby
> Everybody's tryin' to be my baby now

(guitar solo)

I try to get away, I go on home
But they never seem to leave me alone
Everybody's tryin' to be my baby
Everybody's tryin' to be my baby
Everybody's tryin' to be my baby now

I ain't good-lookin', I ain't smart
I guess they're after this poor boy's heart
Everybody's tryin' to be my baby
Everybody's tryin' to be my baby
Everybody's tryin' to be my baby now

("Rock!!")

Here Carl took off into an angular guitar solo, one of his most interesting on record, combining crisp, clear single notes, with double-string runs and sustained single notes hanging and bending before erupting into a flurry of single notes again.

I know I'm not a movie star
I guess they're wantin' to ride in my car
Everybody's tryin' to be my baby
Everybody's tryin' to be my baby
Everybody's tryin' to be my baby now

Well they took some honey from a tree
Dressed it up and they called it me
Everybody's tryin' to be my baby
Everybody's tryin' to be my baby
Everybody's tryin' to be my baby now

The fourth was a strong take. Carl's vocal was loose but knowing: Whenever he returned to the song's title sentiment, he sang it jauntily, with a perceptible chuckle in his voice. Though played for laughs, one lyric phrase cut deep: "I ain't good-lookin' / I ain't smart / I guess they're after this poor boy's heart." Coming in the early stages of "Blue Suede Shoes" 's success, the lyric illustrated Carl's ongoing struggle to understand his achievement in personal terms. Even as his dream was being fulfilled, he was wrestling with the question "Why me?" and finding answers elusive.

From an idea inspired by Curly Griffin, Carl had brought in one of the best songs he had ever written, again drawn from the tonk life, but explicit in its depiction of a charged milieu harboring danger around one corner, drunken revelry around another. Griffin had told Carl he had started a song about being "Dixie fried," a term new to Carl.

"You talkin' about gettin' drunk, Curly?" Carl had wondered.

"Yeah, get fried—Dixie fried," Griffin had quipped, passing him a lyric sheet.

Guitar in hand, Carl took what amounted to an opening verse from Griffin's pen and ran with the idea. He had a completed version written in only a few minutes, and over the next few days rewrote it and hammered out its arrangement in the tonks. In the studio, though, it was transformed from a lightweight, good-time, near-comical bit of tonk schtick into something dark and foreboding, a tale both instructive and cautionary to anyone on the outside looking in.

In the first version Carl sang as if he were a bemused observer sitting out in front of the gas station on a lazy afternoon spinning yarns for the locals. For the second take, he crafted a stinging solo intro and settled into a stomping 2/4 groove with the band. When he entered vocally, it wasn't with the same conversational air he had taken on Take 1. Instead, he came blowing in like rolling thunder at a picnic, with word of evil doings afoot, his language replete with chilling images and one memorable phrase—"Rave on, children, I'm with ya." The band seemed to fade behind Carl's verbal onslaught, quite properly subsuming their personality to the unfolding drama. In urgent, stentorian tones, Carl growled out the specifics of a tush hog's razor-wielding foray into a tonk, his subsequent arrest and imprisonment, and his unyielding disdain for authority—even as he rots away in prison, surreptitiously he sends word back to the tonk for everyone to keep the faith in his absence. Every holler, every little shading of lyric for nuance worked to perfection in controlling the story's mood and pacing; sputtering, crackling guitar solos sent up a report like that of a small handgun being fired repeatedly. It was the most harrowing slice of rockabilly anyone had ever recorded.

After three false starts on the second take—"If I mess up again I'm gonna bust my guitar. This is costin' too much money, isn't it?" Carl laughed after the third miscue—"Dixie Fried" was reconstituted, complete with a new twist on the closing refrain:

> Well, on the outskirts of town
> There's a little night spot
> Dan dropped in about five o'clock
> Pulled off his coat and said, "The night is short"
> Reached in his pocket and he flashed a quart
> And hollered,
> "Rave on, children, I'm with ya"
> "Rave on, cats," he cried
> It's almost dawn and the cops are gone
> And let's all get Dixie fried
>
> Now Dan got happy and he started ravin'
> Jerked out his razor but he wasn't shavin'
> And all the cats knew to jump and hop
> 'Cause he was borned and raised in a butcher shop
> He hollered, "Rave on, children, I'm with ya"
> "Rave on, cats," he cried
> It's almost dawn and the cops are gone
> And let's all get Dixie fried
>
> The cops heard Dan when he started to shout
> They all ran in to see what it was about
> And I heard him holler when they led him away
> He turned his head and this is what he had to say:
> "Rave on, children, I'm with ya"
> "Rave on, cats," he cried
> It's almost dawn, and the cops are gone
> Let's all get Dixie fried—get fried!

Now Dan was the bravest man that we ever saw

He let us all know he wasn't scared of the law

And through the black cross bars

He tossed a note to his dear

It said, "It ain't my fault, hon, that I'm in here"

But hollered, "Rave on, chillun, I'm with ya"

"Rave on, cats," he cried

It's almost dawn and the cops AIN'T gone

And I've been Dixie fried

When it was done, Carl knew he had put all the pieces together in a special way: "I had *nailed* that song. There was no 'Mr. Phillips, let me do it again.' I poured it all out and I got the energy going. I hollered when I needed to and I felt it. But it was one of those things where there was no arguing or no need in going again; I put it all in it."

A second take of "Put Your Cat Clothes On," the first having been cut at the early March session preceding the wreck, was almost a carbon copy of the original. It too was a powerhouse showcase for the Clayton-Fluke rhythm section, and in his lyrics Carl made currency of the wardrobe fetish that was showing up increasingly in his songs and in his audience. As well, the Perkins wit was ablaze, particularly in the near-surreal scenes of toenails and nail polish rent asunder by the big beat:

They took my blue suede shoes

Down to old Mobile

Got to rockin' with the rhythm

Run 'em over at the hill

(chorus:) Ah, put your cat clothes on

'Cause tonight we're really gonna rock 'em right

Kitty, put your cat clothes on

'Cause tonight we're gonna really do it right

Well I slick up myself

Till I look like a dilly

I run downtown and

Get my female hillbilly

(chorus)

Well, come on, cat, get with it
Keep your hand off that fruit jar
Gimme some be-boppin' rhythm
Pick the toenails up tomorrow

(chorus)

Well, my gal's slow and easy
But all the hep cats know
She gets that rockin' beat
She knocks the polish off her toes

Next, Clayton and Fluke went to town again on a breakneck shuffle, "That Don't Move Me," which showed off the fuller sound of Carl's
Switchmaster as well. Lyrically it had little to say—mostly "That don't
get it / That don't move me"—but it was in the pocket with the day's
best dance tunes. The session closed out with two cover versions, one
being a ballad, "Lonely Street," a country song reworked into an over-
wrought style that suggested more than a touch of the Gene Vincent
influence. Wanda Ballman's "I'm Sorry I'm Not Sorry," a mid-tempo
saga of a love affair's unlamented demise, featured Jimmy Smith's
piano prominently, giving the song a honky-tonk edge.

By mid-April, Sam had in the can some of the strongest uptempo
material he had ever recorded on any of his artists in "Dixie Fried,"
"Put Your Cat Clothes On," "Right String, Wrong Yo-Yo," "You Can't
Make Love to Somebody," "Everybody's Trying to Be My Baby"; even
"That Don't Move Me" had a little going for it as a pure dance number. Within these lay a combination that could have been the most extraordinary rockabilly single ever released; instead, as a follow-up to
the scheduled May single release, Phillips chose the routine "I'm Sorry
I'm Not Sorry" to back the definitive rockabilly track, "Dixie Fried,"
and scheduled it for an August release.

One of the new Sun artists Carl met during his early weeks back on
tour appeared to be heading for a hit with his first single, "Ooby

Dooby." Roy Orbison, born in Vernon, Texas, and raised largely in Wink, Texas, had a history that roughly mirrored Carl's own. His family had moved frequently before settling in Wink; money, or lack of it, was an ongoing problem for the Orbisons; Roy had formed his first band, the Wink Westerners, at age thirteen, but had made his first radio appearance when he was eight. The Perkins Brothers Band had headlined their own sponsored radio show, while the Wink Westerners had their own weekly television show. Carl had written out his life's plan at age eight; Roy had expressed his own in verse in his high school yearbook: "To lead a western band / Is his after school wish / And of course to marry / A beautiful dish."

Unlike Carl, Orbison had continued his education. After graduating from high school he had attended North Texas State for a year before transferring to Odessa Junior College, where he majored in geology. If he didn't make it in music, he would join his father in the oil fields. At Odessa JC, Orbison's three roommates were also musicians; adding a rhythm guitarist to their lineup, they formed the Teen Kings and landed their own local television show. One of their guests in 1955 had been Johnny Cash, who suggested they go to Memphis and seek out Sam Phillips. When they did, Phillips had sent them away, saying, "Johnny Cash doesn't run my record company."

Orbison returned to Texas, where he cut a demo for Columbia in Dallas in 1955. One of the songs he recorded was "Ooby Dooby," a novelty dance number written by two fraternity brothers at North Texas State. In March of '56 Orbison and the band went to Clovis, New Mexico, to work with producer Norman Petty. They cut several songs, including another version of "Ooby Dooby," which was subsequently released as a single on the Je-Wel label, an independent operating out of West Texas. A friend of Phillips's played the record over the phone for Sam, who was impressed with the odd quality of Orbison's voice. He brought the Teen Kings to Memphis and cut "Ooby Dooby" and "Go! Go! Go!", the latter a song cowritten by Orbison and his drummer, Billy Pat Ellis. Released in mid-April, it started percolating in Memphis and other southern markets, prompting Phillips to get the band out on the road through Bob Neal's Stars, Inc., agency.

Carl remembers hearing "a demo" of Orbison's at Sun in April, which was either the Je-Wel or Sun version of "Ooby Dooby," since Orbison hadn't submitted any demos to Phillips. Regardless, Carl, like Sam, was taken with the voice. "Man, he can sing!" Carl said. "He's got that Bill Monroe high thing goin'."

"I really like that voice," Sam concurred. "But you know," he added, "he's not a good-lookin' boy at all." He handed Carl a photo that showed Orbison to be a tad chubby in the face, with a shock of brownish-blonde hair greased back on his head, narrow eyes, and an odd, sad, recessed smile. Never one to be judgmental after having seen Elvis and himself standing side by side in a mirror, Carl had to agree with Sam nonetheless. "Well, if he don't make it, it'll be because of the way he looks," Carl said.

When they met at a show in Little Rock, Carl found that Orbison's photo hadn't lied about his looks, but he hadn't expected a man of such gracious and gentle manners. Orbison spoke softly, haltingly, and seemed to Carl to be even more introverted than Jay. His shyness extended to his stage show too: He tended to stand behind the microphone and barely move a muscle, even when playing "Ooby Dooby." But as Carl got to know him during their travels, he found Orbison to be as decent a man as he had ever met. What he lacked in personality he made up for in strength of character—he knew what he wanted, was fixed on his goals, and worked hard at his music, especially songwriting, his true passion. In concert his original ballads were well received, mostly because he had an enviable gift for communicating the deepest feelings implied in the lyrics. Of the cover versions Orbison performed live, one that "absolutely warped" the audience, as Carl recalls, was "Indian Love Call," a song popularized in 1936 by Nelson Eddy and Jeanette MacDonald in the film *Rose Marie:* "It was a killer," Carl says. "When he sang, 'I'm callin' you-oo-oo-oo,' you could hear a mosquito in that building, it got so quiet. People recognized something special. Roy was maybe one notch under raw greatness at that time."

Orbison's passivity made him an easy target for Carl's needling jokes. Having learned that Roy's eyesight was bad, Carl used this information to his advantage whenever possible.

"Man, if I looked as good as you do," Orbison said during one of their trips together, "I'd have it made. Big, broad-shouldered, long, tall man—you know, you should comb your hair fancier."

"I ain't got enough, Roy!" Carl answered, patting his thinning locks.

"You got enough!" Orbison insisted. "Shoot, man, what you got's dark. You got plenty of hair. You look great."

Carl laughed at the idea of Roy Orbison giving fashion tips. "That's one thing I got going with you—you about half-blind!" he said, as Orbison chuckled. "You can't see good. I can see myself in that mirror. I don't like to even walk by one."

Road trips were often enlivened by the mind games Carl played on a love-smitten Orbison. In Odessa he had a girlfriend, Claudette Frady, whose hold on him was complete—she was the "beautiful dish" of his high school dream. They planned to get married as soon as Roy was making enough money to support her. On the road, he called her every night, no matter the hour. Carl got used to seeing Roy staring in dazed silence at her photo in his wallet; miles and miles they would go down the road before Roy would look up.

"Carl, oh, I love her so much. What a gift to see Claudette," he sighed to Carl on one such occasion.

"Boy, you drivin' me crazy about that ol' ugly girl," Carl kidded him. "Lemme see her picture," he asked, knowing Roy's eagerness to show off his girlfriend to anyone who would look. "Man," Carl gasped as he studied the photo, "those are some pretty lips."

Roy smiled beatifically.

"Look like peaches," Carl continued, making sure to sound like he was impressed. "Look like a peach just split right down the center, don't it?"

"Man, and they taste like a peach," Roy bragged.

"Well I don't know about that," Carl said, "but I will if I ever get around her, 'cause I'm gonna kiss her. You talk about them lips so much!"

Of his love life, Orbison's main concern, often voiced to Carl, centered on the trajectory of his career relative to Claudette's patience. "I wanted to get myself set up in the music business to making good money if I could" went a familiar refrain. "We're gonna marry—she's done said yeah."

"Roy, I'm gonna tell ya somethin'," Carl would offer in his most sagacious manner. "You're gonna fool around and be out here on this road, and you're gonna go back to Wink one of these times, and as pretty as she is, some ol' long-legged cowboy's gonna have her around the waist. If she loves you like you say she does, and if you love her like I'm believin' you do, you better get back to Wink and forget how you gonna live. That will fall in place. Instead of that hamburger you chewin' on there, tear it in two and give Claudette half of it. And both of you can live on love and half a hamburger. It'd work. You can do it."

Orbison would ponder this before responding. "Carl, you givin' me some good, sound, fatherly advice there," he would nod in agreement, deadly serious. "Dadgum, she's not used to that. She's from a pretty wealthy family."

"Well, you can use that too!" Carl would point out. "She can borrow a little from her dad and see you through. *You got to go where love leads you, man!* And if you don't . . . "

As Carl expected, this seed, once planted, would sprout quickly. Concern etched on his face, Roy would suggest they stop for a Coke. While the others went in the store to make their purchases, he would head for the phone. Someone in the group would ask, "Where's Roy?" and when they went back outside, he would be found yapping away long distance to Claudette.

as rock 'n' roll swept over America; as black artists gained access to the mainstream of the new pop culture; as the once-dominant and lily-white Hit Parade shrunk to meaninglessness, opposition to the new music mounted from coast to coast. From pulpits "the devil's music" was reviled by the clergy as a corrupting influence on the nation's youth; newspaper editorialists inveighed against the declining morality in the wake of rock 'n' roll's advent; some radio stations banished rock 'n' roll and emphasized the point by smashing records on the air. After his television appearances, Elvis, the lightning rod for most of the anti-rock sentiment, was being ridiculed by the national press: "For the ear he is an unutterable bore," wrote Jack Gould of *The New York Times*, adding: "His one specialty is an accented movement of the body that heretofore has been primarily identified with the repertoire of the blonde bombshells of the burlesque runway." The New York *Journal-American*'s Jack O'Brien stated flatly, "He can't sing a lick," and at the same time revealed his own prejudice in describing Presley's stage movements as "the weirdest and most plainly planned, suggestive animation short of an aborigine's mating dance."

The ill-disguised subtext in most anti–rock 'n' roll diatribes related to its derivation from black sources. Having failed before—in the late twenties Ralph Peer, the man who first recorded Jimmie Rodgers, described the father of country music's repertoire as "nigger blues" to no noticeable effect on Rodgers's appeal to his white audience—this old and disingenuous tack was failing again. Carl and Elvis made no attempt to hide their influences, and their record sales continued apace. In 1956 Elvis told the Charlotte *Observer*, "the colored folks been singing it and playing it just like I'm doin' now . . . for more years than I know. They played it like that in the shanties and in their juke joints, and nobody paid it no mind 'til I goosed it up. I got it from them." Speaking that same year to *Rock 'N' Roll Jamboree* magazine, Carl said: "It's a lucky thing for me that the people came 'round to liking music with a beat like I've got. My style hasn't changed. I'm playin' what I've always played. It's still the same rhythm stuff with some country and blues thrown in."

As the music gained currency in the marketplace, so did it make new and scary enemies. In the wake of the Supreme Court's 1954 school desegregation ruling in *Brown v. Board of Education*, Mississippi farmer Robert Patterson announced the formation of the first White Citizens' Council, and like-minded organizations began springing up throughout the South, ostensibly bent on using entirely legal means to resist the Court's directive. Its leaders were town merchants, farmers, politicians, and bankers; its mandate was to strangle blacks economically. "These leaders denied credit, provisions, employment, and services to blacks, and their purview extended far beyond school desegregation to include every aspect of racial etiquette, including suffrage," notes David R. Goldfield in *Black, White and Southern: Race Relations and Southern Culture, 1940 to the Present.* The councils were particularly hard on black parents who dared to send their children to white schools—overnight they found themselves virtually shut out of the world, as white merchants refused to allow them to shop for even basic necessities.

As they sensed their power increasing, the councils began assessing other aspects of white society threatened by the black menace. White boys like Presley and Perkins warranted investigation for singing black music and bringing young girls to their knees with suggestive gyrations. In short order rock 'n' roll would take its place in the councils' eyes as a threat even more insidious than school desegregation.

Enter Asa Earl (Ace) Carter, a journeyman radio broadcaster, full-time Commie hunter and rabid anti-Semite, who in 1955 had broken off from the Alabama White Citizens' Council (one of whose members had denounced him as a "fascist") to form the North Alabama Citizens' Council. Among the many bogeymen Carter expected to find hiding under his bed was rock 'n' roll—"Bebop Promotes Communism" was his watchword. Writing in his NACC magazine *The Southerner,* Carter expanded on his novel theory. Describing rock 'n' roll as "sensuous negro music," he declared it was eroding the "entire moral structure of man, of Christianity, of spirituality in Holy marriage . . . of all the white man has built through his devotion to God." Not to be outdone, the Alabama White Citizens' Council established its own committee to, in the words of one member quoted on local television, "do away with this vulgar, animalistic, nigger rock 'n' roll bop."

Nat King Cole was the most prominent victim of the racism directed at music stars. Hardly a rock 'n' roll artist by any definition of the term, Cole had begun his career in the late thirties leading a jazz trio and recording several sides for Decca that showed him to be a scintillating and inventive pianist. In 1943 he had shifted gears entirely, signing with Capitol and transforming himself into one of pop music's preeminent vocal stylists. His path crossed that of Asa Earl Carter's, indirectly, on April 14, 1956, when he was attacked and beaten onstage in Birmingham, Alabama, by six of Carter's followers. Their arrest spurred Carter to set up a White People's Defense Fund and to excoriate the mild-mannered Cole as "a vicious agitator for integration." Cole would not be intimidated: He stayed on the road, keeping his commitments throughout the South and refusing to stoop to the race baiters' level in subsequent interviews. "I'm interested in doing something positive," he told reporters.

In the late spring of '56, Carl had difficulties of his own with the councils, one of the most memorable encounters taking place in Meridian, Mississippi, birthplace of Jimmie Rodgers. Prior to a show Carl was scheduled to do an interview with a local newspaper reporter. Instead, he was confronted backstage by four of the town's prominent community leaders, one of whom Carl suspected of being a preacher by virtue of his fluid patter and omnipotent air. He steered the discussion as his partners sat scowling at Carl throughout the "interview."

"We just want to talk to you about this music you're playing," the preacher began.

"Yes sir, be glad to," Carl said courteously. "What is it you want to know?"

"Do you not know that you are defiling the minds of our beautiful teenagers?"

"No, I don't know that I have," Carl said calmly.

"In your song you say, 'Drinking liquor from a fruit jar.' That's horrible!"

"You never tasted none out of a fruit jar?" Carl queried, feigning surprise at finding someone who hadn't engaged in this noble pursuit.

"No waaayyy," the preacher replied. "But our children! We are responsible for them."

"I've got children. I'm not givin' 'em liquor out of a fruit jar."

"You must pull this music. We have to find out what is happening to our youth!" the preacher intoned gravely.

Having struggled to keep his cool during this colloquy, Carl went on the offensive, fuming at the suggestion that he abandon his music. "It's people like you—that's what's wrong," he said. "Trying to make something out of nothin'. Leave the kids alone! What's wrong with them out there in that gymnasium in sock feet enjoyin' themselves? They ain't twistin' nothin' that you ain't tried to twist. And when I said, 'drinkin' liquor out of a fruit jar,' man, I was lookin' for a word to rhyme with '*car.*' I'm not tellin' 'em to go do it, I'm sayin' [they] *could.* But you don't step on my shoes! See what I'm sayin', man? Do I have to break this down for you? If you're that dumb, you believe what you want to believe."

Carl offered no concessions, and after further fruitless interrogation the meeting ended and the show went on. A few days later he had a similar small-town run-in on the Texas circuit, when he emerged from a radio interview to find a local dignitary awaiting him. "*Why,*" he asked Carl straight out, "are you singing this black music?"

"What I sing is not black music. It's black and white music," Carl explained.

"You have stated you were influenced by the black gospel singers."

"And I *still* state that," Carl shot back. "I was. What else have you got to ask?"

"What are you gonna do next? Indian music?"

Bigoted questioners got the response they deserved—none. From the outset, Carl regarded the rock haters with disgust and contempt. Of the Meridian incident, he says: "I knew what they were and I didn't think they were invited there and didn't have no right to be condemning my music. That fella needed to be out there preaching what he knew. He didn't know what he was talking about with me. I didn't do a lot of interviews back then because I didn't like those things happening. The kids were keeping the music alive; it wasn't the local papers and it wasn't the people that owned the radio stations. It was the pressure being put on those disc jockeys by those teenagers, that's what did it. The *kids* brought us through and kept the music alive."

Music wasn't the issue—rather, sex and race were the twin poles of the rock haters' fury. At a time when the burgeoning civil rights movement was focusing the country's attention on the social and political inequities imposed on the black population, rock 'n' roll was bringing an aspect of black culture into the consciousness of young white Americans for the first time in the twentieth century. It's difficult to distinguish whether the music's detractors were more disturbed by this politicization of the rock 'n' roll audience or by what had been properly observed as the "sensuous" quality of the music. Sex, race, and rock 'n' roll were linked in ways the bluenoses insisted were unheard of in this country's history, and the music's black roots provided all the necessary evidence to prove that blacks lived a base, prurient existence from which segregation had protected white society, and never the twain should meet.

Through ignorance or the passage of time or both, those who attacked rock 'n' roll could not afford to point out that Jimmie Davis, the composer of "You Are My Sunshine"; the beloved singing cowboy Gene Autry; and the putative king of country music, Roy Acuff, had all recorded bawdy songs early in their careers, before fame struck. Even the most revered of all gospel composers, Thomas A. Dorsey, penned a double-entendre classic, "It's Tight Like That," in his secular incarnation.

On the front lines, among the artists in the cross-hairs of the debate's scope, private conduct versus public behavior was more than an evolving philosophical concept. It was a daily battle. Carl and Elvis exemplified two extremes of choices as their professional paths ran parallel and then diverged. Elvis's even caught the attention of the Federal Bureau of Investigation following a May 14 performance in La Crosse, Wisconsin.

Two days after Presley's appearance, FBI director J. Edgar Hoover received correspondence on the letterhead of the La Crosse *Registi*, the official newspaper of the Diocese of La Crosse. Contained in Presley's FBI file, its author's name has been blacked out. In it Presley's performance is attacked as "the filthiest and most harmful production that ever came to La Crosse for exhibition to teenagers."

It goes on to note:

Eye-witnesses have told me that Presley's actions and motions were such as to rouse the sexual passions of teenaged youth. One eye-witness described his actions as "sexual self-gratification on the stage"— another as "a strip-tease with clothes on." Although police and auxiliaries were there, the show went on. Perhaps the hardened police

did not get the import of his motions and gestures, like those of mas-
turbation or riding a microphone . . .

Indications of the harm Presley did just in La Crosse were the two
high school girls (of whom I have direct personal knowledge) whose
abdomen and thigh had Presley's autograph. They admitted that they
went to his room where this happened. It is known by psychologists,
psychiatrists and priests that teenaged girls from the age of eleven,
and boys in their adolescence are easily aroused to sexual indulgence
and perversion by certain types of motions and hysteria—the type that
was exhibited at the Presley show . . .

From eye-witness reports about Presley, I would judge that he
may possibly be both a drug addict and a sexual pervert. In any case
I am sure he bears close watch—especially in the face of growing ju-
venile crime nearly everywhere in the United States.

I do not report idly to the FBI. My last official report to an FBI
agent in New York before I entered the U.S. Army resulted in the ar-
rest of a saboteur (who committed suicide before his trial). I believe
the Presley matter is as serious to U.S. security. I am convinced that
juvenile crimes of lust and perversion will follow his show here in
La Crosse.

Dead center on page one of the *Tribune,* surrounded by the
columns of type describing Presley's concert and the ensuing tumult,
was a story the letter's author seemed to have overlooked. A three-tier
headline said it all:

Lack of Discipline
in the Home Fosters
Crime—FBI Agent

Carl understood the frenzy attending Presley's appearances. He had
once been part of those shows, and was now seeing it on his own as a
headlining act. During his tours with Presley and afterwards, it was a
common practice for kids to line up backstage for autographs—one
photo shows Elvis and Carl together signing for a group of teens—and
for many of the girls to request the signatures on something other than

a piece of paper. Carl remembers girls raising their skirts to ask for an autograph on their "show panties." He would oblige, often to find Elvis's signature already there: "I've signed their bodies all over. That was a fad. I've signed many a panty right above 'old glory'—that's a red-dog term—that's where they wanted it. Yes sir. That was a must. They were special panties to 'em then. They had autographs all over 'em. They would maybe just wear them to a special show. That never really aroused me. Believe me, I never really enjoyed this; I knew it was a waste. I knew it was a fad. Elvis got to signin' undergarments and bare breasts; they'd just do that. It got out of hand. But the human element goes with you wherever you go. And the manly figure of an ol' red dog don't ever go away. But I've never had affairs."

Carl's policy was to sign only at the show venue; girls often found their way to his motel room, but he refused to allow them entrance; he signed autographs outside. Given his admitted red-dog habits, he struggled with the temptations before him, because he, like Presley, could have had any of the females who came his way. Unlike Presley, though, he had a wife and three children waiting for him at home. Valda had made it clear that if he cheated on her, she wouldn't be there when he came home, nor would she be talked into coming back once betrayed. Both Carl and Jay made it a practice to get back to their rooms quickly after the show and call home. When Carl would hear Valda's voice, and then hear one of his children squeal into the phone, "Hi, Dad-eeee!", he knew he wouldn't stray: "I took my marriage vows very seriously. I knew if I wasn't true to them that Valda wouldn't stay with me a second. It would kill her and it would kill the love she has for me. I didn't know about me when I was drinkin', and I knew that I just didn't need to take a chance. Because I went with a lot of 'em before I went with Valda; a lot of 'em. That was one of the things I enjoyed doing, going with different ones. And I played the field; to be an ol' red dog I did all right, I think. Presley? He took advantage of quite a few. I think that's pretty well documented. I've seen him with a lot of beautiful girls, so I've just let my imagination satisfy itself, by knowing him and hearing him talk some. He was pretty hot to trot. You can't blame a man for picking out the best one in the crowd when every one of 'em wanted him. And there's no law says you can't. I know if I hadn't been drinkin' and hadn't had kids and that wife at home, I'd have taken advantage of it as much as I could've."

The assault on Nat King Cole weighed on Carl's thoughts as he headed out in July for the Top Stars of '56 tour. In the weeks after the attack on Cole, Carl had been told of threats on his life from persons unknown who objected to his black-influenced music. He had told Jay, who was coming back into the lineup, albeit with a neck brace, "Somebody's gonna shoot me from the audience." Having Jay at his side again was a great comfort, and the money wasn't bad either—$1,000 a day to play two songs as the show's headliner, with his new agency, GMAC in New York, taking twenty percent. Still he worried about his and the band's safety in the southern states. Columbia, South Carolina, was the first date of the tour, and as Carl studied his road map before leaving, he thought to himself, *I'm gonna be the white Nat King Cole.* He had been taken to task enough by racists to feel the fear of action replacing words.

On a brighter note, he had his new Cadillac, his older brother on rhythm guitar again, an open road, and the prospect of making a bundle: "It was the ultimate, top money anybody in America was making. Presley wasn't doing no more than that; that was it. Big stuff. All we had was an old road map and a new Fleetwood Cadillac. We wrote the rules. We hadn't done this before, and nobody told us anything."

When they finally made it to the auditorium in Columbia on the night of the show, Carl, Jay, Clayton, and Fluke came in the backstage entrance and found their way to the dressing-room area. They could hear Frankie Lymon and the Teenagers harmonizing in one room, the Cleftones working out on "Little Girl of Mine" ("doodle-lootle-lootle-loo-lit") in another, and they saw the Spaniels huddling in their red silk suits in still another.

"Whatta we got into here?" Jay asked Carl. "We might get killed if this is a black audience. They might not like us. You better check and see if we're in the right place."

"I'm not askin' 'em, Jay," Carl answered. "That's the way this thing works."

Nevertheless, Carl sought out the road manager, a young black man everyone called Charlie. After welcoming Carl to the tour, Charlie ran down the rehearsal schedule. He also had a warning for Carl: "I'm gonna tell you, I suspect this thing's sold out and they may be a little wild here in South Carolina. They may rush the stage on you, Carl."

"Whatta you talkin' about?" Carl asked.

"Well, you bein' the only white act on the bill, I don't think we'll have any problems once we get up past Norfolk, goin' up North," Charlie said. "Everything'll be smooth after that."

(Cathy Carr, also on the bill, was white, but she didn't mingle with the rest of the troupe; her manager brought her to the venue only minutes before she went on and sang her hit, "Ivory Tower," and then whisked her away immediately afterwards.)

"You mean they're really gonna rush the stage and try to hurt us? You think that?"

"No. No, I don't," Charlie replied. "But I think it's gonna be wild and frantic by the time it gets to you. The kids are gonna be so up, they're gonna see so many of their favorites that they're gonna be pretty rowdy by the time you get on."

"And always look to your right," Charlie instructed. "I'll be standin' there, and when I do this,"—he extended both arms and brought them back towards his body rapidly—"run. Drop that guitar and go! Toward me. I'll have an escape outta here for you. That's my job."

When Carl and the band came out, the crowd was on its feet and roaring; many had left their seats and were pushing towards the stage. While plugging in his guitar, Carl looked back and saw one of the kids' faces pressed against the lip of the stage, blood dripping from a cut on his chin. He was prepared to perform two songs—"Honey Don't" and "Blue Suede Shoes" (released in May, "Boppin' the Blues" had already faded from the pop chart after peaking at seventy; on the country chart it had risen to number nine before dropping, but had failed even to chart nationally on the R&B side)—and the band was fired up. Clayton, inspired by the big payday, "hit the stage in fifth gear," Carl recalls, and the rest were "ready and charging. We gave it all we had."

During his first guitar break in "Honey Don't," Carl noticed Charlie waving him offstage. The musicians unplugged (save for W.S., who had to leave his drum kit behind), ran to the wing, and were directed upstairs, where they parted a double line of police officers and took over a vacant dressing room, slamming the door shut behind them. While running for safety, Carl could hear the kids tromping on the stage he had abandoned.

"It was terrible, it was very frightening, and the music was being mistreated," Carl asserts. "It was sickening to see pretty girls with their faces smashed against the stage. I couldn't stand to look at it, but I had to. Every once in a while you'd play a place that had an orchestra pit and that kinda stopped it. They'd start jumping off into the orchestra pit and stand up on each other's shoulders. It was dangerous. Lot of kids got hurt. There was a lot of rioting going on, just crazy, man! The music drove 'em insane."

In the dressing room, all was quiet. Carl, Jay, Clayton, and Fluke sat stunned at the scene they had witnessed. Carl knew what he was going to do: He was going home. An hour later, Charlie came in and told them it was safe to go out to their car. They made their way through a police cordon to the Cadillac, which had been vandalized. It had scratches all over the body from either knives or fingernail files, or both. In lipstick adoring messages had been written—"We love Carl," "Liz loves Carl."

As Carl eased in behind the wheel, Charlie came over to the window. "Carl, y'all got rooms at the hotel downtown," he said.

"I won't be needin' 'em, Charlie," Carl told him.

"What?" Charlie said.

"I'm goin' to Jackson, Tennessee. I don't belong here."

"You're *what?*"

"I'm goin' home," Carl said again. "I don't like this. This is not the way I wanna make my music. This is not right. I saw too many kids get hurt and I'm not gonna be a part of it. If that's what my music's gonna create, then I won't make it no more. It's over. I'm going home."

With that, Carl drove away from a $1,000-a-day obligation and arrived back in Jackson the next day. Sam Phillips was already calling when Carl got there and continued to call nearly every hour regularly as the day wore on, warning Carl he would be sued if he didn't return to the tour, and his career damaged severely. "What's wrong with you?" Sam inquired.

"Stomach ulcers are startin' to bleed," Carl lied.

"Carl, you're gonna get in trouble," warned Sam.

"No, sir, I'm not," Carl said. "I got a doctor says I ain't able to go."

"I don't believe you got that."

"Well I do have it!"

"Then you've developed that damn ulcer in the last week! You didn't have it two weeks ago!"

"Well, I got it now."

Sam asked to talk to Valda. "He's sick," she assured him.

"Look, man," Carl began when he came back on the phone, "I got my reasons. I'm not gonna stand on the stage trying to sing my song and watch them kids get hurt. Make them people hire enough cops to make the kids sit down! There's got to be a way to do this. There's got to be some rules. When they buy a ticket, tell 'em if they stand up, they're gonna get throwed out. It's too loose. Mr. Phillips, it's crazy out there; they're wild!"

Sam tried to reassure Carl that in other regions audiences would be calmer. Inadvertently he gave Carl an out by citing a clause in the contract binding the artist to the terms therein save for "an act of God," sickness being one. In short order Carl had in his possession a note from his doctor indicating he had been diagnosed as being on the verge of a nervous breakdown, for which complete bedrest at home was pre-scribed.

After pleading and cajoling for a week, Sam convinced Carl to re-turn to the tour, avoiding a threatened lawsuit. He rejoined the show in Pittsburgh, where he found the audience wild but controlled—no riots. A July 12 show near Annapolis, Maryland, demonstrated rock 'n' roll's enormous appeal and produced no casualties either. *Billboard* reported:

Annapolis city and Anne Arundel county police reported that the July 12 r&b show at the Amphitheater at Carrs Beach, southeast of Annapolis, played to a sellout crowd of 8,000, while they had the al-most impossible job of handling an overflow crowd of 50,000 to 70,000.

County police said that the turnout jammed approach roads for five miles on route 655 and blocked all entrances into the route. The

Annapolis police said that it wasn't until 3:30 o'clock in the morning, approximately seven hours after the jam began, that normalcy was restored ...

The turnaway is estimated to be double that of the entire Annapolis population and is reported to have come from four neighboring states.

Without incident the tour wound its way through New York— Syracuse, Rochester, Buffalo—and into Canada, came back down through Cleveland, Chicago, and Minneapolis, and made stops in Iowa, Nebraska, and Kansas before concluding in Houston, Texas. Three weeks solid on the road, generating good response at every stop, had calmed down Carl considerably since his first traumatic experience in Columbia. In August he returned to Pittsburgh to play a date that had been booked for April but that had been canceled after the wreck, and also signed to play his first dates in California come fall. Praising him in its September issue, *Song Hits* said:

He is a sincere, down-to-earth fellow and insists that he's just a 'Country boy.' His humility at the success that is coming his way is amazing—and heartwarming to see. He is a little overwhelmed by what is happening to him and can hardly believe it is real. And he experiences a little fear before each appearance, especially before a new audience—afraid that they won't like him. But those fears are always unfounded; for when Carl and the band go into their routine (and quite a show it is!) the crowds go wild and he returns for encore after encore, with part of the audience usually "bopping" in the aisles.

Hit Parader, in noting his June guest appearance on Red Foley's *Ozark Jubilee* and Elvis's appearance the same month on *The Dorsey Brothers Stage Show*, opined, "There is still room in country music for good new artists."

In the fall of 1956, he finally made it to the Como show, but it was anticlimactic, "useless," in Carl's estimation, because "Presley had done knocked the nation cross-eyed with all his TV appearances on [Ed] Sullivan, [Jackie] Gleason, Tommy and Jimmy Dorsey."

In addition to the better-behaved audiences above the Mason-Dixon line, Carl's tour experience was smoother, in part because of the friendship he had struck with Chuck Berry. Since his strong debut with "Maybellene" in 1955, Berry had had only one other song crack the top 40, "Roll Over Beethoven," but other, less successful singles had knocked Carl for a loop with the quality of their writing. Berry had an eye for detail and a flair for wordplay that Carl envied: His songs limned social issues (racism, for example, in "Brown-Eyed Handsome Man") and chronicled the new youth culture in terms incisive, insightful, inventive, and humorous. In addition, he was a compelling live performer who excited the crowd by folding himself into a slight crouch and marching back and forth across the stage, jerking his head to and fro as he did—the "duck walk," he called it. Along with Carl and Scotty Moore, he had become one of the architects of rock 'n' roll guitar with a fluid solo style blending aspects of country with rhythm and blues and a signature sound in the form of wailing three-note chords.

Berry had come out of his native St. Louis in 1955 to record for Chess Records in Chicago. Familiar with a number of musical styles, he was joined at Chess by his longtime pianist Johnnie Johnson, who was equally at home in blues, boogie-woogie, R&B, and rock 'n' roll. In the studio he worked with some of Chess's front-line players, including Willie Dixon, Fred Below, and Jimmy Rogers. Berry had a voice—as a singer, as a writer, as an instrumentalist—that marked him for greatness in Carl's eyes. As well, Carl appreciated the country influence in Berry's playing: "I knew when I first heard Chuck that he'd been affected by country music. He had three-chord songs, not hard to play. Chuck made it sound hard, but he's taking that pick and hittin' three strings at the same time. Sounded way big for the time, but it was not really that hard to do. But his guitar playing ain't what made him—it was his songs. And live he was very exciting with his duck walk. Chuck made a lot of mistakes in his playing, but he made 'em at the right time. I respected his writing; his records were very, very great."

Their introduction had come backstage at the Columbia show when Berry knocked on Carl's dressing room door and peeked inside, asking, "Who Carl?"

Seeing a handsome face with prominent cheekbones, bright, intelligent eyes, thin moustache, and long hair slicked back, Carl sprung to his feet and cried, "Chuck Berry!"

"You know, I thought you was one of us," Berry said as he gripped Carl's hand.

"Well, just below the surface of this skin, I think we're about the same color," Carl said with a laugh. "Pink meat and red blood. Wouldn't that be about right?"

"I like your attitude, brother," Berry said, nodding his head. *"Love your attitude."*

When Carl returned to the tour, Berry asked if he could ride with him instead of in the bus with all the other artists. Carl was happy to have him along, as he was Al Hibbler, the blind R&B stalwart whose latest single, "After the Lights Go Down Low," was then approaching the pop chart's top 10. One or the other would share the Cadillac's smooth ride, and most of the time it was Berry. Conversing on the road, Carl found out that Berry not only liked country music, he knew about as many songs as did Carl. Jimmie Rodgers was one of his favorites. Once when Carl broke into a Rodgers Blue Yodel, Berry told him he had the verses wrong.

"That second verse belongs in 'Blue Yodel No. 4,'" he corrected Carl.

"Chuck knew every Blue Yodel," Carl says, adding that Berry knew most of Bill Monroe's songs as well. The two often found themselves rolling down the highway harmonizing together on "Knoxville Girl" and "Blue Moon of Kentucky." A warm friendship formed: "We talked about everything," Carl remembers. "I felt very free around him. He told me about how he was raised, very poor, very tough. He had a hard life. He was a good guy; I really did like him."

August brought mixed blessings. "Dixie Fried" was released to a positive review from *Billboard* ("a solid country rockin' tune"), but was dead in the water as a pop record. Again no R&B play ensued, but the single did rise to number ten on the country chart. Sam's best guess was that the song was too raw for the pop market, an instinct borne out by a review in *Hillbilly and Western Scrapbook*, which observed: "*Dixie* carries too much in its lyrics about drinking, thus obviating much dj play and possible promotion."

"For its day it was a little bit too dark," Carl says in reflecting on "Dixie Fried" 's fate. "Disc jockeys kinda cringed a little when they laid it on the turntable; we had a little trouble gettin' it played. I had to work that record—I'd stop and thank the DJ, let him meet you, and see that you was a country boy and that really was an experience song. So they got to saying, 'Hey, that Carl Perkins swung by yesterday, and I'm gonna play his new record, it's called 'Dixie Fried.' Carl told me it was kinda like the way he was raised playin' in the honky-tonks. So here it is now, we know what it's all about.'

"When it first came out it was a little heavy—that cat born and raised in a butcher shop and slicin' them dudes. I guess that was pretty strong stuff. But I'd seen it happening, that's the way it was. Dan was just a tush hog. I didn't write it about anybody—I wrote it about a group of somebodies, you know. That's why the song appealed to them people that go to tonks at night. They listened to radio by daytime; they got the message. In the South it was a big record."

The month was brightened by the arrival of Carl's first royalty checks from Sam Phillips. Two envelopes were mailed, one bearing the Sun Records logo, the other a different-colored envelope from Sam's publishing company, Hi-Lo Music. The Sun check was for an amount slightly exceeding $12,000; the Hi-Lo check for a little more than $14,000. An accounting of royalties, showing their source and amount, was included with the Sun check.

"Well, this is about half of what we thought it would be," Carl told Valda as he stared at the two checks totaling more money than he had ever imagined would be his at one time. "But ain't it somethin'? *Ain't it somethin'?!*"

First he wanted to bring the band members in for individual shares. He would give Jay and Clayton $5,000 each, and W.S. $2,000. At the Jackson Bank of Commerce, Carl opened the first bank account of his life and deposited the checks.

Valda thought something was amiss. While attempting to deci-
pher the accounting statement, she told Carl, "There's no way this
can be right." Carl admitted that other artists had told him he would
probably make $100,000 from his first royalty payment, given how
mammoth a record "Blue Suede Shoes" had been out of the box. To
Valda he suggested this might be the first of a series of payments.
As they looked at the accounting together, one item caught their attention: Sam had deducted the price of the Cadillac from Carl's
artist earnings. So much for the grand gesture honoring Sun's first
million-selling record. (Shortly after receiving the royalty checks,
Carl wrecked the Cadillac on Highway 70, requiring extensive re-
pairs.) "The accounting that Sam Phillips gave Carl was not to where
you could really even count it up yourself," Valda recounts. "It was
just so vague. Even without it, there was no way that amount of
money could be right. But Carl was just thankful to have that kind
of money, even though he was not properly paid. I was thankful, but
I didn't want Sam to cheat him out of his money, which is exactly
what he did."

Urging Carl to question Sam, Valda emphasized to Carl, "Look, it's
your money. He's made a lot of money off you and he should be willing to give you your part of it, because it is yours."

Carl declined to pursue the matter, because he could not make himself believe Sam would cheat him: "I didn't feel right to question Sam
about too much of anything, really. I trusted him. I was making more
money than I'd ever made in my life. My dream was coming true. So
why did I ever want to say anything to him about anything, other than
being totally happy?"

Rather than hounding Sam for a proper accounting, Carl did something he considered more important to his and his family's immediate welfare: He made a $10,000 down payment on a house on Jack-
son's Park Avenue—his own house, not a government-subsidized
apartment, not one side of a duplex. It wasn't spacious, but it was the
first real home for the Carl Perkins family. For Carl it was another
dream realized: "It was brick and it had trees and a yard. To me it was
the prettiest house in this town. I didn't have to go drive around look-

ing at pretty houses anymore. I'd drive up to my own. I was a happy man."

That fall the moment Carl had been dreaming about from his youth, that had driven him from age six, arrived when Sam secured a booking for him on the Grand Ole Opry. Roy Acuff—*the* Roy Acuff— would introduce him, and his mother, father, and wife would be sitting in the front row watching him.

Since the Opry did not permit drums on stage, W.S. stayed home. Carl, Jay, and Clayton were escorted to their dressing room, and learned an early lesson in the difference between myth and reality. However grand the Opry, however hallowed the Ryman Auditorium, the Perkins brothers found themselves sharing a room that was hardly larger than two outhouses put together. Still, Carl was rendered breathless as he greeted the idols of his youth—Acuff and Bill Monroe—who were strolling casually around the backstage area.

"We made it!" Carl exclaimed to Jay and Clayton. "This is it!"

Clayton had a different perspective. "We worked awfully hard to land in this little hole," he told Carl. "Wonder what they're gonna pay us for this?"

"I don't think they're gonna pay us," Carl answered, realizing he had failed to tell either brother about the honor of playing the Opry being reward enough, in the eyes of the Opry management anyway.

"Well, hell, let's go home then!" Clayton said, heading for the door.

"No, man!" Carl said. "We're doin' it for the great thing it is to play the Opry."

Clayton laughed ruefully. "Yeah," he huffed. "It's a killer alright."

Before going onstage, Carl took a swig of Early Times—"a drink of courage"—and listened as Acuff rendered one of his gracious introductions. Carl stepped to the microphone, greeted the audience, and said, "I want to sing my new record," and began: "Well it's one for the money . . . " After polite applause for the opening lines, the largely middle-aged audience sat respectfully and quietly as Carl performed. He stayed on to do "Honey Don't," and it generated more buzz than did "Shoes." Even so, "polite" best describes Carl's reception, "muted" his reaction. So much had happened to him since "Shoes" broke big that the Opry paled in comparison. Years later he would say it "rocked the bottom of my soul" to have been invited on the Opry, albeit less than if he had appeared before "Blue Suede Shoes" had made him a household name.

between December 4 and the end of January 1957 Carl returned to the studio for extensive sessions once again aimed at getting some material in the can in advance of his heavy touring schedule in the first half of the year. Two new faces showed up for the first session, one to play, one to watch. The latter was Buck Perkins, making what would be his only appearance in a recording studio. Carl had brought his father there for the purpose of showing him the recording side of the business; Buck had been sought out for interviews in the wake of Carl's success and was distressed that he had come off sounding ignorant about his son's work because he had no idea how a song became a record.

The new addition to the instrumental lineup was also new to the Sun artist roster. He was a piano player from Ferriday, Louisiana, named Jerry Lee Lewis, whose first single, "Crazy Arms," a country hit earlier in the year for Ray Price, had been released on December 1. Then twenty-one years old, Lewis played a fiery, almost baroque style, heavy on glissandos and other right-hand flourishes, and sang in a clear, high tenor, somewhat conversational in tone, projecting no quality so much as attitude—a freewheeling, rollin' and tumblin' attitude, cocky, full of feeling for life, with an element of the salacious in his sly phrasing. His cousin Carl McVoy had been his earliest tutor on piano, and his technique owed something to that of Moon Mullican; in later years he would point to Al Jolson, Jimmie Rodgers, and Hank

Williams as having had the greatest impact on his vocal approach (and would always add his name to the list in enumerating America's greatest singers).

Carl came to the studio knowing Jerry Lee would be on the session, but never having met the man himself. In late November Sam had called and told Carl, "I got an ol' boy down here that can beat a damn piano up and I'd like to hear him playin' with you." "Bring him on," Carl said. At their introduction to each other, Carl found Jerry Lee "a very self-assured fella. He didn't have any doubt about what he could do."

Of the numerous songs he expected to record in December and January, Carl is certain of only two being cut early in the afternoon of the December 4 session. "Your True Love," a straight-ahead, swinging paean celebrating love and devotion, was enlivened by Carl's edgy guitar solos and some catchy call-and-response between the brothers Perkins on the choruses. It was made up on the spot.

When the song ended, Sam's voice came over the studio speaker. "That's a hit," he told the band.

At the piano, Jerry Lee raised his head. "That song ain't worth a damn," he announced.

Carl was stunned. "I thought to myself, *Okay, you'll be alright.* I didn't know whether he was good or not, and I didn't talk to him a lot during the session because I detected that I would have trouble with him being a smart aleck. To me that's what a smart aleck was—somebody who would jump in and give his opinion of a record when it was *my* record. But he opened all them smart-aleck doors to start. I didn't pick at him. I didn't act like the guy that had 'Blue Suede Shoes' and coulda said, 'Hey, you're in here to play piano and *shut your damn mouth!*' I didn't do that. I tried to make him feel welcome and comfortable, but I saw that that's what he was. I'd done been around too many like him."

During a break, Buck approached Carl with a suggestion. "Carl, you oughta do that old song, 'Matchbox Blues.' You know—'I'm settin' here wonderin', would a matchbox hold my clothes.' "

Carl remembered hearing Buck singing that same lyric around the house on occasion, but had never heard the complete song. "What else does it say, Daddy?" he asked.

"I ain't got no matches, but I got a long way to go," Buck warbled in response.

"What else?"

"That's about all I know," said Buck.

"That don't make no sense," Carl said. " 'Matchbox hold my clothes. I'm settin' here wonderin', would a matchbox hold my clothes.' "

As Carl sang the lyrics to himself, Jerry Lee slipped in behind his tentative vocal with a restrained boogie-woogie riff. Nodding encouragement to Jerry Lee, Carl began picking out a melody on the guitar and improvising lyrics. A few minutes later he had constructed a complete song:

> I'm an old poor boy
> Just a long way from home
> I'm an old poor boy
> Just a long way from home
> I'll never be happy
> Everything I do is wrong
>
> (chorus:) I'm settin' here wonderin'
> Would a matchbox hold my clothes
> I'm settin' here wonderin'
> Would a matchbox hold my clothes
> I ain't got no matches
> Got a long way to go
>
> Well let me be your little dog
> Till your big dog comes
> Let me be your little dog
> Till your big dog comes
> When the big dog gets here
> Show him what this little puppy done

The verse Buck had learned, either off the radio or in the cotton fields, was from a 1927 recording by Blind Lemon Jefferson, a towering figure as a blues guitarist and, as a writer, a wise and often witty commentator on the life and follies he observed in his wanderings through the South. Carl maintains he had never heard Jefferson's song at the time he wrote his own "Matchbox," and apart from the first verse supplied by Buck, the two brook no comparison. Jefferson's "Match Box Blues" is a quintessential mean-woman blues (make that a mean, peg-legged woman), a far cry from Carl's depiction of a rootless, lovelorn "poor boy" with limited prospects.

In the first take of "Matchbox," Carl tore into a steely bass string triplet, repeated twice before the band came clattering in behind him, a little sloppy but roaring; Jerry Lee began filling gaps with right-hand runs across the keys, a glissando here, a walking blues line there, a boogie-woogie riff that dropped off into another glissando—every trick in his repertoire, it seemed. On a second take, Jerry Lee dispensed with all the embroidery and settled into a solid, pumping boogie-woogie riff. Carl attacked the song vocally and instrumentally as relentlessly as he had "Dixie Fried," firing off the lyrics like a man completely fed up with his station in life and aching to hurt someone—the first verse was delivered contemptuously and with searing anger; on his guitar solos—heralded by his cry of "Let 'er go, boy! Go! Go!"—single- and double-string notes slashed and burned their way around the relentless, pulsating rhythm, each musician answering Carl's challenge with a ferocious assault of his own, none more so than Jerry Lee, who supplanted Clayton in having the last word by firing off another glissando *after* the bass lick sign-off.

When it was over, Carl turned to Jerry Lee. "Boy, I like what you're doin,' " he said.

"Hell, that ain't all I can do," Jerry Lee shot back.

Again rocked by Jerry Lee's arrogance, Carl regrouped and mentioned that Dale Woods, a Nashville session player who graced her recordings with numerous glissandos, had a style similar to Jerry Lee's.

"Aw, hell, she can't do it," Lewis scoffed. "This is the way to do it." With that he began running his right hand rapidly back and forth across the keyboard. Back and forth, back and forth, all the while fixing Carl with a beady-eyed, confrontational stare, thin lips set in a smug half-smile. His long, wavy blonde hair, swept straight back on his head when the session began, was unkempt and hanging off the sides of his forehead.

"That's the way he was," Carl says. "Jerry Lee didn't manufacture Jerry Lee. Jerry Lee *was* Jerry Lee, I guess, from when he was a kid. His attitude was, 'You think you can play that sumbitch? You let me sit down.' And you know, he was right. He was cocky, but he fulfilled what he said. If he told you, 'Get up and let me play,' you'd just get on up because he could beat you. And he beat you with a style. He wasn't copying anybody else. Dale Woods had that thing of slinging her thumb down them keys. But Jerry Lee perfected it."

Over the speaker Carl heard Sam call him into the control room. "Man, listen to this!" he said as he rolled Take 2 of "Matchbox." As Carl's voice came in after the intro, Sam began shaking his head. "That sounds like the South comin' back to fight the North again! Listen to that damn blonde-headed fool play that piano! And what are you doin' on your guitar?"

"I'm just on the bass string. I don't know," Carl answered.

"God, it's an awesome sound! This is a smash hit! If there ain't nothin' but an intro, if you never said a word, you'd have a hit! Just keep that intro going for two minutes. That's it!"

Out in the studio, blissfully oblivious, sat Jerry Lee at the piano, singing "Crazy Arms" for the rest of the band. Sam laughed as he watched the performance; he had taken to Jerry Lee in a way Carl found inordinately intense for Sam. "Listen to that damn fool sing," he said. "Carl, that boy can sing. He sure can."

Carl's initial impression of Jerry Lee was more measured than Sam's: "Jerry was a hell of a piano player but he wasn't much of a singer, because he didn't know who he wanted to sound like. He was using that Hank Williams yodel too much—'Cra-a-azy h-arms, reach to ho-old somebody new.' He was trying to bust his bubble with every word he said. I thought, *Oh, we got us a copycat here but we don't know who it is. I hear a bit of me, I hear a little bit of Elvis, he's just a little mixed up.*

But there was and is no question in Carl's mind of Jerry Lee's contribution to "Matchbox," attitude and all. "I don't think 'Matchbox' would even have been a record if he hadn't been there. It wouldn't have fired me up to start writin' and makin' it up and doin' it like I did it. No way. And I wouldn't have played them hot, fiery guitar breaks. I took some of my best guitar breaks on that song. Triple string is what I was doing, playing all three strings at the same time with a pick, which is usually done finger-style. But foolin' around and practicin' I knew it would work, and that was the time to try it, 'cause I was shootin' at Jerry Lee's head. It was never rehearsed."

In what will remain one of rock 'n' roll's great, unanswerable "What if?" questions, Carl says "Matchbox" had a moment when Jerry Lee could have taken over and left his mark in a more pronounced way than he did. The tush hog in Carl didn't allow it to happen, because he still resented Jerry Lee putting down "Your True Love." As his first guitar break approached, Carl intended to give Jerry Lee a piano solo after his: "But I thought, *No, you smart aleck, I'm gonna play both breaks on this guitar. Next time I'm gonna try to burn the neck off of it.* I knew he was itchin' for me to holler, 'Get it, Jerry!' I kinda wished I had of; I'd like to have seen what he would've done, 'cause he was hot that day. He was going after it. I let myself get in the way of probably a phenomenal piano break. He would've *shown* me how to play a piano. So the world probably missed the greatest piano break Jerry Lee would have ever taken."

Shortly after "Matchbox" was complete, Elvis walked into the studio, taking everyone by surprise. Seeing Presley for the first time since he had left Sun, Carl found the change in his friend's appearance startling. Elvis's hair, sandy-colored in 1954, was jet-black, a deeper shade than the black he had sported in his latter days at Sun; his skin was smooth as china, and the acne on his neck had cleared up—he wasn't even wearing his collar up now. Dressed casually in black slacks, a white shirt, and a light-colored jacket, Elvis cut a striking figure—the Hillbilly Cat had ascended to the media-anointed title of King of Rock 'n' Roll. The professional makeover was impressive: "They had glamorized what was there," Carl says. "The features looked right, the hair looked so great, no bumps on him anywhere. Man, he looked sharp and great."

Elvis had been out of town, busy with personal appearances and preparing for his first movie, and had stopped in Las Vegas on his way back to Memphis. This bit of information he passed on to Carl and the band by way of introducing his female companion, a striking, well-appointed brunette who told Carl she worked as a dancer in a Vegas nightclub. Her name has been widely published as Marilyn Evans, but Carl remembers her surname being Miller, prompting him to ask if she were related to the dancer Ann Miller, to whom she bore a physical resemblance. "We're sort of in the same business, but I'm not kin to her and I'm not near the dancer she is," Carl recalls her saying. "She's a wonderful dancer."

Making a beeline for the piano, Elvis sat down and played a quick run of notes across the keys.

"So you're Elvis Presley, huh?" Jerry Lee said, strolling over casually.

"I ain't nobody but," Elvis answered, smiling.

"Well, I'm Jerry Lee Lewis. I'm playin' piano with Carl today. I play on everybody's records down here at Sun. Man, I didn't know you could play."

"Aw, I can't," Elvis said sheepishly as he noodled a melody.

"Well, then, why don't you let me sit down?"

Elvis looked up at Jerry Lee and laughed softly. "Well, I'd like to try," he said, as he continued playing.

"So Jerry didn't sit down then, but he smarted off to Elvis," notes Carl. "He wanted to show Elvis what he could do. Right off, Elvis didn't really go for him. Elvis was a humble guy, raised that way, and when he was cocky he didn't mean to be. He wasn't cocky with his mouth. He was cocky with his hips and his legs and his moves. But it was 'Yes sir,' and 'No, ma'm,' and 'Thank you, ma'm.' And he wasn't hateful with waitresses, which rockabillies and rock 'n' roll people make me sick doing. And Jerry Lee would be. There's a way to get anything done, and there's that smart-aleck way, and that was Jerry. And it was so natural to him to be that way that people just accepted it. That's the way he was. But Elvis didn't have to accept it, so he just put him in the file of being a smart aleck and stayed away from him. I did hear him brag on [Jerry Lee's] piano playing to him. I heard him say, 'Boy, you can play. I heard you playing. It was great.' Jerry Lee said, 'You ain't heard nothin' yet.'"

As Elvis played and Carl strummed along on guitar, Sam came out and said he'd like Elvis to hear what Carl had recorded earlier in the day. Elvis listened to "Matchbox" and declared it a "killer" track; the harmony singing on "Your True Love" impressed him. "Man, who's doin' them voices?" he asked Carl. Told it was Jay and Clayton, he said, "God, them boys can sing! Carl, you got you some killers comin'!"

With that, Elvis returned to the piano. As he and Carl harmonized on a gospel song, Sam told engineer Jack Clement to start a tape rolling—"We may never have these people together again." Through the late afternoon and early evening others came and went—Charles Underwood, a writer for Sam's publishing company, was present at the outset and stayed for the duration; Sun artist Smokey Joe Baugh stopped by briefly in the afternoon and teamed with Carl on rhythm guitar for a few songs; Jay, Clayton, and Fluke played on some songs before the tape started rolling, then left the studio, either to get food or to take Buck home (on the tape someone asks, 'They went with Clayton?"); Marilyn perched herself seductively on the top of the piano while Elvis played, and occasionally pitched in on harmony vocals.

The core and the focus, however, remained Presley, Perkins, and Lewis; Johnny Cash had dropped by before Elvis's appearance and stayed long enough to sing with Carl and Elvis on "Blueberry Hill" and "Isle of Golden Dreams" before the recording began. His presence was brief because he had to leave shortly after Elvis arrived, to go pick up his wife Vivian when she left work. Knowing Cash was preparing to take off, Sam called the *Press-Scimitar*'s Robert Johnson with news of the goings-on at Sun. Johnson arrived with a photographer, who snapped Elvis sitting at the piano, Carl behind him on acoustic guitar, and Jerry Lee and Cash flanking them. In his next day's story, Johnson referred to the artists as the Million Dollar Quartet.

For the near-seventy minutes recorded that day, the quartet ranged far and wide. On the tape they are loose and relaxed, out of the spotlight and simply enjoying each other's company, lending credence to Carl's assertion of there being a strong, unyielding bond among this most individual group of first-generation rock 'n' roll artists. Even newcomer Jerry Lee, born of similar roughneck stock as the others, makes an immediate connection with the more experienced hands and is treated as an equal. By any reasonable standard the music these men made together on December 4 reflects nothing so much as their deep immersion in matters spiritual and in songs reflective of their rural background and values.

In their song selection they moved through about thirty years of American music history. Gospel figured most heavily in the repertoire. "I Shall Not Be Moved" was done at a stomping pace; "Down by the Riverside," one of the songs that helped get Carl through the cotton fields, was energized by his tasty electric guitar solo; as Carl and Jerry Lee echoed Elvis in "As We Travel on the Jericho Road," Elvis stopped and said, "Takes young Johnny Cash to do this." Elvis tried out Thomas A. Dorsey's "Peace in the Valley," which he would record at RCA for an extended-play album the following spring.

The gospel road took them into Bill Monroe country. Elvis did his high lonesome Monroe voice on "Little Cabin Home on the Hill," sounding much as he did on his Sun recordings and phrasing in Monroe's style; he sang Monroe's "Summertime Is Past and Gone" straight, then had Carl supply high harmony to the plaintive "Sweetheart You Done Me Wrong." Carl has praised Elvis as a first-rate mimic, and this talent was on fleeting display not only in "Little Cabin on the Hill," but also in Ernest Tubb's "I'm With a Crowd But So Alone."

Carl jumped in with a stunning version of Wynn Stewart's country hit "Keeper of the Key," accompanying himself on acoustic guitar, with Elvis and Jerry Lee harmonizing. At the end, as Carl's and Elvis's voices rose sweet and high, Jerry Lee blurted out, "Yeah, that's the way I done it on a piano awhile ago. That's the way I done it on a piano."

Carl remarked: "Boy, that's a beautiful song. Wynn Stewart. I'm gonna cut that record."

Jerry Lee started Chuck Berry's "School Day" and sent Carl into a rapturous account of his high regard for "Brown-Eyed Handsome Man."

"You oughta hear some of his stuff settin' around," Carl told the others. "I just come off a tour with this guy, Chuck Berry. Man, he sat down behind the stage and just, ah, I—" and the tape ran out.

During his stopover in Vegas, Elvis had gone to see Billy Ward's Dominoes, one of the pioneer R&B groups. He came away talking up the lead singer, who had performed some of Elvis's songs in his show, including "Hound Dog" and "Don't Be Cruel." Recalling the singer's performance, Elvis said: "He was trying so hard and he got so much better, much better than that record of mine. He had it a little slower than me. He was real slender, he was a colored guy." He began imitating the singer's stilted phrasing on a slow, bluesy reading of "Don't Be Cruel," singing, "At least please telly-phone" at the end of the first verse.

"He was just a member of Ward's Dominoes," Elvis said. "He'd already done 'Hound Dog' and another one too and he didn't do too well. He was trying too hard. But he done that 'Don't Be Cruel' and he was trying so hard. But he got better, boy. Whoo! Man, he sung that song! That chorus just stand in the background, you know—*ba-dop-ba-dop /ba-dop-ba-dop*—and he was out there cuttin' it, man, and I was goin' way up in the air! Boy, he sung the hell out of it, man. I went back four nights straight, man. I went back four nights and heard that guy do that. He'd soften up—" and Elvis sang a verse in a lighter voice, then rose up and up on "hmmmmmm" before the second verse.

On January 6 Elvis would make his final appearance on *The Ed Sullivan Show* and sing "Don't Be Cruel" in much the same way he had heard it sung by Jackie Wilson, then lead singer of Billy Ward's Dominoes (having replaced Clyde McPhatter, who left to found the Drifters), who would soon go solo and become one of the most important singers and performers of his generation: "Elvis was affected by Wilson," says Carl. "Wilson had some slick moves. Wilson was as authentic as a man could be. And Elvis liked that high stuff he did. Elvis also liked Bill Monroe; he *loved* Dean Martin. He even said later on he liked Mario Lanza. He liked a lot of different people and incorporated them in his voice. [But] the old Sun Elvis was rockabilly and a little Bill Monroe bluegrassy—that whang. He knocked all that off there."

Jerry Lee finally took over the piano when Carl and Elvis went into the control room, and proceeded to do a three-minutes-plus version of "Crazy Arms," the longest song of the day, and followed it with a bluesy country torch number, "That's My Desire"; the B side of "Crazy Arms," his self-penned "End of the Road"; a lively taste of Jelly Roll Morton's "Black Bottom Stomp"; and closed the session out with an uptempo version of Gene Autry's "You're the Only Star in My Blue Heaven."

As Jerry Lee hit the final glissando on the Autry song, Elvis prepared to leave. It was nearly eight o'clock, Carl recalls, and Elvis told him that his female companion was hungry. He referred to her as his "house guest," an exalted rank, as Carl recalls: "People like Natalie Wood come home with him as house guests. Lot of pretty Hollywood girls. He had a lot of pretty 'house guests.'"

Carl was not so far removed from his red-dog days that he couldn't appreciate a good euphemism, particularly when he knew Elvis had a different girlfriend for every season and "his seasons were short."

"Good luck, boy," Elvis said on his way out. "See you again, y' hear? Jerry, glad to have met you."

"Glad to have met y'all," Jerry said sincerely. "I got to go myself."

"Come out," Elvis said to Carl.

"Okay," Carl replied.

"Whenever you're ready," Elvis added.

"Okay, I might come out," Carl answered.

Before the tape rolled, Elvis had talked to Carl about his unsuccessful appearance in Las Vegas the previous spring. In April he and the band had appeared for two weeks at the New Frontier, playing in a lounge in the casino area, with comedian Shecky Greene. Elvis had bombed.

"We shouldn't have been booked in there," Scotty Moore says of Elvis's ill-fated Vegas stand. "I blame [Col. Tom] Parker for that. As smart as the guy was he should've been able to figure that out. Those people are in there eatin' like we sit now and eat with the television on. They were anxious to get back to gambling. I never did consider that a failure; it was a mistake."

Elvis didn't leave Vegas humiliated or humbled; he left mad. "About this Las Vegas thing, I wanna tell you about it, Carl. I'm gonna play it again," Elvis asserted. As he talked he held one hand out and pointed with his pinky finger, an odd gesture Carl had seen only Elvis use. Even onstage, he would point with the pinky and make the girls scream.

"My fans can't get in back there," he explained of his poor showing. "You gotta be eighteen. And Shecky Greene's not funny. Carl, y-y-y-you don't wanna fool with that place out there. They ain't no good. People eatin', drinkin', they don't show their appreciation, man. I don't care about that place. It's dead, it's hot, it's terrible, man. Ain't nothin' to do, nothin' but sand. It's pretty at night. But it ain't nothin' in the daytime."

He paused and played a soft melody on the piano. "Let me tell you something," he said, again pointing the pinky at Carl. "When I go back, they'll be screaming for me, and I'll be the highest paid guy that ever played there."

"Man, they pay Sinatra lots of money," Carl noted.

"I know. I know," Elvis nodded. "But when I go back, they'll give me more money than they ever paid anybody."

Fifteen years later, Elvis was true to his word.

The downside of the Million Dollar Quartet event was that it brought a halt to what Carl thought was shaping up to be his best session at Sun. Carl's memory, and the session records, are spotty as to the exact dates of the January sessions, but there were probably two, one of the all-day variety, the other a short one yielding only a song or two.

As he had vowed, Carl recorded Wynn Stewart's "Keeper of the Key," cutting a slower, more traditional country version than what he had sung with the Million Dollar Quartet, complete with a melodramatic recitation midway through the song, inspired by the religious recitations that were part of Red Foley's repertoire. Apart from Carl's strong vocal performance, though, there was nothing to separate the cover version from most of the weepy country fare on the market. The looser, more spirited Million Dollar Quartet rendition was the better of the two, even in its truncated form. A more interesting cover version Carl cut was of Chuck Berry's "Roll Over, Beethoven," goosed along by Jerry Lee's bracing piano support and Carl's variations on the Chuck Berry guitar stylings as played the Perkins way, combining single-string and triple-string solos.

The number of covers creeping into Carl's session has puzzled Perkins researchers through the years, some suggesting Sam might have been trying to find material that would be a better commercial balance to the raw force of Carl's self-penned songs. In fact, Carl enjoyed recording other writers' songs that were favorites of his. "Sweethearts or Strangers," by Governor Jimmie Davis, had been part of the Perkins Brothers' tonk sets for years by the time Carl cut an inspired rockabilly version of it in January '57, his razor-sharp solos answered by Jerry Lee's in-your-face riffing. Two takes were cut, the second being in-the-pocket country, but both were powered by Carl's loose, spirited vocal performances, ranking with his best. With his voice heavily echoed, Carl delivered an urgent reading of "Be Honest With Me," a song written by Fred Rose and originally cut by Gene Autry. In Carl's rockabilly version, key changes are employed throughout to heighten the mood, and Clayton keeps the momentum going with his walking bass lines. Trying out "Caldonia," a 1945 hit for Louis Jordan, Carl, who had been performing the song in tonks, screamed and hollered his way through a rhythm raveup, as Clayton and Fluke pushed the song forward and Jerry Lee darted in and out with glissandos and boogie-woogie lines.

On two new takes of "Put Your Cat Clothes On," Carl and Jerry Lee demonstrated the remarkable chemistry between them as musicians. Even though Carl had cut two fine versions of the song the previous March, Sam thought Jerry Lee's presence should generate some special sparks, and he was right. Carl delivered another top-notch vocal, the rhythm section kicked in mightily, and on each of the new takes Carl's sputtering, white-hot guitar solos were answered in force when he screamed "Rock it!" at Jerry Lee and sat back as the piano man worked the keyboard its full length, right to left, and punctuated each hand's soloing with emphatic glissandos. It was a battle royal between two stone rockabillies, neither one bowing to the other, Jerry Lee exacting retribution for the solo he had been denied in "Matchbox," Carl countering with a hailstorm of double and single notes up and down the neck.

In the early morning hours, under the influence of Early Times, Carl cut his most exotic Sun track, "Her Love Rubbed Off." Exhausted and irritable, he growled at the end of Take 1, "Let's get this son of a bitch finished! If I can get that damned key, we can get it!"

He got it, and it was stunning, industrial-strength rockabilly. Minor key verses dissolved into major key choruses; Carl's guitar solos were

jagged, trembling, dark, angry, threatening; Fluke layed down a double-time shuffle beat; and Clayton, using an electric pickup on the bass,
stalked along furtively, enhancing the song's menacing air. Carl's vocal
was a performance in the truest sense—calm and measured, betraying
only a hint of excited anticipation as he set the scene; brooding and frustrated in the chorus; swinging and swaggering in describing himself,
bemused and perplexed in bemoaning his woman's flighty behavior.

> Well I'm strollin' 'long in a city park
> Grabbed my baby, sittin' in the dark
> Took my lovin' baby by the hand
> I let her know that I'm a lovin' man
>
> (chorus:) That lover rubbed off on me
> That baby wouldn't LET ME BE!
> That baby took me by the hand
> That woman took me, lovin' man,
> That woman wouldn't let me know
> That baby hollered 'Go, go, go!'
> Oh-ho
>
> Well I'm a hot-rod fiend for fancy cars
> Drive-in movies and caviar
> Big sport coats and a lotta things
> Lotta lovin' and a diamond ring
>
> (chorus:) That lovin' rubbed off on me
> That baby wouldn't LET ME BE!
> That woman wouldn't tell me no
> That woman wouldn't LET ME GO!
> That woman wouldn't let me be
> That lover rubbed off on me
> Well, I'm a happy man, I'm so in love
> Get my strength from the man above
> He's the one that teach me how to give
> Learned me how to love and live

(chorus:) That lover rubbed off on me

That baby wouldn't LET ME BE!

That lover wouldn't let me go

That baby hollered no, no, no

That baby wouldn't let me stand

She took away all I had

That woman wouldn't let me see

That baby . . . (fades out)

This uncommon manic-depressive narrative line, notably innovative in the way the story is developed more in the choruses than in the verses, had no parallel in Carl's previous work. Even the seemingly incongruous reference to "the man above" makes sense if the song is seen as a metaphorical journey through a life sustained by faith in God's blueprint and a woman's love. If "Dixie Fried" was rockabilly's most powerful moment, "Her Love Rubbed Off" was its most surreal. Even Carl's guitar work seemed to have come from a dark place in his soul, with notes bending and moaning, then erupting in sharp, angular bursts of violent emotion. Heavy on the tremelo and the treble, its sound was ahead of its time. Link Wray and Duane Eddy were still a year away from appearing on record with individual guitar styles that could have been linked to "Her Love Rubbed Off," had it been issued. Even surf guitar would have owed a debt to Carl Perkins if Sam Phillips had seen fit to release this oddity. Instead, it remained in the can, deemed to have little commercial appeal. To Carl the song sounded "strange": "I should have been drug out onto Union Avenue and whipped by my daddy with that same belt he wore me out with in Lake County, then sent home till I got right. It's crazy, man. It sounds like a bunch of drug addicts so high they don't know where they're at . . . Well, we were pretty high. I remember that session. I slept on the studio floor that night."

Late January saw the single release of "Your True Love" backed with "Matchbox," Sam opting for the softer pop-country of the former as the A side over the rockabilly fireworks Carl and Jerry Lee had supplied on the latter. Reviewed in the February 16 issue of *Billboard*, the favorable critique described "Your True Love" as "a swingy blues with an attractive off-beat quality and interesting backing by a youthful sounding vocal chorus," while "Matchbox" was trumpeted as "a driving blues, featuring Sun's familiar sound with heavy emphasis on the beat." *Billboard* concluded: "Both sides should grab off plenty of attention in the field. 'Your True Love' is also a possibility for the pop market, à la Perkins' big hit, 'Blue Suede Shoes.' "

"Your True Love" made a strong showing on the country chart, rising to number thirteen, and topped out at sixty-seven on the pop chart. For Carl, it was a minor but hollow success. Sam had speeded up the tape in mastering, raising the timbre of the singing voices so much they could have been mistaken for teenagers—hence *Billboard*'s description of the backing vocals as "youthful sounding." Contrary to the review's prediction, "Matchbox" gained no attention at all in the field, any field.

As he had in acquiescing to Sam in the Denny matter, Carl accepted Sam's decisions with regard to his single releases. Sam was supposed to be the authority on the marketplace; Carl was trying to keep his head above the water of rock 'n' roll's rapid current. He had all he could handle in being a dutiful father and husband, and in being the mealticket for his band. Lacking any kind of business sense, however, he relied on Sam's expertise to steer his career in the proper directions. Childhood lessons continued to guide his conduct: He respected authority and followed orders to the letter. He never had a problem being tough and uncompromising when it came to defending his family's interests, only his own.

It is one of show business's oldest and saddest tales, that of the unsophisticated, unassertive, unlettered artist taken advantage of by savvy, duplicitous businesspeople who enrich themselves at their charge's expense. Carl was hardly the first whose gratitude blindered him to the fine print of his career. When Sam's conduct and methods appeared questionable, he could always find an explanation to support his faith in the man who had believed in his music when other record companies had rejected him. If the "Blue Suede Shoes" accounting was short, Carl was sure more payments were on the way (his publishing contract gave him the right to hire a certified public accountant "for the purpose of verifying royalty statements rendered or which are delinquent under the terms hereof," but he had not read the contract); if Carl was slotted in as Sam's country act in 1954, even though he had been doing Elvis's style of music years ahead of Elvis, Carl willingly became a traditional country artist for the purpose of getting on record; if his best studio work remained unreleased, or was released as the B side of a single, well, Sam knew what he was doing: "my job is to go play the hell out of this record on the road and get some people interested in it." With each excuse, Carl's personality as a recording artist became more schizophrenic. Was he a country singer? A rock 'n' roller? With "Your True Love" in its speeded-up form, was he trying to move into the pop market?

Carl believed he could do it all, and he was trying to accommodate Sam's sense of the marketplace. Ultimately, though, he was losing his foothold on rock 'n' roll radio, as the complete wipeout of "Matchbox" indicated. To listen to Carl Perkins's music was to hear an artist traversing the increasingly disparate universes of country and of rock 'n' roll without ever landing firmly in either one. He was as rhythm-bound as any rock 'n' roller, but his best writing was so explicitly personal and so rural in detail that it belonged in the country ranks. But now, even country was changing—Eddy Arnold had pointed the way to pop success, but in 1957 Jim Reeves, whose early hits were uptempo country songs, introduced an even lusher country-pop sound in "Four Walls," which nearly made it to the pop chart's top 10. Who was Carl Perkins, circa March 1957? No one seemed sure. Least of all Carl himself.

Nevertheless, as a performing artist he remained in demand, almost solely on the basis of "Blue Suede Shoes" 's enduring popularity. He wasn't making $1,000 a day anymore, but he rarely made less than $500 per show, and often saw $750 paydays. Even as his lagging record sales nagged at his conscience and pride, he was still seeing hundreds, thousands of happy teenagers enjoying his music. With this, he convinced himself everything would work out for the best in time and did nothing more than to keep pace with his demanding tour schedule.

Jerry Lee remained true to form when he joined Carl and Cash on the road in early '57. On the day they were to leave Memphis, he and his band—bassist J.W. Brown and guitarist Roland Janes—pulled up at Sun thirty minutes after the scheduled departure time. Carl, for whom tardiness was inexcusable, was fuming. He was getting ready to take off without the others.

"How do y'all think we'd of found our way down there if you'd left?" an irritated Jerry Lee asked.

"Get you a damn road map like we got," an equally irritated Carl answered. So it began.

Some two hours out of Memphis, on their way to Birmingham, the troupe stopped for gas. Jerry Lee, climbing out of his Ford for a stretch, circled Carl's Cadillac, studying every feature. "I'm gonna get me one of them," he said.

"Yeah, that's the thing to have, boy. Go get you one," Carl said. "In fact, you oughta stop and get one after while."

"I could if I wanted to," Jerry Lee insisted. (Says Carl: "He probably had thirty cents in his damn pocket.")

Before they left, Carl told Jay he wanted to ride with Jerry Lee. "I believe I'll see if I can get to know him."

Jerry Lee was happy to have Carl's company, and suggested he bring his guitar along.

"Naw, naw, I don't wanna play," Carl said, depositing himself in the back seat next to Jerry Lee. "Let's look at this pretty country down here." For the next few minutes the two artists sat there, Carl recalls, "Just chit-chattin' about a little of nothing. I was kinda feelin' him out; wanted to know what made him how he was, find out how many brothers and sisters he had, and what caused this boy to be so cocky."

Carl, in a passing comment, said, "Well, you know the Bible says we'll get weaker and wiser."

Jerry Lee shot to attention. *"What!?"*

"The Bible says we'll grow weaker and wiser," Carl repeated.

"Where you hear that!?" Jerry Lee demanded. Carl could see his eyes jumping, flashing angrily at him.

Carl shrugged. "I don't know."

"That ain't in the Bible."

"It ain't?"

"Hell no, it ain't!"

"Well, excuse me," Carl said, backing off. "I was just quotin' something I had heard my ol' grandma say many times."

"Well, you tell your ol' grandma she's a damn liar. It ain't in there." Jerry Lee sat back in the seat and would have bored a hole through Carl with his white-hot stare if Carl hadn't been riveting him in place with one of his own.

"Wait just a damn minute here!" Carl steeled himself for a fight. "You're gettin' a little *stout*. That's a little strong. I won't tell my grandma that she lied, 'cause I think if there's a lie being told, *you're* tellin' it." Carl was "ready to choke his damn head. I was raised that when somebody hurts your feelings and he does it in a smart way, pop him. Or get away from him. Well, I'm sittin' in the damn car! I can't get away."

Telling Jerry Lee to change the subject, Carl apologized for mentioning the Bible and admitted his own knowledge of the good book was slight. Then he added: "And you don't know near as much as you're trying to make me think you do. I don't care what you know. I don't *need* to know your opinion about things. That ain't gonna help me a damn bit, and it ain't gonna help you to express 'em, 'cause I ain't listenin' to 'em. I don't give a damn."

Neither man could let it go. When Jerry Lee came back with what Carl perceived to be another smart remark, Carl ordered J.W. Brown, who was driving, to pull the car over.

"Listen, you son of a bitch," Carl growled at Jerry Lee, "if you got any guts, get out here in this gravel and let's get this damn thing over with. I ain't puttin' up with your mouth. I'm gonna warn you right now, I'm gonna knock that damn jaw of yours loose."

"I'll damn sure be out there," Jerry Lee promised.

As soon as Jerry Lee emerged from the car, Carl grabbed his shirt and faced him nose to nose. "First of all, I'll choke your damn head off," Carl said. "Take back what you said about my grandma!"

"I ain't takin' it back!" Jerry Lee sputtered, struggling to free himself.

Jay, Clayton, and Fluke pulled in behind Jerry Lee's car. Jay jumped out and sprinted to Carl's side. Shouting, "What's goin' on here!" he pulled his brother away as he pushed Jerry Lee, who lost his balance and righted himself seconds before he would have fallen into a nearby ditch.

"Ah, that crazy bastard," Carl said as he straightened his shirt. "He ain't got no sense, man. Let's go." To J.W. he said, "Y'all find your way the best way you can." When he returned to the Cadillac, he ordered Jay to "outrun 'em, lose 'em." Jay sped off and was soon beyond Jerry Lee's sight.

Over time, Carl found Jerry Lee more bluster than action, then and in later years as the latter's fame and infamy grew: "He will try you if you're a rank stranger, but unless he's got the upper hand, he'll cool down. He has a knack of knowing who's around that's gonna stop it when he bellows. I would say you could search the history of rock 'n' roll and you wouldn't find where Jerry Lee stood toe to toe and fought. That's smart, 'cause he don't have no scars on him. I'm not saying he's wrong for that. And I'm not saying he's wrong for being like he is. It just don't work with a Lake County fella who was at the bottom of the totem pole all those years. I wasn't gonna take nothing off of him."

Anyway, Carl had all he could handle on the road with Cash continuing to inspire Clayton to ever greater heights of chicanery. An otherwise unremarkable date in Omaha, Nebraska, entered into legend when Cash and Clayton came back from a sightseeing trip with two hundred baby chicks, which they loosed throughout the hotel. At another stop, disgusted by the color of their rooms, they spent the early morning hours changing the color scheme from peach to solid black. In some cities hotel guests awoke to find themselves imprisoned in their rooms after Clayton had tied adjoining doorknobs together with a length of rope.

Even Cash was fair game. Seeing his friend pull up in a new Lincoln, Clayton walked over, tore off the driver's side rear-view mirror and handed it to Cash. "Here's your mirror, John," Clayton said solemnly as Cash doubled over in laughter. Cash later pulled the same prank on Carl, only to have Carl chastise him with a severe, "John, that's not funny. You messed up my car." Cash stood mute, looking like a baby who'd had his candy taken away from him.

It fell to Jay and Carl to smooth over the problems Clayton and Cash left behind. Carl felt their conduct reflected poorly on everyone, but especially on himself, being the headliner. Cash would shrug off the more destructive episodes—like the room painting—saying he would pay for any damages; the man would do anything for a laugh.

Clayton was less of a problem to Carl when he was carrying on with Cash, but the brothers' relationship had little of the warmth of Carl and Jay's. The youngest Perkins brother was too much the loose cannon, drinking inordinate amounts of alcohol, smarting off and always looking for a fight in return. Sometimes in the car he would pick an argument with Carl over the most inconsequential comments or issues; Carl would try to reason with Clayton as he drove, only to be rocked in mid-sentence by the young tush hog (who always shared the Cadillac's rear seat with Fluke) popping him on the back of his head. Angered to the boiling point, Carl would then pull off the road and start slugging it out with Clayton, while Jay tried to play peacemaker. Jay had a calming effect on Clayton, according to Carl, because he knew from personal experience that when Jay hit you, you stayed down.

Since returning to the lineup, though, Jay had not been himself. Never loud or assertive, he nonetheless had always been one of the boys, enjoying a good drink without going overboard, telling a story or joke with the best of them, and laughing as hard as anyone at Clayton and Cash's outlandish shenanigans. Onstage and in the studio, he was solid and serious, the quintessential rockabilly rhythm guitar picker. But after the accident he had been plagued by frequent, recurring headaches. He found it more difficult to get in the spirit of things when the horseplay began; in the car he slept more and laughed less. He was consuming aspirin at an alarming rate, taking four or five at a pop, several times a day. He shrugged off his maladies as passing annoyances, nothing to worry about. But Carl, so dependent on his older brother, worried about the change. Something was not right, and Carl soon found himself unable to look at Jay without feeling uneasy.

By contrast, Jay's aspirin habit was small potatoes compared to what was going on in Cash's corner. On some of their stops, Cash would purchase his own box of St. Joseph's, consume its entire contents, and wash it down with a Coke. To Carl's warning that he was going to blow off the top of his head, Cash would reply, with a blissful smile on his face, "Naw, man, it's alriiiight, make you feel pretty good."

Aspirin was a minor vice, though; while on tour with some Grand

Ole Opry artists, Cash had been introduced to amphetamines, "speed," by a friend who worked for Faron Young. On the road he seemed to have an endless supply of pills of every color; he took them before shows, during long drives, any time he needed to get pepped up. On a car trip to California, he gave Carl a large black pill, a "West Coast turnaround" Cash called it, explaining how it was reputed to keep the user awake and alert for the duration of a round trip from the midwest to the western United States. Carl, whose mainstays were Early Times and cigarettes, remembers being awake for at least two and possibly four consecutive days after popping the black pill, then crashing hard. Awakening with a splitting headache, he swore off speed forever and stuck to the bottle.

While drinking and drugging, Carl and Cash came up with another song, one of the quickest Carl ever wrote or had a hand in writing. It started with a line Carl improvised while sitting in the back seat of the Cadillac with Cash. With guitar in hand, he hit a rapid series of chords, then stopped and sang:

> I get off at four o'clock
> Just a little before dark
> Standin' on my steps at
> Four-thirty-five sharp

"You got a song goin' there," Cash said. "But you gotta have—" and hummed a bright melody. "That's the melody for it right there. Just hit that lick."

Doon-da-do-down-do. They started trading verses, Cash printing every word on a scrap of paper.

> Lucy, gal, you better get decked out

he sang, and Carl rejoined with:

> Tell ol' lover boy he can get checked out!

"Yeah!" Cash laughed as he wrote. The tag line for each verse was the phrase "That's right!" sung high and emphatically. In its final form,

"That's Right" was another dark, backwoods tale of betrayal and revenge, but one driven by a cheery melody and a gently stomping rhythm. Carl's vocal was wry and knowing—the song is a satiric take on the red dog's visceral response to presumed infidelity: Not only will he inflict pain on his woman's lover, but he will turn around and prove he has no equal in the sack, so she knows what she's been missing (there's a suggestion as well that he's going to take out some of his anger on the woman).

Carl came off the road in late March for another session at Sun, and cut two takes of "That's Right," the first being the more assured. Only minor lyric changes were made from the version Carl and Cash wrote in the car, most significant among them being the time of Carl's arrival home. Also new at the end of Take 1 was the spoken-word wisdom, so nonsensical it made perfect, brilliant sense:

> I get off at four o'clock
> Just a little before dark
> Standin' on my steps at
> Four-o-five sharp
> Lucy gal you better get decked out
> Tell ol' lover boy to get CHECKED OUT!
> Cause that's right!
> Well, that's right!
>
> I got a funny feelin'
> I wanna go home
> When I get there I find you on
> On Mr. Bell Telephone
> Lotta people been tellin' me what to do
> But when it comes to lovin' gal,
> That's me and you—and that's right!
> Uh-huh, well, that's right
>
> In my vocabulary you been ratin' fine
> But it seems to me I been walkin' the line
> When it comes to lovin' I'm dumb in spots
> But I get mad, gal, I sho' get hot!
> That's right!

> If what they say is true and there is another joker
>
> Well you's a number five in this game of poker
>
> When I find the cat that's gettin' my sugar
>
> It's gonna be rough when I catch that booger
>
> That's right!
>
> Ah, ha, huh, that's right!
>
> (spoken:) You know, did you ever stop and think about, when
>
> somethin's right, it's just flat right, honey?

Carl also brought in "Forever Yours," one of the best ballads he had ever written. Another love song to Valda, its strength was Carl's pleading vocal and the heartfelt sentiment he poured into every line of his pledge of endless love in 2/4 time. It was as simple, sweet, and honest as they came in 1957:

> I'd like to go someplace
>
> Where we can be alone
>
> To hold you in my arms
>
> And call you my own
>
> I know this love of ours
>
> Will always endure
>
> And I'll forever stay
>
> Forever yours
>
> (chorus:) I die a thousand times
>
> Just to prove you're mine
>
> And just to let you know I care
>
> My life is in your hands
>
> Please, darling, understand
>
> That I'm sure I'll always be
>
> Forever yours

A tender love song, "Y.O.U.," was one of the rare Perkins songs on which an acoustic guitar was featured prominently. Take 2, the strongest of two versions cut in this session, found Carl singing in a style combining vocal techniques associated with both Hank Williams and the Platters' Tony Williams. Odder still, Jay and Clayton's backing choruses were right out of the group harmony textbook, much in the manner of the Jordanaires, who had been backing Elvis on his RCA recordings. Carl had another song in the ballad mode, again heavy on the acoustic guitar, in "I Care." Its lilting, shuffle rhythm, acoustic fills, and smooth backing choruses were reminiscent of Sonny James's chart-topping hit from January 1957, "Young Love" with a taste of Eddy Arnold's "Cattle Call" thrown in on Carl's high, yodeling vocal bridges.

During the playback of "That's Right," Elvis came by the studio. When he picked up the rhythm he began dancing across the floor, hips and shoulders shaking, hair flying, pinky finger pointed at Carl.

"What a beat!" he cried out. "That's a Perkins song there!"

"Sure is," Carl acknowledged.

"Perkins, good gracious! Mr. Phillips, play that again!"

"I've got a cut on this one, Elvis," Sam said. "Come on back here."

As they listened to the second take, Elvis began shaking his head left and right. "Mmm-mmm-mmm. I'd kill for that song!"

Sam boxed the tape and the three of them headed out to Elvis's Cadillac to drive to WHBQ. When the trio walked into the studio at the Chicsa Hotel, Dewey Phillips broke into the record he was playing and announced: "Somebody lock the door! Don't let 'em out! Got 'em both down here, burnin' them jukeboxes up with songs like—" and he had "Hound Dog" cued up and ready to rip. As it played, Sam handed the tape to Dewey and said, "I think this is the one of the best records that will ever come out of Sun."

"Well, I'll tell you what," Dewey said when he came back on the air. "Elvis told me a minute ago this new song's gonna be a smash hit. Elvis, you tell 'em about this song."

Elvis moved close to the mic. "Well, ladies and gentlemen, if this ain't gonna be a hit record I'm gonna be fooled. I-I-I-I-it's really got a different beat and all I know is the name of it's 'That's Right.' Here's Carl Perkins." After the first airplay, Dewey interviewed Carl and Elvis on the air, and devoted a good portion of his show to their music, coming back frequently to ask them questions.

When they left the station, Elvis, Carl, and Sam found the street mobbed with teenagers who had been listening to Phillips's show. They ran for the car and drove back to Sun, where more cars and teenagers were lined up. "Boys, I gotta go," Elvis said, declining Sam's invitation to come in. Carl and Sam made their way through the crowd as Elvis sped off into the night, a line of hot rods following behind him.

Once again Carl had a heavy touring schedule ahead of him almost immediately following these sessions. He had barely had time to decompress after the previous trip, it seemed, before Valda was washing and ironing his stage clothes and helping him pack again. Jay was starting to bristle over the constant touring too, at one point pleading with Carl to tone it down.

"Man, I want to stay home some," he said. "Really want to stay home. Carl, you're the boss. Tell 'em. Tell 'em."

▶ THE VOICE OF CARL PERKINS

Life was very good and very exciting, but empty in a way. 'Cause I wasn't home enough. I had three children, and I wasn't there. And my woman was raising 'em. And they'd look at me strange when I'd go in the house—"Oh, that's Daddy. That's who I talk to on the telephone." And I felt very dirty, very guilty. I was having to split Carl Perkins and take him away from them and leave part of my soul at home.

How can you feel like a good father? I wasn't there to take 'em fishing. I wasn't there to teach 'em how to ride bikes. I bought the best bikes money could buy, but they'd run into trees and skin their knees, and I wasn't there to catch 'em when they fell and their mama wasn't strong enough. They needed me. And I needed to back off and say, Wait a minute. I'm gonna give this music business half of my life. It's too late when a boy's ten to wish he was five.

I've spent many lonely nights. If I hadn't went ahead after I talked to Valda and got pretty drunk, I'd probably have got on an airplane and come home. I was toying with it very very much. I'd come home and I'd hold her for five minutes in my arms at the back door. I'd say, "This is it." I said it every time I come back. I said, "Let me get out of next month's contracts. I ain't leavin'." 'Cause I really loved my wife and kids. But the music and the promoters and the people pulled me away. I didn't enjoy it like Elvis and the single boys. And I was feeding my sorrow by drinking.

Carl and Cash helped effect a startling transformation in Jerry Lee Lewis when they got back on the road together following the "That's Right" session. Carl remembers the troupe being in Canada when it happened. It was early 1957 and when the moment had passed Jerry Lee was a changed man, ready to ride to stardom on the crest of his new single's burgeoning popularity.

As much as Carl and Cash admired Jerry Lee's playing and singing, they saw that as an opening act, he wasn't getting the crowd worked up. The arrogance and seeming self-confidence he displayed offstage weren't translating into dynamic live performances; in fact, he was as riddled with stagefright as Elvis, Carl, Cash, all of them. But where they fought it and used it to their advantage, Jerry Lee gave in to it. He angled his piano in such a way that the audience had a better view of his back than they did his face.

On this particular night, the three were booked to do two shows in one evening. Jerry Lee was moping around backstage after his opening set. Questioned by Carl as to why he seemed so low, he replied that his show wasn't "right." He didn't have a chance, he groused. "Elvis goes out there with a guitar, he can move and go; you can jump around; Johnny Cash can spin around, throw that guitar behind him. I can't pick up that damn piano. I can't do nothing with what I play."

Carl thought for a second. "Well, have you ever tried standin' up and playin' the damn thing?" he asked. "Can you do that?"

"I can play the piano, man. Ain't no man on the face of the earth can beat me at it. I can play it layin' on top of it!"

Carl laughed. "Well, you oughta crawl on top of it and play it. That'd be very unusual."

"That'd be somethin'," Cash added, laughing at the image. "You mean you can play it like this?" He raised a booted foot and moved the toe up and down, as if he were tapping on something.

"Hell yeah!" Jerry Lee exclaimed. "I can play the sumbitch with *my feet* better than most people can play it with their hands!"

"I believe that," Carl said. "I believe every word you're sayin'. Now just prove that to them. If you can stand up when you start singin' 'Shake, baby, shake,' then stand up!"

Carl and Cash stood together in the wings watching Jerry Lee's next set. He did a good version of his own "End of the Road," a couple of other songs, as Carl recalls, a strong take on "Crazy Arms," then started pumping out the intro to his new single, "Whole Lotta Shakin' Goin' On." As Carl watched, he knew instantly that nothing would ever be the same: "I told him the wrong thing to do, 'cause when he started to get up, he turned his piano stool over. That wooden piano stool hittin' on that ol' stage popped, and he'd done gone into that, 'I say shake, baby, shake,' and he just started slingin' his head. I told John, 'He's goin' crazy as hell,' and the audience *went wild!* And that pretty hair that he had all of a sudden looked like a mop! And when he'd sling his head they'd scream. I said, 'There it is.'"

"You may have told him the wrong damn thing," Cash said to Carl as they watched the spectacle unfolding. "You've got to follow him now."

"That's alright," Carl said. "He's doin' it. He's knockin' 'em outta their seats. Watch him. Look at him!"

As the song was playing out, Carl recalls, "[Jerry Lee]'d walk back over and kick his piano stool. He wound up and the damn piano stool's back there where we was. Every time he'd kick it he'd just go crazy. That was not Jerry Lee's act, but he quickly made it his and never stopped doing it; he went from that to throwin' piano keys out there to 'em. He'd get up on it with his feet, I've seen him kick the ivory off 'em, I've seen him turn 'em totally over. The big uprights, he'd get his knees under 'em and get 'em to rockin' and they'd be layin' on their back when he walked off the stage. And that was it! The writeup the next day, it wouldn't be 'Johnny Cash and Carl Perkins . . .' It'd say, 'Jerry Lee Lewis, who calls himself The Killer, killed a piano last night. Promoter says it wasn't worth fixing.' They wrote about it; that electricity went through the news media, man—'watch this wild man from Memphis.'"

Jerry Lee had indeed taken to referring to himself as the Killer, but it wasn't a nickname that excited the public's consciousness until his stage show took on the added flamboyance of destruction. On the road Carl and Cash tolerated him when he was obnoxious, laughed at him when he was outrageous. They never doubted his talent, but they did see a lack of self-discipline and an outsized ego they regarded as, at the very least, disruptive, and possibly dangerous.

A case in point occurred in early June at a County Fair show in Caruthersville, Missouri. Carl was headlining a bill that also featured Jerry Lee and another Sun artist, Warren Smith, whose third single, "So Long I'm Gone," was climbing regional charts neck and neck with "Whole Lotta Shakin' Goin' On," although neither song was doing much on a national level. Posters announcing the show had Carl's name at the top, Smith's below his, and below Smith's, "Rockin' Sensation Jerry Lee Lewis." According to Carl, Smith took this to mean he would be appearing second on the bill, following Jerry Lee and preceding Carl.

When Carl arrived at the Fairgrounds tent that served as a dressing room, Smith told him to expect some trouble out of Jerry Lee "about who's gonna open the show.

"I ain't openin' the damn show," Smith declared. "Your name's up there first, in big letters. You're the star of the show, and I'm second on there."

Carl told Smith it was up to the promoter to decide the pecking order. He wanted to stay out of the argument, knowing Jerry Lee and having been around Smith enough to know he was "a little cocky too. His eyes were close together and he thought he was cute. He had black hair and he dyed it a little bit." Before he could leave, though, Smith called Jerry Lee into their conversation.

"Jerry, I guess you open tonight, and I close the first set," said Smith.

"HELL NO! I ain't openin' the show!" Jerry Lee exploded, his face turning crimson. "I don't open a show for *no*-body. Them days is over!"

"Well why?" Smith wondered.

" 'Cause my record is bigger than your record!"

"No, no. Mine was about number fourteen last week and yours was about seventeen."

"Next week I'm gonna be ahead of you 'cause they done checked it out!"

"But this is *this* week!" Smith pointed out. "This is now!"

Carl wanted no part of it. Spotting the promoter standing nearby, Carl interrupted him. "Look, you gotta couple damn fools on your hands. That's exactly what you've got," he said, pointing to Smith and Jerry Lee. "They ain't growed up yet. They're back there arguing."

"Are they really arguing?" the promoter asked.

Carl explained the nature of the disagreement and offered to kick off the show while the promoter sorted it out with the other two. Showtime was near. The promoter refused to allow Carl to open. "You're the star of the show. *By far.* I'll put 'em both out there together," he said.

"Well, they'll fight. That's what's gonna happen," Carl told him, adding: "*If* Jerry'll fight. And I don't know whether that other one will either. I've never seen 'em blow; I've heard 'em go with their mouths like they're goin' now."

Behind them in the tent Carl and the promoter could hear Smith and Jerry Lee in heated negotiation.

"You're not opening," the promoter emphasized to Carl. "Whatta you suggest I do?"

"Flip a damn coin—heads Jerry Lee, tails Warren," Carl said with a shrug. "And tell 'em. Let 'em puff up. If they wanna go, I'll play a little longer. I'm sorry you're having trouble outta these two bastards."

Carl was getting the band together to go on, over the promoter's objections. Smith and Jerry Lee were no longer arguing—Jerry Lee had left the tent and was sitting in his car. Smith emerged from the tent wearing his stage clothes.

"You gonna open?" Carl asked.

"Yep," Smith answered. "I'll get the sumbitch back tomorrow night."

After Carl had closed the show and everyone was preparing to hit the road to the next date, Smith cornered Carl and said, "Now I done bent as far as I'm goin' to. I'm not openin' the next show. I'm gonna split it with him. I done opened at Caruthersville, he'll open tomorrow."

Jerry Lee had other ideas. Backstage before the next evening's show, he went on at length about how well he had done in Caruthersville. "Man it worked really great," Jerry Lee said to Smith. "You see how I closed that first half?"

"I'll see how you do, because I'm gonna close it tonight," Smith responded.

Jerry Lee jumped to his feet. "No, hell no, it's gonna be just like it was! It worked perfect last night. Then Perkins comes out and closes the second half. I'm a *closer*, man, I'm not a opener."

Smith charged at Jerry Lee. As he did, Clayton and Carl leaped in between them. Carl picked up a metal folding chair and slammed it to the floor. The room grew quiet.

"Now listen. Enough is enough!" Carl shouted. "I'm gonna open this sumbitch myself because I'm ready to go home. I wanna get away from both of you damn fools! You're worryin' this promoter here and probably neither one of you will get to work for him again."

Clayton turned to Carl and said loudly, "Which one of 'em you gonna whip? I think I'll take Jerry."

With that, Jerry Lee and Smith walked off in different directions. When the promoter arrived, he directed Smith to open, and had Jerry Lee close the set. Before Carl went onstage, he was handed his night's pay in cash.

"What's this? You aren't supposed to do this, are you?" Carl asked, taken aback.

"Well, I can pay you any time I want to," the promoter told him. "You're wantin' to get on home, so I'll just pay you now and when the show's over you can take off.

"Now them other two," he added, "I don't know if I'm gonna pay 'em or not. They've caused me some difficulty. I think I'm gonna try to break those two boys from bein' stars when they ain't neither one of 'em a star."

A few days later, Smith caught up with Carl and told him he and Jerry Lee hadn't been paid for their last shows together. After learning that Carl had been paid, Smith vowed he would get his money. "I played," he said. "I opened the show."

"Good luck," Carl replied.

After a late July appearance on Steve Allen's television show, where his performance of "Whole Lotta Shakin'" was a leering, lustful display of rock 'n' roll fury—complete with the piano stool being booted

offstage only to be sent flying back across the boards by the host—
Jerry Lee's career hit high gear. The single topped the country chart,
and peaked at number three on the pop chart. Jerry Lee was a star,
and began to be treated as such, to the chagrin of those who had to
endure his boundless egocentricity while touring with the new Sun
king.

Carl's and Jerry Lee's paths crossed again in August, when Sam got
a call from the producers of *Jamboree*, a rock 'n' roll film then beginning production in New York. They wanted to feature the two Sun
artists in the cast of musical performers. Having seen a few of these
jukebox musicals, with their insipid plots and lip-synched musical in-
terludes, Carl was reluctant at first; he changed his mind when he
learned his brief appearance would merit a $1,000 payday. He had his
choice of two songs that had been demo'd in New York, "Glad All Over"
and "Great Balls of Fire," the latter written by the movie's musical director, Otis Blackwell, composer of Presley's "Don't Be Cruel." Carl
winced when Sam played the demos, which might best be described
as penthouse rockabilly: "Both of 'em was done with somebody in New
York on piano. They wasn't rockabilly. Didn't have no fire. I thought
both of 'em was junk, but I told Sam I'd take 'Glad All Over.' "

Sam had Jack Clement, who was assuming more of the producer's
functions at Sun, work with Carl on the "Glad All Over" session. In producing Cash, Clement was broadening out the sound with vocal choruses and additional instrumentation. With Carl, he did little more
than bring the rhythm section out front in the mix, romping in support of the lively lead vocal. At a shade over a minute and a half, it was
one of the shortest songs Carl had ever cut, and featured his guitar in
only one perfunctory solo. Still, as nothing more than a pop confection with a rockabilly swing, "Glad All Over" got the job done.

Jerry Lee's "Great Balls of Fire," on the other hand, captured in its
studio version every bit of the unharnessed energy of the Killer's live
performances. Neither pop confection nor counterfeit rockabilly, it
was Lewis at the boiling point, hollering "Goodness gracious, great
balls of fire!" in a voice that rose from a clear tenor to an orgasmic
falsetto shriek in a dramatic stop-time measure. Squeezing and com-
pressing the lyrics to create tension and release, Jerry Lee employed

every vocal trick at his command, from suggestive whispers to wanton howls, punctuating these with frequent glissando runs, mixed crisp and clean to underscore the singer's erotic anxiety.

Released in November concurrently with the movie, the singles took dramatically different courses. Carl's "Glad All Over" was paired with another cover, "Lend Me Your Comb," and sank without fanfare. "Great Balls of Fire" (with the artist identification reading "Jerry Lee Lewis and His Pumping Piano") topped many regional charts, and had a four-week stay at number two on the national charts before dropping slowly. Along the way Jerry Lee became the highest profile rock 'n' roller in America, save for Elvis.

"Glad All Over" was the beginning of the end for Carl at Sun. As far as he was concerned, Sam was expending too much effort on Jerry Lee and too little on his troubled career at a time when he needed support and encouragement. Cash felt likewise, despite having had more recent success than Carl. In August, when both artists were in California for a series of shows, they were approached by Don Law, one of the Nashville music industry's most important executives as the head of Columbia Records's country A&R (Artists & Repertoire) division.

Four years prior to meeting Carl and Cash, the British-born Law had taken over all of Columbia's country recording, which he had been sharing with his mentor, Art Satherly, following the latter's retirement in 1953. Like Satherly, Law loved traditional music. Hence his interest in the two country-born and -bred Sun artists he was pursuing.

Law offered Carl and Cash recording deals that would commence with the expiration of each one's Sun commitment. After several conversations, both signed Columbia contracts; Carl's deal was set to begin January 1, 1958, Cash's to follow in August.

Through the grapevine, Sam got wind of Law's maneuvering. He called Carl and found out everything he had heard was true, and asked Carl to come to Memphis to talk it over.

The two men drove all over Memphis as Sam enumerated every reason he could think of for Carl to stay on Sun. "I think you're makin' a bad mistake. You're gonna get up there and get lost," he said. "Now it's okay for Johnny Cash—and I understand John's leavin' too."

Carl confirmed Cash's signing, and Sam stepped up his entreaty. "Now it'll work for John," he observed. "But I'm tellin' you, it's a mistake for you. 'Cause I know how you play, and I know what you do they don't understand in Nashville. If anybody does, it's Chet Atkins, and you not goin' on RCA Victor. There ain't nobody over at Columbia Records knows anything about rockabilly music."

Carl, for whom Sam Phillips had been an authority figure very nearly the equal of his parents, wavered. He had stood at this crossroads before, as a child whose reverence and respect were so complete, that when his own father had tried to order his second son to play music the way it was played on the radio, he felt terror as he refused. That same feeling gripped him again as Sam pleaded with him to stay with Sun. At the same time, though, another inner voice spoke, reminding him he was no longer Sam's golden boy.

"Mr. Phillips," Carl said, "it ain't gonna do me no good to stay down here."

"Why would you think that?" Sam asked. His tone of voice suggested disbelief.

" 'Cause you got Jerry Lee Lewis of the brain," Carl answered, his anger rising. "That's all you talk about when I'm in here, and it has been that way for the last year. Every time I come in here you wanna play me somethin' he's done. All you braggin' on is him. I'm sure he's makin' you a lotta money. I know he's got hit records. But you even put on his records 'Jerry Lee Lewis and His Pumping Piano.' You ain't never said nothin' about me and my guitar."

"We'll change that," Sam vowed. "I'll start calling you 'The Rockin' Guitar Man.' "

Sam delivered, affixing the honorific below Carl's name on the "Glad All Over" single. In interviews he has admitted to focusing a good deal of his energy on Jerry Lee. In his defense, as he indicated to Escott and Hawkins in *Good Rockin' Tonight*, he felt both Carl and Cash had let ego obstruct clear thinking: "I had given [Carl and Johnny] a lot of time [when they were] getting started. Then I gave Jerry Lee Lewis a lot of time, and they saw it as if we were petting Jerry Lee. They had forgotten that we had brought them along in the same way. They were young people and there was an awful lot of jealousy."

Cash has a more complex answer as to why he and Carl left Sun, and it has nothing to do with jealousy and everything to do with opportunity and artistic growth. His is a memory tinged with sadness over the unpleasant end of his Sun tenure and with reverence for the history he saw unfolding in those years: "Everybody was leaving. We didn't like the royalty rate we were getting. I'm not saying I was underpaid as an artist. I'm saying I was paid according to what a small, independent label could pay me at the time. We didn't think it was fair. I'd been talking to other record companies about things I wanted to do as an artist, and I knew I wouldn't be able to do 'em on Sun. Sam had sold Elvis's contract, and there was not that much excitement around there. It just didn't feel like the place to be anymore. Had a great, fun three years on Sun Records. It was a blast. But when I moved on, it was definitely time to move on.

"It was like Camelot: For one shining moment in history there was a unique situation, never before and never after. Sam's a genius. And he was the man that brought it all about by recognizing artistry when he heard it. What are the chances in two years' time one person will discover and record Elvis Presley, Carl Perkins, Jerry Lee Lewis, Roy Orbison, myself? Of course Elvis was the beacon that brought us all there. We were out there just waitin' for our chance to do it the way we felt it. Elvis opened the door and Sam let us stay."

Sam's effort at appeasing Carl was too little, too late. Carl saw himself being left behind as the music he helped create mutated into new forms, as artists he had started out with sustained their popularity through single after single, as his strongest studio efforts wasted away in a tape box, unissued and apparently forgotten.

At the end of 1957, the topography of the rock 'n' roll landscape was rich and varied, although some disturbing elements were starting to erode its sharp edges. Teen idol Pat Boone, a smooth-voiced, plain-faced, straight-laced, Tennessee-born, Ivy League–educated descendant of Daniel Boone, had been on a roll since mid-'55 with vapid cover versions of black artists' music. Wooden actor Tab Hunter had usurped Sonny James's "Young Love," reconfiguring it into an insipid pop song bearing little resemblance to James's stark, plaintive country ballad; it was number one for six weeks. Rockabilly had been gobbled up by way of Texan Buddy Knox, whose chart-topping "Party Doll" fused a feisty rhythm to a plain vanilla voice free of the deeply felt emotion characteristic of roots rockabilly as played by Carl Perkins.

On the other hand, numerous established and new artists were cutting enough inspired rock 'n' roll to keep the music's detractors busy denouncing it. Chuck Berry had hit the top 10 twice, with "School Day," an eloquent account of the tedium of the classroom and rock 'n' roll's place as an emotional outlet, and "Rock & Roll Music," wherein the music's appeal was described in compelling, concise fashion. Ever-reliable Fats Domino, whose records rarely sold less than a million, kept pace with the many white artists covering his material by racking up four top 10 hits and four others that entered the top 30 before the end of '57. With "Jenny Jenny" and "Keep A Knockin'," Little Richard cracked the top 10 twice. Elvis, no longer the raw rockabilly of his Sun years, was cutting some tough sides at RCA with Scotty, Bill, D.J. Fontana, and the Jordanaires backing him—four number ones in '57 alone, including "Jailhouse Rock," one of his most inspired performances. Singer-writer-guitarist Buddy Holly, a native Texan, and his group the Crickets had released some razor-edged bits of self-penned rockabilly-rooted rock 'n' roll in "That'll Be The Day," "Oh Boy," and, under his own name, "Peggy Sue." Oklahoma City–born rockabilly Eddie Cochran, like Carl and Holly a triple-threat artist, hit the top 20 with his debut single, "Sittin' in the Balcony," its heavily echoed vocal and stark background reminiscent of a Sun record. Don and Phil Everly, brothers hailing from Kentucky and steeped in traditional country through their father, guitarist Ike Everly, had blended rockabilly and folk in cutting two of the top singles of the year in Felice and Boudleaux Bryant's "Bye Bye Love" and "Wake Up Little Susie."

The juggernaut had not slowed, despite preachers preaching against it, parents fearing it, and racists preying on it. What had been a renegade subculture was moving into the mainstream of American life as its commercial potential became apparent. Magazines were launched featuring rock 'n' roll stars on their covers, gossip and feature stories about the artists on the inside, and, in some, advice to the teen lovelorn. Elvis's face and name showed up on everything from clothing and perfume to lunchboxes and trading cards, and as a film actor he was proving to be a box office smash.

Only Carl was absent from the pantheon. On the road he was continuing to draw sizable, enthusiastic audiences, making his dismal showing on the charts all the more puzzling. A case can be made for the music changing and Carl not accommodating the marketplace. Having purveyed the purest form of rockabilly, having defined the style, he hadn't thought to evolve it, as Holly seemed to be doing, or, for that matter, as Buddy Knox had done in introducing a softer pop element into the formula. While chart failings dismayed him, his sense of himself as a still-vital artist remained unwavering—"Dixie Fried" and "Matchbox" were as good as rockabilly or rock 'n' roll could get. He believed that sitting on Sam's shelf in the Sun studio were some tracks, still unheard, hot enough to melt the disc jockeys' needles.

Could Carl have polished the rough edges of his style without losing his uniqueness as an artist? It was one thing to try to follow up "Shoes" with other fashion-oriented themes—such as "Put Your Cat Clothes On," or "Pink Pedal Pushers," cut during one of his final Sun sessions but, like "Cat Clothes," unreleased—it was quite another to sit down and write a song that existed solely for the sake of the song, rather than as a statement of personal experience. Of the early rock 'n' roll songwriters, Carl's songs were the most subjective in narrative line. He didn't have Chuck Berry's gift for translating the teen experience and the teen culture, or even the beauty of the rock 'n' roll experience, into what amounted to folk anthems. He wasn't Fats Domino and Dave Bartholomew, penning sunny, good-time rockers with only a hint of melancholy here and there, only a hint of his own life therein. He wasn't Little Richard, in any way, shape, or form.

He was an artist who drew his best material from his own life in the fields, in the tonks, and from having inhabited the lowest strata of the American working class. His memories were of a time and a place quickly receding into history; to the rock 'n' roll audience, "Movie Magg" would have seemed hopelessly antiquated. Holly's "Peggy Sue," by contrast, said nothing about the artist's environment, offered nothing explicit in the way of details about his background, even said little about the girl in question beyond her being "pretty, pretty, pretty,

pretty." But it had the big beat, and a spirited, honest, unusual, and irresistible performance to get it across vocally and instrumentally. Carl could never have pulled off "Peggy Sue"; his least successful Sun recordings had been his least personal songs, in which he had struggled to find common ground between his experiences and those described in the lyrics. For the most part, these were songs he had had no hand in writing and no point of shared memory with the composer.

His was a dangerous position to be in, given the drift of the industry towards more pop-influenced sounds and more teen-related themes. In 1957, Carl Perkins was a twenty-five-year-old man with a wife and three children to support; a man whose family's woeful poverty had denied him anything approaching a normal childhood; a man whose teenage years, instead of being the final, carefree ramp into adulthood, were spent in toil, in cotton fields and in honky-tonks, so that parents and siblings might have the most basic necessities.

After dropping off Sam Phillips in front of the Sun studio, close to the same spot where he had parked in 1954 and begged for a tryout, Carl drove away towards Jackson, on Highway 70, the same two-lane road that had brought him to Sun in the first place. There he had collided with history and had made a difference. America had changed, was still changing, especially its youth. "Blue Suede Shoes," and by extension its composer, had been one of their touchstones. Now, less than two years later, as he sped through the night in the Cadillac purchased by his achievement, Carl Perkins was nothing so much as a man out of time.

3

RESTLESS

1958–1980

The harvest is past, the summer is ended, and we are not saved.

—Jeremiah 8:20

Carl's initial Columbia session took place in early February 1958. His first intimation that things were going to be different here came when he saw the inside of Don Law's preferred studio, the Quonset Hut, owned by producer Owen Bradley, another Nashville music-industry pioneer whose production credits included Bill Monroe, Ernest Tubb, and Kitty Wells, and an extraordinary young singer from Virginia, Patsy Cline (and, a rare failure, Buddy Holly, who headed back to Texas after cutting nothing useful with Bradley in a 1956 session). The facility was large enough to house two or three studios the size of Sun's. There were *two* pianos. Extra guitars. And a clock—*a clock in a recording studio!* This was a daunting place.

Augmented by session pianist Marvin Hughes, the band cut four songs during an afternoon session. The clock, as Carl learned, was there to time the session. Other artists were coming in to record when Carl was finished. There would be no all-nighters, no extended jams being worked into songs over the course of several hours and a fifth of Early Times.

After signing with Columbia, Carl had been urged by Law to write some new material and "give me another 'Shoes.' " Carl delivered four songs, all uptempo, three of them consciously directed at the teen audience, including an updated but less seductive version of "Pink Pedal Pushers," originally cut at Sun in late '57. "Just Thought I'd Call" had a tight, driving rhythm and a melody and vocal performance reminiscent of "Put Your Cat Clothes On," and a brief, sizzling guitar solo from Carl before the final verse; "Rockin' Record Hop," offered an inspired vocal and a good guitar solo run from Carl, but little else. It sorely missed a character like "Dixie Fried" 's razor-happy Dan, and the artist who had fashioned that brutal, knowing portrait of an American subculture was here reduced to:

> Wake up, little Susie, and tell her the news
> Tell her don't be late
> Take your hair down and get prettied up,
> Sugarfoot, and meet me at the gate

The best song of the four Carl brought in was a kindred spirit to his best Sun work in that it had character, detail, humor, a smidgen of anxiety, and a point of view relevant to the working life Carl knew well. Titled "Jive After Five," it was only partly Carl's song. The lyrics were written by his cousin Martha and her husband, George Bain. Having once worked at a soda fountain, Martha had the idea to look at the soda jerk's job from the viewpoint of a modern teen eager for the day to wind down so he could meet his girlfriend for a dance. The soda fountain having become the locus of much after-school socializing among fifties teenagers, Martha, with George's assistance, not only described the tedium of the job but also threw in references to the most popular items on the menu. Time has proven it to be an interesting look at a minor facet of early pop culture, with references to friends dropping in "for sodas and pop" and "talkin' plans about a new record hop." Carl energized the story in its chorus, delivering his lines with a chuckle that evolved into a slight sneer, as if he couldn't decide whether he loved or loathed his routine:

> All day long I'm fillin' orders
> Takin' nickels, dimes, and quarters
> Cherry sodas and a chocolate shake
> Strawberry sundaes and a lemon phosphate

Oddly, for an artist who was proving to be one of the most influential of all the early rock 'n' roll guitarists, Carl had no solos on "Jive

After Five," and was barely audible on his instrument after the introduction. Hughes's piano and the Clayton-Fluke rhythm section dominate the track: No Jerry Lee, Hughes played clean, brisk boogie-woogie lines with little emotion or individual flourish.

Released March 10, 1958, "Jive After Five," backed with "Pink Pedal Pushers," barely made it onto the pop chart, peaking at ninety-three before dropping out of sight. Its lackluster showing confirmed Carl's feelings about the session: "I had to do four songs in three hours in Nashville. Hell, at Sun I'd do four hours and might not even get a song. There was no time limit. That put a fear in me when I walked in that studio. I thought, *God, four songs. I gotta do 'em right the first time.* So I didn't holler; I didn't enjoy it. See, I wasn't free. And those restrictions just flattened that music out to where it didn't have the fire."

Touring from late winter through spring, Carl entered the studio again in June for two lengthy sessions; went back in November and cut four songs; and in mid-March of 1959 laid down four more. In this period—June 1958 through March 1959—he recorded only two self-penned numbers. In addition to working some interesting rockabilly variations on early rock 'n' roll tunes—"Tutti Frutti," "Shake, Rattle and Roll," "Long Tall Sally," "That's All Right," and "Whole Lotta Shakin'" being the most convincing tracks—he cut material penned by Nashville-based contract songwriters. Despite some credible performances—"Where the Rio De Rosa Flows" had a loose, lively feel, and "Honey, 'Cause I Love You," written by Wayne Walker and Mel Tillis, two of Nashville's most successful songwriters, was suitably poignant—Carl began to suspect that financial incentives may have dictated Don Law's preferences in song selection:

"[Don Law] was a wonderful man, and I loved him, but he did favor Peer Music. I would hate to think he was gettin' a cut, and he certainly didn't come off as that. I never argued about it. I never went there planning to record [the songs Law suggested]. I'd always have my songs ready. But it seemed like he always had three or four he wanted me to do. And he'd play me a demo of a song and say, 'Sing it like this guy here's doing it on the demo.' That really was not Carl Perkins. For the most part, an artist shouldn't copy what the demo singer is doing; he needs to sing it like he feels it. I let myself record some things I never did like. I should have been totally sold on every song I ever sung. My career suffered because I wasn't so choosy."

Producers having a stake in song publishing would hardly have been big news, but other factors were undercutting Carl's career as well. When "Jive After Five" failed, and was followed into the cutout bins the following summer by Carl's second Columbia single, "Pop Let Me Have the Car" b/w "Levi Jacket (And A Long Tail Shirt)," Law appears to have lost faith in Carl's style of rock 'n' roll. For sessions in June and the following March, he added saxophonist Andrew Goodrich to the lineup (in addition to Hughes) in an effort to reconfigure the Perkins sound.

By March of 1960, a little over two years after he had joined Columbia, Carl, widely admired for his songwriting and instrumental brilliance, was rarely recording his own material and wasn't playing at all on his sessions. Law had brought in one of Nashville's legendary stylists, Grady Martin, to direct Carl's sessions and play guitar in a band that included a number of the town's finest session men, including Owen Bradley's brother Harold on guitar, Floyd Cramer on piano, and Boots Randolph on saxophone. Typical of Carl's plight was his first Columbia album. Issued in November 1958, *Whole Lotta Shakin'* consisted entirely of the rock 'n' roll standards Carl had cut in mid-year. The cover photo showed him wild-eyed and decked out in a sport coat with alternating black and red stripes. In production the photo negative had been flopped, resulting in Carl being pictured on his own album as a left-handed guitarist.

(Sam's parting shot at Carl had been to issue the first and only Perkins Sun album after Carl had left the label. Titled *Dance Album of Carl Perkins*, it featured the A and B sides of his issued Sun singles and other gems such as "Right String Baby, Wrong Yo Yo," and "Everybody's Trying to Be My Baby." Curiously, "Dixie Fried" was omitted, and "Her Love Rubbed Off" remained in the can, but the material chosen—apart from the speeded-up version of "Your True Love"—offered a broad overview of the breadth of Carl's art from 1954 to 1958. The classic cover art consisted of line drawings of teenagers dancing, decked out in their best cat clothes, with a photograph of Carl's handsome mug beaming in the lower right corner. The album was later reissued as *Teenbeat—The Best of Carl Perkins*, with the line drawings replaced by actual photos of dancing teenagers. Although Carl didn't approve of some of the material, *Dance Album* was one of the best rock 'n' roll longplayers of the fifties, completely eclipsing *Whole Lotta Shakin'* in every aesthetic aspect and offering in its song selection the most compelling proof available of how much first-rate rock 'n' roll Carl had cut during his Sun years.)

Roland Janes, Jerry Lee's guitarist, visited Nashville during Carl's early Columbia days, and saw problems immediately. For one, Carl had switched from a Gibson guitar to a Fender Stratocaster, one of the first on the market, presented personally to Carl by its inventor, Leo Fender. As Janes related to Escott and Hawkins: "The Gibson had a much better sound for what [Carl] was doing. He'd also bought one of those Echoplex amps that sounded great when Scotty Moore used them but didn't suit Carl's style at all."

One of the first contract songwriters Carl met in Nashville was Mel Tillis, who was signed to Jim Denny's Cedarwood Publishing. Well aware of Carl's work at Sun, Tillis found common ground immediately in sharing tales about their past. Carl's slow footing in Nashville puzzled Tillis as much as it did everyone else, and he suggests, as do others, that Nashville's system was to blame: "I'd be up at the old James Robinson Hotel with Don Law, playing my songs for him. Carl would come in with his songs, and he'd say, 'I got one here, I think.' And he'd play it and we'd agree it was a hit. Then he'd cut it and it just seemed like nothing would ever happen. I never could understand that. There was a little clique in those days around there. It was Grady Martin or Hank Garland playing guitar on most of the records. Grady was good—most of the hits that came out of Nashville at that time, most of the new sounds were thought up, if that's the word, by Grady Martin. So I guess Mr. Law said, 'Well, if you can do it for these other acts I guess you can do it for Carl.' But it took away from Carl, because he had a style, that was him."

Ed Cisco, who played rhythm guitar with Carl on the late fifties and early sixties Columbia sessions, remembers Carl being disappointed constantly by what was going down in the studio: "We'd leave the studio to drive back to Jackson, and all the way home Carl would be shaking his head and saying, 'It ain't right, Ed. It ain't right.' "

In April 1959 Carl cut through with an original song that hearkened back to his finest Sun material but sounded thoroughly contemporary. Fashion again provided the theme—shoes, in fact. On his rousing vocal he sounded more alive than he had since "Jive After Five," reveling in his playful, colorful slang, and stepping out in the chorus to declaim his prophecy like a preacher in the pulpit announcing Judgment Day at hand. Everything about "Pointed Toe Shoes" was "all reet," from its galloping, scattershot guitar intro to its stop-time breaks in the verses, to its proselytizing vocal, to its final, fleeting reference to an earlier shoe fad:

> Well there's a brand new style goin' round
> Hypnotizin' cats in town
> Livin' end, walkin' dream
> Pointed toe and that'sa WHAT I MEAN!
>
> I said, Pointed toes are comin' back again
> Pointed toes are comin' back again
> Everything's all reet
> When I got 'em on my feet
> I say the point's comin' back again
>
> Well they're made from hide
> Cow that died
> Long and lean, narrow and keen
> Some are brown, some are black
> A cat start's a-walkin'
> He's EASY to track
>
> I said the pointed toes are comin' back again
> Pointed toes are comin' back again!
> Everything's all reet
> I got 'em on my feet
> I say the points are comin' back again—ROCK!!

Well I'll be sharp-toed and high-heeled

And buckled on the side

Zip 'em up, lace 'em up or any ol' style

I won't have to worry

About you steppin' on my blues

A keen cuttin' cat in my POINTED TOE SHOES!

"Pointed Toe Shoes" broke out quickly upon its release and was strong enough in major markets coast to coast for a Columbia executive in New York to call and ask Carl if he was ready to have a smash-hit record. To push the single the label planned a major promotional campaign that featured, among other elements, the manufacture of hundreds of pairs of pointed-toe suede shoes—colors selected by Carl—to be given away to fans and disc jockeys while Carl was out touring. On the road Carl visited every television and radio station in every town he played. A month after its release, "Pointed Toe Shoes" was a bona fide "turntable smash," that is, a frequently played single on radio coast to coast. It entered the national pop chart in the lower reaches of the Hot 100, rose only slightly, and disappeared altogether in less than a month.

On the professional front, Carl approached the end of the fifties unfulfilled. After his first session in the Quonset Hut, he gave serious thought to backing out of his Columbia deal and returning to Sam Phillips's fold. But by then his heart had hardened towards Sam, because the royalty payments from Sun and Hi-Lo were so infrequent and, Carl suspected, short of what he was due. Raised to honor his word, he stayed put at Columbia, his faith in Don Law and in himself wavering with each new session. Unwilling to assert himself on his own behalf, Carl Perkins had become the architect of his own despair.

Nevertheless, his artistic breakthroughs at Sun had created the literature of rockabilly that was forming the primary text for new artists working in the same style and trying to broaden its boundaries—Eddie Cochran and Buddy Holly, for instance, who were as comfortable in the control room as they were in front of a microphone and insisted on having greater control of their finished work.

When Carl landed on Columbia, rockabilly's golden era was over. Rock 'n' roll, after its first brilliant burst of incandescent, individual artistry, was losing its character and its characters to mainstream tastes. What the preachers, White Citizens' Councils, and other anti-rock crusaders could not do, time, circumstance, greed, tragedy, and rapacious businesspeople did, and that was to eviscerate the music until it barely resembled its original form.

Between 1958 and 1960 alone, the toll was staggering: Drafted into the Army in 1958, Elvis essentially went on ice for two years and came out neutered for mass consumption; also in 1958, Jerry Lee Lewis found his records banned from most playlists across the country and his concert bookings canceled after the news broke that he had married his thirteen-year-old second cousin; in late January of 1958, Little Richard underwent a religious conversion, renounced rock 'n' roll as "the devil's work," enrolled in a Bible college in Alabama, and stated his intention to labor thereafter on God's behalf as a minister preaching His word. In February 1959, a plane carrying Buddy Holly, the impressive seventeen-year-old Mexican-American singer-writer-guitarist Ritchie Valens, and disc jockey turned novelty recording artist J.P. Richardson (the Big Bopper, as he was known) crashed shortly after takeoff in Clear Lake, Iowa, killing all on board; late that same year Chuck Berry was indicted under the Mann Act, which prohibits the transport of minors across state lines for immoral purposes, and in 1960 was sentenced to a two-year term in a federal penitentiary. Also in 1960, Eddie Cochran, while touring England, was killed in a car crash that left fellow traveler Gene Vincent seriously injured and nearly crippled with a leg injury.

A new decade was ushered in with a federal inquiry into allegations that radio broadcasters were taking under-the-counter payments—dubbed payola—from the labels in turn for favoring certain records in their programming choices. Dick Clark, host of the Philadelphia-based, nationally broadcast *American Bandstand*, which regularly featured rock 'n' roll artists in performance, was an early target of a House of Representatives committee investigation into the payola issue, but ultimately emerged unscathed professionally. The real victim turned out to be Alan Freed, whom a New York grand jury served with a twenty-six-count indictment (more properly, commercial bribery informations, a misdemeanor) for receiving illegal gratuities. Coming in 1960, it was the beginning of an arduous legal process that would break Freed financially and emotionally and end his radio career on a disgraceful note.

Finally, at the same time New York was producing some scintillating studio-crafted pop records—well written, expertly and energetically played, convincingly performed—Philadelphia labels began cashing in on the bankability of vacuous but good-looking singers modeled after Pat Boone. Calling them singers is something of a misnomer, because so few had anything to recommend them as musical artists. Their appeal was blatantly keyed to their matinee-idol good looks and innocuous, boy-next-door charm; personable, believable singing was a secondary concern, as was proven when the likes of Fabian, Bobby Rydell, and Frankie Avalon tried to warble their saccharine, assembly-line teen love songs. In contrast to Carl and his peers, who had traveled thousands of miles by car to gain exposure, inventing their own career promotion as they went along, the teen idols had a ready-made national platform in *American Bandstand*, which beamed rock 'n' roll's new conservatives coast to coast.

Quite distinct among the teen idols was West Coast–based Ricky Nelson, who had risen above his stumbling start covering Fats Domino's "I'm Walkin' " to cut some admirable pop records backed by redoubtable instrumentalists (and, on background vocals, by the Jordanaires), among them James Burton, a resourceful rockabilly-rooted guitarist whose links to the hard-edged styles of Carl Perkins and the Memphis-bred Rock & Roll Trio were obvious on Nelson's uptempo material. (The Trio's members included brothers Dorsey and Johnny Burnette and a marvelous guitarist, Paul Burlison, who bore a close physical resemblance to Carl and whose soloing demonstrated the same fluid, inventive melding of various roots influences. The Burnettes wrote the Nelson hit "Waitin' in School.") Nelson had a smooth way with a ballad and could put across his rockers with great feel, despite his monotone singing voice. He too had the advantage of national television exposure by way of his own family's high-rated weekly series, which he used to good advantage in debuting new material. As something of a standard bearer for a genre under siege, Nelson cut eleven top-20 singles between 1958 and 1960, almost all of them inspired performances of a piece with rock 'n' roll's finest mid-fifties offerings.

I n 1957 Roy Orbison fulfilled his pledge to marry Claudette. He wrote a song for her, titled it "Claudette," and pitched it to the Everly Brothers. They cut it as the B side of "All I Have To Do Is Dream," a number-one single in 1958, and with its success Orbison was able to buy out his Sun contract. Like Carl, he felt mishandled at Sun, where Sam pushed him to record rock songs rather than the ballads for which he had such a natural feel. Also like Carl, he was having trouble finding a follow-up to his first hit: "Ooby Dooby" had sold nearly 300,000 copies, but three subsequent singles had flopped.

As a songwriter, however, Orbison was beginning to have some success apart from "Claudette." Warren Smith hit the Hot 100 with "So Long I'm Gone"; Jerry Lee reworked "Go! Go! Go!" into "Down the Line" and cut it for the B side of "Breathless," which went to number one; Johnny Cash, during one of his final Sun sessions, cut "You Tell Me." On the strength of "Claudette," Orbison became convinced his future lay in Nashville, and possibly out of the spotlight, as a writer.

Once free of Sun, Orbison signed with the Acuff-Rose publishing company, hoping he could get his songs placed with other artists. Through Wesley Rose he landed a recording contract with RCA, but a one-year tenure produced only two forgettable singles. Orbison was then signed by the fledgling Monument label. After the Everlys declined to cut a new song he had cowritten with a Texas friend, Joe Melson (and following unsuccessful attempts to get it to Presley, for whom it was intended), Orbison cut it as his first Monument single. "Only the Lonely" sold a million copies, rose to number two on the Hot 100 and showcased the singer's overpowering vocal instrument.

Although their careers were going in different directions on different labels, Roy and Carl remained close—close enough that between 1958 and 1964 Roy and Claudette often stayed with Carl and Valda for days at a time. During a memorable two-week visit to the Perkins house in 1959, Carl and Valda learned something else about Roy: Claudette had him under her thumb, so much so that he even asked her permission to go with Carl to see a new fishing spot outside of town.

For her part, Valda was run ragged taking care of her own brood and of her visitors, including their baby boy. While Valda worked, Claudette whiled away the days relaxing on the couch, reading, and watching television. Valda was used to having guests—at one time or another almost all of the Sun artists and musicians, excluding Elvis, had been over for dinner—but Roy and Claudette strained her patience to the breaking point. Finally, she ordered them out: "I told Carl, 'They're gonna have to leave. She won't help me and I can't see after her child and my three and try to keep something cooked for everybody. I'm just not gonna do it.' So they packed up their suitcases and left, but they came back again after that. It seemed like they stayed here three-fourths of the time. I know Johnny Cash discussed it with Carl—what time they weren't with us they were with him!

"Claudette was a beautiful woman. Her face compared to Elizabeth Taylor's. She had real black hair and almost purple eyes, violet, like Liz Taylor's. But as a woman, she wasn't my kind. That means she was just hard and lazy.

"I never will forget one time we had been to the grocery. We pulled up in the driveway, and they pulled in right behind us. I said, 'Carl, who is that?' He said, 'You don't want me to tell you.'"

Having spent so much time with Roy on the road, Carl understood why he was such a frequent visitor. "Roy liked to save a dollar," Carl says. "Roy put his hand in his pocket slow-ly when it come time to go to the counter."

In the fall of 1958, less than six months before the "Pointed Toe Shoes" session, Carl had suffered a blow that nearly destroyed him person-ally and professionally and would haunt him the rest of his life. While touring earlier that year, Jay's headaches became more serious. Mul-tiple doses of aspirin couldn't alleviate his pain, and his mood had turned dark and depressed. At a show in St. Paul, Minnesota, Carl no-ticed Jay "really fighting his guitar," and thought for a moment that maybe the impossible had happened and Jay had taken one drink too many before the show. When their eyes met, though, Carl saw only sad-ness in Jay's countenance.

Between shows, in the dressing room, Carl asked Jay what was bothering him. Jay said only that he had had a tingling sensation in his foot for the past couple of days and it was getting worse. As he spoke, "big tears fell down his face," Carl remembers.

Carl insisted Jay go home immediately. Jay disagreed, vowing to finish out the tour's final few dates. Carl prevailed: "I called the air-port that night and got him a flight early the next morning. Took him to the airport. Clayton and Fluke was still in bed. Bought his ticket and walked him to the gate. He was kinda draggin' his left leg. He hugged me, I hugged him. I said, 'Jay, go straight to the doctor. Don't wait around and wait for it to get better. It's something. When you're tin-gling you're losing feeling, it's serious.' He really wanted to stay and try. But he never played again. He waved at me, sittin' inside that plane. God, I can see his face now. I stopped a couple of times on the way back to the hotel, so I could see how to drive, I was crying. Terrible day. Terrible, terrible."

Jay returned to Jackson ("He could not walk straight when he got off the plane," Valda recalls) and went on to Vanderbilt Hospital in Nashville, where a physician diagnosed his problem as being a nervous condition. He was advised to give up the road and to "put that guitar under your bed. Forget about it," as he told Valda.

When Carl came home after the tour, he found Jay failing fast. He took his brother to the Jackson hospital, where a visiting neurosurgeon recommended he go to Memphis to be examined for "a brain problem," as Carl was told. After tests in Memphis, surgery was recommended because, as a doctor told Carl, Jay had a tumor "anywhere from the size of a marble to the size of a sausage."

On the day of the surgery, Carl, Valda, and Martha maintained a vigil at the hospital. Hours later the doctor emerged from the operating room with the news that the tumor had been removed, tested, and was found to be malignant. Carl shook the doctor's hand and thanked him for his effort.

As they walked to their car, Martha and Valda looked at each other warily. Carl seemed strengthened by the doctor's words and had said he was happy that it was only "a malignant tumor."

Valda stopped suddenly and looked at Martha. "Oh, no," she moaned.

"Uh-huh," Carl said jauntily. "It was malignant. Little ol' malignant tumor. Yeah, that's what it was, Val."

"Carl, honey," Valda said, "do you know what 'malignant' means?"

Carl looked puzzled. "Well, it's a tumor, isn't it? What is it?"

"Carl, that's cancer."

"No, it's a tumor," Carl corrected her.

Valda touched Carl's arm. "Carl, malignancy is cancer."

"No."

"That's what it is," Valda said.

Two days later Carl called the doctor for a final prognosis. Valda stood nearby: "You could see the paleness on Carl's face. He didn't have to tell me after he got through with the conversation with the doctor. [Carl] said, 'He's got about six months to live.'"

Most of the tumor was too deeply embedded to be removed, and it was growing in the area of Jay's brain that controlled his motor functions. Carl was told Jay would be given morphine to ease his pain, but was forewarned that his brother would "die tough. He's a strong boy. It's gonna be a hard go. He may go blind. He may lose his hearing. If he's fortunate it will attack him massively and kill him quickly, and he won't dry up and have to suffer so long."

Apart from honoring recording commitments in early June, Carl stayed by Jay's side constantly. In February Sam Phillips had sent a $20,000 royalty check, allowing Carl to take on financial support of Jay's family during his brother's illness.

Jay struggled after his surgery. His weight dropped precipitously; with his sunken, dark eyes and hollow cheeks, he had the appearance of a living corpse. Morphine dulled the pain, but as the months passed the medication became less effective. Yet he rarely complained, even when he had every reason to and no one would have begrudged him doing so. In his most desperate hour, Jay was as unyielding as he had been as a boy toiling during the long, hot afternoons in the Lake County cotton fields.

So deep was Carl's concern for Jay's welfare that the only good news he received during this time passed with little celebration. In late spring Valda learned she was pregnant again. The baby was due in January. Whenever Carl would be overwhelmed with grief after spending a day at Jay's bedside, Valda would try to comfort him by reminding him of their unborn child. "Remember one thing," she would say. "You're gonna have a new baby, and the baby will be a boy. He'll replace your brother." It was a mantra she would repeat over and over as the weeks passed, Carl straining to find a reason to believe in anything about the future beyond Jay's passing.

One of Jay's first visitors upon his return from the hospital was Johnny Cash, who came to effect a plan: "The last time I was with him, Carl, Clayton, Marshall Grant, Luther Perkins, W.S. Holland, and I went fishing on the Tennessee River, below Pickwick Dam. I'll never forget—we helped Jay in the boat that day. Everybody was determined to take Jay fishing. It was kinda like our last hurrah. Caught some big catfish too—twenty-, thirty-pounders. We had a big time that day. Jay really enjoyed himself. And we all knew it was kinda . . . Nothing was said about his health that day that I can remember. We just really enjoyed him and enjoyed being with him. I guess all of us wanted him to know we loved him."

In mid-October, Jay, now bedfast with paralysis in both legs, told Carl to keep the Martin acoustic guitar he used onstage, and gave Clayton his outboard boat motor. After a short visit with Buck and

Louise, he lost consciousness. His final words: "See that Carl and Clayton don't kill each other."

On October 19, Carl sat beside Jay's bed, holding one of his brother's icy hands. He felt Jay's legs under the covers, and found them cold from the feet to the knees. That afternoon Clayton came to visit, and the brothers were all together for the last time—on one side of him Carl saw Jay, the man he wished he could be; on the other, Clayton, the man he feared he would become.

Carl went home late in the evening to get a short nap. In his room he fell to his knees in prayer: "I talked to God so deep that I thought God had told me he wasn't gonna take my brother. That's what I made myself believe I heard God say—'Don't worry. I'm gonna get him back on his feet and I'm gonna heal him and you'll have him for as long as you live. You'll die first. I'm not takin' Jay.' I made myself believe that."

At the hospital on the morning of the 20th, Carl found Jay still alive. Again he sat next to the bed and placed Jay's hand in his. After some time had passed Carl felt his hand being squeezed tightly. Jay's eyes were open, and his mouth was moving, as if he were trying to speak. Carl leaned in close. "Carl! Carl!" Jay said in a strangled voice, looking Carl straight in the eyes. Suddenly his body went limp, and his eyes closed. James Buck Perkins, age twenty-eight, died holding his brother's hand. In tears, Carl said good-bye. "Part of me went to the grave with him," Carl says. "It all flashed back to me when he went. I saw him in Lake County trying to pick as much cotton as I could, working harder than me. What a brother I had. I remember Jay healthy and happy and flailing that good rhythm. And I very well remember the wonderful fella he always was, to *everybody*. He was the kind of fella you'd throw your hand up whether you knew him or not, because he had a good, wonderful, innocent sweet face. And he backed that face up—he was good man. He kept me from maybe being as bad or worse than Clayton. He was somebody special. He was somebody I needed the day I was born. God knew that."

When he got home, Carl "fell into" the house, then parked himself on the floor. Valda sat next to him, trying to offer some consolation. "I'm so thankful that he's over all that suffering, Carl," she said. "And you should be."

"I can't live without him," Carl sobbed.

"Yes, you can," Valda stressed. "You will make it. Just remember, you've got me, you've got three kids, and you're going to have another one and it will be a boy." Nothing Valda said seemed to work. All his mother's assurances that God would help if you call on Him in prayer . . . all seemed like a crock now.

Placed alongside the many wreaths and sprays at Jay's gravesite on the day of his funeral was a lone weeping willow tree, with a dozen papier mâché redbirds affixed to its limbs. The attached sympathy card was signed, "With love, Elvis."

On November 23, 1958, Johnny Cash organized a benefit concert in Memphis to help defray the cost of Jay's medical and household expenses. Held at Ellis Auditorium, the show's lineup included Jerry Lee Lewis, Webb Pierce, Hawkshaw Hawkins, Lefty Frizzell, Curtis Gordon, Thomas Wayne (Luther Perkins's brother), Slim Rhodes, Sonny Burgess, Merle Travis, Dickey Lee, Curtis Gordon, the Collins Kids, and Joe Maphis. One of the special guest artists on hand was Ernest Tubb, Jay's inspiration. In the dressing room, Carl heard Tubb at the microphone announce, "In honor of a great man, I dedicate this song," and then sing the opening lyrics of "Walking the Floor Over You." As Tubb performed, Carl buried his face in his hands and wept uncontrollably.

▼ a r i o u s news blurbs tell the story of Carl's movements in the aftermath of Jay's death: December 27, 1958—an appearance on Tex Ritter's *Ranch Party* television show; June 1, 1959—*Billboard* reported Carl flying to the West Coast "to begin work in a Hawaiian flicker. Carl, whose latest on the Columbia label is 'Pointed Toe Shoes,' will make several personals while in California" (the film in question was titled *Hawaiian Boy*, in which Carl had a bit part as a bartender and performed "Y.O.U." and "Where the Rio De Rosa Flows"); August 17, 1959—a *Billboard* tour item: "George Morgan and Carl Perkins are set for a four-day stand at Springlake Park, Oklahoma City, August 20–23 . . . Brenda Lee and Carl Perkins take their group to the Clinton County Fair, Wilmington, O., August 25–26."

The itinerary doesn't reveal the diminishing interest Carl brought to his work during this period. He performed concerts "only when I got hungry or saw I was gonna lose the house," then got back to the bottle of Early Times as quickly as possible. Sensing little enthusiasm on Columbia's part to support his studio efforts, and tumbling into an emotional freefall without Jay, he had scant motivation to keep it going on the road. On January 15, 1959, Valda gave birth to a boy, as she had predicted. He was named Gregory Jay Perkins. Even this blessed event failed to snap Carl out of his doldrums.

Less than a year after Jay's death, Fluke Holland left the band to manage Carl Mann, a teenage singer he had heard performing on a Jackson radio station. Holland offered to continue with Carl as his schedule permitted, but Carl encouraged his drummer's new career, saying, "Don't worry about me, man. Take that boy down to Sun."

Signed in 1959 to Sam's new Phillips International label, Mann had a top-30 hit with his first single, an uptempo reworking of Nat King Cole's "Mona Lisa"; a follow-up single, "Pretend," another Nat King Cole cover, peaked at number fifty; each of three subsequent singles charted lower than its predecessor. Meanwhile Mann was becoming an alcoholic at an early age and undermining his livelihood in the process—he wound up playing piano in Carl's band briefly in the early sixties before being drafted in 1964. After completing his tour of duty, he was signed to Monument and ABC/Dot, affiliations producing neither a hit nor enough momentum to sustain a career. Eventually he conquered his alcoholism, married, found God, and retired to a quiet life in Huntingdon, Tennessee.

When Mann's career foundered, Holland decided to leave the music business entirely. In 1961 he was getting ready to go to work for the city of Jackson when Cash called with an offer to join him on a concert date at the Steel Pier in Atlantic City. Following that successful engagement, Cash invited Fluke to stay on and transform the Tennessee Two into the Tennessee Three. There he remains today, now introduced by Cash as "the original rockabilly drummer," still playing the high hat on the right, still hitting the bass drum pedal with his left foot, still solid, on and off the stage.

To Carl, only the bottle mattered. When he was off the road he would get strong moonshine from a Madison County bootlegger. On the road it was Early Times, morning, noon, and night. Dismissing Valda's assurances that God would help him if asked, he quit attending church. The more he contemplated the terrible wrong God had done him in taking Jay, the more bitter he became towards his maker, the more resolute he became in his quest for a never-ending alcohol high.

Despite his career ups and downs, Carl had kept his professional concerns apart from his family life after he returned from sessions or tours. But with Jay's death and the frustrations building up over his poor showing at Columbia, he began drinking at home, starting in the morning and continuing through the day. He was mean drunk, and Valda bore the brunt of his anger. On several occasions his verbal abuse escalated into the physical, when Valda would plead with him to stop drinking and he would respond by slapping her across the face. At first she took it, but when it continued, she fought back: "I was never afraid of him. I should have been. He never hit me with his fist, but he has bruised me. Course he's got a few on himself too. That was a really low time for me when he was drinking so much. And I did not know what to do about it. Deep inside he felt guilty, and he was mad at himself. He would be so sick the next day, just so sick, till it got to the point where I said, 'I'm not helping you anymore. If you wanna drink and be sick, you can wait on yourself. I will not go get you soup and try to get you over this to get you drunk again.'"

It fell to Valda to hold the family together when Carl was doing his best to destroy everything they had gained. They were now living in a $32,000 house on Crescent Street, owned a Lincoln Continental, and the kids had all the toys they wanted. As a husband and a father, though, Carl was not only coming up short, he was terrorizing his own. Stan, particularly, being a high-strung child, feared his father's wrath and would question Valda incessantly as to the sudden change in Carl's temperament.

"You know your dad, when he's sober he's not a mean person. What he's puttin' in his body is what's makin' him mean," Valda would answer Stan.

"Why doesn't he quit, Mama?" Stan would ask in return.

"Well, honey, he's got a bad habit. You just keep prayin' and I will too. One day he will quit and then you'll have Daddy like he is when he's sober all the time."

Completely out of character, Carl would disappear for two or three days. Outside the city limits, so far off the road he couldn't be seen, he would park under a tree and drink himself into a stupor, pass out in the car, wake up the next day, start drinking again, pass out again, and the cycle went on. Finally, if her husband hadn't already staggered into the house on his own, Valda would send a family friend out to find him and bring him home.

To an outsider, it would have appeared that Carl was doing nothing more than staring off into space while he drank himself comatose. Inside the car, though, the radio would be playing. Alone with his thoughts, Carl was torn apart by what he heard: "I'd get mad. Turn on the radio and get hit with a song and say, 'I can beat it. God, you know I can beat it. And I ain't got nothin'.'" I never listened to rock 'n' roll. Rockabilly had died down and it had jumped over to another vein, and I didn't like it. I was a million miles from what they were doin'. I just recognized 'em as being people that took what I had and run off and got rich with it and I was going the other way."

Every day he visited Jay's grave, plopped down next to the tombstone, and talked to his brother, reliving old memories. During his infrequent live appearances, Carl would be in the middle of a song and suddenly see Jay walking down the aisle, stout, strong, and smiling, making his way to the stage to take his position behind and to Carl's left, strapping on his guitar and banging out a rockabilly rhythm pattern.

▶ THE VOICE OF CARL PERKINS

I said, "Am I gonna ride this out, or will I be brave enough to drive off somewhere before it gets worse and put a barrel to my head?" I thought [my family]'d be better off. At least they'd get a lump sum of insurance that

I kept. I knew I couldn't think those thoughts very often and I couldn't dwell on 'em because [suicide] was my ace in the hole. Before I would be totally washed out, throwed in a cell, be forced to have to shoot somebody, steal or rob, or turn out to be something I never wanted to be, I knew I did have [suicide] left. And those thoughts came and I'd push 'em away. No, it ain't time for that. I'd pull myself up and go out and work a few dates. Kept things together somehow. I really don't know how.

Let me rephrase that: I still had that woman believing in me. Valda never gave up on me. The only way I wasn't totally trapped was I had that woman and those kids who could somehow look at me and give me a push to say, "Oh yeah, I'm gonna get it together now, and when I do get me a few shows I'm gonna change them people to the point where they'll get me back there next week." Took shows for little or nothing, whatever they offered me. I had to because I couldn't get the money that was due me from Sam. See, Sam was not the man I had known in the beginning. If he had been, we all could have survived very easy. Instead I was a turmoiled, mixed-up man who was trying everything he possibly could to get back in the music business where he could make a good living.

If I had a bottle in my back pocket, or in my possession, under my car seat, or in my suitcase where I could get it, then I was me. I thought I was total then. There was an arm gone, there was a limp in my walk, there was a slowness in everything I did without it. And it was that fuel which I named the Devil's Fuel. It was the Devil's Fuel that gave me the rushes to where every time I'd take one, Wham! Almost a song! Not quite. Another one. Rowr! "Get back on that ladder of success. You can do it. I'm your buddy; I'm with you. You've got me clutched there right where I wanna be. I fit your hand, your hand fits me. We're pals. Together we can get outta this." No, you can't. That's where it lets you down, see. It builds you up and it's very good to do that. But it puts you a little bit too confident. And then all of a sudden you're either drunk or you don't have no more in the bottle.

I had voices talking to me. Real feelings. Very deep feelings. And when they'd get loud and chattering, I'd say, "I don't wanna hear you, you get outta me. Just don't talk to me." And I'd turn that bottle up.

They were saying, "You might as well go on and walk on off into these woods and become a tree—you ain't nothin'. You can't do nothing no more. You've tried it all. You've been to the biggest label there was; you had the biggest producer; you couldn't do it." But something always said, "No, you're not." I had that little thing inside of me and then I had this woman who kept saying, "No, no, no."

One night Valda said, "You know, Jay wouldn't have had much of a life if he had lived, Carl. Have you ever thought about that? God knew Jay was just right for Him, so he made an angel out of him. He wouldn't have had much life down here. You wouldn't want him stayin' alive and dryin' up." I hear her voice now talking to me like I was a little kid. Breaking through that cold barrier of solid steel I'd built around myself. Nothing in there but me and my guitar and some songs.

I laid down on the bed one night and I thought, "Wait a minute. Did she say he wouldn't have had a life? You know, he wouldn't have." It started opening up in my brain. How wonderful God was that He picked him at the right time. All of a sudden because of what Valda said, one night, and this is very vivid, it scared me:

God, you did love him, and you loved me! And I've still got mine and I've got a little boy Jay and I can love him for the rest of his life, for the rest of my life. Where have I been? I've been in such a terrible trance. I've been wantin' to please the Devil because I hated you! Oh, God!

On come every switch I'd shut down. Pow! Pow! Pow! Back to life Carl Perkins came. Out of total darkness. If I'd've died during that time I'd've been burning in Hell all these years. I believe that. I'm not saying that's true, but it's right for me. I turned Him on. Oh, how wonderful I felt when I turned Him back on! It was a night to remember. It was a night to re-member when I turned Him off when Jay died. But, oh, it was a long, dark Hell.

Carl struggled to bring himself out of his "long, dark Hell." From the beginning his original songs had been a means of taking stock of his life, and in the bleakest hours after Jay's death he turned for help to himself, the songwriter. Shortly after Holland's departure, and at Valda's urging, Carl visited Jim Denny at Cedarwood Publishing, and found Denny eager to sign him on as a writer—"You look like you might still rock a little," Denny kidded Carl, dismissing Carl's apology for turning down his management offer two years earlier.

His association with Cedarwood marked the beginning of Carl's return from the brink of his own demise, personally as well as artistically. For the first time in his career he began crafting songs, consciously developing themes and ideas in his lyrics, working out the music, rewriting, editing, trying to discipline himself to go from A to Z by way of B, C, D, and so on.

Jim Denny turned out to be precisely the right person for Carl at a time when he most needed guidance professionally. Having someone of Denny's standing believe in him spurred Carl to stay sober for long stretches. He became a prolific writer: In the four years between 1959 and 1964, Carl published nearly three hundred songs he characterizes as "studied, pretty well written, and well constructed." Some of his writing sessions were fueled by alcohol, and it wasn't unusual for a writing session to end with Carl passed out on the Cedarwood floor for the night.

At their worst, Carl's songs were maudlin and self-pitying, showing the influence of too much alcohol mixed with overwhelming sadness. Most, however, were remarkably tough and restrained, given Carl's wild mood swings during a period when he was grappling with a shaky career, and all were deeply reflective of the inner man's longings, his troubled heart, and his memories of a better time. Occasionally he went overboard with the sentimentality, but more often than not he walked gracefully on a line between the cloying and the genuinely measured in examining his reason for being. Some of these, particularly a number of religious recitations he recorded under the name C.D. Cedar, were among the most personal and self-revealing writings he had done in his life, and in keeping with their intimate nature, none has ever been released and the master tapes have remained Carl's personal property.

Musicians who worked with Carl during this time say he was most always prepared, and never at a loss for new songs, much to the amazement of his cohorts at Cedarwood. One of those who visited him in Nashville in 1963 was Les Paul, who was in town seeking material for a new album. Friends in the music community had directed him to Cedarwood, with instructions to seek out Carl Perkins.

He showed up at the office early one evening with Chet Atkins in tow. Carl had started drinking in the afternoon when he found out who would be visiting him later and was flying high by the time they arrived. As the night wore on, Carl, Paul, and Atkins sat in the Cedarwood studio playing every kind of song that came to mind, including a few new Perkins originals. From Cedarwood they journeyed out to Music City nightspots, playing short sets in each one before finally calling it quits sometime near sunrise. Fascinated by the guitar solos on "Blue Suede Shoes," Paul asked Carl how he got his sound. Carl's answer: "My guitar neck was warped," a response that can only be ascribed as alcohol-influenced, since Carl was playing his sacred two-year-old Gibson Les Paul at the time. At the end of the night, Paul left impressed by what he had heard of Carl Perkins's newest music and by the man's ability to assimilate new instrumental ideas into his own music.

"Carl was in the back room with a guitar, a jug, and a recording machine, and he was writing some very good songs," Paul says. "I thought he was a good player and a good writer, and when we went around to all the different clubs and sat in and jammed we had one hell of a time. I think he was picking up on some of the things I was doing. I remember we were talking about multiple tracking that night, and I found out he really had his ear to the ground and knew what was happening. I thought he was very valuable."

Jim Denny was also responsible for opening Carl's eyes to the truth Valda had always suspected: He wasn't receiving near what was due him in royalties from Sam Phillips. Carl's first clue came when Denny made an offhand comment that Carl's BMI check on "Shoes" must have amounted to "a fortune."

To which Carl replied: "What's BMI?"

After explaining Broadcast Music International's function as a licensing agency that registers songwriters' material and collects fees due them and their publishing companies for use of the material, Denny pointed out, "You get paid half of what your publisher gets. 'Blue Suede Shoes' is probably one of the most played records that's been out in years. What did you get off that in fifty-six?"

Carl related the figure on his first Hi-Lo check. Denny's comment: "You've got to be kidding." When Denny checked with BMI, Carl alleges, he found more than $60,000 having been paid to Sam Phillips in 1956. Less than $15,000—less than half of the fifty-fifty split with Sam's publishing company—had made its way into Carl's pocket that year.

To Carl's dismay, he found Sam beyond reach, owing to the expiration of BMI's three-year statute of limitations provision for protesting royalty payments. Denny offered to hire a lawyer to go after Sam directly, but Carl declined, not wanting to owe Denny the lawyer's fees and feeling that he was getting a fair shake at Cedarwood and would eventually recoup his lost earnings. At Cedarwood he saw his first thorough accounting, with listings of all his songs, where they were being played, and how much he had earned off each one.

Having found an honest man and a staunch supporter in Jim Denny, it was a blow to Carl when Denny died of cancer in 1963. He had left the business in good hands, though, with his sons Bill and John assuming the reigns upon their father's passing. Bill handled the business affairs (he had an economics degree from Vanderbilt University), while John tended the creative side of the operation as producer and engineer at Cedarwood's recording studio. The mantle of leadership rested easily on Bill, who maintained his father's policy of respecting every aspect of the artist's career, particularly relating to finances. It was not only Jim Denny's practice, Bill insists, but one common to the Nashville music industry: "The music industry to me was almost a family business—in our case it *was* a family business. But I felt that the industry itself in Nashville was kind of a great big family business. And we made a real effort in Nashville among the publishers and the record labels to make sure people didn't get taken advantage of. It was probably the only town you could go to as far as the music industry's concerned where there's never been any really big lawsuits, writers suing publishers because of nonpayment, or suits against managers, and so forth. Because people in Nashville just didn't treat each other that way."

Las Vegas proved to be an important destination for Carl in the early sixties, when he began appearing regularly at a lounge in the Golden

Nugget casino, playing six hours a day, forty-five minutes on stage, fifteen off, for three to four weeks consecutively. From being the opening act on a package that included Hank Thompson's western swing band, country singer Judy Lynn, and a house comedian, Carl's popularity elevated him to headliner status after only a couple of appearances at the Nugget. The money was good, the audiences appreciative, and the work grueling. So grueling, in fact, that Carl cut down on his drinking so that he could get enough rest to endure each day's grind. Even though he was treading water as an artist, maintaining his sobriety was a major achievement.

Even Clayton was somewhat becalmed by the rigors of the Vegas schedule, although he was still Clayton. During one set, a drunk in the audience fired a shot glass towards the stage and knocked a hole in Clayton's bass. Clayton dropped his instrument and took off after the fellow, bounding across table tops, streaking through the casino area and out to the street, where he pummeled the man senseless as a crowd gathered. The police arrived and took the man to jail; he was bailed out the next day by Clayton, in a rare moment of compassion.

Clayton had taken to singing in the late fifties after hearing Don Gibson's first hit, "Oh Lonesome Me," and finding he possessed a voice nearly as dark and compelling as Gibson's. Carl was willing to give Clayton a solo spot in the show, but Clayton would take it only when he decided he was ready to sing. Carl usually learned of Clayton's intentions between songs; on a few occasions he was interrupted in the midst of an introduction, Clayton butting in with, "I'm ready to sing me one now." He did this once at the Nugget, and was rebuffed by Carl. Never one to give up easily, he proceeded to push his brother away from the mic, telling him, "Yeah, hell yeah, I'm fixin' to sing!" To the audience he announced: "I'm Clayton Perkins and I'm gonna sing this song, and I don't give a damn whether you like it or not." With this, Carl recalls, the audience erupted into wild applause: "Automatically he had 'em right in the palm of his hand. And a lot of times they stood up and applauded for him. I saw it happen right there in the Golden Nugget in Las Vegas many times. There were nights when he would absolutely just about take the thing. Except for 'Blue Suedes' and 'Honey Don't' and 'Matchbox,' he just about had the rest of the hour. Either with his fiddle or he'd sing. And he'd get up and talk to 'em and he'd tell some dirty jokes. People loved him. 'Oh Lonesome Me,' he loved to play that. 'Legend in My Time,' I can hear him singing it now. He could sing it as good as it's been sung. He had three or four songs that he liked to do. But he didn't want to do 'em unless he'd reached a certain high."

Among those warning Carl to keep Clayton under wraps was Patsy Cline. Astutely guided by producer Owen Bradley, she had, by the early sixties, become the most important female singer in country music history. Hers was a style that merged pop and country and was being accepted by both audiences, overwhelmingly so, causing the Nashville music industry to rethink the scope of its music's potential. Cline had a natural affinity for country blues, swing, and traditional country, but with Bradley's encouragement she began cutting other types of material that challenged her interpretive skill—Cole Porter and Bob Wills showed up in her repertoire alongside songs by Don Gibson and Hank Williams. The qualities apparent in her voice mirrored the woman offstage: A bulwark of feminine fortitude, she combined strength and self-sufficiency with forthright expressions of vulnerability, longing, and desire. With her dark hair, dark, piercing eyes, and the natural grace with which she carried herself, she projected exactly what she was: a sensuous, straight-shooting, intelligent woman who would be accepted on her terms or none at all.

In January of 1962, Carl had been on a two-week package tour with Cline, Cash, George Jones, and Bill Monroe that wound through the Midwest and into Canada. At the end of the year, from late November to late December, during one of his engagements at the Golden Nugget, Cline was across the street making her Vegas debut at the Mint Casino and paying frequent visits to the Nugget to hobnob with Carl between sets. On the road she heard Carl arguing with Clayton backstage and cautioned him, "You better watch that boy. He'll cause you trouble, Carl. That boy is flat mean. You sure he's your brother?" Cline shook her head in dismay and told Carl: "He damn sure don't favor you. And he damn sure don't act like you."

"I got a good mama, Patsy," Carl answered. "He's my brother."

"Aw, I didn't mean anything," she said apologetically. "You get in trouble just openin' your mouth, really. That was stupid of me. Why'd I say it like that for?"

"That's all right," Carl said. "He *is* a little different."

In Vegas Cline brought her mother to see Carl's show, and the three of them were photographed together in the Nugget lounge. An attractive, persuasive woman, Patsy even coaxed Carl into performing two of his unrecorded spiritual recitations, "Today You're Twenty-One" and "The Lord's Fishing Hole," not the sort of fare the casino patrons expected. Reveling in Carl's stories of the hard times in Lake County and of his years at Sun, she would often refuse her husband-manager Charlie Dick's requests to discuss upcoming business until she had heard a few more tush-hog yarns.

She also teased Carl about his singing, accusing him of holding back on his country ballads. "No I'm not," Carl assured her. "I'm wide open. You're the one holdin' back. Just go ahead and tear the world up with one of those songs. That's what you're gonna do anyway. What are you waitin' on? Just destroy everybody with that voice you got. It's there. You're just slightly usin' it."

"Yeah," she said, laughing. " 'Slightly usin' it.' You said you was wide open? I'm using every gear I've got when I'm in that studio, hoss."

"Hoss" was omnipresent in Cline's vocabulary, along with stronger epithets, none of which Carl remembers ever being directed at him. Patsy called him "Perkins," and was mild-mannered in his presence—even motherly, in her advice to him to "hang around smart people who can stimulate your mind. No sense wastin' your time with a dud."

While on the road in January, Carl hit on an idea for a song backstage in either Omaha, Nebraska, or Wichita, Kansas. On the guitar he strummed a slow, minor key melody, and began improvising lyrics, singing:

> I was so-oh wrong
> For-or so-oh long
> Thought I could live
> Without the love that you'd give
> I was wrong, oh, so wrong

I've been so wrong
For-or so-oh long
I didn't know
That I loved you so
I was wrong

From the other side of the dressing room wall Carl heard a squeal of delight as he sang, and then Cline's voice shouting, "Perkins! Whose song is that?"

"Just mine," Carl answered.

"Damn you! When did you write that?"

"I haven't," said Carl.

"Well you better do it," Cline ordered. "And don't sing it so loud! Don't let nobody else hear it! You'll get that one stolen!"

Carl returned to Nashville to cut a demo of "So Wrong" at Cedarwood before resuming his tour. He gave the unfinished song to Mel Tillis, who completed it with another Cedarwood writer, Danny Dill. Over a wash of crying strings and a tinkling piano—one of Bill McElhiney's most sensitive arrangements—Cline gave it a performance for the ages at her February 28 session, her voice caressing the lyrics to underscore the feelings of guilt and resignation Carl described in his sad saga of bad judgment in matters romantic. Released in July 1962, it peaked at number fourteen on the country chart, and number eighty-five on the pop chart.

To Owen Bradley the "So Wrong" session stands out for Cline's reaction to the finished product: "I liked the song, and I remember a comment that was made when we were making it. The Jordanaires were on the record, and we had their voices down real low, singing a low chord on the words 'so wrong.' We came into the control room and had a playback, and Patsy said, 'It has balls,' and the Jordanaires' bass singer held up three fingers. It was so virile, that background. Patsy liked the way that song was written."

At the close of their stands in Las Vegas, in late 1962, Carl bid Patsy good-bye, telling her, "I never worked with a greater lady and I thank you for being so kind to me. I'm gonna call you my friend from now on."

Waving farewell and winking at Carl, Patsy said, "Hoss, you better," and was gone back to Nashville.

On the morning of March 6, 1963, Carl left his house at four a.m. to spend the day fishing with his friend and new drummer, Tony Moore. On the way to Moore's house, Carl heard a news bulletin on the radio reporting the deaths of three country-music stars in a plane crash near Camden, Tennessee: Hawkshaw Hawkins, Cowboy Copas, and Patsy Cline, along with the pilot, Randy Hughes, Cline's manager.

Carl slumped in his seat, numb with disbelief. At Moore's house, he unhooked his boat trailer and told Moore they were going to the crash site. Having a state government license plate as a result of his friendship with Tennessee's governor, Carl was waved through the Highway Patrol blockade and parked near the area being combed for remains. The plane had crashed to the ground after hitting a tree about three miles west of the Tennessee River; its fuselage bore a hole in the earth some three feet deep. "It wasn't something I'd rush to see again," Carl says. "I had nightmares about it, thought about it a lot. I remember a black slip hanging high in a big tree with a foot or two of human intestine hanging from the tree. I remember Hawkshaw Hawkins's big white hat sittin' up in the top of a tree just like it was sittin' on top of his head. I picked up a few pieces of a guitar neck that I know was Copas's, because it had his name on it—C-O-P was part of the fingerboard. That was the biggest piece of the guitar I found. Picked up Patsy's compact—it said 'Made especially for Patsy Cline'—lipstick, hair brush. The smell of death was all over that hillside. It was hard to leave it. It's hard to explain standing in the middle of where such a tragic thing happened, and you steppin' around blood, and you see an ear with a piece of hair hanging on it that came off her head.

"I don't know really know how to describe it. Every memory you ever had of 'em is right on the tip of your tongue and right on the front of your brain and you just say, 'Why, why, why?' And there are no answers that come. I just sat down and said me a little prayer and came back home."

In the years following Jay's death, Clayton's behavior had taken an ugly turn. Drinking heavily, the rough-cut prankster had turned violent and surly. By 1963 he had taxed his brother's patience to the limit.

One summer evening in Las Vegas, during a card game with Hank Thompson's band, Clayton spent his time hurling insults at Carl, denigrating his music, his lifestyle, his lineage, anything and everything that came to mind. Carl tried to deflect the insults with jokes in an effort to keep things light around the table. Clayton persisted in his attacks. Finally fed up, Carl invited him outside to talk it over. Together they walked to their motel's rear parking lot.

"Alright," Carl said, squaring off, "you been wantin' to fight me ever since we got out here. Let's go. Just help yourself and get all you want, 'cause I'm gonna hurt you if I can."

Clayton swung wildly and ferociously, but missed. Carl landed his first punch to Clayton's jaw, spinning him on his heels. Then he connected with two more blows in succession near Clayton's eyes, before Clayton doubled him over with a solid punch to the abdomen. As Carl struggled for air, Clayton knocked him to the concrete with a slap to the back of his skull. On his hands and knees, Carl crawled away from Clayton, then rose up to his full height again. Fists pumping like pistons, he landed blow after cutting blow to Clayton's face. But the youngest Perkins brother took the shots and began scoring some of his own to Carl's jaw and torso. For several minutes the brothers stood toe-to-toe, pounding each other, both men bloodied but undeterred. Suddenly Carl ducked, lunged at, and tackled Clayton, throwing him to the ground. Immobilizing him by sitting on his chest, his knees pinning down Clayton's shoulders, Carl gasped for breath as his brother tried to squirm free.

"You know, I could finish you right here," Carl said. "I could knock every tooth outta your head."

"You got me. You got me," Clayton moaned. "This one's yours. You won."

"Alright, Clayton. This is the last one we'll ever have. And just remember: If you wasn't my brother, I'd kill you."

Carl apologized, Clayton said nothing—"he found it very hard to ask for forgiveness"—and both men started back to their room, Carl walking several feet ahead of Clayton. Hearing footsteps behind him, Carl instinctively ducked to one side at the moment Clayton's fist came whistling by him and slammed into the motel's brick wall. Without breaking stride, Carl went on his way, while Clayton stood screaming for help in the breezeway, holding onto his bleeding, fractured hand. The Las Vegas dates went on with Jimmy Martin on bass. A musician by trade, Martin had been hired as road manager by Carl, whose hunch it was that someone would be needed to replace Clayton on a moment's notice.

Near the end of the year, after a date with Red Foley and Ray Price in Cincinnati, Foley came to Carl and Clayton's room, asking Carl if he would do some of his recitations. When Foley entered, Clayton was sprawled on the bed, stinking of alcohol, apparently passed out. He began stirring as Carl played. Suddenly he shot up and attacked Foley with his fists, knocking Foley's false teeth across the room. Reacting swiftly, Carl slugged Clayton and sent him sprawling; with a second blow he knocked him unconscious.

"Send that boy home. He's gonna pull you down. He drinks too much," Foley told Carl as he pulled himself together. Apologizing profusely, Carl dragged Clayton out to the car, loaded the bass in the back seat, and headed for Jackson. Clayton slept through the ten-hour drive, awakening only when Carl pulled to a stop in front of their parents' house. With Buck and Louise looking on, Carl ordered Clayton out of the car, then handed him his bass.

"Well, this is the end, Clayton," Carl said. "This chapter of our lives is finished."

Clayton grabbed the bass and flung it towards the house. As it bounced around the yard, he stormed inside, slamming the door behind him.

Turning to his mother and father, Carl waved. "I'll see you in a few days," he said. "Take care of yourselves, and watch him." Carl drove away, fighting back tears: "That was the end of the Perkins Brothers. Jay was dead, Clayton and I had stretched the string till it broke. I knew I'd be lonesome. I knew it'd be tough. I loved him, he was my brother, but I was told by that sweet old man [Foley], and by some others, 'Carl, he's like to kill you one of these days.' So I just kept on working, got me a drummer so I wouldn't be riding alone."

W i t h the expiration of his five-year Columbia contract in early '63, Carl signed a two-year deal with Decca and was told by his new producer, Owen Bradley, to cut and play on his own songs. Bradley also questioned Carl closely about his recording sessions at Sun. Like most everyone Carl came into contact with, Bradley was surprised to learn how much of the Sun material had been composed on the spot in the studio. He urged Carl to proceed the same way and to try to get something going with the musicians Bradley would hire for the sessions. Many of these turned out to be the same players Carl had worked with on Columbia, including Grady Martin and Harold Bradley on guitars, the Jordanaires on background vocals, Buddy Harman on drums, Floyd Cramer on piano. Trumpeters Carl Galvin and Don Sheffield were the most notable of the few new faces on the first Decca session in August 1963, which produced three first-rate cuts on new original material and an odd cover song, "I Wouldn't Have You," which sounded suspiciously like a slowed-down version of Presley's "(Let Me Be Your) Teddy Bear." Carl's latest efforts were in a pop-country vein—the evocative trumpet lines floating around in a couple of the songs added an interesting bit of jazz flavor to the tracks—and he delivered spectacular vocal displays of deeply felt country singing. One song, "After Sundown," spoke to the emptiness Carl still was feeling five years after Jay's death. The pain in his voice was nearly palpable when he sang:

After sundown, when darkness closes in on me
Oh, and I'm left alone, with just my blue memories
I look at your picture 'cause that's all I have around
Life is so, so blue, mighty, mighty blue after sundown

I make it pretty good when my friends are around
They don't know I'm hurt, because you let me down
They think I'm doin' fine, and happiness I've found
But my world stops turning 'round, after sundown

The rather ornate production of some of the Decca sides was Bradley's attempt to augment Carl's sound without altering its essence. With a career possibly hanging in the balance, Bradley felt bold strokes were necessary: "The music business is a whole bunch of ups and downs, and it was sort of in a down. I let Carl do what he wanted to. He had made some very good records, and his guitar was a part of those. We'd have almost every artist either sing or play, but in Carl's case I felt it was important that he play. Grady Martin's one of the greatest guitar players I ever worked with, but he didn't play like Carl, and Carl doesn't play like Grady. They're like chocolate and vanilla— they're both great. I did an experimental thing with some trumpets, just trying to find something—when you're drowning you kinda grasp at anything you can. And if you don't try something different, you never know. I doubt if we captured the real Carl. The bottom line was we didn't know what the hell to do with Carl. I didn't."

Although Carl had a regional hit with "After Sundown'" b/w "I Wouldn't Have You,'" his tenure with Decca was even less successful commercially than his Columbia years, producing a number of tracks that remain unissued. An interesting idea that never came to fruition was a duet album featuring Carl with Brenda Lee, another Bradley-produced artist. Lee had begun her career in the mid-fifties, when she was barely in her teens, singing rockabilly (one of the few females to venture into those waters); in the early sixties she had followed Cline into the pop-country arena and couldn't stop having hits. But nothing worked for Carl, no matter whether it was music with a hard edge or Bradley's tasteful, glossy productions. Drinking heavily again, Carl was losing momentum every time he went into a studio, and becoming more discouraged as his records failed.

Various theories have been advanced as to why Carl could make so many good records without having any of them be hits. Puzzled yet, Carl believes his lack of assertiveness coupled to his drinking undercut his career in the sixties as much or more than the record companies' failure to support his records with adequate promotion. Others who worked with Carl agree up to a point, and then struggle for answers. Bill Denny, for example, recalls that "Carl was having a problem with alcohol, and his reliability status was a problem for him. But that was a problem that a lot of people in the industry faced, so you just kind of lived with it and worked around it."

Harold Bradley suggests Carl bent too much to meet Nashville's standards: "I always felt badly about Carl not making it. Not that we did anything wrong or did anything bad—we gave him our heart. How could you not with a guy that's laying down the beat that guy is? But we already knew what the record producer wanted. Carl was very laid back in not bringing forth any musical ideas. As opposed to what Roy Orbison did—he came in and he had a lick or an idea and he had the song real constructed. When he quit bringing them in is when he quit being successful. But we didn't get that input from Carl. I felt he was very much trying to please Don Law and also join the Nashville party. It's awful to say this, but maybe if he had stayed in Memphis and recorded . . . Maybe he didn't write any more hits. I don't know. But I didn't feel like we really captured the man that he is. He played wonderful guitar, he sang with such soul. Maybe we watered him down trying to make him commercial. I don't know that we helped Carl."

Reflecting on Carl's approach to recording, Owen Bradley seconds his brother's assessment. Producing major artists, and having been a working musician himself, had given him an informed perspective. Ultimately, he admits, if Carl in his role as featured artist failed to communicate effectively, so did his producer: "Carl would leave it all up to me, maybe leave me more authority than I could handle. Maybe I expected him to say more and he didn't. Or maybe he expected me to do more and I didn't. But it takes a pretty sharp guy to figure that out when it's happening, and I've never been that sharp. If he'd been a little more aggressive, maybe it would have been different."

Of those closest to Carl, Johnny Cash was least surprised by his friend's difficulties in Nashville. Cash's music always had been closer to traditional country than to rockabilly or rock 'n' roll, easing his transition from Sun to Columbia. Carl's was a more difficult gap to bridge, Cash asserts: "Carl is unique, and the music scene in Nashville was not then or is not now conducive to propagating his style of music. I don't know if Carl ever had the right producer; I don't know if he ever had the right record company behind him to understand and care what his talents were. It seemed to be a struggle for him to find somebody that really wanted to bring out the best in him as an artist. I didn't hear a lot of that. They should've just let Carl be Carl."

With "After Sundown" 's poor showing, Carl hit bottom emotionally. He told Valda he was going to look into buying a farm near Jackson, retire from music, and go back to working the land full time. She told him to follow his heart, but added, "You'll never stop playing music." In March, Bill Denny called with an offer for Carl to do a tour of England with Chuck Berry, newly released from prison. Believing he was even more forgotten overseas than he was at home, Carl thought the whole notion insane. Only Valda saw a silver lining.

"I've got a feeling about you going over there," she told him. "They're bound to know you; they're bound to love you. You don't know but what you might go over there and find you're a big star."

Valda was right. The English rock fans embraced Carl with a fervor he had not experienced since the mid-fifties. Backed by the young British rockers the Nashville Teens, Carl threw himself into his shows as if he were back in the tonks, and had the fans not only dancing in the aisles but storming the stage. At the Hammersmith Odeon, where he appeared with John Lee Hooker, the Animals, the Swinging Blue Jeans, and Kingsize Taylor and the Dominoes, a banner unfurled in the audience that read: "Carl Perkins—King of Rock." At another date on the tour, a banner was hung from the balcony, greeting Carl with "Welcome Carl 'Beatle Crusher' Perkins." Carl knew a little about the Beatles, mostly from his son Stan, who loved the Liverpool quartet's music. "Them boys could use haircuts" was Carl's initial response to seeing a photograph of the group, but when he listened to *Meet the Beatles*, the band's first U.S. album, he heard echoes of the Sun sound, and in particular his Sun sound, in George Harrison's tense, trebly, single- and double-string solos. (Later he would learn that in the Beatles' early days, the guitarist had dispensed with his own first name and billed himself as Carl Harrison.) At every stop in England, he offered tearful, heartfelt thanks to the fans, saying, "You don't know just how happy you've made this ol' country boy feel."

The good feeling carried over to a studio date Decca arranged for Carl on May 22, with the Nashville Teens joining him. On six songs, including "Your True Love" and "Blue Suede Shoes," Carl sounded revitalized, singing with unbridled passion and constructing fuzz-tone guitar solos with a fury rivaled only by his finest Sun sides. The Teens were a perfect fit for Carl, because they, like the other young British bands Carl encountered, had learned every rockabilly nuance in the book from listening to Sun records; the Nashville studio pros were superior technicians, but the young rockers coming up in England had the energy that was the bedrock of Carl's music. Two new songs, "Big Bad Blues" (which Carl had written hoping to pitch to the Beatles) and "Lonely Heart," were top-notch rock 'n' roll efforts, the Teens and Carl demonstrating their unusual synergy in flamboyant style throughout; even more impressive was a new country weeper Carl had written, "A Love I'll Never Win," with a melody reminiscent of Floyd Cramer's "Last Date," and a narrative line that Carl sang like a man who was ready to open a vein.

> I'm as lonesome as any man's ever been
> Like an autumn leaf that's tossed around by the wind
> Please don't ask me why I cry
> These are real tears in my eyes
> And I'm waitin' for a love I'll never win
>
> It's like waiting for a ship that don't come in
> I'm just watchin' the tide rise on the sand
> The rushing waters of the sea and no one to comfort me
> Oh, I'm waiting for a love I'll never win
>
> My reason for living I don't know
> Her sweet love was my memory
> Oh how will I ever escape
> When our love just lingers on the leaves

Mr. Blue, move on in

Guess we'll have to be friends

Cause I'm waitin' for a love

For a love I'll never win

On June 1, Brunswick (Decca's British division) released "Big Bad Blues" as a single backed with "Lonely Heart." Little noted at the time was a recording session taking place that day at Abbey Road recording studios wherein one of rock 'n' roll's founding fathers passed the torch to the most important of the newest generation of rock 'n' roll bands.

As the last night of the tour approached, Carl and Chuck were invited to attend a post-concert party, at which the Beatles would be present. Both accepted, Carl reluctantly because he was anxious to get home after being away nearly five weeks; Chuck, Carl says, was even less enthusiastic than he. Prison had changed Chuck Berry, and the bright, spirited man who had graced Carl's Cadillac on the Tour of Stars in 1956 was now reclusive and withdrawn. He barely acknowledged Carl's presence in England, and when Carl asked good-naturedly why he didn't go back and write some great songs like he had done in the fifties, Chuck glared and snapped, "Do you mind if I don't answer that question?"

At the party, Carl was introduced to George Harrison, who wasted no time in interrogating Carl about the finer points of his Sun material. What key was "Honey Don't" in? Told it was in E, George turned to John Lennon, standing nearby, and said, "I told you we weren't doing it right." The Beatles had been playing the song in clubs and concerts in the key of G, with Ringo Starr doing the vocal. How do you play the intro? George's scrutiny of Carl's fingering patterns reminded Carl of how as a boy he had eyeballed Uncle John's solos.

John interrupted. "If you want to, we'd like you to come over to Abbey Road with us," Lennon said. "We're recording. You're welcome to come. We'd be honored."

Carl spent the afternoon, and most of the evening, of June 1 at Abbey Road. When he arrived at the studio, Paul McCartney was at the piano, John off to one side, finishing a run-through of his vocal on

Larry Williams's 1958 rocker "Slow Down." George was unwrapping a new Gretsch guitar sent to him by Chet Atkins—"You gotcha a hoss now," Carl told him. "I played one of those a little bit."

Carl took a seat next to an idle Ringo, who asked him more questions about Sun, and addressed him as "Mr. Perkins."

"Mr. Perkins is my daddy," Carl told Ringo. "I wish you'd call me Carl."

Ringo hesitated and then said, "This is hard for me to do."

"Shoot, spit it out, man!" Carl said with a laugh. "What is it?"

"Would you care if I sang some of your songs?"

"You mean you want me to write you some songs?" Carl asked.

"Well, that would be fine," Ringo began, "but I really love 'Honey Don't' and 'Matchbox.' "

"Do I care if you do those songs!?" Carl said, arching his eyebrows at the nervous drummer. "Shoot, no, man. I'd love it!"

During the afternoon the Beatles recorded five takes of "Matchbox." Between seven and ten p.m. the group recorded a Lennon-McCartney original, "I'll Be Back," in sixteen takes. Carl's recollection is of staying at the studio until close to three a.m. the following morning, joining in on guitar while the Beatles played early rock 'n' roll songs, including several Perkins compositions. They played "Blue Suede Shoes" "in the old Perkins style," according to Carl, with the stop-time pauses, and each Beatle taking a line of the intro, with Ringo having the honor of shouting "Go, cat, go!" As night melted into day, other Perkins songs were given vigorous treatments, including "Honey Don't," "Everybody's Trying to Be My Baby," and "Your True Love." (The Beatles performed still more Perkins songs on their frequent BBC Radio appearances, including a stunning version of "Sure to Fall," complete with the distinctive Jay and Carl harmony singing—swapping lead tenor roles seamlessly—as interpreted by John and Paul.)

As the Beatles continued questioning him, Carl noticed looks of absolute astonishment on their faces. "Where did you get the idea for 'Everybody's Trying to Be My Baby'?" John asked.

"I just said that on stage one night and my brother said, 'That's a song title,' " Carl answered.

An outtake from the Million Dollar
Quartet Session, December 1956.

The Million Dollar Quartet plus one: Elvis's female companion, identified as Marilyn Evans
in most reports, although Carl remembers her last name being Miller, was perched on the
piano for a while as the musicians worked their way through gospel and early country songs
that had influenced them.

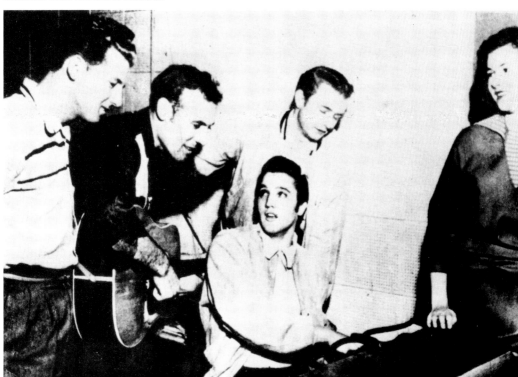

Carl performing at the Golden Nugget in Las Vegas in the late '50s.

The Martha Perkins Bain Collection

Carl and Jay onstage, late January, 1958. This is the last known photo of Carl and Jay together. Shortly after this date, Jay, who had been suffering from severe headaches and increasing weakness in one of his legs, left the tour to return to Jackson for a medical checkup. Diagnosed with a malignant brain tumor, he died on October 19, 1958.

The Martha Perkins Bain Collection

Carl in 1957 with country artist Wynn Stewart, whose hit song, "Keeper of the Key," Carl performed during the Million Dollar Quartet session and later cut for Sun.

The Jim Bailey Collection

(*Above*) **E**nd of an era. A publicity still from *Jamboree*, a 1958 rock 'n' roll musical featuring Carl, Fats Domino, Buddy Knox, Jerry Lee Lewis, and lesser lights. Given a choice of songs to perform, Carl picked "Glad All Over," leaving "Great Balls of Fire" to Jerry Lee Lewis. "Glad All Over" was released as Carl's final Sun single.

The Jim Bailey Collection

Carl posing in front of his new house on Park Avenue in Jackson.

THE JACKSON SUN/The Jim Bailey Collection

In 1965 Johnny Cash invited Carl, then recuperating from a gunshot wound to his foot, to join him for a couple of shows. The weekend gig turned into a fruitful ten-year association. The Cash troupe is shown here backstage before a show in the late '60s. Front row, from left: (unidentified), June Carter Cash, Johnny Cash, (unidentified), drummer W.S. Holland. Back row, from left: Carl Perkins, Don Reid of the Statler Brothers, Helen Carter, Phil Balsley of the Statlers, Bob Wootten, Harold Reid of the Statlers, Lew DeWitt of the Statlers, Mother Maybelle Carter, Anita Carter.

The Carl Perkins Collection

Carl caught in a quiet moment in the late '60s, writing a new song, using the back of his guitar as a desktop.

The Jim Bailey Collection

Johnny Cash and Carl backstage with a
fan in England, May 1968.

The Carl Perkins Collection

In the late '60s, Carl's son Greg took up playing the bass, with his father showing him the fundamentals on electric guitar. In the mid-'70s, he and his brother Stan would join their father professionally in the C.P. Express. They continue to play with him today.

THE JACKSON SUN/The Carl Perkins Collection

△ publicity still from Carl's mid-'70s stint with Jet Records.

The Jim Bailey Collection

In 1981, Carl's career received a boost from Paul McCartney, who asked Carl to play on his *Tug of War* album. They are shown here during rehearsals in the Montserrat studio where the sessions took place.

The Jim Bailey Collection

Carl and Chuck Berry greeting each other in November 1986 after Carl received a Lifetime Achievement Award from the Academy of Country Music.
The Carl Perkins Collection

The gymnasium at Gladewater, Texas, High School, 1993, looking virtually unchanged from the way it appeared in the mid-'50s when it was one of the regular stops for Sun Records artists on tour. In January 1956, teens attending a Carl Perkins show at this venue were the first to hear "Blue Suede Shoes" in its final version, as recorded by Carl the previous month and released at the outset of the new year.
Jim Bailey/The Jim Bailey Collection

The Gladewater motel where Elvis, Carl, Johnny Cash, and other Sun artists stayed after their shows at the nearby high school.
Jim Bailey/The Jim Bailey Collection

In October 1981, the Exchange Club Carl Perkins Center for the Prevention of Child Abuse opened in what was once a dormitory room on the campus of Union University. In 1994, ground was broken for a new building on the site of what was once Hardeman Music Store, where Carl bought his first Gibson Les Paul electric guitar. Each year since the Center opened, Carl has headed up a day-long fundraising telethon on a Jackson television station. In this photo, taken in the mid-'80s, he is shown near tears, greeting a girl who had come to the center a year earlier with cigarette burns over most of her body.

The Jim Bailey Collection

Even though weakened by radiation treatment for throat cancer, Carl summoned the strength to appear periodically throughout the day on the August 1991 telethon for the Center for the Prevention of Child Abuse. Among the special guests that day were Wynonna and Naomi Judd, shown here with Carl in the offices of WBBJ-TV before their appearance.

Courtesy Naomi Judd

"Then you sat down and wrote it?" George asked.

"No, I started singin' it."

"What?"

"I said I started singin' it."

"Live? On stage? Without writing it first?" George's voice rose in disbelief with each question.

"I wish I had my first version of it," Carl said. "It was much better than the one I recorded."

"What about the melody?" asked John.

"It came at the same time the words did," answered Carl.

"You must be kidding," said George.

So it went through the night, an event whose symbolism is without parallel in rock 'n' roll history: one of the artists who helped define the genre in its most basic form dispensing wisdom and sitting in on an early recording session with the artists who would build on his foundation and take it to places previously unimagined. The Beatles released "Matchbox" on their *Something New* album, recorded "Honey Don't" and "Everybody's Trying to Be My Baby" in two October sessions and released both songs on their *Beatles '65* album. No other writer had more of his songs covered by the Beatles than did Carl Perkins.

The high Carl felt on his return to the United States, knowing that somewhere at least his work hadn't been forgotten, recharged him. He went back on the road, working shows with country artists such as Webb Pierce and Faron Young, honing new material and anxiously awaiting his scheduled fall return to England, where he was set to tour with the Animals and Tommy Tucker (of "High Heel Sneakers" fame).

At the moment he was feeling revitalized, though, his career nearly came to an end. He was performing in Dyersburg, about sixty miles north of Jackson, at a political fund raiser. At the close of his set, Carl bowed to the audience, then stood up and raised his left hand to wave. As he did, the exposed blades of a rotary fan onstage tore through his hand. Blood splattered Carl's clothing and the stage around him. He was rushed to a local hospital, but when the examining physician ordered him transferred to a clinic in Memphis, Carl refused. Despite having suffered severe bone damage and losing blood so fast it formed pools on the floorboard of his Buick, he was adamant in demanding to go home to Jackson.

Suddenly, he felt a wonderful calm come over him: "My spirit left my body and went out that car window, through a dark tunnel. I went all the way through that tunnel and it opened up into the most beautiful sight I have ever seen. It was like being in the center of a rainbow. I can see it anytime, and have since then. The prettiest colors of blue and purple. There again I wasn't scared. And then all of a sudden it just [snaps fingers] was gone."

The Buick threw a rod on the ride down, and Carl, by then unconscious, was driven to Jackson by a highway patrolman who had been clearing a lane for his car from Dyersburg. In the emergency room he was given three quarts of glucose and five pints of blood—over half of his body's capacity.

When Valda arrived at the hospital and finally saw Carl, she gasped, "Oh, my Lord!"

"I got hysterical because he just looked dead," Valda recalls. "He had that yellow color that people get just before they die. He kinda came out and said, 'Val,' and then he went back under. The doctor told me, 'We can't operate on him. He's lost so much blood.' They were giving him glucose then. During the surgery the doctor had to stop three times because he thought Carl was dying. He did say, 'I did his surgery exactly like I would want somebody to do me, because I make my living with my hands.' I said, 'Don't cut off any fingers.' "

Carl's fingers were spared, even though all the tendons had been severed in the third finger and the pinky and both had deep cuts into the bones. Two months later, when his cast was removed and he began an arduous physical rehabilitation, he had feeling only in the tip of his second finger—"a little tingling." Useless after the accident, the pinky was permanently bent inward after its tendons were surgically severed and tied to prevent it from interfering with Carl's playing. Part of his hand had no feeling, and never would again.

As he had re-created himself as a songwriter after Jay's death, so did Carl set out to re-create himself as a guitarist now. Only his thumb was free of the cast that extended up to the elbow, so he tuned his guitar to an open E and began exercising the thumb by pressing on the top strings. When the cast came off nearly two months later, the hand, Carl says, "looked like a skeleton."

Constantly squeezing a rubber ball to build up the hand's strength and flexibility, he gradually began to practice on the guitar strings. In what seemed to Valda to be a remarkably short time, he was sounding like the Carl Perkins of old, only with three fingers instead of four.

"I have never seen anybody as determined," Valda says. "Deep in my heart, I didn't think he'd ever be able to play anymore. I don't know how he did it, 'cause I know it had to hurt so bad. He said, 'I will play again.' I like that determination in him, but there was that thing in my mind that said, I don't think he ever will be able to. But I didn't say that to him."

It was a moment of triumph, then, when Carl was able to return to the stage in time to fulfill his British tour commitment in the fall, the response to which almost mirrored that of the previous summer. Nevertheless, his near-death experience occupied most of his thoughts: "I made it through [the injury]. But what I would constantly go back to was that beautiful rainbow that I was taken away from. I liked that place. I fell in love with it. Quiet, most peaceful, restful, there was nothing scary about it. If death is like that, man, it's not bad. It's not bad at all."

A little over a year after his hand injury, Carl's left foot was nearly severed by a blast from his shotgun. He was on a hunting trip with a friend, and had laid his weapon against a fence while he climbed over. The gun fell to the ground and discharged, hitting Carl square in the left ankle. He was told he might not be able to walk again without assistance, but in another remarkable bit of self-rehabilitation, he was mobile in a matter of weeks, moving around on his own strength and with only a slight limp.

During his recovery, he was visited by Johnny Cash, who invited Carl to join him for a show in Chattanooga. The visit was well timed, because Carl was getting restless at home, and inconsiderate: He would wake up hungry at three or four in the morning, and roust Valda by pounding on their bedroom wall with his crutches and repeatedly screaming out his order of "Biscuits! Meat! Eggs!" Valda would usually oblige, but she was getting frustrated with Carl's impatience and wild mood swings. Sometimes he would get so fed up that he would fire a crutch end over end across the living room into a wall. Valda was as thankful for Cash's offer as Carl was.

It was 1966, and for Carl other battles loomed, but some had ended. In the wake of his warm reception in England, he set out to find what he thought was a missing piece of his life's puzzle. Never again would his music tap into the cultural and political climate of America as it had in the fifties. The moving hand, having writ, moved on.

Elvis was now a sure-fire box office attraction and occasionally made some interesting records, proving that the flame still burned. He was coasting, almost lost in the changing of rock 'n' roll's guard. After his late-fifties disgrace, Jerry Lee was mounting a comeback as a country artist; he too had been energized by the tumultuous receptions accorded him in the early sixties by British rockers. Roy Orbison had cut one masterpiece after another for Monument through the early sixties, all showcasing not only his remarkable gift as a writer, but also his powerful, unusual voice. Cash was proving himself one of the most literate and adventurous country artists of his generation, his 1965 *Orange Blossom Special* album featuring three songs by Bob Dylan.

Carl was still in the hunt, but on its fringes. Thus did the search begin.

W h a t Carl thought was nothing more than a diversion during his recuperation became a place he called home professionally for nearly ten years. With the Cash show, the pressure was off—he knew where he was going, what he would be doing, and when he would be doing it. No matter the fate of his own records, there would always be work, because Cash toured constantly and recorded regularly and wanted Carl part of both pursuits. With the royalty checks from Sun coming infrequently (despite Valda's persistent calls to Sam to demand he honor the twice-yearly payment schedule spelled out in his publishing agreements with Carl), touring with Cash also offered much-needed financial security.

Moreover, Carl and Cash were addictive personalities trying to gain some measure of control over their demons. They could and did try to support each other in getting straight, but both were backsliders. Cash was sometimes so drugged up he couldn't make a show, and left it to Carl to explain away his absence to bad weather or a missed airline connection. The concert would go on while Cash lurched around his tour bus parked outside the auditorium, ransacking its interior and destroying anything he could get his hands on. Carl would return to find Cash sitting on the edge of his bed, abject and bawling like a baby, only to be reduced to tears himself as he tried to commiserate with his friend in their mutual misery.

Eventually Cash sought the help of a psychiatrist, Dr. Nat Winston, and urged Carl to do likewise. Carl, however, preferred to help himself, and in comparison to the amount of alcohol he had consumed during the late fifties and early sixties, he seemed to be nearing recovery. Never an avid book reader, he took a friend's suggestion to try Norman Vincent Peale's 1952 self-help best-seller, *The Power of Positive Thinking*, and it struck a chord.

"I picked up some wisdom from that book," Carl says. "Positive thinking is what I needed when I started in this business. I didn't have enough of it then, and I'm still working on it. I've flashed back to that book several times in my life since I read it."

In a generous portrait published in the December 7, 1968, issue of *Rolling Stone*, reporter Michael Lydon captured the essence of Carl's spirit during the Cash years. He is on the road, lonesome for Valda and the kids, but forever the good soldier, his deadpan, self-deprecating wit providing welcome comic relief on the long bus trips.

"I don't know what we'd do without you, Rock King," Cash says.

"Laugh," Carl is quoted, "but that's what they called me, and that's what some people still call me, the King of Rock and Roll."

Lydon observes: "They all laughed. Carl Perkins is a natural born straight man . . . He reads *Positive Thinking* seriously, but it's like Mr. Peepers reading Charles Atlas. Yet he is never pathetic."

At the close, Carl turns philosophical in a revelatory comment: "It's all in how you look at things," Carl finished, picking up *Positive Thinking* again. "I figure I went from low to high to low to just about right in the middle. That's an advance, isn't it, and maybe now I'm inching forward again."

Carl had every reason to be upbeat. In addition to working with Cash, he had signed with the Dollie label, founded in the late fifties by Jim Denny but dormant for years until being reactivated under his son Bill's aegis. Coproducing with his brother John, Denny attempted to recreate the feel of a Sun session, dispensing with the clock, encouraging Carl's songwriting, putting the guitar back in his hands and urging him to tell his story any way he wanted to. Supporting Carl were veteran session players James Colvard (guitar), Bobby Dyson (bass), William Ackerman, and Jerry Kerrigan (drums); Ron Ochs and Larry Butler (keyboard); Walter Haynes and Pete Drake (steel guitar); and background singers Jan Crutchfield, Delores Denning, and Hershel Wigginton.

The Dennys succeeded in capturing the pure country soul of Carl Perkins better than anyone since Sam Phillips. Over the course of two years, Carl dug into his past and set down in lyric form a clear statement of where his heart was at—no surprise then that most of the songs spoke of home and family and the power of love as a guiding force. The titles told a story: "Home (That's Where the Heart Is)," "Poor Boy Blues," "You Can Take the Boy Out of the Country," "Back to Tennessee," "Mama and Daddy," "An Old Fashioned Sing-A-Long," even "Valda" ("A real true wife / for the rest of her life / she'll be there").

Plagued by poor distribution, however, Dollie was a commercial failure. Of the thirty-some Perkins recordings cut for Dollie, only ten were released as singles. Discounting the few that lapsed into overweaning sentimentality, the work illuminated Carl's evolving artistry: His singing voice had deepened to a world-weary baritone, and he was phrasing and varying his timing with a stylist's assurance; his guitar solos displayed an economy of expression without losing the individual stamp associated with Carl's unpredictable choices; his writing, always reflective, displayed a more profound understanding of life's drift and the eternal verities.

"The simplicity in Carl's music came through and he just motivated people to do things," says John Denny in recalling the artist at work in the Dollie sessions. "The best way you could produce Carl Perkins was to turn the tape machine on and shut up. Put him in the studio ten, fifteen, twenty minutes before you turn on the tape machine and let him get a rapport with everybody in the room. Everybody gets in the same mind-set and simplicity becomes art."

Carl reached down for a definitive personal statement to conclude his last Dollie session, on April 16, 1968. Roots and family were long-standing topics in his songs, but "Lake County Cotton Country" cut to the bone in bearing witness to the strength of his dream:

> I nearly 'bout remember the day I was born
>
> Mama, Papa said it was early one morn
>
> Pop liked his boy; I'd soon be a man
>
> He started me out in that cotton land
>
> He put a nine-foot tarbottom on my back
>
> He said, take your hand, boy, and fill that sack
>
> I worked my fingers down to the bone
>
> Folks, that ain't funny
>
> But it's about the only way I had
>
> To make a living in the Lake County cotton country
>
> I finally saved enough nickels, got myself a guitar
>
> I had visions of the Opry, I'd soon be a star
>
> Picked cotton by day and guitar at night
>
> I got my lessons on the floor by a coal oil light
>
> I wore hand-me-down britches every day to school
>
> That's enough to disillusion any ordinary fool
>
> Kept on pickin' my old guitar
>
> It meant that much to me
>
> Lord, I kept on pickin' my old guitar
>
> In the Lake County cotton country

In 1966, shortly after joining Cash and making steady money again, Carl was able to move his parents out of a government-subsidized housing project in Jackson and into a home on a sixty-six-acre farm near Clarksburg, Tennessee, about thirty-five miles from Jackson, neighboring Ed Cisco's place. Carl paid $6,500 for the land and the dilapidated house. Standing on the porch with his parents at twilight, after all their few worldly possessions had been put in place in their new home, Carl said: "Well, you don't know what this means to me. You don't ever have to change addresses again. Your next address can be Heaven, 'cause this is y'all's. This is a dream come true."

Throwing himself into the remodeling of the house helped Carl "back off the bottle quite a bit" and gave him new purpose, for a cause he believed in, namely, giving something back to Buck and Louise: "For one time in my mama and daddy's life they wasn't second class. I loved to go up there, because, man, we worked. We put white fence all around it. I loved every nail I drove. Life was very special to me during that time. I stayed busy helping my dad clean up that little farm. It had grown up a lot, and my three little boys were up there working, sweating and just loving the action. Every Friday, when them boys would get in from school, my daddy would be sittin' in my house, waitin' to take them to the farm. See, they looked out across them fields and they saw Jay, Carl Lee, and Clayton. But under a different set of circumstances. They saw them little boys with new shoes and nice little short pants on that Valda saw they had. We all fell in love with that place."

In his self-rehabilitation, Carl was surrounded by sobriety in the Cash troupe. While Johnny was still battling an amphetamine addiction, around him were people who stayed straight—Mother Maybelle Carter and her daughters June (whom Johnny was courting, having divorced Vivian several years earlier), Helen, and Anita; and the Statler Brothers (Harold and Don Reid, Lew DeWitt, and Phil Balsley). Among the Tennessee Three, only Luther Perkins indulged in alcohol or drugs of any kind.

Cash was over the edge. Before he married June Carter in 1968, he lived alone in a large house on Old Hickory Lake in Hendersonville, Tennessee, a few miles outside Nashville's city limits. Roy Orbison lived a short car ride down the same road. On the few days they were off the road and out of the studio, Carl became accustomed to Cash calling at odd hours of the day or night and asking him to come visit.

Always obliging, and bringing along Fluke Holland for good measure, Carl would find Cash in the kitchen, cooking country ham and eggs, tromping barefoot on a grime-covered marble floor, blinking his eyes rapidly (as he did when he was on something), and talking a mile a minute. The house had hardly any furnishings and Cash could be said to be negligent in his cleaning duties. It was, as Carl notes, a comical scene: "He'd make biscuits big as saucers, and get flour all over that marble floor. Cut that ham thick. It was hilarious to watch him. He'd be barefooted and you'd see them ol' big crooked feetprints in the flour on the floor. And he'd cook up the awfullest platter of that ugly-looking ham. He'd start out thick and come down to the width of a cigarette paper. Throw it in that big iron skillet. He'd fry a dozen eggs. He'd make a lard stand full of them biscuits. He thought he was a wonderful cook. That bread was so hard I could have throwed it right through the wall. He'd say, 'How's that?' I'd say, 'It's mighty good, mighty good. You didn't make enough.' If there had been any furniture in the house he'd of tore it all to pieces. Had one big ol' round bed upstairs, and that's what he had. Out there in that mansion by himself."

Outside the confines of his home, Cash was dangerous. A man of conscience, he had made the rights of Native Americans his cause, and, with the same commitment he brought to his vices, had thrown himself into a study of the various tribes' histories. Carl remembers Cash standing with the toes of his bare feet dangling over the edge of a cliff on Old Hickory Lake, arms outstretched towards the sinking sun, mumbling something or other about the Great Spirit giving him wisdom and guidance on his life's journey. Completing his benediction, he would then leap several feet from one rocky precipice to another. Other times the conscience would drop away and he would be crazy Johnny Cash, thrill seeker, driving his jeep into Old Hickory Lake, submersing the car, himself, and Carl, and climbing out, saying, "You know, that's something I've always wanted to do—I've *always* wanted to drive this Army jeep off into that lake." It was the typical pattern Carl had long observed: "He'd stay straight for a few dates and then he'd turn into that wild Indian again," Carl recalls. "We'd travel in an old Dodge motor home, and it was all to pieces. He'd lock himself inside that thing where [June] couldn't get in to him, and he'd hide his drugs from his own self. He'd take a speaker off with his old pocket knife and put them in a speaker, put the cover back over it. When the radio would play, you could hear the bennies rattlin'. He was comical, but I loved him. And I didn't want him to hurt himself. He'd break a thumb and wouldn't even tell you about it. He didn't know—he couldn't feel no pain."

Carl was keeping up by drinking beer, lots of beer—in the late sixties his weight ballooned to 230 pounds, 60 pounds more than he weighed during his Sun years. Beer was a substitute for whiskey in Carl's effort to wean himself from the bottle. Whiskey did him in quickly, but with beer he could drink for hours and get only a mild buzz.

In his struggle with alcoholism, he found it easier to stay straight for long periods of time being around the Carters and, especially, the Statlers. Mother Maybelle was both tough and gentle with Carl, one moment lecturing him on the damage he would do to his career if he didn't stop drinking, the next plying him and the others on the tour with her fried chicken and home-cooked vegetables and telling Carl how much he was loved by everyone. Having been an important participant in the birth of modern country music, her stories of the old days kept Carl connected to his own roots.

More than any others in the Cash troupe, the Statlers offered Carl laughter as a cure for what ailed him. Unlike Cash, the Statlers and Carl were in the same boat in being separated for long stretches from close-knit families. At these times, when Carl was at his loneliest and most vulnerable, Harold, Don, Lew, or Phil provided solace. "We knew what Carl was feeling and he knew what we were feeling," says Harold. "I think that's the reason we were so comfortable with each other: All of us had those same kind of longings and those same kind of things we were missing out on."

Of the quartet, their longtime producer Jerry Kennedy says, "They're crazy and they don't use drugs or alcohol." By all accounts the Statlers are unpredictable when it comes to the frequency and inventiveness of their practical jokes. It wasn't unusual for Carl to come back to his hotel room and find Phil Balsley sitting there in a chair, his pants off, carrying on a one-sided conversation with one of Carl's toupees, which he would have perched on his knee.

"You little son of a bitch!" Carl would exclaim. "You're lookin' up under that thing just like you do when it's on my head!"

Harold, the bass singer and comic foil in the group, created an alter ego named Snappy Simmons, who dressed in knee-length overalls and an old baseball cap turned sideways, and had singled out Carl Perkins as his favorite artist of all time, because he was "a rock 'n' roll star" (unlike Johnny Cash, whom Snappy disdained because "he thought he was rock 'n' roll, but he wasn't"). Snappy was liable to appear anytime, anywhere. Once on an overseas flight, Carl was awakened by a tap on the shoulder and heard Snappy say, "Carl Perkings, Carl Perkings, deen-deen-deen-deen, he a rock 'n' roll star" ("deen-deen-deen-deen" was supposed to be the sound of Carl's guitar).

Though the Statlers' friendship sustained him through countless dark hours ("They were strength for me"), Carl's memory of their time together drops off into sadness—not because their time ended, but because his addiction took hold and once again led him to a personal and professional precipice.

In the summer of 1968 the Cash show made a stop in Tulsa, Oklahoma. Carl, deep into a bottle of Early Times, left town drunk, heading for the next show in San Diego several days later. In California, he hooked up with an old friend, John Swanner, whom he had met at the Golden Nugget in the early sixties. At that time Swanner, a native of Cullman, Alabama, was in the Air Force and stationed at a Nevada base. Almost every show Carl played, Swanner would be standing at the end of the bar. Eventually they became drinking buddies.

With Swanner at his side, Carl stayed drunk for four consecutive days, up to and including the moment he was supposed to open the show for Cash in San Diego. All the years in the tonks, on the road with Jay and Clayton, and touring after Jay's death, Carl had always been sober for his shows. Now, disheveled and in tears, he tried to beg off when Cash came into the dressing room to summon him for his set.

"John, I can't go out there," Carl said. "I'm so drunk I can't stand up. I'm too weak. I'm drunk and I'm sick. You been there."

"Yeah," Cash admitted, "but Carl, this thing is sold out, man, and they wanna see you. Go out there and don't jump. Don't talk. Just do four songs and turn around and come off. You don't look that bad. Look in the mirror."

Carl remembers seeing "four or five of me in the mirror. But I put my guitar on, took a deep breath, walked out on stage, done what he told me, done four songs, the people looked like a haze to me. I'm sure my movements were slow, because I didn't want them to know I was drunk. Got a good round of applause, I remember that; I remember how sick I was to think that I'm standing out here and I cannot see nothin' but a blur. I didn't want that ever again in my life. I was ashamed to the pit of my stomach. I went straight to the bus, and crawled in the back. When we got back to our motel rooms, I looked across the street and saw a liquor sign flashing. I said good-bye to [John Swanner] there."

Carl left the bus, bought a pint of Early Times, came back, drank it all, and passed out. When he woke up, he found the bus was parked at a beach. The entire Cash troupe, save him, was outside eating and lounging in the sun. Head pounding from a hangover, he staggered outside, was blinded by the bright light, went back to the bus, headed straight for the bed in the rear, and fell into a deep and troubled sleep.

▶ THE VOICE OF CARL PERKINS

Then I started that hallucinating. I saw them big spiders, and dinosaurs, huge, and they were gonna step on me. I was trying to scoot away from them. My hand was probably asleep hanging off the bed and there was a dinosaur standing on it. I thought, "This is it. I'm not gonna live through this one. I'll die before this day's over. And I thought, "I gotta go to God. Gotta go to God. Gotta get through to Him."

So I prayed, just as serious as I possibly could. I said, "God, if you'll let me get home to see Valda and the kids, then I won't argue with You if You take my life. I want to die at home. Not out here. Not here, Lord, please."

And after I prayed I sat up on the side of the bed, and I felt a little stronger. I had vision. I could see out the door to the ocean, saw John and them out at the picnic table, the Statler boys playing volleyball, beautiful day. Then I started getting a little sick to my stomach. Used the bathroom on the bus, sat down, head started spinning again, started going back the other way. And I thought, "Man, if I had one drink, just to settle my nerves." I was a nervous wreck, I was shaking—and there sat my little black bag. And I picked it up; I had totally forgot I had put a pint of whiskey in there. It had one big drink took out of it.

Oh, boy! Lookee here! And I got the top off of it, and I got it within a foot or closer—I could smell it—my hand just stopped. Something went off in my brain, said, "Okay, Carl. You gonna drink this, you gonna want another bottle, then you die. If you wanna get home to Valda and them kids, put the bottle back, and I'll see that you get home."

I put the top back on the bottle, and I stuck it in my back pocket. I walked, I had to hold on the inside of the bus to keep from falling. I saw a rock that was a lot further than I thought it was. But that's where I wanted to get. And my track across that sand was like where a snake had crawled. I fell on my knees on that beach, hid from everybody but Him. And I said, "Lord, You heard my prayers and I heard what You said to me. You better get me home. And I'm gonna throw this bottle. I'm gonna show You that I believe You."

I sailed it into the Pacific Ocean. It took three skips, a wave got it, and that was it. I got up, I knew I had done the right thing. I knew I was gonna make it home. That's what happened to Carl Perkins on a beach in Los Angeles.

John came to the bus and said, "Carl, we're fixin' to eat. Boy, it's good to see you up. You're lookin' pretty good. I been checkin' on you; you looked bad."

I said, "John, I'm gonna make it. I'm gonna make it."

1968. Life just really changed again for me. I hit it sober. I leaned on John; he said, "You don't take a drink, I don't take a pill." That's how I did it. And many times I'd say, "John, you gonna take a pill tonight?"

We've talked about it. He said, "I knew if I said yes that you had a bottle and you would've hit it." And I would've. And times he'd come in my dressing room and he'd say, "I bet you're gonna take a drink tonight, ain't you?" I sensed he was gettin' nervous. "No way. It's over." So we made it the rest of the tour, got back home, I really sobered up and that was it. It

was probably one of the happiest days of Valda's life when I told her. She
said, "I knew it. I knew you was gonna do it." My family rallied around me.

Carl's whiskey days were over, but the turning point wasn't complete.
In the mid-seventies, while being booked as a solo act by Swanner
(who had moved to Nashville and was then running a successful
agency business), he began developing a taste for screwdrivers. But he
stopped himself before falling into the trap again. His oceanside conversion became the stuff of legend, so dramatic was Carl's account of
his turmoil. An amused Harold Reid of the Statler Brothers verifies
most of the specifics, but one: "We know the story. The more Carl tells
it the more people get to go to the picnic. And the further out into the
ocean the bottle goes. No, we were not there."

Cash looks back on that episode with admiration for Carl's sheer
will power: "He was standing way down there by the waves and we
were at the camper. When he came back, he looked like he felt better
about everything. I had a feeling that this was it, too. I don't remember where we were going, but I remember June and Marshall and
Luther were hugging him and telling how proud we were of him, because we believed he meant it, and he did."

Luther Perkins died a little over a year later. Cash's beloved guitarist fell asleep while smoking and was asphyxiated when his couch
caught fire. Despite his limitations, Luther could play the Cash beat
better than anyone, and it was with some trepidation that Carl agreed
to step in for him when asked to do so by Cash.

Using Luther's old Fender, Carl surprised no one by being an able
replacement—more than able, his muscular playing brought grandeur
to Cash's sound at the moment it needed most. In the late sixties,
timing and talent merged and Cash's popularity soared, propelled by
the 1968 success of two live albums, *Johnny Cash at Folsom Prison*,
with its hit single, "Folsom Prison Blues," and *Johnny Cash at San
Quentin*, and from it the single "A Boy Named Sue," which had a
three-week run at number two on the pop chart in addition to being
a number-one country single. ("A Boy Named Sue" existed only as a

Shel Silverstein poem when Cash decided to perform it as an encore; Carl fashioned a melody and rhythm and directed the band as Cash read the words.) "Hello, I'm Johnny Cash" became as familiar a salutation as could be heard in America at this time, being the first words uttered on his live albums and the greeting for his popular ABC variety show, which ran for two seasons (1969–70). Cash had taken to wearing black outfits on stage in symbolic protest of the world's ills, from famine to war, and it turned out to be a smart commercial ploy as well—"The Man in Black" (memorialized in a Cash song explaining his philosophy) was so towering a figure of moral authority that one expected to hear news of him being measured for Mount Rushmore.

To Cash's success Carl contributed more than a few guitar licks and his unwavering friendship. In December of '68, near the end of a tour, Carl sat alone in his dressing room, strumming his guitar before being called on stage. Humming the melody to "Will the Circle Be Unbroken," a Carter Family gospel standard, he began improvising a verse:

> I remember when I was a lad
> Times were hard and things were bad
> But there's a silver lining
> Behind every cloud
> Just poor people
> That's all we were
> Trying to dig a living
> Out of black land dirt—

Carl stopped and wrote the words "black land dirt" on a paper towel, then continued:

> And we'd gather in a family circle
> And sing out loud:

Kicking the rhythm into a strutting tempo, he composed a chorus:

> Daddy sang bass, Mama sang tenor
> Me and little brother would join right in there
> You know singing seems to help a troubled soul
> One of these days, and it won't be long
> We'll rejoin them in a song
> And we'll sing again up yonder around the throne

Breaking into the chorus of "Will the Circle Be Unbroken," he looked over to see Cash, outfitted in black from head to toe, at the door. "Now that is a hell of a song," Cash said.

"Wait a minute, John," Carl said. "How about if I sing,

> Will the circle
> Be unbroken
> By and by, Lord
> By and by
>
> (Chorus:)
> Daddy sang bass—

"June, come here," Cash called out to June Carter. "Carl, do that song. But that 'Circle Will Be Unbroken,' that's it!"

Carl played what he had written. When Johnny and June left to prepare for the show, Carl wrote a second verse, thinking of Jay as he did:

> I remember after church
> Mama would call in all of us
> And you could hear us
> Singin' for a country mile
> Now my brother's done gone home
> We'll be together 'fore too long
> We gonna sing again up yonder
> By the throne

He did a quick rewrite of the first version, smoothing out the lyrics, and was getting ready to go onstage when Harold Reid stopped to ask if the Statlers could record the song. Carl replied that Cash had "insinuated" his interest in the song, but that the Statlers could have it if Johnny decided otherwise. Cash felt strongly enough about "Daddy Sang Bass" to insist on recording it against the wishes of Columbia executives who feared him following "the mud, the blood, and the beer" of "A Boy Named Sue" with a religious-oriented song. Cash's single, though not a crossover hit, was a number-one country record for nearly three months, and a Country Music Association nominee for Song of the Year in 1969 (in a major disappointment to Carl, it lost to Porter Wagoner's "Carroll County Accident").

"Daddy Sang Bass" indicated Carl's undiminished talent as a writer. The December release of his new single, "Restless," the initial effort in a new five-year deal with Columbia (he was re-signed to the label by Larry Butler, who had played on some of the Dollie sessions), proved him still formidable on his own. From its opening flurry of double-picked notes, the song was unadulterated Carl Perkins. The lyrics showed the skewed sense of humor that had informed his best rockers, from his inspired response to a ticket agent's question to the left-field reference to a Greyhound bus:

> Well I walked up to the window
> I said, "Gimme a ticket please,"
> She said, "Where to, mister?"
> I said, "That's all right with me,
> Honey, I'm just restless, I need
> To get on out of town, I need to
> Go right now—
> Take me where the livin' 's easy
> Baby, that's where I'll be found"

> I said, "Honey, tell that driver
> Put his big foot in that gas
> And run this grey dog
> Just as long as it will last
> 'cause I'm just restless"

I said, "Honey, take this grey dog

Any place it wants to go

Drop this ol' country boy

Off farther down the road"

All right, chillun, let's go now!

With the command to "go now!" Carl launched into a solo that would be diminished by being described in musical terms. In the blustering, sputtering notes he fired off in working his way up the neck, Carl answered everyone who had doubted him as he fought to stay alive as a working artist in an industry that seemed more comfortable forgetting his contributions. Even more, this was the rage of his cotton patch days in Lake County's deep poverty given fiery expression; the pain of Jay's death, the sorrow of Clayton's squalid fall given loud, howling voice; the self-inflicted misery of his years in the bottle given a torturous exorcism. It was a man suddenly finding himself on the road home, and refusing to be denied his sanctuary. In the end, it was an artist in full command of every aspect of his art reasserting his claim to greatness.

After Carl heard the playback, he turned to look at Denny in the control booth and said coolly, "That's pretty good." He knew his assessment was an understatement, and years later would reflect: "My guitar playing on 'Restless' was as strong as it was on any piece of music I ever wrote in my life. The fire jumped back in me when I took that break; I didn't know where I was going and I pulled some Sun Records stuff. I went off down on that guitar neck and found some things right on the spur of the moment in that studio that day. I had two guitar breaks in there that were about the best I ever did on record. No question about it. I got to flying on that thing and everything just fell right in place. I didn't make a mistake on either one."

"Restless" was included on a Bill Denny–produced album, *Carl Perkins' Greatest Hits*, released to negligible notice in May 1969. In most respects, *Greatest Hits* was a step backwards: the repertoire consisted largely of re-recordings of Carl's Sun material, all of which suffered in being translated to the poppish Nashville sound, and pointed up how critical a role Jay, Clayton, and W.S. had had in firing up the spirit of the original recordings (Early Times played its part as well)—only "Turn Around" arrived in agreeable form, underscoring its staying power as a pure country song.

Another Bill Denny–produced album, *On Top*, released in late '69, proved to be one more well-intentioned but misguided effort to re-shape Carl's sound and style. Only two new Perkins compositions were recorded—the spirited "Soul Beat," and "Power of My Soul," a moving account of the strength he gained from Valda's unconditional love—and Denny added an organ to the instrumental lineup, imparting a jazz feel to a couple of tracks. Carl responded with appropriately measured, easy-swinging vocals, but he was out of his element. On sounder footing, from the Cedarwood catalogue Carl pulled an obscure Buddy Holly song, "I'm Gonna Set My Foot Down" (cut during Holly's ill-fated Owen Bradley sessions in 1956), and scorched it with a tough-sounding arrangement and rowdy vocal; also, he finally recorded Chuck Berry's "Brown-Eyed Handsome Man" after having raved about it years earlier in the Million Dollar Quartet session.

Little noted upon the album's release, or since, was the song "Champaign, Illinois," a collaboration between Carl and Bob Dylan. The two had met earlier in the year on the set of a Johnny Cash television special, and a strong friendship ensued. Inviting Carl to his dressing room, Dylan said he had been working on a song, but couldn't come up with more than one verse. To Carl he sang, over a ragged rockabilly rhythm:

> I got a woman in Morocco
> I got a woman over in Spain
> But the girl I love
> That stole my heart
> She lives up in Champaign
> I said Champaign,
> Champaign, Illinois

"That's as far as I got," Dylan said. "You think you can do anything with it?"

"You can!" Carl said. "Go ahead and finish it!"

"You think it's any good?"

"Yeah. Let me see your guitar a minute."

Dylan sat transfixed as Carl worked out a loping rhythm on the bass strings with his thumb, filled in with some quick, stinging runs on the treble strings, and improvised a verse-ending lyric:

> I certainly do enjoy
>
> Cha-a-am-pai-hane, Illinois

Dylan said: "Your song. Take it. Finish it."

Cash recorded Dylan's "Wanted Man" on his San Quentin album, then dueted with Dylan on the latter's *Nashville Skyline* album. Dylan appeared on Cash's television show—for a couple of years, as Carl recalls, Dylan was around Nashville frequently, recording on his own and hanging out with Cash. On more than one occasion Carl says he, Dylan, and Cash recorded together (cutting mostly old blues songs) at the Columbia studio under Bob Johnston's production aegis. (These tapes have never surfaced. "There's a lot of missing stuff from that period of time," Dylan confirms. "I know there was some stuff done in the Columbia studios, but I don't have it and I haven't heard it.")

During one of their sessions together, Dylan told Carl a story about "Matchbox" inspiring him to make his first record. As Carl recalls it: "He told me, 'It cost me two hundred fifty dollars, and I went in a little studio somewhere in Minneapolis, Minnesota, and cut 'Matchbox.' That's the first song I ever recorded.' Him, his guitar, and his harmonica."

Dylan, who says his memory of those years is "really primordial," doesn't dispute that he may have recorded "Matchbox" early in his life as a musician. The circumstances were a bit less glorified than in Carl's version. "I could've done it before I started playing folk music," he says. "That would have been in the band I had with my cousin, and we probably did play that. But that was long before anybody started recording me. Unless it was in one of those little booth studios; they were almost like a telephone booth and you could go in and for a quarter make a floppy-disc record. I might've done that."

Dylan's most vivid memories of Carl in the late sixties center on the live performances he witnessed: "To me [Carl] looked like he was in his prime. He was lookin' good and he was playing that jet-propelled guitar, which, even at that time, was really outstanding. He never really fell into that oldie trip. He was just playing with a bass guitar player and a drummer. He would open the shows, do five or six songs. He would blow the place down. But he would just play radiant, you know, and he never lost that. Even at that time he would affect the people in the crowd the same way. I saw him before that when he was playing with the original band, before he had that accident. That to me was the quintessential sound of what could be gotten at that time. They were amazing."

But Carl meant more to Bob Dylan than good showmanship. To the question of what Carl Perkins stood for when he first encountered his music in the fifties, Dylan offers luminous affirmation of his profound influence: "He really stood for freedom. That whole sound stood for all the degrees of freedom. It would just jump right off that turntable; live, it would create such a thump in your belly, you know. Everything—the vocabulary of the lyrics and the sound of the instruments. Where I particularly came from I don't know a lot of people who listened to it; I think myself and a few of my mates were definitely in the minority. But it made us feel less like wanderers around, that there was definitely a sun out there and a moon and there were celestial elements to life that were being expressed in just a small group of people, like Carl; I guess you could just about count 'em on one hand. It was everything. It was almost like another party in the room. It was coming from somewhere that we wanted to go; we wanted to go where that was happening. As opposed to a record on the radio where it might sound nice, but it doesn't give you any answers or make you think that there are any really. Or any other place to go besides the place you're perfectly adapted to."

A busy year of recording concluded in late fall when Carl cut an album titled *Boppin' the Blues* that teamed him with NRBQ, a young quintet celebrated for its raucous brand of updated honky-tonk and rhythm-and-blues-styled music. Impressed with the band's grasp of rockabilly nuances, Carl got over his initial misgivings about the project and threw himself into the sessions. Some of the old problems resurfaced, however: Carl appeared with NRBQ on only six of the thirteen tracks, and on four of these NRBQs Steve Ferguson took the lead guitar role; the song selection was weighted in favor of Sun material ("All Mama's Children," "Boppin' the Blues," "Turn Around," "Sure to Fall"), even though Carl's new songs, "Sorry Charlie" (an all-stops-out rocker inspired by the Charlie the Tuna TV commercials) and the roaring "Allergic to Love," turned out to be the strongest performances on the album. Having the last word, Carl was given the closing track, a meditative instrumental in the melodic, lyrical Chet Atkins style, the sort of thing Carl would sit at home and pick out effortlessly but rarely played in public. What could have been Carl's commercial resurrection at a time when a new generation was rediscovering blues and rock 'n' roll pioneers turned out to be nothing more than an interesting but failed interlude. Reviewing *Boppin' the Blues* in *Rolling Stone*, Peter Guralnick praised Carl as "always engaging," but added: "[The album] might have been better if [NRBQ] had shown themselves a little less presumptuous."

In late 1968 Carl had accompanied the Cash troupe on a tour of the Far East, which took them, briefly, to South Vietnam. In addition to playing for the U.S. forces at Long Binh Air Force Base in Saigon, Carl, Johnny, and June had visited a hospital where wounded servicemen were being treated; Carl brought his acoustic guitar and they all sang songs for the soldiers. On his own Carl returned to the hospital with an Army-supplied tape recorder and taped "sixty-five or seventy" of the wounded sending messages to their families back in the States. When he returned to Jackson, he called each soldier's family and played back their son's spoken letter. Said one thankful parent, upon hearing his son's voice: "God's gonna bless you, Mr. Perkins, because we're gonna pray for you for the rest of our lives. It's a wonderful thing you're doing."

For Carl, the response to his selfless gesture marked the first stirrings of a spiritual awakening that would reshape his life by inspiring deeper reflection on the purpose of his earthly days: "In my life I've done a lot more wrong things than right. But there's no words to

say what that did for me and I know for Valda and for my own kids
to think their Daddy would think of something like that and carry it
through—come back and call every single family and tell 'em. I did
not do it to call and say, 'Hey, look what I did while I was in Vietnam.'
When you give out of love, you do it because God is tinkerin' away at
you. Even then I hadn't turned it over to Him. I was just takin' little
hints from Him."

On February 2, 1969, the city of Jackson declared "Carl Perkins
Day" and celebrated with an evening banquet attended by five hundred of Carl's professional and personal friends and acquaintances,
various political dignitaries, and family members. Among those sending telegrams of congratulations and appreciation: Tennessee governor Buford Ellington; Senator Howard Baker; Senator Albert Gore;
Johnny Cash; Marty Robbins; Jerry Lee Lewis; Sonny James; Chet
Atkins; Eddy Arnold. In *The Jackson Sun*'s February 3 edition, reporter Jim Vann described one of the evening's most memorable moments:

> *During the narrative "Blue Suede Shoes Turns To Gold" (The Life of*
> *Carl Perkins), several country music singers and writers along with*
> *many of his West State neighbors heard how the Jacksonian over-*
> *came hardships and poverty to become known and respected in his*
> *field in the U.S. and abroad.*
>
> *Both voices and persons from his past were recalled as Perkins,*
> *his eyes filled with tears of appreciation, relived the years during his*
> *climb to fame. Among his many friends Perkins had surprise visits*
> *from a former grammar school teacher, Miss Lee McCutcheon, who*
> *took him out of school and brought him to Jackson to appear over*
> *WTJS Radio, his first radio appearance.*

Grown frail in old age, Miss Lee was slow getting to the podium.
But when she spoke, her voice rang clear and proud as Carl sat trembling, overcome by the emotions her presence summoned.

"I had a brilliant little boy in my class," Miss Lee began. "He didn't
think he was. He didn't act like he was. But he was a star pupil. He
was a wonderful little fellow. And I kept this, and I would like to share

it with you tonight, to show you that at an early age you can build your dream and go after it. Carl Perkins had a dream of being a nationally known star when he was in my class in fourth grade in Tiptonville Elementary.

"I assigned my students on a Friday to put a little picture of themselves at the top, put your name, age, and write some things about yourself. Things that you like about yourself. Turn them into me on Monday morning. This is what Carl wrote."

After reading Carl's eighty-two-word marvel of self-definition, Miss Lee added: "There were literally hundreds of students in my classes through my years of teaching. Ask me why I kept this one paper. It had to be destiny, that I could turn around and hand it to the man who has blessed his own little home town of Tiptonville that we call the home of Carl Perkins. You people here in Jackson like to say this is the home of Carl Perkins. We had him first. Carl has said I started him, I gave him hope. If I did," she concluded with a gentle smile, "I did a wonderful job."

With that she turned and handed Carl the paper he had dutifully composed according to instruction as a fourth grader, along with another piece of his past he thought long lost: "She bent down, her old hands were shaking with palsy. But that brain was still right on the money. She kissed me on the side of the face, and she handed me a little cap and a little cape that I wore in the fourth-grade band. She said, 'No other student ever wore this. It was special.' Since that happened, I have wondered many times what made her think I would achieve any part of my dream. But I never saw her again. She died shortly after that."

Carl's second association with Columbia again produced good reviews but disappointing sales, and his contract was not renewed. With Bill Denny's representation and the Statlers' recommendation, he was signed by the Mercury label in 1973 and teamed with producer Jerry Kennedy, who had revived the Statlers' waning career after their unproductive stint with Columbia (they had gone seven years without a hit when they moved to Mercury and cut a chart-topping single, "Bed of Roses," with Kennedy behind the board). Kennedy was also producing Jerry Lee Lewis, who had left Sun in 1967 and was now doing well as a pure country artist.

Kennedy seemed like a good match for Carl. Growing up in Shreveport, Louisiana, he had been a fan of the early Sun artists, notably, Elvis Presley (a guitarist himself, Kennedy claims he used to go see Presley at The Louisiana Hayride so he could pick up on Scotty Moore's technique; also, as a session player he had worked often with Presley in Nashville in the early sixties). In Carl he had an artist whose writing and playing he admired equally. He pushed Carl to bring in original songs, unless he had others he wanted to cover: "I can remember gettin' with Carl and him playing me songs, and I never really looked beyond what was right there. I wanted to keep it as close to what Carl wanted to do, rather than me going out and saying, 'Okay, here's the way I hear you.' I wanted him to be comfortable. Carl had been around, he knew what was happening. I wasn't going to be presumptuous enough to tell Carl Perkins, 'Here's how you need to be doing it, buddy.' You can't do that."

By urging Carl to get comfortable and play whatever he liked whenever he liked (without concern for the clock or the presence of Nashville's busy A-team studio musicians), the low-key Kennedy engendered a relaxed atmosphere during sessions at Mercury's Custom Recording studio. It took several weeks to get enough songs done for a complete album, and that suited Kennedy fine. Recalling the sessions, guitarist Harold Bradley says the unstructured feel "was the closest stuff to Memphis that Carl had experienced, the free playing. Jerry would encourage spontaneity."

Energized by Kennedy's sympathetic approach, Carl delivered what amounted to a concept album of intense, personal revelations (even covers of Cash's "Goin' To Memphis" and Mel Tillis's "Honky Tonk Song" related to the themes Carl explored in his own songs; only Tillis's morbid "Ruby, Don't Take Your Love To Town" was out of place). Of the rock 'n' roll pioneers, only Presley had so consciously constructed a personal portrait in song over the course of an entire LP—1971's *Elvis Country*—the most fascinating aspect of which was the revealing snippets of a song titled "I'm 10,000 Years Old" weaving between the individual tracks. But Elvis hadn't written his own songs.

Torn from personal history, Carl's songs bemoaned his spiritual and moral failings, indicating the squalor he felt he had made of his life by turning to the bottle. The simple, eloquent lyrics betrayed an unbecoming self-pity, but Carl's dark, impassioned vocals, and the musicians' sensitive support, lent a grim nobility to his quest to find inner peace amidst turmoil. Two songs, "Love Sweet Love" and "Help Me Dream," detailed how the strength of Valda's love was keeping him afloat as he sought direction; others detailed a landscape as stark and bleak as T.S. Eliot's "The Wasteland." A sampling:

(From "You Tore My Heaven All To Hell":)

> Everything that's ever mattered
> I've watched it slowly die
> And last night, just like a baby
> Girl, I sat right down and cried

(From "One More Loser Goin' Home":)

> The Georgia sun is shinin' through the pine tree
> As I slowly walk this blacktop goin' home
> I don't have no fancy story for the home folks
> 'Cause I'm one, one more loser goin' home

> I'm goin' home to spend my life with wife and baby
> Oh they have been through livin' hell since I've been gone
> And I hope my boy won't be ashamed of Daddy
> 'Cause I'm one, one more loser goin' home

(From "Never Look Back":)

> Oh, the Springtime of your life is gone
> I want you, girl, around
> And I'll love you
> When the whole world turns us down

(From "Lord I Sinned Again Last Night":)

> Now when you catch me flyin' that high
> Please, clip my wings, Lord
> And don't ever let me fly from Your sight
> I tried, I tried but I still fail You
> And Lord, I sinned again last night
>
> The crowd all drinkin' sang with laughter
> They only called Your name in vain
> I guess the Devil made me join them
> Look down, look down, I'm so ashamed

(From "Help Me Dream":)

> Things ain't what I thought they'd be
> And this loneliness is killin' me
> And I'm like a bird that's lost its way in flight

As he was listening to the playback with Kennedy one evening, Carl observed that the songs were "my kind of country. It's a little different to Nashville, but it blends well with it."

"You just took a burden off me," Kennedy said. "You just named your album—*My Kind of Country.* How do you like it?"

"It's the truth," Carl said.

The cover photos, shot at the farm Carl had bought for his parents, show him in trimmed-down condition—laying off the bottle had helped him reduce his weight to slightly under two hundred pounds—all broad, strong shoulders and chiseled jawline. On the front he is crouching near the remnants of an old tractor he had found on the property; on the back he is standing in the driveway, facing the camera, with Buck and Louise visible behind him, sitting on their front porch. In both poses, his steely-eyed, grave mien suggests the forcefulness he brings to his performances here.

As much as he thought the cover captured the spirit of the album,

Carl was most impressed with the music inside, one of the few times he had ever been completely satisfied with his performances: "We took time to cut it right. It was done so clean and pure. It's really a vision of my life. Most of the things I wrote touched on my own soul. I'm roamin' around in those songs. That's what was goin' on in my life—I was out there trying to make a living, but the nights after the shows when you couldn't see the countryside and you was out there ridin' to another town, it wasn't fun. And I didn't like it. I didn't like music anymore. But I'd get these little lifts from people like Bill Denny and Jerry Kennedy."

Recalling his work on Perkins sessions for three different labels, Harold Bradley came away from *My Kind of Country* sensing Carl might have made his breakthrough record as a country artist: "They were the best we had done on the three labels. Jerry Kennedy's one of those people who's good at bringing people out as songwriters and putting them in a situation where they can be themselves. If they've got something to offer, maybe it will sell. The odds should have been in favor of that happening."

But it didn't, neither the album nor its three singles. In mid-'75, Carl went in with a band featuring himself, Scotty Moore, and D.J. Fontana, and cut a song he had written whose lyrics were comprised almost entirely of Elvis Presley song titles ("Well I put my hound dog on your trail / I found it out at Heartbreak Hotel / But that's alright now, Mama, any way you do"). An inspired performance, "E.P. Express" was breaking on the country chart when Kennedy learned that Mercury's new management had decided to drop Carl and a number of other artists from the country roster. It should have been a crushing blow, but Carl had been through it so many times before that he accepted it and moved on without rancor: "There wasn't any need in us sittin' and cryin' about it; it was over. But it liked to have been a good thing, it really did. Everything I dreamed of to get back on the ladder of success I had with Jerry Kennedy, except it was the wrong time for me, with the label becoming part of a big conglomerate."

Five years would pass before Carl landed on a major label again. In the interim, Bill Denny sold Cedarwood and accepted an offer to become president of Nashville Gas; John Denny established himself as an independent producer of small label projects, but without Cedar-wood the Denny family's impact on the mainstream country music business effectively ended. Carl became a partner in Jackson's Arlue recording studio, thinking he might be able to build it into a profitable operation and full-time occupation. Specializing in jingles and gospel recording, the business thrived until the previous owners' undeclared Tennessee State tax debt sank the entire operation. At Arlue he launched his own label, Suede, and released a few singles and two albums, *The Carl Perkins Show* (1976), which was sold only at his concerts (1,000 copies were pressed, making it one of the rarest of all Perkins collectables) and *Carl Perkins and the C.P Express Live at Austin City Limits* (1981), also a limited edition; in late 1976 through early 1977, he cut four singles for the Nashville-based MMI (later Music Mill) label. These were barely noticed. In 1978 he was signed by a fledgling British label, Jet Records, which was making its American push with the benefit of CBS distribution. Working with Elvis's longtime producer Felton Jarvis, and a host of Nashville's top sessions players, Carl cut *Ol' Blue Suedes Is Back*, for which he wrote one new song, "Rock On Around the World," as the closer to a collection of some of his favorite songs by other artists, including "Rock Around the Clock," Fats Domino's "I'm In Love Again," Chuck Berry's "Maybellene," Hank Williams's "Kaw-Liga," and Chuck Willis's "Hang Up My Rock & Roll Shoes." Aesthetically it was little more than a holding action, as Carl's restrained performances suggested. Respectful reviews greeted the album's U.S. release, and Carl toured incessantly in its support, gaining new fans as the music press trumpeted his standing as one of rock 'n' roll's founding fathers. Only the British music press, always so loyal in its support, wavered, and cruelly so. An unsigned review in the March 25, 1978, edition of *Melody Maker* said, in part: "Time's run out for Perkins. Let's face it, there's got to come a stage when a 48-year old rock 'n' roll pioneer just can't put over teenage rebel-rock songs the same way he did when he was 21 . . . The time has come for him to hang up those rock 'n' roll blue suede shoes."

Undeterred, Carl moved on in 1979 and cut some interesting new material at the Music Mill studios in Muscle Shoals, Alabama. An anticipated label deal failed to materalize (most of the Muscle Shoals work surfaced on bootleg albums over the next few years), and a decade that had begun in the glow of "Restless" and "Daddy Sang Bass" ended ignominiously. Carl, extolled by Bill Denny for "creating an industry with his songs," was adrift as an artist.

t h e aimlessness of Carl's post-Mercury recording history in the seventies was more than an indication of a wayward artist. He was sober, he was working, but he was hollow at the center, almost disconnected emotionally from his professional life as he struggled to make sense of a changing world and his purpose in it.

On Christmas Day in 1973, Carl was scheduled to fly to California to film an episode of the *Columbo* TV series with Cash. After the kids had opened their presents, he drove to a gas station to fill the tank for the drive to the Memphis airport. On his way, he passed near Clayton's apartment, close enough to see his brother, wearing jeans and a leather jacket, getting into his car.

Clayton had remained unemployed since being fired by Carl almost a decade earlier. Ruby Sue had long since divorced him, leaving under cover of darkness after Clayton had threatened her with a gun. When he passed out after firing several shots into the floor of their house, she escaped to safety with their three children and never returned. Eventually she remarried and moved to another city, where she was living well with a prosperous new husband. With his wife and children gone, Clayton hit rock bottom, according to Carl: "He lived the life of a hobo. He slept in boxcars. He'd go home with old women, lay around a year or two with one, go get him another one. And stay pretty well out of it most of the time. He just layed around with the winos and he was a superstar. The old train station was his home. If you wanted to find him, you'd find him sittin' out on the front, maybe with an old guitar, singin' to them fellas. He was a star in that world."

Though he had remarried, Clayton's second wife, Carolyn, was an afterthought. He continued to spend most of his waking hours with the drifters at Jackson's Union Restaurant, near the abandoned railroad station. Carl saw his brother becoming "old and crusty" as his alcoholism worsened. The final breach in their relationship came when Clayton, in a scene frighteningly reminiscent of the one that had occurred in 1954 in Bemis, showed up at Carl's house one day with a loaded pistol, which he brandished in front of the Perkins children. "He was not threatening me, but letting me know that if he needed anything, he knew how to get it. See, that line had been drawn. He would've had to pull it out and use it, but use it quick, because I had my reasons for living. I had my plans for the future. I was sober then. I had some openings in my life, and I wanted to live, wanted to raise my family, wanted to love my kids and Valda and be somebody. I think I would've had to done something terrible."

Carl flew to Los Angeles with Fluke Holland and Marshall Grant. When they arrived at the terminal, W.S. was being paged to the phone. Carl heard him exclaim, "Oh, no! No! No!"

"What is it?" Carl asked. W.S. handed him the receiver. Cash was on the other end of the line.

"Carl, are you sittin' down?" asked Cash.

"God, no, man, I just got off that airplane," Carl said. "My rump's sore and burnin'. No. I'm standin' up."

"Sit down, Carl," Cash said in his low monotone.

"What is it, John?"

"Carl, it's Clayton."

"What about him?"

"He's been shot."

"No. No, John. Huh-uh. Is it bad?"

"He's gone."

"*Gone?* Clayton dead?"

"Yeah," Cash answered. It was one of his most wrenching hours:

"I always regretted that I couldn't be there to tell Carl in person and to put my arms around him. I knew how he loved Clayton. And I *really* loved Clayton."

Carl, after calling Valda and hearing her say straight out, "Clayton killed himself," remembers little of the plane ride home. "I just got in a frozen state of mind," he says. "Thought about all the records, I thought about all the good times, I thought about . . . it was just terrible. When I got in, about three, four o'clock in the morning, lights was on in the house, Valda was sittin' in the den, children were laying around in the floor, they wanted to stay near their Mama. They were tore up too."

Greg, then fourteen, and Stan, then twenty, had found Clayton's body. Carolyn had spent the afternoon with her mother at a nursing home, and came home to an eerily quiet scene—even Clayton's pet chihuahua didn't bark as he normally would at the slightest sound outside. Fearing foul play afoot upstairs, she called Valda, who sent Stan and Greg over to check on their uncle. They found Clayton face down on the bed, a .22 pistol in one hand, an empty whiskey bottle lying near the other.

Debbie and a friend drove over to the farm and brought Buck and Louise back to Carl's house. Louise was expecting Clayton for dinner that night. Debbie, as she had been instructed, told her grandmother that Clayton had become ill and was in the hospital. Back at the house, Valda had called the family doctor over, knowing how hard Buck and Louise would take the news. Indeed, they had to be sedated after Valda told them of Clayton's demise.

Typically, the suicide was unforeseen and raised more questions than it answered: Why would Clayton tell his mother and father to expect him for dinner, then shoot himself? What did he mean after he had been examined by a doctor for a stomach ulcer and emerged saying, "I will not suffer like Jay B. did," even though he was never diagnosed as having cancer?

Carl went so far as to hire a private detective to investigate the possibility of murder, suspecting Carolyn knew more than she was telling. After two days of searching, the detective could find nothing implicating Clayton's wife or anyone else in the shooting; at the same time, the city coroner and chief of police told Carl that all the evidence and the autopsy findings were consistent with suicide. Reluctantly, Carl dismissed the detective, although he clung to the opinion that Clayton's death was accidental: "The bullet hole in his T-shirt was about in the middle of his stomach. I believe when he got ready to do it, he got over and flinched and turned the gun up and [the bullet] bounced in his rib cage and popped in his heart. The coroner said it went in his rib cage and didn't penetrate out. I believe Clayton meant to shoot through his stomach so he could get back in the hospital and get some of the good drugs they gave him when he was in there, because he'd run through several prescriptions. He had an ulcer. His health was really failing him; he was falling apart from so many years of rough treatment."

Once past their predictable anguish, only the method of Clayton's passing surprised anyone close to the family, least of all Valda: "I felt there would be a tragedy; I just hoped it wouldn't involve Carl. Clayton was trouble to whomever he was around. He was trouble. And no one could get close to him. As much as it shocked me the day he killed himself, after he was buried, a week later, I knew that was the perfect way God had to do it. That was the only way that it could not involve Carl."

Clayton was buried next to Jay. Cash offered to come off the road to attend the funeral, but Carl urged him to honor his commitments. Elvis again sent a weeping willow tree populated by thirteen papier mâché redbirds.

▶ THE VOICE OF CARL PERKINS

I loved Clayton, and I suffered a lot when he [committed suicide], for many years. I'm suffering today, because I'm not sure that he got it totally right with God before he left here. I'd sure like to know that he'll be playing in my band up in Heaven; I know Jay will. But there's some doubt in my mind, and I pray every day that I'm wrong. Maybe, just maybe, in the solitude of being alone he asked for and got forgiveness.

I could have spent more time with him. I tried to. I'd drive by his house, he'd come out and I'd smell alcohol on him and I'd say, "Well, I gotta go." I know from experience that it does no good to talk to a drinking man about drinking. If he's drinking he will say, "Oh, yeah, I'm gonna quit." You gotta catch him sober. I never deserted Clayton. I'm proud of everything I did for him, proud of everything I had the opportunity to do for him.

Clayton was not bad all the time. When he was good, he was as good a man as ever breathed. He would give you anything. He was only bad about half the time. So you'd put up with the bad to get to the good of him. He was that way. But he was as good as he was bad, he really was. And he had people that liked him, loved him.

Life was lived on Clayton's terms all of his life. He did it his way from as far back as I can remember until the day I put him in the ground. He was an individual, good-time-loving guy who had a wonderful side. He was two people in the same shell. He could be tough, mean, angry, hateful, couldn't get along with him. He was suffering a little. And then there's days as you would drive the car, lost way off on some long road in Texas, that he'd be takin' his finger and popping you behind the ear. "Now you do that one more time and I'm stoppin'." And he would do it one more time. If you told him not to do it, he would do it. He was that way as a little boy.

But it was a beautiful life; it was a success story, thirteen-year-old, mean, white-haired Lake County boy that made good.

The Perkins family's earthly circle was shattered further a year later. In May 1974 Buck was diagnosed with bone cancer and given no more than six months to live. Carl left the Cash show to care for his father in his last days, and the entire family pitched in to take turns staying at the farm. Finally, to ease the strain of traveling every day, Carl decided to move Buck to an apartment in Jackson, where he would be within blocks of his son and grandchildren. As the ambulance eased down the road towards Highway 70, Buck's friends came out of their houses to wave good-bye; Buck had barely enough strength left to wave weakly in return.

By January 1975 Buck was fading fast. Carl had been asked to play a benefit in Memphis for the Cancer Society, and on the night of the show he stopped by the apartment to visit his father before driving on to Memphis. "Well, Daddy, I'll do a song for ya," he said as he was preparing to leave. Buck handed him five one-dollar bills and asked that they be contributed to the cause.

Less than a week later, as Carl sat by his father's bedside, Buck, his voice trembling and soft, looked over at Carl. "Well, it ain't gonna be long now," he said.

"You don't know what the good man has in store for you," Carl said, trying to be strong. "He's gonna heal you. Can't you believe He's gonna heal you?"

"Naw, I'm a little too far. I'm past that, boy," Buck said. "This is it; I ain't gonna make it. But I want to tell you, I've never been ashamed of you, not one day in my life. I'm proud that you took the years to learn to play the guitar like you can. Proud of the songs you wrote. I'm gonna go on over yonder where Jay is, and I'm gonna pick out the finest guitar that God's got. And it's gonna be a perfect team. I want you to stay like you are, 'cause I'm gonna hand it to you when you get to Heaven."

It was their last conversation. Buck went into a coma shortly afterwards, and died on the same day as Johnny Cash's father-in-law, Ezra P. Carter.

Smith Funeral Home was packed with mourners. Buck had a winning way with people and was well loved by those who knew him. At the cemetery, flowers covered his grave and lapped over onto the surrounding plots on all sides. In the midst of them was a large weeping willow tree with thirteen papier mâché redbirds perched on its limbs. From Elvis, with love.

Buck's death devastated Louise. She insisted on moving into the apartment where Clayton had died. Against his better judgment Carl acceded to her wish. A year later the police found her one afternoon wandering on the other side of Jackson, near the city limits. They drove her back to the apartment, and Carl arrived to find her sitting in a chair, staring blankly out the window. Carl tried to get her attention. "Mama?" he called. She didn't respond.

"There's an old saying, She had enough to drive her crazy," Carl says. "In Mama's case, it did. It was like a little bird that had fell out of a nest. After Daddy died, she didn't talk a lot. My mama went crazy. She didn't know nobody—not me, nobody."

Carl and Valda brought Louise to stay with them, but she required constant attention. Finally they had her admitted to Maplewood Nursing Home. Carl's frequent visits were always painful: "I stayed out there with her a lot. I'd hold her hand and try to get through to her, about Jay and about Clayton—'Mama, you remember those sweet potato pies you made me when I was a little boy? You better get well and make me some sweet potato pie.' She looked at me like I was a hundred miles away. It was a horrible, trying, soul-shaking experience to see somebody you love and you can't get through."

Diagnosed with Alzheimer's Disease, Mary Louise Perkins died at age seventy-nine in 1991. Carl's final tribute to his mother came in the form of a poem he composed the night before her funeral and read to those in attendance while standing beside her coffin:

She was weak, worn and weary from years of failing health
A common simple woman who hardly knew the meaning of the word wealth.
Caring for her family and sharing was her job
Mama got promoted today; she's gone to live with God
Even if I could, I wouldn't stop her
Cause today she's Heaven-bound
But Mama if you could take just one second
To stop and look back around.
Look back at all your pretty flowers
Look at all your friends that are here
I bet you didn't know so many wonderful people cared
Mama you didn't live forgotten, although there were times you were alone
But you were loved while you were living
And I'll miss you while you're gone
Mama say hello to Jesus for me
Tell him I love him too—

I'll always love you Mama

Some day I'll be seeing you.

To Mama,

Your son,

Carl Perkins

July 29, 1991

I n 1975 Carl's ten-year association with the Johnny Cash show ended. Cash's brother Tommy was having personal problems, and to help him get back on his feet Johnny had brought him into the troupe. To keep the budget in line, someone had to be cut, and the show was top-heavy with guitarists: A year after Luther Perkins's death, Cash had hired a young picker out of Tulsa, Bob Wootten, who had memorized every lick of every Cash record ever made (he was playing in a Cash cover band in Tulsa) and even emulated Cash's dress, mannerisms, and speech patterns. Having modeled his playing after that of *Luther* Perkins, Wootten wasn't as inventive or as resourceful as Carl, but he was more than a serviceable player in the style Cash liked. Unbeknownst to Cash, Carl had been pointing towards the day he would leave Cash's employ; the crisis with Tommy merely hastened his planned departure. For Cash, Carl's exit was a sad day, but an inevitable one. The love the two men shared for one another remained undiminished, but their day-to-day relationship had cooled under the strain of constant touring and recording.

"I had it in mind that we'd be just buddies and partners and that it'd be like it was in the mid-fifties and we'd get out there and we'd have *fun*," Cash says. "But then touring became like a machine, and I had a lead guitar player, so Carl was relegated to the position of opening the show, singing three or four songs and standing out there playing second guitar with me, which was not a good position for me to put Carl in. For a long time we were really close, but then it became halfway an employer-employee relationship, and halfway a friend relationship. There was never any hard feelings, no argument at all, never had a cross word between each other, but we both felt a strain. I wanted him to cast his own shadow. He deserved that."

It wasn't without emotion that Carl cut long-standing ties with a friend he loved like a brother and who returned his feelings in kind. Being with Cash had allowed Carl to sustain his own career, albeit on a diminished plateau, and had kept him busy constantly at a time he needed it most. With Cash he had sobered up; had played prisons (and hated them so much he stopped—he didn't like donating his services to men and women who had broken the law); had played the White House for President Richard Nixon in 1970 ("He had the same expression on when I met him as he had when he was sittin' out there listenin': no expression. He had bulldog wrinkles that were permanently embedded, and if he smiled you never knew it. Didn't mess up them permanent wrinkles."). He had experienced grand times in the major cities of Europe, and soul-shaking times in Southeast Asia; had been witness to and part of Cash's ascension from country-music star to American legend. He had been given career opportunities that might otherwise have passed him by: He and Cash had written music for the Robert Redford film *Little Fauss and Big Halsy,* Carl contributing the theme song and three others (including one of his strongest efforts, "True Love Is Greater Than Friendship"), and Carl had been an important presence on Cash's albums since joining the troupe in the mid-sixties (never better than on 1970's *Hello, I'm Johnny Cash,* particularly on the cut "Blistered," where Carl did exactly as the song title indicated in fashioning a song-length backing solo that was fast, clean, imaginative, and completely breathtaking in its power and momentum—without Carl's guitar, "Blistered" wouldn't exist).

What he had been keeping largely quiet was the growing confidence he had in his sons Greg and Stan as musicians. Stan had started playing drums in the late sixties, after having demonstrated his aptitude for percussion years earlier—before his tenth birthday, in fact—by beating out rhythm on Clayton's bass during his father and uncle's practice sessions in Carl's den—shades of Fluke Holland's introduction to the Perkins Brothers Band. By age five Greg was showing some aptitude on piano, watching Valda play and then picking out the melodies by memory. In 1969, when he was ten, he was asked by Carl if he would be interested in learning to play bass. Being left-handed, Greg found it difficult to convert Carl's instructions on a right-handed instrument, but he persevered and in time was able to hold his own in jam sessions with his father and brother. If there was an obstacle to overcome, it was the normal generation gap with respect to music. Stan and Greg were very much products of their generations—Stan being the Beatles fanatic, Greg being a devotee of Led Zeppelin and British progressive rock. But although Carl may not have understood his children's musical taste, he never criticized it either.

Because Stan and Greg had grown up with their father's music as part of their lives, they didn't have to travel far to understand the spirit and simple complexities of rockabilly, or to learn to love it. If any two people were to rockabilly born, they were Greg and Stan Perkins. By the time they joined Carl's band in 1976, both boys had had experience playing in local rock bands, especially the older Stan, who was working full time during the day and playing in tonks at night. For Greg, playing in his father's band became a full-time occupation in 1977, when he dropped out of twelfth grade to go on the road.

Although Valda was disappointed by Greg's decision to quit school, she knew the boys were fully capable of playing professionally and that they might be the best company for Carl as he sought to re-establish himself as a solo act on the concert circuit. For Carl, there were no pangs of conscience over his son leaving school. He saw a future he wanted, for himself and for his family, and they would be part of it. "I just knew music was in them boys' blood, and it was gonna be their livelihood," Carl says. "I just felt that. I felt we could make it, or I wouldn't have walked back out on that thin ice again. We'd played enough together at home, I knew we sounded as good as I'd ever sounded in my life. The first night in Alexandria, Louisiana, I got 'em in a little circle and said a prayer: 'God, give us all the nerve we need to do a good show. Thank You for putting us together and may this last a long time.' "

Greg saw a greater purpose to his and Stan's joining Carl: "You want your children to grow up decent, and you want your children to succeed in life. I think it was my dad's whole life plan, to have us in the band, and it was a pleasure to try to fulfill that. The first time we went onstage and fulfilled that dream was like the essence, for me, and I know it was for Stan. We knew that was gonna happen. I knew he wanted that dream. He wanted to some day walk on the stage with his kids and say, 'Okay, I've given you the chance, take it, let's do it.' And it was the most overwhelming feeling."

Carl rounded out the band with drummer Gary Vailes (Stan was the rhythm guitarist, playing three chords "my wife had shown me") and keyboardist Lee McAlpine, friends of Stan's from playing the tonks, and with multi-instrumentalist and vocalist David Sea, recommended to Carl by a mutual friend. (On *The Carl Perkins Show* album they cut for Suede, the band was joined by Stan's wife, Judy King, on vocals.) The Alexandria date, on a bill headlining Willie Nelson with T.G. Sheppard as a supporting act, took place on January 14, 1976, followed the next day by a show at Jackson's Civic Center (where Nelson was mistaken for a drifter and refused admission to the backstage area). John Swanner, Carl's drinking buddy from the Las Vegas years, came back in the picture at this time as the band's booking agent and succeeded in getting dates in some of the most depressing places in America, as Stan recalls: "When we first started out, we played places where our spotlight would be a number-three washtub with three 100-watt bulbs in it. A wrestling arena. We did some bad places. There were places we played where, after we'd get through playing, they didn't want to pay us. We were traveling in a 1975 GMC motor home, pulling a trailer. If we had a breakdown, there'd go the profit you'd make, trying to get it fixed. We were in the position that time where Mom and Dad were struggling, I was married and had a family, had obligations—they were paying me weekly when they couldn't really afford to pay me. I was making like two hundred fifty dollars a week in 1976, '77, and my mom and dad couldn't afford to pay me. There were times that my mother tried to beat the check back to the bank. I mean it was tough."

Everything was in short supply for the group Carl dubbed the C.P. Express, but the work, though low paying, was constant. The hard times brought everyone closer, Greg recalls, even at the most dismal points, when one sandwich would have to feed three starving musicians: "I knew the talent in my dad. I knew he wasn't a quitter. He doesn't have that in him. He was raised hard, very hard, and even at that time, it wasn't as hard as it was when he was growing up. He never, ever gave me a look that said, 'Son, I can't handle this anymore.' Never."

Playing lowbrow places again, Carl would appear to have sunk to the bottom level of the entertainment world, back where he started with Jay. Again he was without a recording contract, and desiring one. When he left Cash, he was no longer a teenager, but a forty-five-year-old man working in an industry infamous for treating its aging giants like yesterday's papers.

And yet Carl was feeling curiously fulfilled on the road with his sons. "Man, them boys know where I'm goin' before I do—it's so much like it was with Jay and Clayton," Carl says. "Jay sensed, Clayton sensed, they knew where I was goin'—these two boys know, and have, ever since they started playin' with me. Jay and Clayton, and here God came along and gave me two sons that provide the exact same thing them two brothers did."

It would be over a decade later before he came up with his elegant formulation that "if a man lives long enough, he'll run into himself," but he was doing precisely that as the seventies wound down. Seemingly back at square one on the career track, he was experiencing the fullness of life he had felt in his own youth, when he seemed to have less than nothing, save riches uncounted in his family's love and compassion for one another. Now, as then, he reached out for that love, and returned its blessings manifold. In his own home, Carl Perkins was as big a man as walked the Earth.

Carl had other reasons to be optimistic. In the weeks before his father's death, and a full year before going out with the C.P. Express, he had taken a step he had explored tentatively in 1970. After years of fruitless attempts to collect royalties on his Sun recordings according to the twice-yearly schedule set out in his publishing contracts, he filed a complaint against Sam Phillips with the Chancery Court of Shelby County, asking for a complete accounting of "all monies and property of every kind and from every source" collected by Phillips and his publishing companies over the years. The case received little notice, but it showed Sam Phillips to be as devious in his business practices as he was brilliant in his musical instincts.

Carl's relationship with Sam went downhill steadily after 1958. In legal documents submitted in the case of *Carl Perkins, Plaintiff v. Samuel C. Phillips, Defendant,* Carl asserted Sam "refused to discuss or account to" him any information regarding his publishing royalties, and added: "At one time Defendant said he was taking BMI money and using it to promote future songs." To the Court he claimed his efforts to be paid properly had been notably unproductive, producing only one check a year, "around Christmas."

Harsh words passed over telephone lines were simply that—harsh words. Physical violence nearly ensued when Carl decided to confront Sam personally over the unpaid royalties. In a November 1977 response to questions from Phillips's attorneys, reference is made to Carl visiting Sam at the studio in 1959; Carl says the confrontation occurred sometime in the early sixties, when Sam had moved from the Union Avenue facility to a larger building on Madison. Carl was accompanied by Dewey Phillips, and both men had been drinking when they confronted the Sun owner. As Carl tells it: "I went down to get me some money for Christmas, for my family.

"Sam said, 'You ain't got nothin' this year.' I said, 'Oh, yeah. Mr. Phillips, don't do that. You know I have. Give me my money.'

"He said, 'You ain't gettin' nothin' this year.'

"Dewey said, 'Sam, you oughta pay the boy what you owe him.'

"And Sam said, 'No, this is one year I ain't gonna give him a damn thing.'

"I said, 'One year you're gonna give me all of it. Or I'm takin' you back to Jackson, and you'll be folded in the back of my car. You gonna pay it all. Get the checkbook.'

"And he *jumped* behind his desk and quickly opened a drawer.

Dewey got his hands under my arms and behind my neck, pushed me out the door and said, 'Perkins, he's got a gun! Let's go! Let's go!'

"I was in some kind of state of shock. The car was parked out front, he got on the steering wheel, Dewey did, said 'Gimme the key! Gimme the key!' I handed him the key, and didn't look back. When he said [Sam] had a gun, I figured he did and I said, 'He may use it. I don't wanna die.'

"I got in my car, he screamed the tires out and went down the street, and I was sittin' there, man, I was in a daze. I said, 'Did he have a pistol?'

"He said, 'He has one in that desk. Did you know that?'

"I said, 'No, but I don't care. Take me back. I wanna face him with his pistol and the whole works. I just wanna get my tire tool outta the back. Just stop.'

"He said, 'No, I'm not stoppin'.' I said, 'It's my car. Stop it!'

"He pulled over to the edge and said, 'Perkins, somebody's gonna get killed. I don't want you to get killed, and I don't want you to kill him. You don't need to see him tonight; he ain't gonna give you no money.'

"I kinda knew he wasn't. I knew we were hittin' on something we'd never been that close to. I had those vibes, those feelin's, like a black velvet curtain that fell down in front of my eyes and all over my soul. It was crossbones and skulls. It was a bad, icy night, really was. And I said, 'Well, let me walk around. I don't wanna drive. Let's walk around.'

"He pulled in a service station and stopped. I walked around, guys worked there said, 'You're Carl Perkins. Give me your autograph.' I was so nervous I couldn't even hardly write. And I was drinkin' too.

"So ol' Dewey got out and went to the dressing room. That put me behind the wheel of my car. He come back out and said, 'You don't want me to drive?' I said, 'No.'

"He got in. I said, 'Well, I'm goin' back to Sun Records.'

"Dewey said, 'Well I'm gettin' out.'

"'Why don't you go with me? I need a witness to this.'

"He said, 'I don't want to be a witness to this. No.'

"I said, 'Well just sit down. Let's talk a little longer.'

"I knew something bad was gonna happen. I cranked up the Cadillac and we eased down the street. And he said, 'Now Perkins, if you pull in here, I'm gone.' I just drove slow. Sam had double glass doors in his new studio over on Madison, Phillips International. He was standin' in the door with his hand down beside him. Whether he had a pistol in his hand, I don't know. I drove slow, and Dewey said, 'Go on, Perk. Go home, Perk. Go on.'

"Something took over and I said, 'He's right. Don't go over there. You'll get your day.' So I came on back to Jackson. I stopped out on Summer and got a pint of whiskey and me and [Dewey] drank and sang all the way to Jackson."

"After that episode," according to answers to interrogatories posed to Carl by Phillips's attorney in 1977, "Defendant for the next three years did not pay Plaintiff anything."

Near the end of 1967, after years of persistent calls, Carl received a check for $12,000 from Sam's publishing companies, Knox Music and Hi-Lo Music. In the lower left corner was written: "Accepted in payment as full for all royalties due through December 31, 1967." Suspicious of this, Carl consulted a Jackson attorney, who advised him, erroneously as it turned out, to cash the check, because it would not have any bearing on any lawsuit Carl might file in the future. (In July 1969 Sam sold Sun Records to Nashville music executive-entrepreneur Shelby Singleton, although he retained his music publishing companies and a small percentage of Singleton's Sun operation, renamed Sun International Corporation.)

From January 1975 through the early months of 1978 each side's respective attorneys shot paper bullets at each other. Sam's defense, in a nutshell: He did what he had to do as a small, underfunded, understaffed business to broaden the prospects for his songwriters by striking a deal with the New York–based publishing concern Hill and Range to exploit worldwide the catalogues of all writers published by Sam's companies; that in doing so he allowed writers to realize more income than would otherwise have been possible with Sun's limited resources; that Carl understood the contracts he signed and had since chosen not to exercise rights stated therein; that Carl didn't read the contracts (as Carl admitted in his answers) but was content to reap the accompanying rewards; that Carl was paid all revenues according to the contracts' terms and had no proof to the contrary; that the December 1967 check satisfied all obligations on Sam's part; that Carl had, in effect, slept on his rights for so long that the statute of limitations prohibited him from bringing any action at this late date.

Carl's attorneys countered Sam's claims by alleging that Carl was not advised of the deal with Hill and Range and thus had been improperly paid when he was paid at all. Under the terms of the Hill and Range agreement, twenty-five percent was taken off the top as Hill and Range's commission, with Sam receiving the remaining seventy-five percent, out of which he was paying Carl fifty percent. However, Carl's publishing contracts stipulated a fifty-fifty split on the royalties with Knox and Hi-Lo, not Hill and Range. The assertion was that Carl was paid half of seventy-five percent (or thirty-seven-and-a-half percent) rather than half of one hundred percent.

In a late-spring hearing in Chancery Court with Chancellor W.V. Doran presiding, Carl gave moving testimony in stating his position. Those attending regard it as one of his greatest performances. After all the claims and counterclaims (some particularly painful to Carl personally, as Sam's attorneys assailed his intelligence and integrity), Carl spoke from the heart in revealing himself as a man of principle.

"The allegations you're making against [Sam Phillips] are very severe," said Sam's attorney, Saul C. Belz, in addressing Carl on the stand. "You are accusing him of thievery, of a form of robbery, of taking from you—"

"I sure like the last way you said that—'taking from me' makes sense to me," Carl interjected. "Now that's not saying he did. I'm saying I *think* he did. All this hearing is about, as far as I'm concerned, your Honor"—Carl turned on the witness stand to look at the Chancellor—"is to see who owes who. I don't feel like there's been a fair and just account given to me. I'm not saying Mr. Phillips is cheatin' me. He might have overpaid me. This works both ways, and he just might have overpaid me. And if he did, I wanna know about it. I feel as an artist who was signed to him, who had privilege to my money before I saw it, I have a right to get a full accounting, which I never got. I don't know how many records Elvis sold; I don't know what the Beatles sold.

I do know, sir, that I wrote a song, he published my song, he sold over a million of my own records of my song. Of that one song. I don't know how many more. But the one we're talkin' about here is 'Blue Suede Shoes.' It's caused the most commotion of any of 'em. And it just might be, sir, that I owe him. And if I do, I make this statement in your court, I will walk from Jackson, Tennessee, back to your courtroom, your Honor, this very room, in this courthouse in Memphis. I will walk the median of I-40—I will not drive—I will *walk* if he overpaid me one dollar." Carl raised a hand in the air, his thumb and forefinger grasping an imaginary dollar bill. "I'll bring it and hand it to you, sir. That's all I ask. I want to know who owes who."

On August 10, 1978, Chancellor Doran ruled "that Defendants owed to Plaintiff an obligation to publish his music and distribute to him 50% of all money generated by mechanical licensing of his music whether received by Defendants as Publisher, or from Hill and Range as their assignee." He added: "Defendants shall account for and pay over to Plaintiff an amount of money which when added to that heretofore paid would represent 50% of all royalties generated by mechanical licensing whether foreign or local earned by the songs composed by Plaintiff."

He ruled further that Carl's attorneys had failed to prove fraud on Sam's part or the existence of a fiduciary relationship between publisher and writer "merely because Plaintiff entered into contracts with Defendants." In upholding the statute of limitations on Carl's claim, he limited damages to the period beginning January 5, 1969, and awarded Carl $36,182.46, "which sum represents the difference between those sums heretofore paid to Plaintiff by Defendants and fifty per cent of the revenues generated by mechanical licensing . . . for the accounting periods ending June 30, 1977."

The Chancery Court ruling was an important victory, but less significant in the long run than one negotiated by Carl's attorney, Stanley Chernau, in the weeks after the hearing, when he threatened yet another lawsuit against Sam for full recovery of Carl's publishing. Sam acquiesced ("for a little money," says Chernau) and Carl was given full control of the copyrights on all of his Sun songs. Free and clear of Sam's influence, Carl Perkins Music was formed and the titular artist never again had to beg for what was his. In November 1977 he was able to buy his dream house, a modest, rambling, one-story brick structure on Country Club Lane, to which later he added a personal recording studio–recreation room. In time he would acknowledge, with genuine appreciation, Sam's contribution to his music—would even tell reporters that the biggest mistake he had made in his career was leaving Sun Records—but he would never forgive him for taking money he needed to support his family.

On the morning of August 16, 1977, Carl passed the morning hours leisurely. He was relaxing in his favorite recliner, drinking his eye-opening cup of coffee, when, unannounced, Greg burst through the front door.

"Daddy, did you hear about Elvis?" he called out urgently.

"No, what about him?" Carl asked.

"He's dead."

"What??"

"He died awhile ago," Greg said.

"Boy," Carl said, his tone severe, "you're kiddin' me."

"No I'm not," Greg assured him. "Fella just told me he saw it on television."

Carl turned on his set and filling the screen was a head shot of the young Elvis, "a beautiful picture of him," Carl recalls, and beneath it the dates 1935–1977. Dead at age forty-two.

Elvis's physical deterioration had been well publicized in recent years, and through the grapevine Carl had heard tales of Elvis's insatiable appetite for drugs. None of it made sense to someone who had known the King of Rock 'n' Roll not as an icon but as one of the guys. Six months earlier, after seeing pictures of Elvis in his bloated condition, Carl had made a trip to Graceland, determined to get his friend out of Memphis so that he could "take him fishing, feed him some beans and cornbread, and talk to him." At the gates of Graceland he was met by Elvis's uncle, Vester Presley, who called to the house to announce Carl, but reported back that Elvis was still asleep. At seven o'clock in the evening. After signing autographs for fans waiting on the street for a glimpse of Elvis, Carl drove back to Jackson.

He never got through to Elvis, but he did get to see him, from a distance, at a concert in Memphis. Sitting with Valda near the back of the arena, he peered through binoculars, sadness enveloping him.

▶ THE VOICE OF CARL PERKINS

I couldn't believe what the other end of them things was showing me. This guy so fat that he couldn't even make his moves. He was like some big, grossly overweight Presley imitator that did a bad job of imitating him. I left out of there just heartbroken, and I kept telling Valda, "I'm gonna go get him, there's something bad wrong with him." But I kept puttin' it off. There would have been a way I could've got in to see him, if I'd pressured for it, I believe, every day. Finally he'd of said, "Well let the old bastard up here, then he'll leave me alone." But I didn't. When his death came, Valda said, "Carl, you shoulda tried a little harder." I said, "Don't tell me. I know."

I don't know what happened to his life. I don't know how it happened. I don't know how it happened that I became an alcoholic. But I don't condemn Elvis; I don't condemn any man. I know one thing: The Elvis I knew was a very sick man or he'd of never let himself get that much overweight. The Presley I knew would've stayed up night and day doing backflips off his bed to the floor before he'd let himself get in that kind of condition. He was very ashamed of his size. I saw it in his face at that concert. He didn't like that big fat fellow he was. But there again, he showed me something. Even so grossly overweight and hurt to the bone when he'd glance down and couldn't even see his feet, but yet as the sweat rolled off of his fat jaws and dropped to the ground or on his fat belly, he gave those fans his soul.

I guess we all thought that maybe somehow Elvis would never die. But when it hit me, man, there'd be no more Elvis, I toted the guilt around that I didn't get to him. I couldn't describe it then and, really, I still can't and give that feeling justice, the emotional drop that took place inside of my soul when Greg walked into my house and told me Elvis was dead.

4

HOME

1981–Present

Oh when I was a young man
Searchin' for fame
Thought I'd make myself a name
Might even make a marquee
Out in Hollywood;
Now the road ain't smooth
Boys, it's been rough
I hit a lot of spots
Sure been tough
Now I find that ramblin's no good;
And I'm headed home, home
That's where the heart is
That's where I really want to go
Home, home, that's where my love is
I found out there ain't no place like home

—Carl Perkins, "Home (That's Where the Heart Is)"

What had it all amounted to, this journey from the Lake County cotton fields into the tide of America's cultural and musical history? Swept along by forces beyond his control, Carl had been too consumed by the recurring dramas of his career to enjoy, or even to recognize, his own achievements. In his deep-seated humility, only grudgingly would he concede music historians' view of "Blue Suede Shoes" as an important statement—he felt he had written and performed better songs, considerably better, than the one for which he was recognized internationally. If only the public had been given the opportunity to hear them . . .

Still, in the wake of Elvis's death, when he weighed what had been lost and what had been gained, he found the scale tipping in his favor. The family's stability and love were his rocks in hard times. With the resolution of his conflict with Sam Phillips, he could now live comfortably; more significant, he could now act when he chanced upon others less fortunate than he in their efforts to escape a hellish life.

In 1980 a front-page story in *The Jackson Sun* described a long history of abuse a four-year-old boy had suffered at his father's hands, which finally resulted in the child lying in Jackson Hospital in a coma from severe head trauma. Accompanying the story was a photo of the boy, sandy-haired, bright-eyed, and smiling broadly. Below it was the caption "Near death."

Carl walked into the kitchen, where Valda was preparing supper. "Who does this look like?" he asked, holding the paper for her to see.

"It looks like Stan," Valda answered, studying the uncanny likeness to her firstborn.

The next day brought news of the boy's death. Carl "just got absolutely tore up. It seemed I could see a billboard with a telephone number and a message—'If you have hurt a child, call this number.' Let help get there and get the kid in the hospital. That was all of my intention. All I could see was that telephone number on billboards around this town."

Spurred by that vision, Carl imagined not merely a billboard, but an entire facility devoted to aiding abused children. Influential friends and the reservoir of good will he had built through his support of other charities served him well as he moved his dream forward. For several years he had been playing benefit concerts at Reelfoot Lake, with proceeds going to the disadvantaged children populating the still-depressed area of his birth. Since 1976 he had been appearing with local celebrity Doris Freeman ("Cousin Tuny," as she is known in west Tennessee) on yearly telethons raising funds to support children afflicted with cerebral palsy. This work had gone unnoticed by the national press, but his celebrity and growing legend had led to him being befriended by important politicians at every level of local and state government.

At the time he began investigating the viability of creating a shelter, the Exchange Clubs of America, a Toledo, Ohio-based civic organization modeled after the Rotary- and Lions-type Clubs, was looking for a national project that would define it much in the same way the Shriners were noted for aiding burn victims. Carl's interest reached the Toledo headquarters through a friend, Henry Harrison. Lengthy discussions and mounds of legal paperwork later, in October 1981, the Exchange Club Carl Perkins Center for the Prevention of Child Abuse opened in what was once a dormitory room on the campus of Union University. Carl headlined a fundraiser that also featured the Statler Brothers, and brought in $33,000 of seed money, to which the Exchange Club added $26,000 in grant money to fund the opening. In Tennessee, the Jackson facility was the first such center concentrating solely on abused children, and only the fourth in the entire United States. Four years later it moved to more spacious quarters on the second floor of downtown Jackson's McLellan Building. From a single director, its staff has grown to fifteen full-time workers and two part-timers, all degreed professionals.

Most of the Center's children are under twelve years of age. Consistent with Carl's vision, a twenty-four-hour hotline operates seven days a week. Now serving 250 families a month, the Center has grown to include fully staffed satellite offices in Gibson County, Henderson County, and Haywood County, and on a part-time basis provides services to eight other counties. As a nonprofit operation, its primary source of funding comes from donations generated each year in mid-August during a day-long Circle of Hope telethon whose headline attraction is Carl Perkins, who stays before the camera for virtually all of the show's ten hours on the air.

In appealing for support, Carl stares straight into the camera, tears welling in his eyes, and offers a folksy appeal, utterly sincere, that tugs at the heart and loosens purse strings across the station's viewing area. He's Andy Griffith in *A Face in the Crowd* without the malevolence. A sample monologue: "Are you tellin' me that by not ringing that phone that you don't care? If everybody watching would just give one dollar, do you realize I could go off the air and I wouldn't have to ask you no more? I'm pleading for the kids who can't help themselves. My name is on the building, but it's not mine. That Center is called that because somebody decided to do it. I'm telling you, it belongs to you. You may need that Center, or you're gonna know somebody who needs it. But if you don't give, if these phones don't start ringing, then we won't have one. You'll drive by where it used to be, and you'll say, 'Well, ol' Carl wanted us to have a child abuse center here but I didn't care enough to call him and give him a dollar.' Is that what you're tellin' me out there?"

The first telethon, held in 1983, raised $33,000; the tenth, $160,000. In toto the telethons have brought into the Center's till close to $1 million.

By 1993 the Center was beginning to outgrow its offices, and an architect had drawn up plans for a new facility with an estimated cost of $600,000. One year later ground was broken on a new, permanent home for the Center; a year later, in 1995, the facility opened. The first $64,000 earmarked to pay for its cost came from sales of a "Classic Carl" limited-edition Coca-Cola bottle with Carl's likeness on one side and a list of his achievements on the other. The building is erected on the former site of the Hardeman Music Company, where Carl purchased his gold-top Gibson Les Paul electric guitar in 1954, shortly before recording "Blue Suede Shoes."

Around the time of the Center's opening in 1981, Carl's career received a boost when Paul McCartney invited him to Montserrat to play on his *Tug of War* album. The ensuing publicity (and good reviews) boosted his concert bookings considerably, putting him in better venues for a higher guarantee (from this point on his price per night would never be less than $10,000); he also began making his first appearances on college campuses, where the young audiences greeted him with the same enthusiasm—and respect for his legacy—as had British audiences in the early sixties.

Though he had never given up the dream of again having a hit record on his own, he didn't fool himself. Most of the living rock 'n' roll pioneers had disappeared from record completely, although a few were still hacking away on the oldies circuit and in small clubs; those who had gravitated to country were finding it increasingly difficult to be noticed among the influx of new talent.

Even this historical pattern was changing by the mid-eighties under the full force of the New Traditionalist movement, a backlash against the soft, pop-influenced country that had been dominant since the seventies. Although its roots could be traced in the rock realm to the Byrds' 1968 album *Sweetheart of the Rodeo* (which was inspired by a brilliant but bedeviled young musician named Gram Parsons, briefly a Byrd before going solo and cutting some of the most haunting country songs of his or any other time; he died of a drug overdose in 1971), its most resonant echoes were heard in the mid-seventies' Outlaw movement. Spearheaded by Nashville outcast Willie Nelson, along with Waylon Jennings, Kris Kristofferson, Gary Stewart, and a handful of other artists, the Outlaws' lyrics spoke frankly and often explicitly of personal traumas, sexual and otherwise, and their music harkened back to the stripped-down, basic band approach of honky-tonk. Fittingly, one of the Outlaws' seminal documents came from Hank Williams's son, Hank Jr., whose 1975 album, *Hank Williams, Jr. & Friends*, was a tour de force of raw, emotional power, and hard-edged playing.

Gram Parsons's spirit and passion persisted in his friend and confidante Emmylou Harris, whose eclectic taste defined the broad parameters of New Traditionalism and from whose band sprang two of the most important New Traditionalist artists, Ricky Skaggs and Rodney Crowell, the latter a songwriter of uncommon sensitivity and insight whose writing betrayed as strong a strain of Lennon-McCartney influence as it did Hank Williams. In the eighties, country gave rise to a host of compelling young artists, be they gifted interpretive singers such as Randy Travis and George Strait, or, shades of Carl Perkins, self-contained artists who could write, play, and/or sing with authority: K.T. Oslin, Dwight Yoakam, Steve Earle, and Johnny Cash's daughter Rosanne, whose soul-searing writing had few peers.

Carl's path intersected that of the New Traditionalists in 1985 with his introduction to a mother and daughter duo whose acoustic-based music had jetted them into the front ranks of country's most popular new artists. The Judds (Naomi, the mother; Wynonna, the daughter), Kentucky natives both, were more than a couple of attractive, sexy women. Working with producer Brent Maher and their associate producer–musical mentor Don Potter, the Judds favored a sound that remained close to country blues and to Byrds-style country rock while updating both. Moreover, they projected an image of strength and self-sufficiency in their choice of material and in their public posture, and were unabashedly spiritual in their outlook on life. Following the release of a six-song EP in '84, they were becoming fixtures in the number-one spot on country charts.

In early '85 the Judds came to Jackson to open a concert for Conway Twitty. As Harold Jenkins, his real name, Twitty was signed to Sun shortly after Carl left the label, but success came much later, following a name and label change. By the the mid-eighties, Twitty was one of the best-selling artists in country-music history. Carl had mixed feelings about Twitty, who had heard Carl Mann's version of "Mona Lisa" before it was released and then cut a similarly arranged version for MGM. To Carl this smacked of sabotage, and "I didn't like that."

Nevertheless, Carl buried his feelings for a night and invited Twitty and the Judds to an after-show dinner at the Catfish Cabin, a franchise operation in which he had an investment. There, seated at a long table, Wynonna and Naomi found themselves surrounded by Carl's family and, nearby, Carl himself. Also present was the Judds' manager, Ken Stilts, a Nashville native who had gone full time into artist management following the late-seventies dissolution of his once-successful independent label, Dimension Records. Stilts's introduction to Carl had come in the early eighties, arranged by two British businessmen ("I never could figure out their area of expertise," Stilts says) who had assumed a quasi-management function and were attempting to find new career opportunities for Carl.

Stilts signed the Judds in 1983, and when their EP was released the following year, he sent a copy to Carl, anxious for his opinion. Carl's initial response to the music, Stilts recalls, sealed the mutual-admiration society that had formed between Perkins and the Judds: "Carl recognized that this was unique. He was familiar with the music they had out at that point, and he was really taken back by Wynonna. Carl was one of the first real knowledgeable music artists to recognize Wynonna's talent. They had not met him at that point, but they were big, big Carl Perkins fans."

As much as they had been influenced by country, both Naomi and Wynonna were children of rock 'n' roll (Naomi, born in 1946, gave birth to Wynonna in 1964). Paramount among their influences were the twin gods of Carl Perkins and Elvis Presley. When the Judds finally met Carl, the bond between the artists was immediate and deep, according to Naomi: "Carl called me Mama. I always felt like we had known each other forever. We had that sort of instantaneous relationship, because there were so many similarities—we both obviously believe in family. I remember him telling me that his daughter lives like a door down from his house, and his sons live close by. I thought, *This guy's got it made in the shade—he knows what the priorities in life really are.* Carl and I had that southern sensibility in common, which was an emotional shorthand. Wynonna loved to sit and hear him tell stories—he would regale her with these stories, and I get this real wonderful feeling that he was a bit of a mentor—she called him 'Uncle Carl.' He could be Wynonna's uncle, because he's like our people, but he's also a legend, and he was able to tell her stories that gave her examples of [*laughs*] how she didn't want to be."

Meeting the Judds kicked off what turned out to be one of the most productive years of Carl's career. For the re-formed Dot division of MCA, Carl cut a self-titled album that featured a number of songs cowritten with his son Greg, and one written by Carl, Greg, and Stan, "Texas Women," which was the first time on record that Carl had touched on the western-swing influence in his own music. In his song "If I Had'a Known," a bit of self-deprecating humor rooted in reality, Carl offered a rueful assessment of the price he had paid in his wilder years:

> I ran wide open for too damn long
> If I had'a known I would live this long
> I'da took better care of myself

Once again, a strong effort was in vain: The Dot division folded shortly after the album's release.

The same fate befell the newly formed America division of Polygram, formed by Memphis businessmen Gary Belz (nephew of Sam Phillips's attorney Saul C. Belz) and Herb O'Mell, shortly after the release of the label's first and only album, *Class of '55*, which reunited Carl, Cash, Orbison, and Jerry Lee for two days at the Sun studio and two days at producer Chips Moman's American studio, where Elvis had cut two monumental sessions in early '69 with Moman behind the board. Although it was not the first such project—in 1980, the four had teamed briefly for a segment on a television show honoring Cash's twenty-fifth year in show business; and in April 1981, Carl and Jerry Lee had joined Cash onstage in Stuttgart, Germany, for a show that was released in 1982 on a Columbia album titled *The Survivors*—it was the most ballyhooed. A national press conference held in the lobby of the grand (and Belz-owned) Peabody Hotel produced the first in a stream of reports from major print, radio, and television outlets; in addition the whole enterprise was filmed by Dick Clark Productions. To further hype it as an Event, a grand finale was planned and videotaped in which the four principals were joined in the studio by the Judds, Rick Nelson, British retro-rocker Dave Edmunds, John Fogerty, June Carter Cash, Jack Clement, and Marty Stuart for a near eight-minute raveup on Fogerty's "Big Train (From Memphis)," a metaphorical tribute to Elvis. A more turgid homage to Elvis was provided by songwriter Paul Kennerley (then married to Emmylou Harris) by way of side one's closer, "We Remember the King," on which Cash, among all the soloists, gave the most stirring performance. Later Cash referred to it as "a lovefest. It was really something. There was a lot of crying going on that day, we were all so happy to be together again. We used to work all those shows together across the country, the four of us did, and I had some nice memories of those tours with those guys. And there we were again."

To Carl, the *Class of '55* sessions represented "one of the best weeks of my life and one of the most horrible." The best: seeing Cash "ready to work" and looking healthy, and catching up with Orbison again, to whom the years had been hard, although he gave no outward indication of such. While still slightly heavy of frame, the once-homely youth from Wink had matured into a handsome middle-aged man, thanks only in part to some cosmetic help—in the early sixties he had given in to his poor eyesight and adopted a trademark feature in the form of thick, dark-lensed, black-framed glasses. At the same time, his hair, like Elvis's, lost its light shade beneath jet-black dye.

Physical appearance aside, the sixties had seen Orbison move to the top ranks of rock 'n' roll behind his own songs and stunning displays of vocal prowess. Paranoia, dread, and fatalistic anticipation were the dominant moods of his early-sixties gems—"Running Scared," "Only the Lonely," "Crying," "In Dreams," "It's Over," "Leah"—but there were moments of heart-tugging tenderness in "Blue Angel," "Blue Bayou," and "Dream Baby." Orbison's voice was one of the most remarkable instruments in rock, and he used its full force, most effectively on "In Dreams," when his full-bodied tenor rose from a strong, straightforward delivery to a plaintive wail, followed by a piercing shriek.

All of Orbison's dreams as an artist had come true, and then some. But his personal life had taken tragic turns in the sixties, and Carl knew well the sadness Roy carried inside. In 1966 Claudette had been killed in a motorcycle accident, and a little over two years later two of his three sons died in a house fire while Roy was on tour in England. Always quiet, Roy now seemed frightfully introverted, so much so that he asked everyone to leave the studio when it was time to record vocals on one of his songs for *Class of '55* (he contributed a lovely original ballad in "I'm Coming Home"); uncharacteristically, he was late frequently to the sessions, lingering outside the studio in his bus long after the appointed starting hour, and seemed distracted when not actively engaged in the recording.

The worst: Jerry Lee, who looked healthy enough but was in vintage Jerry Lee form throughout the week. It was what Carl had feared at the outset but had hoped would not be the case when the bell rang: "There's two or three times I could've killed Jerry Lee Lewis, just as easy as I could have walked on by him. He showed out every day, he was wilder than a guinea hen from the very start to the end. He oversang on '16 Candles,' he was gonna show all of us how great he still was. One time he stood on his hands and was gonna walk across the studio floor and ten thousand pills fell out of his pockets in front of the damn *Rolling Stone* camera woman. In one picture he's got on a thin raincoat of some kind, and the pockets are bulged out—that's pills; that's the coat he had on when he stood on his hands, and here come all them pills. Damn plastic raincoat he wore in there one day and it wasn't rainin'. Hell no, there wasn't a cloud in the sky. John said, 'Oh boy, here we go. There's enough pills on that floor to get us all arrested and sent away for life.' "

With these four artists assembled together, it was unsurprising that talk of Elvis dominated their personal conversations and their interviews. Marty Stuart, newly signed to Columbia Records and at that time the guitarist in Cash's band, sat in on the *Class of '55* sessions and was duly impressed by the events he witnessed: "On the planet Earth, Memphis, Tennessee, 706 Union, was *the* place to be that week.

It was great. And the funniest thing is, all the journalists that surrounded the whole thing kept asking the guys, 'Wouldn't it have been great if Elvis had been here?' Carl loved Elvis, and he had his things to say; Cash had some very diplomatic things to say, and Roy finally said, 'Well he is here, we can feel the spirit.' Then Jerry Lee said, 'The boy would've been here if he hadn't overshot the runway!' That pretty well set the tone for the rest of the session."

For Stuart, *Class of '55* brought him in close contact with the music he had grown up loving as a child in Mississippi and the artists whose spirits seemed to him to embody the most vital qualities of rock 'n' roll. Moreover, as Cash's guitarist, he was walking in Carl's shadow. Born in 1958, he had been playing professionally since age thirteen, when he began touring with the Sullivans, a southern gospel duo. From that time forward he has been most vocal about his great affection for the pioneer artists in country and rock 'n' roll—he knows their music, their lives, and honors their work in his own, which leans as much towards Memphis as it does Nashville, blurring the line between rock 'n' roll and country. But when he stepped into Cash's band, he was not yet twenty years old, and had much to learn from those who had come before him. Upon joining Cash, he arranged to interview Carl, whom he referred to as "Daddy Cat," in order to collect the master's wisdom on tape for inspiration and instruction along the way. "Carl's timeless and so real. His playing comes straight from his heart to his hands," Stuart asserts. "It amazes me that there's one little ol' flying saucer out there in guitar land, it keeps buzzin' along year after year with the same sound. That's Carl. I figured if I wanted to do my job better the best thing I could do was get up and go talk to him and see how to do it and get some of his soul on me in general."

At the end of the *Class* sessions, Carl gave Stuart his Fender Stratocaster guitar. "This box has got some songs in it," Carl said, "and you're just the cat that can get 'em out." At the same time, Carl also blessed the prodigious instrumentalist and budding solo artist with the particulars of his personal regimen for wowing an audience: "He told me, 'I put that wig on my knee, I comb that thing out, put that Red Rose hair oil down there. Before I go to the stage I mix nine different kinds of that good smell-on, put my ornaments around my neck, put

my box on, shine them boots. If that don't get 'em, they can't be got.'
You put a Cadillac around that and a hit record, I don't know anything
else a cat needs than that right there."

Carl provided the song that best captured the intended spirit of the
project. "Birth of Rock and Roll" had a three-week stay in the top 10
of the country singles chart, and stands as an eyewitness account of
early rock 'n' roll history, Memphis-style, and of its broad sphere of
influence on a succeeding generation of rockers. In his lyrics, Carl
evoked Elvis, Fluke, Jay, Clayton, Jerry Lee, and himself in describing
the wondrous events on Union Avenue in the mid-fifties, and indulged
in a moment of satisfaction over the music's staying power. Its gene-
sis was in a verse included in the only new song Carl wrote for his *Ol'
Blue Suede's Is Back* album, "Rock On Around the World." For *Class
of '55*, he updated the verse, surrounded it with more personal history
and ruminations on the past, gave it a surging rhythm, a stinging run
of guitar fills, and a strong, playful vocal.

> Well Nashville had country music
> But Memphis had the soul
> Lord, the white boy had the rhythm
> And that started rock 'n' roll
>
> (chorus:) And I was here when it happened
> Don't y'all think I oughta know
> I was here when it happened
> I watched Memphis give birth to rock 'n' roll
>
> Well a cat named Elvis, he bopped in
> To Sun right off the street
> Sang Blue Moon of old K-Y
> But he did it with a brand new beat
>
> Guess he saw him a sleepin' world
> Layin' out there by surprise
> Jerked 'em up and he wrang 'em out
> And he hung 'em out to dry

(chorus)

Well the drummer boy was beatin' on the drums
Just rockin' and a-goin' wild
Bass fiddle picker was clickin' and clackin'
But doin' it in a different style
Guitar strummin', piano pumpin' and the
Lead man kickin' out the blues
Hip-shakin' singer was swingin' and swayin'
Singin' somethin' 'bout blue suede shoes

(chorus)

Some folks called it the devil's music
Others said it wouldn't last long
Thirty-one years since we started shakin'
Proves somebody was wrong
Sixty-four the Beatles were the four
That was rock 'n' roll's best friend
The Beatles and the Stones took the ol' beat home
And the world went crazy again

It all went for nought, however, as a dispute between Moman and the parent company's New York executives resulted in promotional support being rescinded for *Class of '55*. Carl was left with profuse thank you's for his role in what was otherwise regarded as a successful venture, a Grammy Award in the spoken-word category for the quartet's reminiscences about the early days of rock 'n' roll, and some pleasant memories, chief among them his first meeting with Rick Nelson.

Before leaving the studio at the sessions' close, Nelson told Carl it had been his dream to meet the man whose music had so inspired his own (the first record Nelson had ever bought was Carl's "Boppin' the Blues"), and suggested they work some shows together in the future.

"You're the man," Carl told him. "You pull it together. I'm ready."

Less than six months later, on New Year's Eve, Nelson died in a plane crash near Dallas, Texas. Carl was at a friend's house, preparing to go deer hunting the next morning, when a Jackson radio station, through Valda, tracked him down for comment, unaware that Carl didn't know of Nelson's demise. At first Carl thought someone was pulling a tasteless joke on him; when he realized the caller was serious, he made a perfunctory comment, hung up, and went home.

"So much sadness hooked to rockabilly and rock 'n' roll music," Carl says. "[That life is] what everybody wanted; it's what everybody was lucky enough to get. And then let it kill 'em. In a roundabout way it did."

Before the year was out, Carl boosted his public profile further by starring in *A Rockabilly Session: Carl Perkins and Friends* for Cinemax, a tribute to the music he best defined, in which he was joined in a rousing, near free-form, hour-long jam session by George Harrison, Ringo Starr, Eric Clapton, Dave Edmunds, Rosanne Cash, and Stray Cats Lee Rocker and Slim Jim Phantom, two-thirds of a trio from Long Island, New York, who played rockabilly in the authentic Perkins style and had managed the neat trick of having hit records with it in the eighties. (Carl had pulled the show together himself by sending out personal videotaped invitations to each artist he wanted on the bill.) He had a brief turn as a dramatic actor as well, playing a gangster in John Landis's *Into the Night*, which required him to fight, mostly, first with star Jeff Goldblum, and near the end of the film with David Bowie, in which Carl's character was killed (of his limited contact with Bowie, Carl says: "I'd heard his name, but I didn't like his music. Still don't."). It was a brief but meaty role—considerably more satisfying than his previous movie turn in *Hawaiian Boy*—and Carl's performance was mentioned favorably in several reviews, which didn't save the film from a marginal box office showing.

After the brief tumult surrounding the *Class of '55* project and the acclaim for his *Rockabilly Session*, Carl, much to his consternation, began hearing himself spoken of as an important historical figure. Uncomfortable with the superlative "living legend," he was disinclined to lean on the past when all available evidence—apart from album sales—told him he was still improving as a songwriter.

Though he tried to ignore it, his stature was growing at every turn.

A few months after receiving the Grammy Award, he was honored with the Academy of Country Music's Career Achievement Award. Of even greater magnitude was the November 1986 announcement that he, along with fourteen other pioneers (among them Roy Orbison and Eddie Cochran, rockabillies both to varying degrees, and Ricky Nelson, a Perkins acolyte), had been selected for induction into the Rock and Roll Hall of Fame. With Elvis and Jerry Lee among the Hall's inaugural inductees the year before, only Cash remained of Sun's important first-generation artists yet to be honored (his time would come in 1992).

At the ceremony, held on January 21, 1987, at New York's Waldorf-Astoria Hotel, Carl sat at a table with Roy and Bo Diddley, another new inductee. The room was wall-to-wall with a "Who's Who" of the music business, including a host of significant artists past and present, but when Carl looked over the assembled throng, he didn't see big names and powerful executives. In his mind's eye he saw the long road that had led him to this point, from the Perkins Brothers Band tearing down the road in the middle of the night to Elvis, Cash, Jerry Lee, Roy, and himself free and rocking their way across America, making up the rules as they went along. Now here he sat in one of the world's great hotels, an aging rockabilly clad in a tuxedo. How far was this from Tiptonville? From Memphis, 1954?

He turned to Orbison. "Man, this is a great night," Carl said, momentarily shaken by the weight of his history. "Congratulations, Roy. I'm proud of you."

"I'm proud of you, Carl," Roy replied in his soft, gentle voice. "I wish Elvis had lived to experience this. This is mighty high cotton, isn't it?"

"Yeah, it is," Carl agreed. "I couldn't go in with a greater guy. You're the nicest one that ever come through Sun Records."

Orbison was given a heartfelt introduction by Bruce Springsteen, whose description of Roy's singing voice approached poetry. Carl, to his chagrin, was introduced by Sam Phillips, their personal estrangement unknown to the Hall of Fame committee that had planned the program. By the time he got around to bringing Carl up to the podium, Phillips had rambled on so long that "he got a standing ovation just for quittin'," Carl contends. Opting to keep his own remarks brief, Carl said, simply and succinctly: "What a thrill! What a night for a sharecropper's son to be standing in this building. I thank y'all and God bless you."

During the star-studded closing jam session, Carl performed "Blue Suede Shoes," with the Rolling Stones' Keith Richards joining him on guitar.

In October 1987 Tiptonville honored its most famous former resident by opening the Carl Perkins Museum and renaming the area of its location Carl Perkins Square. The centerpiece of the Square was Carl's first childhood home, somewhat restored; inside were replicas of the furnishings in the house when it was occupied by Buck Perkins's family. Carl supplied a wealth of personal memorabilia for the museum, but was on tour with Orbison when the dedication ceremonies were held. At tour's end he returned to Tiptonville to visit the museum and, for the first time in the forty-three years since he had left his home town, to set foot inside his old home. Jo Hanna Coyne, co-owner of the museum, recounted the moment for *The Jackson Sun:* "He walked in and saw the house. He walked right over there and picked up the guitar and sat down on the bed. He said it was so much like home, he couldn't believe it."

One other surprise awaited Carl in Tiptonville. Invited to visit the mayor at his office, Carl entered to find not the mayor but a grey-haired black man waiting for him. His weathered, lined face showed its years, but it was his sad eyes that betrayed his identity. It was Charlie, Carl's boyhood friend. Carl extended his hand, then pulled Charlie to him and the two embraced. Finally, sniffling and wiping his eyes, Carl stepped back and studied Charlie, asking how he had been getting along.

"Well, not nearly as well as you, Mr. Carl," Charlie answered politely.

"You know, you've added something to my name," Carl pointed out.

"What's that, Mr. Carl?"

"That 'Mr.'," Carl said. "I was Carl when we were buddies back when we was growin' up. Did you call me Mr. Carl then?"

Charlie grinned broadly. "No, sir."

"Well, you don't have to now," said Carl. "I'm the same little ol' boy I was then in my heart and soul, Charlie."

"I'm so proud that fame and all of that didn't ruin you like it has a lot of people."

"Well, Charlie, I've been blessed. But I've been aware, and I've tried to stay aware of who I was and where I came from all my life."

"You've done a wonderful job of that," Charlie said, nodding his head. "And I hear tell you have a child abuse center in Jackson, and that's mighty fine of you."

The two friends reminisced for a few minutes more. For a man running into himself, the homecoming was complete.

During the summer of 1988 Carl and Orbison played several shows together, all to sellout crowds. After years of relative quiet, Roy's career had been revitalized, first by the surprising success of an inspired collaboration with Bob Dylan, Tom Petty, and George Harrison in a group dubbed the Traveling Wilburys, then by film director David Lynch's use of "In Dreams" in his offbeat mystery, *Blue Velvet*. Out of this had come a recording contract, and he was to finish a new album for Virgin Records after completing his tour with Carl.

In the late fall they did their final show, at the Wolf Trap outdoor ampitheater in upstate New York. Carl received a standing ovation after his opening set, and came offstage to find Orbison waiting for him.

"You knocked 'em down," Roy said.

"I didn't hurt 'em," Carl said with a laugh. "They ain't a wounded one out there. I got some sympathy."

Roy peered through a part in the curtains, studying the audience now sitting placidly beneath a star-filled sky. "I hate for this night to end," he said offhandedly, wistfully, speaking slightly above a whisper. "Carl, would you do me a favor?" he asked.

"Sure, man," Carl answered, puzzled by Roy's somber tone.

"Be careful. Take care of yourself. Remember I love you."

Carl put his arms around Roy and "hugged him as tight as I've ever hugged Valda." As they stepped away from each other before Roy went on, Carl said, "It's been wonderful. And I love you."

"Winter's comin' on and we won't be traveling that much," Roy said. "But let's work together a lot next year. I really do enjoy you. My boys loved your boys. You got such wonderful boys, Carl. They're just beautiful kids, and I sure do like the man you've become. You're sober, you're doing great shows. I really do love to work with you."

"I'll take you up on that," Carl said. As Roy launched into his first song, Carl stepped onto his bus and headed back to Tennessee.

d e c e m b e r 7, 1988: That morning, as the coffee brewed, Carl turned on his big-screen TV, returned to the kitchen, and filled his cup to the brim. While repairing back to the den, angling for his leather recliner in the corner near the fireplace, he saw Roy Orbison's face filling the television screen, below it the years 1936–1988. Carl felt his knees buckling; his hand holding the coffee cup started trembling, spilling the liquid on the floor in a trail behind him as he staggered in tears to his chair.

▶ THE VOICE OF CARL PERKINS

I lost as good a friend as a man ever had. Being away from home, and being in the situation of traveling and entertaining people, you can become closer to people than you realize. Then when you hear they're gone . . . Regardless of what people think about entertainers, you don't see each other as often as people think you do. You don't hardly ever see 'em, and when you do your good friends are very special, 'cause they remain the same, down or up, rich or poor. Money does not affect that, artist to artist. I've been around. Some of mine I saw at the very beginning, those guys wearing thin britches. I knew 'em when if five dollars worth of gas would get you to the show, that's all you put in there, 'cause you might need the other two dollars to eat on. It's through those times that you can become

very close. If that lasts for fifteen or twenty years, and then one day without warning you look and the [newspeople] are saying he's gone, slowly
but surely it gnaws away at you; but you find a place to put that memory
and you cherish it, and you think of 'em and you grow older and maybe a
little wiser. But love remains the same. And you always say, "Why didn't I
tell him more often that I really did love him?" Then you think, "Men don't
tell men they love each other. We're men." But I know Roy knew I loved him.
Because that's the last thing I said to him.

The connection with the Judds and Ken Stilts proved to be one of the
most fortuitous of Carl's career. In addition to his experience and insight, Naomi and Wynonna valued the spiritual strength Carl carried
so gracefully. Mother and daughter used him as a sounding board for
their own theories about the role of God in their lives and would listen intently as he described how his tribulations through the years had
shaped his religious convictions.

In Stilts Carl had a friend with clout in the industry, who, after
much discussion back and forth, took on Carl for management.
Though the male side of country has since come to rely almost solely
on vacuous hunks and faceless, interchangeable bands lacking an original point of view, in the mid- to late-eighties older artists retained a
tenuous place in the commercial mix. Enough, anyway, to give Stilts
confidence in Carl's prospects.

Typically, Carl responded to this upturn in his career with a song
reflecting the bottom-line philosophy he had learned the hard way,
thanks to his own stubborn nature. Rather than preach, he cast his
message in light-hearted terms, with a sputtering rockabilly rhythm
goosing it along. Given some lyric polishing by Paul Kennerley, "Let
Me Tell You About Love" made its way onto the Judds' 1989 album
River of Time, with Carl playing lead guitar, and into the number-one
spot on the country singles chart and was one of the nominees for Song
of the Year by the Country Music Association. Singing lead, Wynonna
attacked the song with sly understatement, turning on her nasty blues
snarl near the end of each verse to heighten the tension, again dis-
playing an instinct for dramatic interpretation that set her apart from

her peers and marked her as one of the most intelligent singers of her generation in any genre. At the end of the second verse, she backed off to make way for a serpentine, popping solo by Carl and called out in a sultry voice, "Pick it, Perkins," as Carl came sliding in. It was quintessential Perkins in its language and in its humorous, simple reconsideration of history:

> Well ever since the day that time began
> There's been this thing between a woman and a man
> Well I don't know but I do believe
> It started in the Garden with Adam and Eve
> Samson and Delilah had their fling
> Till she cut his hair and clipped his wings
> It don't matter how the story's told
> Love stays young, it can't grow old
>
> (chorus:) Let me tell you about love
> About the moon and stars above
> It's what we've all been dreaming of
> Let me tell you a-bout love
>
> Bonaparte and Josephine
> I believe they had a pretty good scene
> Till she said, "Bonie, boy, we're through"
> That's when he met his Waterloo
> Julie baby and Romeo
> Fell in love and stole the show
> I know they are history
> But there ain't been nothing like you and me
>
> (chorus)
>
> Now Sheba she was a beauty queen
> Prettiest thing that you ever have seen
> Solomon he was mighty wise
> Sheba she done caught his eye

The world would be in a dreadful fix

If it wasn't for the love between cats and chicks

This world wouldn't amount to much

Without a hug, a kiss, and a tender touch

With Stilts funding demo sessions, Carl cut several tracks with Brent Maher that led to a recording contract with the MCA-distributed Universal label founded by Nashville music business power broker Jimmy Bowen. A native Texan, Bowen had been a rockabilly artist himself in the late fifties as a member of Buddy Knox's Rhythm Orchids, and had a solo hit in 1957 with "I'm Stickin' With You." As a producer he had worked with rock and pop artists, including a brief tenure with Frank Sinatra in the mid-sixties before moving to Nashville in the mid-seventies and effecting sweeping changes in commercial recording with his advocacy of digital technology. A complex and controversial figure, Bowen increased recording budgets and championed artists having a say in the direction of their music—this, plus his roots in rockabilly, rendered him sympathetic to Carl's approach and, conversely, made Carl confident that he had landed in the right place.

But history didn't reverse itself: In 1989 Carl, coproduced by Maher and Don Potter, delivered a well-reviewed album in *Born to Rock*, only months ahead of Bowen's departure for the presidency of Capitol Records and the dissolution of Universal. Stilts was less enthusiastic about the album than was the press, saying, "I didn't think it was in the groove of what we needed at that time," but his was a moot point with the label's folding. Shortly afterwards, Carl asked out of his management deal, desiring a clean break with no hard feelings so that he could reassess his future in light of country's youth movement.

Stilts agreed to the split, but he and his wife of thirty-nine years remained close to Carl and Valda, often inviting them to their Florida vacation home and including them in their social events around Judds' activities. Carl came to rely heavily on Stilts's counsel (calling him "as fine a guy as I've ever met in my life"), and Stilts, in return, spoke frankly to Carl about the future, refusing to indulge Carl's propensity for sentimentality as reflected in his original songs of late.

Born to Rock had shown that Carl could still explore his feelings and his past for some tough-minded material, as he did in the title song (cowritten with his sons Greg and Stan), in the semi-autobiographical "Cotton Top," and in a touching love song cowritten with Greg, "A Lifetime Last Night." Stilts sought to cultivate the tush hog, the spirited part of Carl's personality that lay dormant during his day-by-day recovery from alcoholism and abusive tendencies. He had seen enough good work from Carl to know the songwriter didn't need to live on the edge, but only to remember it, in order to produce memorable work.

"Carl is such a sentimental person, and pretty spiritual," Stilts says. "I told him, 'I admire and respect where you're coming from. But I think it's hurt the commercial aspect of your songwriting,' because everything he wrote was very spiritual stuff. I said, 'If you ever get your frame of mind to the point where you were when you were writing things like 'Blue Suede Shoes' and some of the stuff the Beatles did, you can still have big, big hits. Not just country, but pop.'"

Despite Stilts's urgings to back off the "spiritual stuff," Carl went directly to it, inspiration visiting him one night while he was getting ready for bed. As he stepped out of one leg of his jeans, some coins fell out of a pocket and rolled across the floor. His back aching from yard work, Carl thought, *That silver ain't worth me hurtin' my back any more tryin' to pick it up.*

Silver and gold.

Hopping down the hallway trying to tug on his jeans, Carl passed Valda, who saw the anxious look on his face and asked if something was wrong.

"Nothing, nothing," Carl said. "Got a song."

He plopped into his recliner, and, with acoustic guitar in hand, strummed a chord progression to back a verse he wrote extemporaneously:

> I met an old man walkin' down the street
> His clothes were torn and tattered
> With sandals on his feet
> And I stopped to help him

> And lend him a hand
> He said, I love you so much,
> But you must understand

At Valda's urging he wrote the verse on a piece of paper, then constructed another:

> And he said to me, let's rest for a while
> For I have some good news to share with you, child
> He said, you can't change this old world
> The people need to know that a dear savior died here
> A long, long time ago

In two subsequent verses, Carl hinted that the "old man" might be Jesus Christ but left his identity a mystery ("As I watched him walk on, I forgot to get his name"). It was in the choruses, though, that Carl reached down for the plainspoken philosophy that spoke to the faith he had found in his sobriety and to the country boy's simple understanding of his journey. The first chorus:

> Silver and gold might buy you a home
> But things of this world, they won't last you long
> And time has a way of turning us old
> And time can't be bought back with silver and gold

Chorus 2 offered a variation on the first:

> Silver and gold can't buy you a home
> When this life has ended and your time is gone
> But you can live in a world where
> You'll never grow old
> And things can't be bought with silver and gold
> And time can't be bought back with silver and gold

"Silver and Gold" was completed shortly before Dolly Parton came to Jackson for a two-day writing session with Carl, which produced five Parton-Perkins collaborations. During one of their breaks, Carl played the song for Parton, who took it to Nashville and recorded it. Her version became a top-10 single, proving to Carl that in the right hands his message would be heard, regardless of the trends.

S h o r t l y after leaving the Stilts fold, Carl found himself with an-other opportunity to record, albeit with an unknown label out of De-troit, Platinum Records International. The deal had been negotiated by Stan Vincent, a veteran New York producer-songwriter whose ca-reer dated to the late fifties when, while in his mid-teens, he produced the Mystics' 1959 doo-wop classic, "Hushabye," written by the team of Doc Pomus and Mort Shuman, who were then carving out one of the most important songwriting careers in rock 'n' roll history on the strength of songs for the Drifters (including "Save the Last Dance for Me"), Ray Charles, the Coasters, Dion and the Belmonts ("A Teenager in Love") and, not least of all, Elvis Presley. Vincent had gone on to compile an impressive resumé for himself in the sixties, notably by producing numerous hits for Connie Francis and Lou Christie, and had in recent years worked quietly behind the scenes in a number of music-related projects. A low-profile operator who knew his way around every facet of the music business, Vincent had sought out Carl in his conviction that a large market still existed for unsullied roots rock 'n' roll.

To this end he surrounded Carl with a basic instrumental lineup populated by some of the most prominent and respected names in the New York session world—bassist Will Lee, keyboardist Paul Shaffer, guitarists Hugh McCracken and David Spinozza, drummer Allan Schwartzberg, and George Small on synthesizer. Recording in New York and Nashville, he enlisted the aid of several special guest artists, most of them established country names, such as longtime Perkins friends Chet Atkins and Charlie Daniels, as well as Travis Tritt, Les Taylor (the former lead singer of Exile), and Steve Wariner; one of the better New York cuts, a cover of Bruce Springsteen's "Pink Cadillac," also featured Joan Jett. The resulting album, *Friends, Family & Legends*, was a good effort by an old pro, but inconsistent in the quality of its material. Shunned by country and rock radio, it followed form with every other Perkins album in dying quickly.

I t started in the recording studio, 16th Avenue Sound in Nashville, where the *Friends, Family & Legends* vocal sessions were taking place, following the recording of instrumental tracks in New York. Stan Vincent was the first to have any inkling of a potential problem: "Carl would come in occasionally and go, 'I've got this thing here, I don't understand it,' and then he'd go knock the hell out of a song. Finally I said to him, 'You better go check that out,' not knowing what it was or how serious it was. After he mentioned it several times, I got concerned. I told him to get it checked, but he's sort of reluctant with that kind of thing."

Greg and Stan Perkins were on hand for the sessions, and Greg in particular heard something off-kilter in his father's performances: "I was in the control booth and I kept noticing him clear his throat. I've recorded my dad's voice for years, and really know it. Stan Vincent leaned over to me and said, 'You noticing something different?' I said, 'Yeah, something's not right.' He gets hoarse, but he kept getting hoarse in the middle of a song and we'd have to stop. So we finally got through the album and we were flying from New York to Detroit. I asked him, 'Dad, your voice—.' He said, 'Aw, it's just a cold. Sinus drainage or something.' But I knew it wasn't that. I knew there was something not right."

Unaware of these concerns, Valda observed that "at times Carl's color didn't look quite right. He was gray-looking, ashy. I thought maybe it was due to him being tired, not getting enough sleep at times, especially when he did that album. But he really didn't look sick. He had a wheezing sound, bad wheezing sound, and it concerned me because he did smoke. I told him to get checked, and he finally went to a lung specialist."

Reluctantly—because three of Buck's brothers had been afflicted with emphysema and Carl didn't want to hear a doctor give him the same bad news—Carl made an appointment with Dr. Larry Carruth in Jackson. After a routine examination, Dr. Carruth was concerned enough to schedule a bronchoscopy, an internal examination performed with the aid of a tubular device inserted through the nostril into the bronchial tubes. On this closer inspection Dr. Carruth diagnosed chronic bronchitis, but saw no sign of emphysema, news that made Carl feel reborn. On his way out of the throat area, though, Carruth had stopped to examine the singer's vocal cords, not suspecting any problem but merely curious to see how much larger they might be than a nonsinger's. By sheer accident he happened to spot a tiny black dot near a tonsil, where, as Carl remembers being told, "there should only be pink, healthy meat." Probing further, the doctor felt a mass on the upper left side of the neck.

Referred to a local eye, ear, nose, and throat specialist, Carl was biopsied and diagnosed as having a squamous cell carcinoma of the left tonsil that had metastasized to a single lymph node in the same area. Immediate radical surgery was recommended, involving the stripping of generous amounts of tissue around the cancer and jeopardizing Carl's ability ever to sing again.

Carl agreed, but came home and panicked. Seeking a second opinion, he called the Mayo Clinic and received referrals to two doctors, William Permenter, a radiologist based in Jackson, and James Netterville, the director of head and neck surgery in the department of otolaryncology at Nashville's highly regarded Vanderbilt University Hospital. These became the twin pillars he leaned on, as both agreed on a course of radiation therapy over surgery, given that all other tests indicated the cancer was contained in the tonsil and lymph node. Thanks to Dr. Carruth's curiosity and trained eye—"Carl might not be alive without that," says Dr. Netterville—the affliction had been spotted months before Carl would have experienced any symptoms, by which time extensive surgery ("salvage surgery" is the unsettling medical term) and follow-up chemotherapy or radiation would have been the only recourse. Instead, the doctors had a range of options and, as Dr. Netterville notes, a chance to consider other factors in making their decision: "Somebody as famous as Carl, whose life is totally tied up in his voice, the surgery that it would have taken to resect this would have altered his voice forever, and would have destroyed Carl's life. I try to put myself in the position of these patients. Life is worth a lot, but with certain people there's something more important in their life—with Carl, to have messed up his ability to sing because of the treatment of his cancer would have been a terrible thing, especially if there's another reasonable option."

Carl's condition brought the full spectrum of Dr. Netterville's expertise into play. As a partner in the Vanderbilt Voice Center with Dr. Robert Ossof, he had treated a number of singers in their recovery from throat ailments of various sorts, and had gained an informed perspective on the type of personality he would be dealing with in Carl Perkins: "Drinking and smoking are the main causes of squamous cell carcinoma in the oral cavity. Carl has certainly had his share of drinking and smoking in the past. People who are as artistic as he is are far more addictive, far more emotional; and the more emotional you are, the more addictive you are. It's very hard for them to stop smoking, and things like that."

Although he was fighting it every day, Carl had stopped smoking upon being diagnosed with throat cancer. In this and every other respect during his treatment he tried to be a model patient as Dr. Permenter administered a standard regimen—five days a week, using a Linear Accelerator (a machine that directs electrons onto a target to produce a high-energy photon beam) to pump 180 cGy (centiGray) of radiation into the cancerous area over the course of thirty-seven sessions, each lasting approximately twenty minutes.

Two days into his therapy, Carl received an unexpected reality check when he asked Dr. Permenter to move his appointments to an early morning hour so he could spend more days fishing at his place on Piney Lake. He was feeling no ill effects from the radiation and was growing uneasy hanging around the house on warm, sunny days.

"I knew you were going to ask that, because everybody wants to get it over with," said Dr. Permenter. "I have a patient that finishes tomorrow, and I was going to ask you if you wanted his slot. I know you're an early riser, and I know anyone from Lake County will want to fish."

"Wait a minute," Carl said. "How do you know that? We ain't talked about that."

"That's where my family's from," the doctor said, as Carl stared back in astonishment. After revealing that his grandfather recalled giving young Carl and Jay rides to school in his oil truck, Permenter returned the to business at hand. "Let me tell you something, Carl. You have about another week, then you aren't going to want to go fishing."

Carl chuckled as he voiced respectful disagreement. "I can stand more of these babies. I had two and it ain't nothin'. It ain't hittin' nothin' in there."

"Oh yeah, it's hittin'," Dr. Permenter rejoined. "It just hasn't got right yet."

Both doctors had warned Carl of the expected side effects of radiation: loss of salivary glands function and subsequent difficulty in swallowing, along with a complete inability to distinguish flavors; swelling of the larynx; skin irritation; sore throat; earaches; thinning of the mandible to the point where any type of dental problem puts the patient at risk of infection. With the dysfunction of their salivary glands making eating an unpleasant and painful task, radiation patients experience significant weight loss as well. Severe emotional depression usually settles in as the treatment follows its normal, devastating course.

For two weeks Carl breezed through his treatments with no noticeable problem—he was even keeping his weight up, and gaining, as per Dr. Netterville's instructions to put on additional pounds as a safeguard against catastrophic weight loss in the weeks ahead. Then he awoke at two a.m. one morning and everything had changed.

"My throat was *afire*," he recalls. "I thought I was having a nightmare. I'm settin' up on the side of the bed knowing I wasn't, but I said,

Yeah, don't get upset about it. There ain't nothin' that burns that bad. So I went to the bathroom, turned the light on and opened my mouth and I saw ground beef. Tongue, gums, inside of my lips, the whole works. So sore I started to open my mouth wide and could not. When you get enough radiation, your body screams and goes the other way. It did a ninety-degree turn on me. I went to bed, went to sleep, six hours later I was a solid blister. And stayed that way."

Over the course of his two months of five-times-a-week radiation treatments, Carl came to know the love of his family in a deeper, more meaningful way than he could have imagined. Martha cooked and brought meals to Valda. Every morning without fail, Bart Swift, Debbie's husband, drove Carl to his radiation sessions; Debbie and her teenage daughter Suzy took Carl out for afternoon drives around town, showing him new houses, stopping at the Dairy Queen for malts, trying to occupy his mind with something other than thoughts of his own misery.

Stan Perkins's wife had done some research at the office where she worked as an X-ray technician and found that Carl was experiencing all the typical problems of someone undergoing radiation therapy, as both Doctors Netterville and Permenter had indicated. Coming from within the family, this news was comforting. On the other hand, Stan and Greg were now battling their own anguish, their careers being so entwined with their father's.

"Dad would come down to the studio while we were working here and try to sing, and he couldn't do it," Stan recalls. "It would break your heart. You'd put your hand on him and pat him, 'It'll be okay, you'll be alright, sounds good, man.' But you'd hear the breaks in the tape when you listened back, and you know he'd hear it too. Then he'd walk out the door and you'd see him with his head down going back up to the house and gettin' in his chair. And we didn't know if it wasn't always gonna be that way. It started affecting my and Greg's personal life. I was staying depressed. I would go home and just want to sit in a chair—I felt like it was over, I guess. I was grieving to some degree myself with it. Maybe it was self-pity on my part. Greg and I would talk to each other on the phone after we'd go home and I'd say, 'Man, I don't know if I can stand to go over there again.'"

"You wanted to look in the mirror and say, 'Well, you shouldn't feel this way. This guy's going through this, don't start this self-pity thing. He's given you all this," Greg adds. "It was coming home with me. My wife and I had been through this with her dad. She'd say, 'Well, you got the news. He's gonna be alright. Everything will be fine.' But you still didn't know if you were ever going to play together again after seventeen years."

Naomi Judd, who had been forced to retire and break up country music's most successful female act after being diagnosed with chronic active hepatitis, reached out to Carl as she refused to succumb to what doctors believed was a terminal illness. Having once made her living as a registered nurse, she had a natural curiosity about both the physical and emotional aspects of illness, and now had the spare time to investigate matters metaphysical that affected the quality of life. She began communicating her findings regularly to Carl, and sending him gifts designed to stimulate uplifting thoughts: "I sent him some books that had really helped me, a book called *Releasing The Ability of God*, which talks about God being a supernatural being, that the universe really runs on spiritual laws, so Carl wouldn't get flipped out when he got the doctor's report. At that time I was doing research in guardian angels, and found over three hundred scriptures about it, and sent him a guardian angel night light. I just wanted to remind him that there was always light for his darkness, because I know. It's like Carl and I were in this elite little club, when the mirror of truth is held up to you. I call it the End of the Plank Club. We had walked out to the end of the plank and seen the dark, portentous waters and circling sharks and got that tap on the shoulder saying, 'Come on back for a while.'"

For her part, Valda put on the best face she could in her abiding fear that Carl would succumb to his disease. When Carl went on a liquid diet, she plied him daily with a glass of nutrient-rich homemade juice made from carrots and celery ("It tasted like hay," Carl recalls, but he drank it all). More than the kids, she had to endure his wild mood swings—at one point during the radiation Carl started smoking again and was threatening to dispense with his treatments altogether and go off to Hawaii to stay with George Harrison.

Dr. Netterville's sage counsel provided the comfort Valda required to sustain her optimism. His assessment: "Carl was very emotional. Very artistic personality. Very dependent on his wife for strength. Very dependent on other people around him for strength. She would call me and say, 'He's in the lounge chair crying. What can we do?' The main thing I told her was, this is normal. This is what everybody goes through. Don't be alarmed. This is a black cloud that's going to pass away."

The black cloud hung over Carl, though. All around him those he loved and who loved him dealt with the crisis in their own way. Like theirs, his journey was intense and personal too; one he had to confront on his own terms.

▶ THE VOICE OF CARL PERKINS

Death is a very intimate thing when you get throat cancer. And nobody has to tell you that; you feel you know that. So how do you get prepared to talk to the people whose world is built around you? My children sittin' in here, my wife, all of a sudden, man, what if Daddy dies? When will my daddy die? I was so afraid that maybe the doctor was wrong, that it was worse than it was, that after the times they would burn me it was gonna break out somewhere else.

There is not in me the words to put it together to make it sound sensible as to what I went through physically, but more than that, mentally. Mentally it was a stoppage of everything but, oh God, You've worked miracles in my life. Help me to be worth one more miracle. Heal me. And then I will never walk off another stage without calling Your name.

If they had told me how bad I would've burned and suffered, I would've took the knife and said, "I hope I die while they operate." They would weigh me every morning and I was losing seven to twelve pounds a week. Radiation plays devastating tricks on your whole system. I sat out in my back yard with a blanket wrapped around me in ninety-five-degree July temperatures. I would be sweating and freezing. I was pretty helpless. Pretty helpless. And I got some looks from my family, I caught 'em before they could get their eyes off of me. I'm a shifty old man, I'm not smart, but I pick up vibes. I love my family and I caught 'em lookin' at me. I could hear whispers at the table, when I'd be talkin' to somebody else; I could hear 'em say, "Daddy don't look too good."

It was a brand-new world; it was new thinking. Nothing that was was still here. Except more attention paid by everybody that come around. Quickly the news got all over town, people calling, the phone ringing constantly, artists from all around the world, from George Harrison, McCartney, Eric Clapton. The news got out pretty quick—Carl Perkins has throat cancer. It was total newness of life at fifty-nine years old. You really start thinking about that trip you're taking.

The National Enquirer did a story on me, and the mail that came after the story ran was in the thousands. I felt so much love. People would pour their hearts out: "You got it to get well." "I believe you're gonna make it, Carl." Pastors of churches: "Me and my congregation are having special prayer for you Wednesday." That happened all over this country. It was absolutely a feeling of floating on a cushion of love, and there ain't no softer place to be. There ain't nothing more strengthening than to know rank strangers cared enough to go buy a card and mail it. Write personal letters. I didn't know so many people knew me and cared. By the churchfulls praying for Carl Perkins. Awesome. It helped solve the big C for me. It gave me strength.

Love—a man can't get too much of it. The heart can handle every bit that can come. You think after a while you'd get tired of people saying, "I sure do love you." No. 'Cause love's what it was all meant to be.

During seven and a half weeks of radiation treatments, Carl's weight dropped to 160 pounds—60 pounds less than he weighed at the outset of the treatments. His cheeks were sunken, and his eyes seemed hollowed out of his head. Even new clothes hung loosely on his emaciated frame. His voice, once so syrupy smooth and gentle, had become raspy. Although he was allowed to eat solid foods, difficulties chewing and swallowing restricted him to a liquid diet (unable to taste flavors, he found himself, for the first time in his life, losing interest in food). On the positive side, he made it through all thirty-seven radiation treatments without missing or rescheduling a single one, greatly aiding his own chances for recovery by staying the course. And having survived the worst, his depression began to lift as his strength made a slow return.

Even in his weakened state, he worked the Circle of Hope telethon in August 1991, appearing periodically during a four-hour span to sing songs and make appeals to the viewing audience before being overcome by fatigue and retiring for the night. At the telethon's end, pledges had been made to the Carl Perkins Center for the Prevention of Child Abuse totaling over $120,000, $12,000 higher than the previous year's tally.

He returned to public life too, unexpectedly in almost every instance. "Restless" finally became a hit—not Carl's recording, but in a cover version by Mark O'Connor and the New Nashville Cats, a group comprised of the city's finest young country players as assembled by O'Connor, one of the best of the lot. In the Cats' version, Vince Gill, Ricky Skaggs, and Steve Wariner each took three solos and sang a verse as O'Connor and the backing musicians provided rousing support. Theirs was a spirited, workmanlike take in contrast to the cry of the soul that Carl had masked with humor in his 1969 recording, but it was good enough to win Vocal Event of the Year from the Country Music Association. With President George Bush and his wife Barbara in the audience at the Grand Ole Opry auditorium, Carl joined the Cats onstage before a national television audience and delivered some emotional wallop when he stepped up to offer his own fire-and-brimstone guitar solo.

When the Cats' version of "Restless" was released, Parton's "Silver and Gold" was still on the charts, and George Strait was racking up another in his long string of hit singles with a rendition of Carl's "When You're a Man on His Own." It was the best of times and the worst of times, and the irony was not lost on the songwriter himself: "When I had cancer I sat and listened to the radio a lot. So I heard 'Silver and Gold' coming up the charts; 'Restless'; I listened to 'A Man On His Own.' I said, 'What is this? I got three songs on the charts, and I'm takin' my farewell here.' But that helped pull me through. Right when I needed the lift, it came."

In an appearance marked by sadness, Carl joined the Judds onstage in Murfressboro, Tennessee, on December 4 for their final concert together. As he had done on the hit single, Carl played guitar on "Let Me Tell You About Love," and executed his solo with the flair and wit he had brought to the original recording.

On a night of heavy emotions all around, it wasn't easy for Naomi and Wynonna, their partnership ending, to see Carl in his weakened condition coming onstage to play his lick. Although he hardly looked it, Carl was rallying slowly from his brush with mortality; still, periodic newspaper reports offered only bleak reports regarding his future. Anyone outside Carl's immediate circle of friends would have been forgiven for thinking they were seeing not only the end of the Judds, but perhaps one of Carl Perkins's final public appearances as well.

Nevertheless, when Naomi's illness and forced retirement were announced, and a final concert became inevitable, Wynonna's request was, "I want Uncle Carl!" Naomi would have insisted anyway, because Carl had been the first to call with words of comfort, well ahead of her condition being made public, desiring to be as strong in her corner as she had been in his. As Naomi recounts it: "Carl taps into the deepest levels of your emotions, because he's so genuine and so caring. After my diagnosis, I was laying in bed, in a fetal position on a Saturday night. He called and said, 'Mama, I just got the news.' I guess Ken had told him. And he began to weep. He said, 'The first thing I'm gonna do when I get to Heaven is to ask the Master why these things happen to the good ones.' Of course, I'm . . . a mess . . . when I heard him crying, 'cause I'm usually the care provider. He sort of caught himself, and I was silent for a minute, and I heard him blowing his nose, and he came back on the line and said, 'Well, you know what, Mama? Once I meet the Master, it's all gonna be revealed to me. I won't even have to ask him these questions.' Then we had this wonderful conversation and I assured him that somehow I was not only going to survive and thrive, but that we still had a lot of good times left together. He sent me a song that he wrote for me and Larry [Strickland, Naomi's husband]. On the tape, before he does the song, he talks about how much he loves us, that we're almost like blood kin to him. I wouldn't take anything in the world for that tape."

With the release of *Friends, Family & Legends* in December, Stan Vincent organized an industry reception for Carl at the Hard Rock Cafe in New York on January 21, 1992. With a heavy contingent of the music press on hand, Carl, weary but game, performed "Blue Suede Shoes," "Honey Don't," and "Matchbox" to enthusiastic response.

The next night, as Carl and Vincent were preparing to go to the Hard Rock for dinner, the phone rang in Carl's room at the Plaza Hotel. It was Bob Dylan, calling from the lobby. Carl ordered him upstairs; when he opened the door a few minutes later he barely recognized the man standing in the hallway, a guitar case at his side: "Had on an old green Army coat, bent over, looked like seventy years old with his old beard and matted hair, cap on his head. I opened the door and I liked to fell out. I said, to myself, he gained a lotta weight. His face was fat. He sat that guitar down. I put my hand out. He said, 'Uh-uh. We're brothers.' And he hugged me. And I thought he wasn't gonna turn me loose. His beard was scratchin' my damn face—I'd just shaved. And he's sayin' in my ear, 'I love you, man. Oh, how I love you. I love you, Carl.' And had tears in his eyes. 'Let me look at you.' And he just stood there. Said, 'I'm so thankful. You lived through it.' "

Carl tried to persuade Dylan to join him at the Hard Rock. Dylan declined, but then handed Carl a small red jewel box, saying, "This is for you." Inside it was a small gold pin in the shape of a guitar.

"There's three thoughts that go with that little guitar," Dylan said. "One is for gettin' well. Two is for gettin' up and gettin' back out. And number three is so the world can keep lovin' Carl Perkins alive."

"The word 'alive' cracked on him," Carl says. "See, the way he said it says he would have loved me if I had died, he'da never forgotten me. But his way of sayin' it was so poetic, just run deeper, man, right on through to the bone. He hugged me again."

Dylan's explanation of the pin's significance is that "it was kinda like something you give somebody at the beginning of a voyage. That's all it was." His enduring memory of the night centers on his spirits being bolstered by seeing Carl in good health, and hearing him in good voice, when Carl sat down with a guitar and reprised "Champaign, Illinois": "Carl looked good. You know, he sang the song we wrote together. He just happened to be remembering it at the time and he sang it. He's such a great singer. Most people think of him as one of those paragonical guitar players, but to me he's such a great singer. The gospel element in his voice and the mixture of that with his blues singing to me was the essential sound of the rockabilly period."

("Paragonical" is a coinage of Dylan's devising, not contained in any dictionary but understood as the adjective form of "paragon," or, according to Webster, "a model of excellence or perfection.")

When Carl had finished the song, Dylan said, "I still want to learn to pick like you do." With that, he started for the door. "I'll see you before you know it," he said, an expression Carl remembered Dylan using the first time they met. "Keep on that road to wellness. God bless you, Carl."

"Bob, thank you," Carl said. "Mostly for your love, but also for my gift. When they put me in my box, it'll go with me."

"A man can't ask for more than that," Dylan said, turning away.

"Door shut," Carl recalls. "The little bent-over fat man with the Army coat on and ragged guitar case faded into the streets of New York, and nobody knew who he was."

The road back ultimately brought Carl to Memphis, where he would run into himself again on the stage at Cook Convention Center, before some four thousand fans as the headlining attraction of an Elvis Presley tribute concert on August 13, 1992, coinciding with events organized by the Presley estate on the fifteenth anniversary of Elvis's death. Others appearing on the bill included Scotty Moore and D.J. Fontana; the Jordanaires; Ricky Nelson's guitarist James Burton, who had toured and recorded with Elvis through the seventies; Elvis's longtime backup singer Kathy Westmoreland; and Ronnie McDowell, a country artist with a remarkable vocal resemblance to Presley.

Carl was scheduled to do a thirty-minute set with his band. Greeted by thunderous applause, Carl, winking frequently at Valda sitting in the front row (crying), tore into his Sun catalogue, perched on a stool for some ballads, then stood up and rocked some more. A half hour passed, an hour passed, and he was still going strong—weary to the bone and ragged of voice, he pressed on, fueled by the audience's wild response to his every move and utterance. Seventy minutes into his set he paused, and the audience fell quiet. Carl next offered his own tribute to Elvis in his song "The Whole World Misses You." At its end, without pausing, he sang

> Glory, glory hallelujah
> Glory, glory hallelujah

"The Battle Hymn of the Republic" was the centerpiece of one of Elvis's most moving seventies' recordings, "American Trilogy" (comprised of "Dixie," "Battle Hymn of the Republic," and "All My Trials") and a highlight of his live performances. Singing softly and tenderly, Carl felt the weakness leave his body. His voice rose, buoyant and proud, confident and forceful. Behind him the Jordanaires slipped on-stage and began humming harmony; as the refrain "Glory, glory, hal-lelujah" rang out, Carl heard a sound that startled him, and turned to see Kathy Westmoreland standing next to the Jordanaires, singing in a voice so high and pure and aching and lonesome it shook Carl to his core: "I said, 'Oh God, you dropped an angel on the stage. One of 'em got away from you, Lord, she's here.' It was like being in the middle of a powerful, powerful storm and not a drop of rain hittin' me or wind blowin' me. It was coming around me, it was a force. It was an awe-some feeling. And sound coming from behind me, in front of me, I'm right in the middle. It was an experience I may never have again."

For ten minutes "Battle Hymn of the Republic" consumed every-one in the Convention Center, with the audience joining in, the as-sembled artists singing along, and Preacher Carl working the congre-gation, telling them, "One more time, one more time—come on, you can sing it! Oh, if you could just hear yourselves. Get a little louder. Pour your hearts out. Elvis might be listenin' to you now!"

Off to the side, Stan Perkins watched this spectacle unfold, having yielded the drums to D.J. Fontana. Long wondering if this day ever would come again, he had found out not only that his father had a lot left but also that the fans' regard for Carl ran deeper than he had imagined: "It was kinda ironic in a way because the concert was set up as a tribute to Elvis. But you could feel it onstage that while Elvis or his memory was still a part of it, it was also a tribute to Dad."

Two days later, his voice nearly shot after the Elvis tribute, Carl put in another yeoman effort for the Circle of Hope telethon. In early '93 he played two shows in Cincinnati to standing ovations, and gave testimony, as he had promised in his darkest hour the previous sum-mer, of God's mercy and guidance in his life—the boy who had once questioned the very existence of a higher power had come full circle to being a fervent believer, hard experience having taught him the lessons his mother had preached all those years when he doubted her and his own faith.

Finally and irrevocably he rekindled the fire inside during a two-night stand at New York City's Lone Star Roadhouse. It was so good he could have closed his eyes and felt himself back in the El Rancho, blowing away the rowdies with a new song composed on the spot, and a sound they had never heard before, as every fiber of his soul and his spirit felt the love and security of his blood kin rocking next to him onstage. At the Lone Star, Carl became whole again: "It was what I call firin' rockabilly music—I was firin' at my fans. I was diggin' some things off the neck of that guitar that I have never tried to do in the world. Now I run into some areas where I backed out of there and got back in my territory. But there was some Carl Perkins fans told me, 'Man, you really got after that guitar tonight. It's the best you've ever sounded.' They wasn't trying to make me feel good. I knew that. Close, so close and maybe better than me and Jay and Clayton—me and Stan and Greg. It's an awesome place for a daddy to be standing between two sons playing feel-good music when it's right."

In late May 1993, Carl had his regular monthly checkup performed by his long-time general physician in Jackson. The outcome wasn't publicized until his June 17 appearance on the Nashville Network's *Nashville Now,* and the following day on the front page of *The Jackson Sun.* The moment, as Carl remembers it: "[The doctor] said, 'Carl, I've looked forward to telling you this cancer is gone. I can't tell you cancer won't take your life. But I can tell you it will not be this one. This one is over.' And he shook hands with me."

Wh a t had it amounted to? Elvis was gone; Orbison was gone. Jerry Lee had been married six times, death had claimed his two sons, and he was a man nearing sixty still acting "wild as a guinea hen," in Carl's phrase, in his public appearances. Plagued by tax problems, he had emigrated to Ireland for a year, but returned to settle up in early '94. Chuck Berry was playing oldies shows. Little Richard, still strong of voice, had gone completely camp while all the time proclaiming himself the true King of Rock 'n' Roll. Fats Domino was still smiling and living the good life in New Orleans, emerging on his own terms to play whenever and wherever he liked, always for adoring crowds, presiding over the most joyous of rock 'n' roll celebrations when he did.

But among the important surviving artists in rock 'n' roll's first generation, only Carl and Cash had never stopped writing and having new songs recorded. Apart from having seen rock 'n' roll grow from nothing to a multibillion dollar industry, their lives encompass virtually the entire history of modern country music in all its forms. Carl's bout with cancer had the effect of reminding musicians and fans that he was the last of a breed. With his return to live performances, he began receiving calls from other artists interested in writing with him—it became a rarity, in fact, for a day to pass without such an inquiry being made. His publishing company stayed busy with renewed activity on his catalogue—the Kentucky Headhunters cut "Dixie Fried" (but neutered the lyrics); Steve Earle and Joe Walsh teamed on "Honey Don't" for the soundtrack of *The Beverly Hillbillies* movie; and the Mavericks, one of the best new country bands of recent years (who happen to have a bit of rockabilly spirit about them), recorded a sizzling version of "Matchbox" for *Red Hot + Country*, an AIDS benefit album, and brought its composer into the studio to lend his distinctive guitar touch to their effort.

A five-CD box set released in 1990 on the Germany-based Bear Family label, *The Classic Carl Perkins*, provided a sweeping overview of Carl's work, comprising as it did not only the issued recordings on Sun, Columbia, and Decca, but numerous unreleased sides, alternate takes, and home recordings that illustrate how hard-won his gift of simplicity had been. In succeeding years gaps in Carl's body of work have been filled by reissues of Columbia, Decca, and Mercury sides on Rhino's *Jive After Five: The Best of Carl Perkins (1958–1978)* and Columbia's *Restless: The Columbia Recordings;* in 1992 Bear Family issued another Perkins title, *The Dollie Masters: Country Boy's Dream*, a well-annotated collection of thirty Dollie recordings. The 1976 Mus-

cle Shoals sessions, released as bootlegs and on small, now-defunct labels in the late seventies (Sagittarius, Charvan, Accord), received a
more dignified presentation in 1993 when BMG released them in their
entirety on three albums, *Disciple in Blue Suede Shoes*, *Take Me Back*,
and *Carl Perkins & Sons*, albeit minus any explanatory liner notes.

Carl's return to the studio post-cancer brought him back to Sun,
teaming with Scotty Moore on *706 Re-Union: A Sentimental Journey*,
wherein the two guitar legends reprised some of their signature songs
and offered between-tracks reminiscences of their early days. Of the
rock 'n' roll pioneers, none have so assiduously documented their personal histories so compellingly over so long a period of time. The
songs not only endure but underscore how utterly original—touched
by but never imitative of history—and unflinchingly honest Carl's
music has remained over the course of a forty-year recording career.

On the wall of his den hangs the only gold record he's ever received
as a recording artist, for "Blue Suede Shoes." Next to it, framed and
protected by glass, is the brown paper bag on which is written in Carl's
hand the original lyrics to "Blue Suede Shoes," as composed early of
a morning in 1955 in Parkview Courts' Apartment 23D. In 1993,
through friends, Carl located and bought back his original gold-top
Gibson Les Paul (he had sold it in the seventies); it sits on a stand in
the recreation room of his personal studio. The Gibson Switchmaster
used on most of his Sun recordings from 1956 through 1958 is in a
guitar case tucked away behind the couch in the den. His Jackson
restaurant, Suede's (partly owned and operated by Debbie and her husband Bart, with interior design by Debbie), is a virtual Carl Perkins
museum, containing a 1949 set list for the Perkins Brothers Band, photos charting Carl's life and career, the cap and cape he wore in the
fourth-grade band in Tiptonville, the first and second drafts of lyrics
to "Daddy Sang Bass," and other personal effects.

These are a man's memories, memories of a life lived full measure.
Having learned that "time can't be be bought back with silver and
gold," he has given away as much as he has kept, without asking for
or expecting compensation, and would shun it if offered. In his heart
he keeps what cannot be taken away or loaned out. It took a lifetime
for him to realize it was always there. To arrive at this destination, he

had veered off the safe, direct route and struggled over daunting terrain, nearly impassable, with scant resources to see him through. But he had made it. Husband, lover, father, friend—these were all he ever needed to be. He was loved completely and unconditionally for the man he was to his family, not for the applause soaking him like a cleansing rain in arenas and nightclubs around the world.

Shortly after being found cancer free, Carl posed a question to Valda. In their forty years together, he had never asked it, but had always wondered about the answer, never moreso than during his latest misfortune.

"Why would a woman like you ever fall in love with somebody like me? My love is all I had to offer. How did you see in me a hope that I could become more than what I was? And have you been let down?"

"I'll answer the last part first," Valda said. "I haven't been let down, and I did think you could become whatever you set your mind to. You had the talent for it, especially in the music. But if it had not been in God's plan, then let's just put it this way: There's nothing any greater than love. That's a free gift from God—love. So that would have been ample. We would've made it the other way. If it had been that you worked at a service station and I ironed for my family, that's what it would have been. I'm not too good to work; nobody's too good to work. You've got the most important thing, and that's love. So everything else falls under that and everything else will work out if you love."

"I guess it's worked for me," Carl replied, "because I do love you."

"And I love you," Valda said.

They embraced, holding each other close enough to feel their hearts beating, saying nothing. It had all been said.

In his sixty-second year, Carl Perkins, the original cat, was back where he started in 1932; back where he belonged. He was home.

▶ THE VOICE OF CARL PERKINS

My definition for success, I say this without any reservation whatsoever, is a man who is happy with what he's got materially and, more than that, in his soul. How have you treated your fellow man? To me, success is mowing my yard out there and a car going by with its horn blowing and people saying, "Hi, Carl!" Or a stranger coming through, wanting an autograph, and I hop off that ol' mower and sign it for him. I think if a man is happy driving a '58 Chevy pickup truck, he better hang with that jewel. You can go for the new model, but it sometimes don't replace the one you had.

Success is a man who has got, as I've had, a woman for over forty years who loved me in spite of problems I've had with alcohol. Four kids who were never ashamed that Carl Perkins was their daddy. I have been and am to this day a very happy man. That may have stemmed from being brought up so very poor, having absolutely nothing. Longing for a bicycle or a guitar or just average-looking clothes and shoes I didn't have. Growing up under those circumstances, material things and superstardom have never been something I've been tore up about.

I really felt out of place when "Blue Suede Shoes" was a number-one record. I stood on the Steel Pier in 1956 in Atlantic City, followed Frank Sinatra there. The Goodyear blimp, with my name in big lights on it—"Appearing tonight at the Steel Pier, Carl Perkins"—flew overhead. I stood there and shook and actually cried. That should have been something that would elevate a guy to say, "Well, I've made it." But it couldn't. It put fear in me. It makes me feel that I don't belong in that high caliber. I really don't. When guys like Eric Clapton or George Harrison, these super guitar players, say I influenced 'em, it really humbles me. It knocks me kind of way down, because I don't understand how I ever influenced anybody, no more than I can play.

I am rounding the curve of life in many ways, but I've got a lot of livin' to do, got a lot to catch up on. I've got some brain I haven't used yet. But I wanna be happy and relaxed with it. I don't wanna rush nothing. Brushes with death kinda put that attitude to you, and I'm proud of that. I don't get upset with nothing, and I'm not going to. If cancer comes back on Carl Perkins, I'll come through it or I'll go on to be with God. That's what I see.

Well, It's One for the Money . . .

It hurts to see us all gettin' old. I look in the mirror myself, people mail me pictures and people tell me how well I look after cancer. They're just being nice to me, man. I must've really been a dead bastard when this thing was over, because I still look terrible to me. I see myself and I see the way Cash looks with his old broken thumbs and his wrinkledy face, and I think of youth and I think of life back then. Dadgum, I don't wanna give it up. I don't wanna look at no prune in the mirror. I don't want my friends to turn into prunes. I want life to go on, be productive.

You know, life is so short. My goodness, it only seems like yesterday when I walked through that door at Sun Records. It just don't seem possible that we're all old men now. And it really hurts. It makes me about half mad; I can't do nothing about it, but it just makes me want to prove that it's not true. That I'm not through yet, that I'm gonna write some hit songs and I'm gonna have me a hit record before I die. That's my promise to me. I fought to live, and now I gotta give myself a reason for it. I do when I look at Valda and my kids and people that care about me. I live for them. I fought so they didn't have to bury me.

Two for the Show . . .

I could be bitter. I could bow up. But one time I did that and almost destroyed myself 'cause I couldn't be where all my friends were—Elvis, Jerry Lee, Roy Orbison, Johnny Cash were all big stars and moneymakers, and I was a poor helpless drunk in my hiding place. But see, that all-knowing, all-loving God had a plan. And I should be scared as to what He's got left for me, what will happen, but you know, I'm not one bit afraid. I know that whatever it is, He will be with me. Because He's living inside of me. I cleaned a place out of my soul and He came in. I did what He commanded me to do. I got as humble as a man could ever be, and God knew it. And He took the cancer away. Since then I only worry that some of my family will have cancer or something and will suffer like I did. But I can't live my life in fear. And the other thing I think about is, can I make a difference from here on out to mankind? That's strong in me. Those two things.

I guess life is a lot like a glass of tea. You boil it to make it hot, you put ice in it to make it cold, you put sugar in it to make it sweet, and put lemon in it to make it sour. So life has to have a lot of different things. It takes a lot of ups and downs to get a life completed, and so many don't really get to complete 'em, such as Jay. I like to went totally off the deep end when Jay died. That really liked to have been the end of me. Had it not been for that woman in my life there wouldn't have been no more Carl Perkins.

Sometimes I don't know but what a good woman's love is maybe the strongest, most essential thing a man can have. In my case I really think that is true. Valda has rescued me with her faith and her belief in me practically every day since I met her. That is a soul-shaking thing for me to think about, how she came into my life and why God chose Carl Perkins to send Valda to. Me of all people. She'd've had a good life as a doctor's wife; she's a smart woman, intelligent, did good in school, but got hooked up with an old rockabilly and stuck it out forty years. And pulled that old fellow up from his boots when he wasn't worth kicking out. She just kept on believing.

Friends mean an awful lot to me too. That, and a feeling of knowing that you're putting something back into life, like the child abuse center—these are things that satisfy you. If you're not happy with what you have, how can you be happy with more of the same thing? And we're talking about money—money seems to be what everyone is after. They think in their heart that the big house on the hill with the fence around it is the dream. I guess we're all supposed to chase that dream, and I would never tell a youngster not to. But you gotta look at that big house up there in two different ways. That fence keeps the public out, but in a lot of cases it nails you in. To really be happy and successful is to know you are a friend, and you have to be one to have one. There's a lot of people in the business that I really do like, and there's a lot of 'em I don't care to fool around with 'cause of the attitude that they have proven something in their life. No. The only thing you can prove in life is love for your fellow man.

That's the way I see this thing. So who knows? I like the road I'm on. It's not without trials and tribulations. I don't know where it's going. I may wind up back in Parkview Courts, but I'll be happy as long as I got my woman and my children. And I ain't gettin' no worse on my little guitar either.

Three to Get Ready . . .

Talent is appreciated by other people, and I don't think color has anything to do with it. I'm so proud that a black man's nickel played my record on a Wurlitzer jukebox just like any other fella's. And I'm proud that song relieved some of their tension, even if it was only two minutes and forty-five seconds long. 'Cause I don't think anybody worried about anything when they was listening to "Blue Suede Shoes" in 1956. That song was just a very simple little ol' thing that I heard a boy say to a girl, but it was at a time in this country when the teenagers were ready for their kind of music.

If it did anything to change the course of history, so be it. Maybe it made it to happen. I think it was time the engine got off of idle. Some of the preachers around the South and the disc jockeys breaking our records were saying, "This music's got to go," or "It was sent here by the Devil." I was hurtin' because I knew it wasn't. I say it makes people happy, brings back memories, plants a thought. I knew in my soul there was nothing wrong with kids getting out on a floor, dancing, and getting their frustrations out through the beat. I loved it—there ain't nothing prettier than two clean teenagers out there jitterbugging. And if they want to jitterbug at my funeral to "Blue Suede Shoes," I might just raise up and say:

Go, Cat, Go!

CARL PERKINS DISCOGRAPHY

By Jim Bailey and David McGee

▶ALBUMS (ALL AVAILABLE ON CD AND/OR CASSETTE, UNLESS INDICATED OTHERWISE)

DANCE ALBUM OF CARL PERKINS (SUN SLP 1225) 1958 Released in 1958 after Carl's departure from Sun, *Dance Album* is one of the rarest and most important albums of the fifties, containing thirteen examples of prime rockabilly, Perkins style, including powerful tracks that were not released as singles during Carl's tenure at the label—notably "Right String Baby, Wrong Yo-Yo," and "Everybody's Trying To Be My Baby," both of which made their mark at the time on four young British musicians from Liverpool named John Lennon, Paul McCartney, George Harrison, and Ringo Starr. (The speeded-up version of "Your True Love" is here as well.) The cover is a classic of fifties album art, with line drawings of dancing teens decked out in their finest cat clothes, and a photo of Carl's handsome mug smiling out from the lower right-hand corner. Available only as an import CD on the Topline label (TOPCD-503, released in 1987).

TEENBEAT—THE BEST OF CARL PERKINS (SUN SLP 1225) 1958 A reissue of *Dance Album* with new cover art. Stick with the original release. Vinyl only.

WHOLE LOTTA SHAKIN' (COLUMBIA CL 1234) 1958 A mess indicative of the debacle Carl's initial tenure at Columbia would become. In production the cover photo was flopped, making Carl appear to be a left-handed guitar player. Rarely has an artist of Carl's caliber been treated so shabbily by his record company. Reissued on CD by Sony in 1991 (A-1234).

COUNTRY BOY'S DREAM (DOLLIE LP 4001) 1967 The first Dollie sides demonstrate how far off-base Don Law was in trying to conform Carl to the Nashville Sound. Bill Denny let him get loose and play his own songs to his heart's content with a small band and tastefully rendered background choruses. Here is an artist finding his strength again. Vinyl only.

CARL PERKINS' GREATEST HITS (COLUMBIA CS 9833) 1969 Re-recordings of Sun material suffer in being translated to the poppish Nashville sound by producer Bill Denny, but the great, original "Restless" track recommends the album in spite of its failings otherwise. Vinyl only.

CARL PERKINS ON TOP (COLUMBIA CS 9931) 1969   Some jazzy touches on organ throw off Carl's performances, and Carl gets carried away with his wah-wah pedal, but *On Top* remains an interesting if failed experiment. Notable among its tracks: the Perkins–Bob Dylan collaboration, "Champaign, Illinois"; a tough Perkins love ballad, "Power of My Soul," the best song on the album; an obscure Buddy Holly song, "I'm Gonna Set My Foot Down." Vinyl only.

BOPPIN' THE BLUES (WITH NRBQ) (COLUMBIA CS 9981) 1970   Pairing Perkins with NRBQ seemed like an inspired idea on paper, but less than rousing in practical application, mostly because the band plays at rockabilly, while Carl lives and breathes it. Perkins isn't on every track, but his "Sorry Charlie" is a first-rate original, full of wry humor and blistering rhythm. The evocative instrumental, "Just Coastin'," made its debut here.

CARL PERKINS (HARMONY HS 11385) 1970   Columbia's budget line offered reissues of material found on earlier Perkins albums. Vinyl only.

ORIGINAL GOLDEN HITS (SUN INTL LP 111) 1970   Issued by Shelby Singleton after he bought the Sun catalogue from Sam Phillips. Vinyl only.

BLUE SUEDE SHOES (SUN INTL LP 112) 1970   Another Shelby Singleton reissue of original Sun material; marks the first appearance on record of "Her Love Rubbed Off," Carl's strangest Sun track, and one of his best. Vinyl only.

BROWN-EYED HANDSOME MAN (HARMONY KH 31179) 1972; GREATEST HITS (HARMONY KH 31792) 1973   Budget-line reissues, Vinyl only.

GREATEST HITS (COLUMBIA LE 10117) 1973   Reissue of Columbia CL-9833 from May 1969, available only through Columbia Record Club. Vinyl only.

CARL PERKINS (COLUMBIA LE 10159) 1973   Reissue of Columbia CL-9931 from September 1969, available only through Columbia Record Club. Vinyl only.

GREATEST HITS (COLUMBIA C 11309) 1973   Reissue of Columbia CL-9833 and Columbia Record Club LE-10117. Vinyl only.

MY KIND OF COUNTRY (MERCURY SRM-1-691) 1973   Carl's masterpiece of introspective, autobiographical songwriting. Morbid but haunting, it lays bare in explicit detail the demons stalking Carl. By any standard, a great country album. Vinyl only.

THE CARL PERKINS SHOW (SUEDE NR 6778) 1976   One thousand copies of this album were pressed, and these were available only at Carl's live performances. Includes his first recorded version of "Green, Green Grass of Home" (always powerful in Carl's hands, the song was re-recorded for the Dot *Carl Perkins* album), and a medley of Johnny Cash songs, as well as some new Perkins originals. Carl's first professional recordings with his sons Stan and Greg. Vinyl only.

THE BEST OF CARL PERKINS (TRIP TLX 8503) 1976   Double album release of Carl's original Sun material, licensed from Sun International; compilation of Sun reissues Sun 111 and Sun 112. Vinyl only.

MATCHBOX (PICKWICK JS 6103) 1977   Budget release of Sun material. Vinyl only.

CARL PERKINS: THE SUN STORY (GRT 9330-903) 1977   Obvious selections of familiar Perkins material. Vinyl only.

OL' BLUE SUEDE'S BACK (JET KZ 56704) 1978   A selection of Carl's favorite songs from rock 'n' roll's early days. In addition to rock 'n' roll standards—e.g., "That's Alright Mama," "Maybellene," "Whole Lotta Shakin'," and others—Carl serves up Hank Williams's "Kaw-Liga" and Chuck Willis's "Hang Up My Rock & Roll Shoes." The one new Perkins song here, "Rock On Around the World," is interesting mainly as the forerunner of the extraordinary "Birth of Rock and Roll" on *The Class of '55.* Vinyl only.

ROCK 'N' GOSPEL (KOALA AW-14137) 1979   Muscle Shoals sessions. Vinyl only.

SING A SONG WITH ME (KOALA AW 14144) 1979   Muscle Shoals sessions. On side two, four cuts do not feature Carl Perkins; artist unidentified. Vinyl only.

COUNTRY SOUL (KOALA AW 14164) 1979   Muscle Shoals sessions. Vinyl only.

CANE CREEK GLORY CHURCH (KOALA AW 14174) 1979   Secular and sacred numbers recorded in Nashville. Vinyl only.

BEST OF CARL PERKINS (KOALA KOA-14384) 1979   Reissues of Muscle Shoals and other Koala cuts. Vinyl only.

CARL PERKINS LIVE AT AUSTIN CITY LIMITS (SUEDE SLP 002) 1981   A limited issue, the second and last album on Suede documents the C.P. Express in concert on PBS's *Austin City Limits.* Vinyl only.

CARL PERKINS—MR. BLUE SUEDE SHOES (REALM IV 8158) 1981   Out-of-print title available via television marketing campaign. Vinyl only.

THAT ROCKIN' GUITAR MAN—TODAY (SOH AG 9016) 1981   More Muscle Shoals sessions. Vinyl only.

COUNTRY SOUL (CHARVAN AG 8118) 1981   Muscle Shoals sessions. Vinyl only.

PRESENTING CARL PERKINS (ACCORD SN 7169) 1982   Muscle Shoals sessions. Vinyl only.

BOPPIN' THE BLUES (ACCORD SJA 7915) 1982   Muscle Shoals sessions. Not to be confused with 1970 release with NRBQ. Vinyl only.

BORN TO BOOGIE (O'HARA TLA 50135) 1982   Muscle Shoals sessions. Vinyl only.

THE SURVIVORS (WITH JOHNNY CASH, JERRY LEE LEWIS) (COLUMBIA FC 37961) 1982   Recorded in Stuttgart, West Germany, April 23, 1981; features Carl solo on "Matchbox" and "Blue Suede Shoes," with Cash on two cuts (including a strong workout on "Goin' Down the Road Feeling Bad"), and the three principals together on four gospel songs, including Thomas Dorsey's

"Peace in the Valley." An interesting precursor to *Class of '55*, and in some ways better (overall quality of material, primarily).

THE HEART AND SOUL OF CARL PERKINS (ALLEGIANCE AV 5001) 1983 Muscle Shoals/Music Mill sessions. Vinyl only.

GOSPEL (SAGITTARIUS OTD-8635) 1984 More Muscle Shoals material of a religious nature. Vinyl only.

CARL PERKINS (DOT MCA-39035) 1985 Low-keyed and dignified, this one-shot with the Dot label showcases Carl's first songs written with his sons, notable among these being the western swing–influenced "Texas Women," Carl's acknowledgment on record of the impact Bob Wills had on his style of rockabilly. Also contains another strong bit of Perkins introspection in "If I Had'a Known."

UP THROUGH THE YEARS 1954–1957 (BEAR FAMILY BCD 15246) 1986 Twenty-four choice, essential Sun tracks; a precursor to Bear Family's more ambitious 1990 five-CD collection. Import CD.

ORIGINAL SUN GREATEST HITS (RHINO RNCD 75890) 1986 Exactly what it says. Sixteen tracks of choice Sun material, minus some essential gems in "You Can't Make Love to Somebody," "Right String Baby, Wrong Yo-Yo," and "Her Love Rubbed Off."

CLASS OF '55 (WITH JOHNNY CASH, ROY ORBISON, JERRY LEE LEWIS (AMERICA 422 830 002 M-1) 1986 Orbison offers a beautiful original ballad in "Coming Home," Cash does a stellar job on Waylon Jennings's "Waymore's Blues," Jerry Lee flames out, if you will, on a turgid version of "16 Candles," and Carl steals the whole show with "Birth of Rock and Roll," as definitive a statement of rock 'n' roll's origins as has ever been put into song, with a searing guitar solo from Carl to boot. Vinyl, cassette only.

CLASS OF '55 (PICTURE DISK) (POLYGRAM 830002-1) 1986 Same tracks as above. Rumored to be only twenty-five copies of this title pressed.

INTERVIEWS FROM THE CLASS OF '55 RECORDING SESSIONS (AMERICA/SMASH AR/LP 1001(2)) 1986 A Grammy-winning spoken word album of reminiscences of the four rock 'n' roll pioneers assembled for the *Class of '55* project. Out of print.

LI'L BIT OF GOLD (RHINO R3-73015) 1988 A three-inch mini-CD containing a little bit of Carl's best known songs. Now out of print.

18 SUPER HITS (LASERLIGHT 15-034) 1988 Greatest hits collection.

HONKY TONK GAL: RARE AND UNISSUED SUN MASTERS (ROUNDER SS 27) 1989 Less essential now with the release of the five-CD *Classic Carl Perkins* box set, but for those looking for a low-priced alternative, this Rounder collection offers a number of alternate takes and (at the time) previously unissued tracks. Of note here: "What You Doin' When You Cryin'?," "You Can't Make Love to Somebody," "Her Love Rubbed Off," and—well, *everything* is of note here.

BORN TO ROCK (UNIVERSAL UVLC 76001) 1989 Good title track, a wry taste of autobiography in "Cotton Top," and a couple of good Carl and

Greg Perkins compositions ("A Lifetime Last Night" and "Love Makes Dreams Come True") highlight a serviceable effort on the doomed Universal label. Co-produced by the Judds' producer Brent Maher and the Judds' musical mentor Don Potter.

THE MILLION DOLLAR QUARTET (WITH ELVIS PRESLEY, JERRY LEE LEWIS) (BMG2023-2-R) 1990   Long-rumored, finally released, after settlement of a lawsuit Carl initiated to prevent Shelby Singleton from dubbing in additional instruments. Marvelous and essential in every way—a look at rock 'n' roll past and present, as it was in December 1956, by three of its most important practitioners. Gospel, R&B, pop, rock 'n' roll, jazz (by way of Jerry Lee's take on a Jelly Roll Morton song), blues—all are admitted to these premises. Be advised—you are on holy ground when you listen to these voices.

THE CLASSIC CARL PERKINS (BEAR FAMILY BCD 15494) 1990   Five-CD box with extensive and mostly accurate annotation, covering nearly everything Carl recorded for Sun and Columbia, including alternate takes (and home recordings made during the Sun era), plus some of the Decca sides with Owen Bradley as well as those recorded in England with the Nashville Teens. Numerous Decca recordings remain unissued. An essential set for completists, historians, and dedicated fans. Import.

JIVE AFTER FIVE: THE BEST OF CARL PERKINS (1958–1978) (RHINO R2 70958) 1990   Well-considered eighteen-track survey of Carl's Columbia, Decca, and Mercury years, plus two tracks from the 1976 Muscle Shoals sessions ("original release information unknown," says the track list). Value lies in its inclusion of three tracks from the out-of-print masterpiece, *My Kind of Country*.

THE DOLLIE MASTERS: COUNTRY BOY'S DREAM (BEAR FAMILY BCD 15593) 1991   Thirty tracks from one of Carl's most productive periods as a writer, 1966–67. Opening with "Country Boy's Dream" and closing with "Valda," this set is a virtual autobiography in song, almost all written by Carl. Powerful performances belie the purists' sentiment that Carl lost it after leaving Sun. Despite a lack of hits, Carl's writing, playing, and singing were improving with age, a fact made obvious herein. Import CD.

RESTLESS: THE COLUMBIA RECORDINGS (COLUMBIA LEGACY CT 48896) 1992   From "Pink Pedal Pushers" to "Restless" to the lovely instrumental "Just Coastin'," further proof that during Carl's Columbia years the fault lay not with the star. Begs the question, how could so many good records go unnoticed?

FRIENDS, FAMILY & LEGENDS (PLATINUM PRCD 2431-2) 1992   Uneven material mars the album Carl cut before being diagnosed with throat cancer. A scorching version of Bruce Springsteen's "Pink Cadillac" opens the proceedings in fine fashion, and son Greg and daughter Debbie contribute, on the penultimate track, a nice meditation on the power of love in "Of Love." In between it's rough going, even for die-hards.

**706 RE-UNION (WITH SCOTTY MOORE) (BELLE MEADE BMCD 1992)
1992** A convivial look back at rock 'n' roll's roots by two musicians whose work went far towards defining rock 'n' roll guitar. Between songs Carl and Scotty Moore reminisce about the early days at Sun and on the road with Elvis. Available by mail order only.

CARL PERKINS & SONS (BMG 07863-66216-4) 1993; TAKE ME BACK (BMG 07863-66217-4) 1993; DISCIPLE IN BLUE SUEDE SHOES (BMG 07863-66218-4) 1993 Finally a distinguished release for the 1976 Muscle Shoals sessions. Best of the lot is *Disciple in Blue Suede Shoes,* a stirring set of gospel songs. *Carl Perkins & Sons* contains Carl's first professional studio recordings with Stan and Greg. Intermittently compelling, the song selection demonstrates the broad sweep of Carl's thematic concerns as a writer. Ample rewards can be found throughout in the Rockin' Guitar Man's tasty, melodic solos.

BEST OF CARL PERKINS (CURB D2-77598) 1993 Includes the Sun version of "Blue Suede Shoes" and nine cuts from the *Born to Rock* album.

Known Bootleg Albums (as of June 1995):

CARL PERKINS (BOPCAT 500) 1978 Contains ten of the "lost" Decca sides.

THE ROCKIN' GUITAR MAN (BOPCAT 600) 1978

TO ALL MY FRIENDS FROM JACKSON, TENNESSEE (LAKE COUNTY 505) 1978

MR. COUNTRY ROCK (DEMAND 0015) 1983

CARL PERKINS (PICTURE DISC) (NBC AR-30016) 1983

CARL LEE PERKINS—BRITISH TOUR 1964 (DOCTOR KOLLECTOR DK—007) 1984

▶ SINGLES

Title—(Label and Matrix number)—Month/Year of release
1. Movie Magg/Turn Around (Flip 501) 2/55
2. Let The Jukebox Keep On Playing/Gone Gone Gone (Sun 224) 9/55
3. Blue Suede Shoes/Honey Don't (Sun 234) 1/56
4. Tennessee/Sure to Fall (Sun 235—promo only) 3/56
5. Boppin' the Blues/All Mama's Children (Sun 243) 5/56
6. Dixie Fried/I'm Sorry I'm Not Sorry (Sun 249) 8/56
7. Matchbox/Your True Love (Sun 261) 2/57
8. That's Right/Forever Yours (Sun 274) 8/57
9. Glad All Over/Lend Me Your Comb (Sun 287) 12/57
10. Pink Pedal Pushers/Jive After Five (Columbia 41131) 3/58
11. Levi Jacket/Pop Let Me Have the Car (Columbia 41207) 7/58
12. Y-O-U/This Life I Live (Columbia 41269) 11/58

13. Pointed Toe Shoes/Highway of Love (Columbia 41379) 4/59
14. One Ticket to Loneliness/I Don't See Me In Your Eyes Anymore (Col 41447) 8/59
15. L-O-V-E-V-I-L-L-E/Too Much For A Man To Understand (Columbia 41651) 4/60
16. Honey, 'Cause I Love You/Just For You (Columbia 41825) 10/60
17. The Unhappy Girls/Anyway the Wind Blows (Columbia 42061) 7/61
18. Hollywood City/Forget the Next Time Around (Columbia 42403—promo only) 4/62
19. Hollywood City/The Fool I Used to Be (Columbia 42405) 4/62
20. Hambone/Sister Twister (Columbia 42514) 7/62
21. Forget Me Next Time Around/Just Got Back From There (Columbia 42753) 3/63
22. Help Me Find My Baby/For A Little While (Decca 31548) 11/63
23. After Sundown/I Wouldn't Have You (Decca 31591) 2/64
24. Let My Baby Be/The Monkeyshine (Decca 31709) 12/64
25. Mama of My Song/One of These Days (Decca 31786) 5/65
26. Country Boy's Dream/If I Could Come Back (Dollie 505) 8/66
27. Almost Love/Shine Shine Shine (Dollie 508) 2/67
28. You Can Take the Boy Out of the Country/Without You (Dollie 512) 2/67
29. Back to Tennessee/My Old Home Town (Dollie 514) 9/67
30. Lake County Cotton Country/It's You (Dollie 516) 9/67
31. Restless/1143 (Columbia 44723) 12/68
32. Four Letter Word/For Your Love (Columbia 44883) 5/69
33. Soul Beat/C.C. Rider (You're So Bad) (Columbia 44993) 9/69
34. All Mama's Children/Step Aside (with NRBQ) (Columbia 45107) 2/70
35. State of Confusion/My Son, My Sun (Columbia 45132) 3/70
36. What Every Little Boy Ought To Know/Just As Long (Columbia 45253) 10/70
37. Me Without You/Red Headed Woman (Columbia 45347) 4/71
38. Cotton Top/All I Can Give Is My Love (Columbia 45466) 10/71
39. High On Love/Take Me Back to Memphis (Columbia 45582) 3/72
40. The Trip/Someday (Columbia 45694) 9/72
41. Help Me Dream/You Tore My Heaven All To Hell (Mercury 73393) 5/73
42. One More Loser Goin' Home/Dixie Fried (Mercury 73425) 9/73
43. Sing My Song/Ruby, Don't Take Your Love To Town (Mercury 73489) 5/74
44. Low Class/You'll Always Be A Lady To Me (Mercury 73653) 1/75
45. EP Express/Big Bad Blues (Mercury 73690) 6/75
46. Little Tear Drops/Green, Green Grass of Home (Suede 6777-1) ?/76
47. Take Me Back/Born to Boogie (Music Mill 1007) ?/76
48. We Did in '54/Don't Get Off Gettin' It On (MMI 1013) ?/77
49. Standing In The Need of Love/Georgia Courtroom (MMI 1019) ?/77
50. Rock On Around The World/Blue Suede Shoes (Jet 5054) 10/78
51. Mustang Wine/The Whole World Misses You (Jet 0117) 11/78

52. We Did in '54/I Don't Want to Fall in Love Again (Suede 101) 5/81
53. Rock-A-Billy Fever/Till You Get Through With Me (Suede 102) 10/81
54. Get It (with Paul McCartney) (Columbia 38-03325 ?/83
55. Birth of Rock and Roll/Rock and Roll (Fais Do Do) (with Roy Orbison, Jerry Lee Lewis) (America/Smash 884-760-7) 7/86
56. Class of '55/Class of '55 (promo only) (America/Smash 888-142-7) 9/86
57. Charlene/Love Makes Dreams Come True (Universal 66002) 5/89
58. Hambone/Love Makes Dreams Come True (Universal 66019) 7/89

45 RPM Extended-Play Albums:

Whole Lotta Shakin' (Columbia EPB 12341) 10/60
Blue Suede Shoes (Sun EP-115) ?/69

BIBLIOGRAPHY

▶BOOKS

Booth, Stanley, *Rythm Oil*, New York: Pantheon Books, 1991.

Brown, Dee, *Hear That Lonesome Whistle Blow*, New York: Holt, Rinehart and Winston, 1977.

Carr, Patrick, ed., with the editors of *Country Music* magazine, *The Illustrated History of Country Music*, Garden City, NY: Country Music Magazine Press/Doubleday, 1979.

Cash, Johnny, *Man in Black*, Grand Rapids, MI: Zondervan Publishing House, 1975.

Cash, W.J., *The Mind of the South*, New York: Alfred A. Knopf, 1941.

Coppock, Paul, *Memphis Memoirs*, Memphis, TN: Memphis State University Press, 1980.

DeCurtis, Anthony, and Henke, James, with George-Warren, Holly, *The Rolling Stone Album Guide*, New York: Random House, 1992.

Dundy, Elaine, *Elvis and Gladys*, New York: Dell, 1985.

Ehrenstein, David, and Reed, Bill, *Rock On Film*, New York: Delilah Books, 1982.

The Encyclopedia of Tennessee, Nashville, TN: Somerset Publishers, 1993.

Escott, Colin, with Hawkins, Martin, *Good Rockin' Tonight: Sun Records and the Birth of Rock 'n' Roll*, New York: St. Martin's Press, 1991.

Goldfield, David R., *Black, White and Southern: Race Relations and Southern Culture 1940 to the Present*, Baton Rouge: Louisiana State University Press, 1990.

Guralnick, Peter, *Last Train to Memphis: The Rise of Elvis Presley*, New York: HarperCollins, 1994.

Hagarty, Britt, *The Day the World Turned Blue: A Biography of Gene Vincent*, Dorset, England: Blandford Press, 1983.

Halberstam, David, *The Fifties*, New York: Villard Books, 1993.

Heilbut, Anthony, *The Gospel Sound*, Garden City, NY: Anchor Books, 1975.

Hemming, Roy, and Hadju, David, *Discovering the Great Singers of Classic Pop*, New York: Newmarket Press, 1991.

History and Families: Lake County, Tennessee, Paducah, KY: Turner Publishing Company, 1993.

Hurst, Jack, *Grand Ole Opry*, New York: Harry N. Abrams, 1975.

Klein, Joe, *Woody Guthrie: A Life*, New York: Alfred K. Knopf, 1980.

Lemann, Nicholas, *The Promised Land: The Great Black Migration and How It Changed America*, New York: Alfred A. Knopf, 1991.

Lewisohn, Mark, *The Beatles Recording Sessions*, New York: Harmony Books, 1988.

McElvaine, Robert S., *The Great Depression: America, 1929–1941*, New York: Times Books, 1993.

McMillen, Neil R., *The Citizens' Council: Organized Resistance to the Second Reconstruction, 1954–1964*, Urbana: University of Illinois Press, 1971.

Miller, Jim, ed., *The Rolling Stone Illustrated History of Rock & Roll*, New York: Random House/Rolling Stone Press, 1980.

Morthland, John, *The Best of Country Music*, Garden City, NY: Dolphin Books, 1984.

Palmer, Robert, *Deep Blues*, New York: Viking Penguin, 1981.

Parks, Joshua H., and Folmsbee, Stanley J., *The Story of Tennessee*, 6th ed., Norman, OK: Harlow Publishing, 1973.

Perkins, Carl, *Disciple in Blue Suede Shoes*, Grand Rapids, MI: Zondervan Publishing House, 1978.

Rooney, James, *Bossmen: Bill Monroe & Muddy Waters*, New York: Hayden Book Company, 1971.

Sigafoos, Robert J., *Cotton Row to Beale Street: A Business History of Memphis*, Memphis, TN: Memphis State University Press, 1979.

Siler, Tom, *Tennessee Towns: From Adams to Yorkville*, Knoxville: East Tennessee Historical Society, 1985.

Tindall, George B., *The Emergence of the New South, 1913–1945*, Baton Rouge: Louisiana State University Press, Littlefield Fund for Southern History of the University of Texas, 1967.

Tosches, Nick, *Country*, New York: Scribner's, 1977.

Vanderwood, Paul J. *Night Riders of Reelfoot Lake*, Memphis, TN: Memphis State University Press, 1969.

Whitburn, Joel, *The Billboard Book of Top 40 Hits*, New York: Billboard Publications, 1985.

Whitburn, Joel, *Pop Memories 1890–1954*, Menomonee Falls, WI: Record Research, 1986.

White, Theodore, *In Search of History*, New York: Warner Books, 1978.

Williams, Samuel Cole, LL.D., *Beginnings of West Tennessee: In the Land of the Chickasaws 1541–1841*, Johnson City, TN: Watauga Press, 1930.

Wilson, Charles Reagan, and Ferris, Williams, eds., *Encyclopedia of Southern Culture*, Chapel Hill: University of North Carolina Press, 1989.

Wren, Christopher S., *Winners Got Scars Too: The Life and Legends of Johnny Cash*, New York: Dial Press, 1971.

►NEWSPAPERS AND MAGAZINES

Country Song Roundup
The Jackson Sun
Melody Maker
Memphis Press-Scimitar
Memphis Commercial Appeal
Montgomery Advertiser
Nashville Banner
Nashville Tennessean
New Musical Express
The New York Times
Rolling Stone

NOTES

When this project began, a friend said to me, "I really love Carl, but he seems to have about three different versions of every story." Indeed, if anything seems to be a universally acknowledged truth about the original Sun artists, it's that they are all first-rate storytellers who refuse to allow facts to cloud a good anecdote. And Carl, as Marty Stuart observed in our interview, "knows how to make a story fly."

I set out to clarify the alleged inconsistencies in Carl's stories by corroborating his accounts with as many other sources as possible. Along the way, many of those interviewed not only vouched for and amplified Carl's version of events but assured me that "If Carl says it happened that way, it did."

By far the strongest proponent of Carl's accounts was Johnny Cash, who offered additional information about various Perkins Brothers hijinks, and also sat patiently listening to story after story, nodding his head as I went through details supplied by Carl and then offering, "That's right." The more interviews I conducted the more I came to believe that Carl's reminiscences at least had the ring of truth, given that no one's memory of events sometimes forty- and fifty-plus years in the past could be 100 percent accurate.

My one regret is that some key people in Carl's life failed to respond to repeated requests for interviews. Sam Phillips, for one, disregarded requests made through his attorney for his side of the Perkins story; thus his voice is heard only through citations from previously published interviews and court records. Repeated efforts to interview Jerry Lee Lewis failed as well. Ringo Starr declined an interview request, and George Harrison and Paul McCartney, through their representatives, indicated their willingness to discuss Carl and his impact on their music, but the interviews failed to materialize. While Carl has done many print and television interviews over the years, these have tended to be narrow in scope, touching on virtually none of the intricate details of his relationships with Phillips and Lewis, and reducing his Beatles sessions to a sentence indicating that they recorded three of his songs. Again, Johnny Cash was able to verify many, but not all, of the details of Carl's troubled history with Phillips and of Carl's (and everybody's) love-hate affair with Jerry Lee, but, for the most part, it is Carl's voice speaking unchallenged with regard to events and scenes involving these particular characters.

The dialogue re-created in these pages is as Carl remembers it, with corroboration wherever possible. I have, however, ascribed no emotions to anyone save Carl, unless the other party or parties indicated to me their feelings at the time the event(s) in question occurred.

Other sources are as indicated below.

▶ COTTON PATCH BLUES

LAKE COUNTY, 1932–1946

4–10: Background on Carl's lineage and birth, the sharecropper's life, and Lake County, Tennessee, from interviews with Carl Perkins, Martha Perkins Bain, Valda Perkins, and Oma Garner (1990, 1993, 1994), and from Vanderwood, *Night Riders of Reelfoot Lake;* Wilson and Ferris, *Encyclopedia of Southern Culture; History and Families: Lake County, Tennessee; The Encyclopedia of Tennessee.*

10–11: The Grand Ole Opry's birth and growth and the emergence of Jimmie Rodgers, the Carter Family, and Roy Acuff from Carr, *The Illustrated History of Country Music;* DeCurtis and Henke, *The Rolling Stone Album Guide;* Hurst, *Grand Ole Opry.*

11–12: Bill Monroe: Carr, *The Illustrated History of Country Music;* Morthland, *The Best of Country Music;* DeCurtis and Henke, *The Rolling Stone Album Guide;* Rooney, *Bossmen: Bill Monroe & Muddy Waters.*

12–14: Uncle John Westbrook: Interviews with Carl Perkins, 1993; Martha Perkins Bain, 1994.

15–16: Carl as a student: Interviews with Carl Perkins, 1993; Martha Perkins Bain, 1994.

16–17: Charlie: Interview with Carl Perkins, 1993.

17–18: Weekend visits to cousin Delmus's house: Interviews with Carl Perkins, 1993, 1994; Martha Perkins Bain, 1994.

18–19: Buck's drinking, Louise's reaction to: Interviews with Carl Perkins, 1993, 1994; Martha Perkins Bain, 1994.

20: Sharecropper's way of life was ending: Cash, *The Mind of the South;* Lemann, *The Promised Land: The Great Black Migration and How It Changed America;* McElvaine, *The Great Depression: America, 1929–1941;* Tindall, *The Emergence of the New South, 1913–1945.*

20: Mechanization: W.J. Cash, *The Mind of the South;* Lemann: *The Promised Land;* Tindall, *The Emergence of the New South, 1913–1945.*

21–22: Miss Lee McCutcheon: Interviews with Carl Perkins, 1993; Martha Perkins Bain, 1994.

22–23: country music embraced change and innovation: Carr, *The Illustrated History of Country Music.*

23: Bob Wills: Carr, *The Illustrated History of Country Music;* Morthland,

The Best of Country Music; DeCurtis and Henke, *The Rolling Stone Album Guide.*

23: Fair Labor Standards Act of 1938: McElvaine, *The Great Depression;* Tindall, *The Emergence of the New South, 1913–1945.*

23: another type of feel-good music: Carr, *The Illustrated History of Country Music;* Morthland, *The Best of Country Music.*

23: Etymology of "honky-tonk": Tosches, *Country.*

23–25: Al Dexter, Ted Daffan, Floyd Tillman, Moon Mullican, Ernest Tubb: Carr, *The Illustrated History of Country Music;* Morthland, *The Best of Country Music;* DeCurtis and Henke, *The Rolling Stone Album Guide.*

26–27: Jay and Carl: Interviews with Carl Perkins, 1993, 1994; Martha Perkins Bain, 1994.

27: Louise was the family backbone: Ibid.

27–28: Clayton Perkins: Ibid.

29: James Washington leaves Lake County, sons follow: Ibid.

29: Judson Bemis: Various articles in the *Jackson Sun,* 1950–1958.

29: a nation beginning to creak with change: Lemann, *The Promised Land;* Tindall, *The Emergence of the New South, 1913–1945.*

MADISON COUNTY: JACKSON AND BEMIS, 1946–1954

32–33: Day's Dairy: Interview with Carl Perkins, 1993.

33–35: Writing first song: Interview with Carl Perkins, 1993.

35–36: Playing song for Jay, then Buck: Ibid.

36–42: Cotton Boll and tonk culture: Interviews with Carl Perkins, 1993, 1994; Martha Perkins Bain, 1994; Valda Perkins, 1994; Ed Cisco, 1994.

42–43: Moonshine: Interview with Carl Perkins, 1993; Ed Cisco, 1994.

44: Louise's warnings: Interview with Carl Perkins, 1993.

44: Carl transformed by tonks: Ibid.

44–45: Something was happening with the Perkins Brothers Band: Interviews with Carl Perkins, 1993; Ed Cisco, 1993; Martha Perkins Bain, 1994.

45: Red Foley: Carr, *The Illustrated History of Country Music;* DeCurtis and Henke, *The Rolling Stone Album Guide.*

46: Clayton joins band: Interview with Carl Perkins, 1993; Ed Cisco, 1994.

47–49: Carl on radio: Interviews with Carl Perkins, 1993, 1994; Ed Cisco, 1994; Martha Perkins Bain, 1994; Valda Perkins, 1994.

49–50: Hank Williams: Carr, *The Illustrated History of Country Music;* Morthland, *The Best of Country Music;* DeCurtis and Henke, *The Rolling Stone Album Guide.*

50–51: Carl meets Valda: Interviews with Carl Perkins, 1993; Valda Perkins, 1994; Martha Perkins Bain, 1994.

51–52: Crider family background, Valda Crider as student: Interviews with Valda Perkins, 1994; Martha Perkins Bain, 1994.

52–53: Martha and Valda's friendship: Ibid.

53–54: "Rocky" courtship: Ibid.

54: Carl's red-dog habits, feelings for Valda: Interview with Carl Perkins, 1993.

54–55: Jay's marriage: Interviews with Carl Perkins, 1993; Valda Perkins, 1994.

55–56: Memphis became a part of Carl's life: Interview with Carl Perkins, 1993.

56: Rise of independent labels: Tosches, *Country*.

56: Fats Domino: DeCurtis and Henke, *The Rolling Stone Album Guide*.

56–57: Memphis Recording Service: Escott with Hawkins, *Good Rockin' Tonight: Sun Records and the Birth of Rock 'n' Roll*.

57: "There were city markets to be reached": Ibid.

57: A photograph of Sam Phillips: Ibid.

58–60: When Valda came into his life: Interviews with Carl Perkins, 1993; Valda Perkins, 1994; Martha Perkins Bain, 1994.

61–63: Clayton was coming into his own: Interview with Carl Perkins, 1993.

63: Tush hogs: Interviews with Carl Perkins, 1993; Johnny Cash, 1994.

64: Clayton and Carl fight: Interview with Carl Perkins, 1993.

64–65: El Rancho: Interviews with Carl Perkins, 1993; Ed Cisco, 1994.

65–66: Clayton provided the next bit of good fortune: Ibid.

67–68: The most unsettling moment: Interviews with Carl Perkins, 1993; Valda Perkins, 1994.

70: "It wasn't just a dream": Interview with Valda Perkins, 1994.

70–72: Fluke Holland joins band: Interview with Carl Perkins, 1993; W.S. Holland interviewed by Bill Way on "Area Code 901," WBBJ-TV, Jackson, Tennessee, January 12, 1993.

72–73: Stanley Perkins's birth: Interviews with Carl Perkins, 1993; Valda Perkins, 1994.

74: Move to Parkview Courts: Ibid.

75: "Movement was of the essence": White, *In Search of History*.

75: So it was in the boom time of postwar America: White, *In Search of History;* Halberstam, *The Fifties*.

75: Music too was starting to reflect: Escott with Hawkins, *Good Rockin' Tonight*.

75–76: Alan Freed: Miller, *The Rolling Stone Illustrated History of Rock & Roll*.

76: Coinage of rock 'n' roll: Tosches, *Country*.

76–77: Alan Freed's early concerts: Miller, *The Rolling Stone Illustrated History of Rock & Roll*.

77: Muddy Waters: Palmer, *Deep Blues;* DeCurtis and Henke, *The Rolling Stone Album Guide*.

77–78: Bill Haley: DeCurtis and Henke, *The Rolling Stone Album Guide*.

78: The messenger of the covenant: Guralnick, *Last Train to Memphis: The Rise of Elvis Presley;* Escott with Hawkins, *Good Rockin' Tonight*.

78–80: Carl found reason to be upbeat: Interviews with Carl Perkins, 1993; Valda Perkins, 1994; Martha Perkins Bain, 1994.

80–83: Carl had a chance to see Presley perform: Interviews with Carl Perkins, 1993; Valda Perkins, 1994; Scotty Moore, 1994.

▶A SUMMONS TO MEMPHIS, 1954–1958

87–89: Auditioning at Sun: Interview with Carl Perkins, 1993.

88–89: Studio equipment: Escott with Hawkins, *Good Rockin' Tonight*.

91: Urging W.S. Holland to buy drums: Interview with Carl Perkins, 1993.

91–92: Holland's drum setup: W.S. Holland interviewed by Bill Way on "Area Code 901," WBBJ-TV, Jackson, Tennessee, January 12, 1993.

92: Holland's car: Interview with Carl Perkins, 1993; W.S. Holland interviewed by Bill Way on "Area Code 901," WBBJ-TV, Jackson, Tennessee, January 12, 1993.

92–97: First Sun session: Interview with Carl Perkins, 1993.

97–98: Sam did indeed like the song: Escott with Hawkins, *Good Rockin' Tonight*.

98: Between takes, Cantrell coached Carl on his vocal: Dialogue transcribed from session tape released on the five-CD boxed set, *The Classic Carl Perkins* Bear Family Records.

98: "revolutionize the country end of the business": Sam Phillips quoted by Escott with Hawkins, *Good Rockin' Tonight*.

99: Les Paul background: DeCurtis and Henke, *The Rolling Stone Album Guide;* essay by Stephen K. Peeples for Les Paul boxed set, *The Legend and the Legacy*, released by Capitol, 1991.

99–101: Carl buys first Gibson Les Paul: Interview with Carl Perkins, 1993.

101: Sam Phillips acknowledged this: Interview with Carl Perkins, 1993.

101–102: Clayton threatens Carl: Interviews with Carl Perkins, 1993; Valda Perkins, 1994.

103–104: Carl had had a narrow escape: Interview with Carl Perkins, 1993.

104–105: In the drift of time 1954 stands as a watershed: White, *In Search of History.*

105: "an idling engine": Interview with Carl Perkins, 1993.

105–106: Release of first single: Interviews with Carl Perkins, 1993; Valda Perkins, 1994; Martha Perkins Bain, 1994.

106: Dewey Phillips: Booth, *Rhythm Oil.*

106: Carl became a celebrity around Jackson: Interviews with Carl Perkins, 1993; Valda Perkins, 1994; Ed Cisco, 1994.

106–107: Bob Neal: Escott with Hawkins, *Good Rockin' Tonight.*

107–109: First concerts with Elvis: Interview with Carl Perkins, 1993.

109–110: Shopping at Lansky's: Interview with Carl Perkins, 1993.

110–111: Silk stripes on stage slacks: Interview with Carl Perkins, 1993.

111: By the end of 1955: Whitburn, *The Billboard Book of Top 40 Hits.*

112: The difference in America in 1955 was money and time: Halberstam, *The Fifties.*

112–118: Recording session, drinking: Interview with Carl Perkins, 1993.

119–120: Meeting Johnny Cash: Interviews with Carl Perkins, 1993; Johnny Cash, 1994.

120: "I don't feel like anybody discovered me": Johnny Cash, quoted by Escott with Hawkins, *Good Rockin' Tonight.*

119–121: Johnny Cash background: Escott with Hawkins, *Good Rockin' Tonight.*

121–122: Philips was making the most out of low-tech gear: Interview with Carl Perkins, 1993.

122–123: Carl, Cash, and Presley went out on the road together: Interviews with Carl Perkins, 1993; Johnny Cash, 1994.

123: Jay remained unsettled by Elvis's appearance: Interview with Carl Perkins, 1993.

123–124: Elvis using eyeliner: Interview with Carl Perkins, 1993.

124: Cash's fondness for Clayton: Interviews with Carl Perkins, 1993; Johnny Cash, 1994.

124–126: Cash wasn't around for one of Clayton's finest hours: Interview with Carl Perkins, 1993.

126–127: Carl's music . . . finally found a name: Tosches, *Country.*

127: "I knew I was some form of country": Interview with Carl Perkins, 1993.

127–128: Sam received an inquiry from Webb Pierce's management: Ibid.

128: "I had an idea you oughta write you a song about blue suede shoes": Interviews with Carl Perkins, 1993; Johnny Cash, 1994.

128–133: Union University dance, writing "Blue Suede Shoes," teaching song to Jay, calling Sam Phillips: Interviews with Carl Perkins, 1993; Valda Perkins, 1994.

133–137: Shows with Elvis and Cash in Amory, Mississippi, and Helena, Arkansas: Interviews with Carl Perkins, 1993; Johnny Cash, 1994.

137: "I think all of us felt like": Interview with Scotty Moore, 1994.

137–139: In Memphis Sam Phillips was having problems: Escott with Hawkins, *Good Rockin' Tonight;* documents filed in lawsuit, *Carl Perkins, Plaintiff v. Samuel C. Phillips, Defendant,* in Chancery Court of Shelby County, 1977.

139–140: With their finances ebbing: Interviews with Carl Perkins, 1993; Valda Perkins, 1994.

140–148: "Blue Suede Shoes" session: Interview with Carl Perkins, 1993.

148–149: The special feeling Carl felt: Interviews with Carl Perkins, 1993; Valda Perkins, 1994; Scotty Moore, 1994.

149–150: With Christmas then only a few days away: Interviews with Carl Perkins, 1993; Valda Perkins, 1994.

150–151: Invention of 33⅓, 45 rpm records: Miller, *The Rolling Stone Illustrated History of Rock & Roll.*

151–153: So preoccupied was Carl: Interviews with Carl Perkins, 1993; Valda Perkins, 1994.

153–154: Cleveland breakout: Interview with Carl Perkins, 1993.

154–155: Carl's fortunes, literally and figuratively, picked up in the following weeks: Escott with Hawkins, *Good Rockin' Tonight;* interview with Carl Perkins, 1993.

155–156: Bob Neal booked Carl and Cash: Interviews with Carl Perkins, 1993; Johnny Cash, 1994.

156: "Rockabilly was loved in Texas": Interview with Carl Perkins, 1993.

156: *Big D Jamboree* venue: Interviews with Carl Perkins, 1993; Jim Bailey, 1993.

157: Carl made four appearances: Interview with Carl Perkins, 1993.

157: "Man, this is gonna be a million-sellin' record": Interview with Carl Perkins, 1993.

157–158: Carl and Cash aided their causes: Interviews with Carl Perkins, 1993; Johnny Cash, 1994.

157–158: In the first two months of release: Chart information from Escott with Hawkins, *Good Rockin' Tonight.*

158: *Song Hits* review, February 18, 1956.

158: "The last part of January": Interview with Carl Perkins, 1993.

158–159: Four unreconstructed rockabillies: Interviews with Carl Perkins, 1993; Johnny Cash, 1994.

159: *Country Song Roundup,* February 18, 1956.

159–160: Crickets: Interview with Carl Perkins, 1993.

160–161: A bizarre footnote: Tosches, *Country.*

161–162: With his income rising, Carl made two big-ticket purchases: Interviews with Carl Perkins, 1993; Scotty Moore, 1994.

162: By early March "Shoes" was starting to catch on nationally: Escott with Hawkins, *Good Rockin' Tonight.*

162: Cover versions of "Shoes": Ibid.

162: Presley's producer, Steve Sholes, had placed a panic call to Sam Phillips: Peter Guralnick, essay for boxed set *Elvis: The King of Rock 'N' Roll, The Complete 50's Masters, 1992.*

162: It has been reported, and confirmed by Phillips: Escott with Hawkins, *Good Rockin' Tonight.*

162: Scotty Moore discounts other published reports: Interview with Scotty Moore, 1994.

163: "We just went in there and started playing": Ibid.

163: On March 17, Presley introduced the song: from *Elvis—A Golden Celebration,* boxed set released in 1984.

163–165: Recording session, "All Mama's Children": Interviews with Carl Perkins, 1993; Johnny Cash, 1994.

165–166: Curly Griffin: Interview with Carl Perkins, 1993.

166–168: Of those he had taken time to compose on paper: Ibid.

168: "Man, you've cut your next record": Ibid.

168: During a break in the recording: Ibid.

169–170: ("Everybody's Trying to Be My Baby" had a history): John Morthland, liner notes for *Texas Music: Vol. 2. Western Swing & Honky Tonk*, Rhino Records, 1995.

170: "Everybody in there looked to me": Interview with Carl Perkins, 1993.

170–171: "When you've got a hit record out there playing": Ibid.

171: Foley relinquished his role as host: Liner notes for Country Music Hall of Fame Series CD, *Red Foley*, by John Rumble, 1991.

171–173: Arriving for afternoon rehearsal: Interview with Carl Perkins, 1993.

173: Foley in fact was one of the first Nashville establishment country artists: *Memphis Press-Scimitar*, April 10, 1956.

173–174: "If you're going to New York": Interview with Carl Perkins, 1993.

174: The Como show, he was certain, would break open his career: Ibid.

174: The Norfolk promoter was Bill Davis: Hagarty, *The Day the World Turned Blue: A Biography of Gene Vincent*.

174: One of these was Gene Craddock: Ibid.

175: Craddock was also a writer: Ibid.

176: Backstage at the Norfolk Auditorium: Interview with Carl Perkins, 1993.

176: Less than four months later: Hagarty, *The Day the World Turned Blue*.

176–177: Departing Norfolk after another well-received show: Interview with Carl Perkins, 1993.

177–178: On a flat stretch of highway: Interview with Carl Perkins, 1993; W.S. Holland interviewed by Bill Way on "Area Code 901," WBBJ-TV, Jackson, Tennessee, January 12, 1993.

178: The band's Chrysler: Ibid.

178–181: First he saw light: Interview with Carl Perkins, 1993.

181–182: On March 23, Valda spent the day: Interview with Valda Perkins, 1994.

182–183: The staff at Dover Hospital would have welcomed Carl being able to go home immediately: Interview with Carl Perkins, 1993.

182–183: On the evening of March 23: Interviews with Carl Perkins, 1993; Scotty Moore, 1994.

182–183: After Scotty, Bill, and D.J. had left: Interview with Carl Perkins, 1993.

184: On the evening of March 24: Dates from boxed set *Elvis: A Golden Celebration*, RCA Records, 1984.

184–185: Nearly a week after the wreck: Interview with Carl Perkins, 1993.

184–185: He was sifting through his mail when two ambulance attendants arrived: Ibid.

185: At the Wilmington hospital: Ibid.

185–187: While speaking, he became aware of some activity in the hall: Ibid.

187: "came up to and drove right on by": Ibid.

187: While "waiting to heal," Carl saw "Blue Suede Shoes" rise to the top: chart history from Escott with Hawkins, *Good Rockin' Tonight.*

188–189: The trio's leader was Jim Denny: Hurst, *Grand Ole Opry.*

189: Carl invited them in: Interviews with Carl Perkins, 1993; Bill Denny, 1993.

189: "They're wantin' to sign me, Mr. Phillips": Interview with Carl Perkins, 1993.

190–191: Denny accepted Carl's decision: Ibid.

191: At each stop of the tour: Ibid.

191–192: As Carl was preparing for his tour: Ibid.

192–195: "Everybody's Tryin' To Be My Baby" session: Ibid.

195–197: "Dixie Fried" session: Ibid.

197–198: "Put Your Cat Clothes On": Ibid.

198–199: Roy Orbison background: Escott with Hawkins, *Good Rockin' Tonight;* essay by Colin Escott for *The Legendary Roy Orbison* boxed set, CBS Special Products, 1990.

200: "Man, he can sing!": Interview with Carl Perkins, 1993.

200: "I really like that voice": Ibid.

200: "It was a killer": Ibid.

200–201: "Man, if I looked as good as you do": Ibid.

201–202: Road trips were enlivened by the mind games: Ibid.

203: "For the ear he is an utterable bore": *New York Times,* June 6, 1956.

203: "He can't sing a lick": *New York Journal-American,* June 9, 1956.

203: "the colored folks been singing it": *Charlotte Observer,* 1956.

203: "It's a lucky thing for me": *Rock 'N' Roll Jamboree,* fall 1956.

203–204: Robert Patterson announced the formation of the first White Citizens' Council: Goldfield, *Black, White and Southern: Race Relations and Southern Culture 1940 to the Present.*

204: Enter Asa (Earl) Carter: McMillen, *The Citizens' Council: Organized Resistance to the Second Reconstruction, 1954–1964.*

204–205: Nat King Cole was the most prominent victim: Hemming and Hadju, *Discovering the Great Singers of Classic Pop.*

205: His path crossed that of Asa Earl Carter's: McMillen, *The Citizens' Council.*

205: "a vicious agitator": Ibid.

205: "I'm interested in doing something positive": Ibid.

205–206: In the late spring of '56, Carl had difficulties: Interview with Carl Perkins, 1993.

206: A few days later he had a similar small town run-in: Ibid.

206: "I knew what they were": Interview with Carl Perkins, 1993.

207: Through ignorance or the passage of time: Tosches, *Country.*

207–208: Elvis's even caught the attention of the Federal Bureau of Investigation: Correspondence to J. Edgar Hoover from the *La Crosse Registi* is contained in Presley's FBI file, obtained by the author in 1993 through the Freedom of Information Act. The file also contains reviews of and commentary regarding Presley's performance from the *La Crosse Tribune,* May 15, 1956.

208–209: It was a common practice for kids to line up backstage for autographs: Interview with Carl Perkins, 1993.

209: "I've signed their bodies all over": Ibid.

209–210: "I took my marriage vows very seriously": Ibid.

210: "Somebody's gonna shoot me from the audience": Ibid.

210: "It was the ultimate, top money": Ibid.

210–213: Ibid.

213–214: "Annapolis city and Anne Arundel county police": *Billboard,* July 28, 1956.

214: "He is a sincere, down-to-earth fellow": *Song Hits,* September 1956.

214: "There is still room in country music for good new artists": *Hit Parader,* June 1956.

214–215: "Presley had done knocked the nation cross-eyed": Interview with Carl Perkins, 1993.

215–216: Chuck Berry: DeCurtis and Henke, *The Rolling Stone Album Guide,* Miller, *The Rolling Stone Illustrated History of Rock & Roll.*

216: "I knew when I first heard Chuck that he'd been affected by country music": Interview with Carl Perkins, 1993.

216: "You know, I thought you was one of us": Interview with Carl Perkins, 1993; interview with Chuck Berry, 1993.

216: Jimmie Rodgers was one of his favorites: Ibid.

216: "Chuck knew every Blue Yodel": Ibid.

216: "a solid country rockin' tune": *Billboard,* September 6, 1956.

217: "Dixie carries too much in its lyrics": *Hillbilly and Western Scrapbook,* January 1957.

217: "For its day it was a little bit too dark": Interview with Carl Perkins, 1993.

217: The Sun check was for an amount: Interviews with Carl Perkins, 1993; Valda Perkins, 1994; Ed Cisco, 1994.

218: Valda thought something was amiss: Interview with Valda Perkins, 1994.

218: Sam had deducted the price of the Cadillac: Interviews with Carl Perkins, 1993; Valda Perkins, 1994; Ed Cisco, 1994.

218: "The accounting Sam Phillips gave": Interview with Valda Perkins, 1994.

218: "Look, it's your money": Ibid.

218: "I didn't feel right to question Sam": Interview with Carl Perkins, 1994.

218: He made a $10,000 down payment on a house: Ibid.

218–219: "It was brick and it had trees": Ibid.

219–220: Account of Grand Ole Opry appearance from an interview with Carl Perkins, 1993.

220: Buck Perkins, making what would be his only appearance: Interview with Carl Perkins, 1993.

220–221: A piano player from Ferriday, Louisiana, named Jerry Lee Lewis: Background on Lewis from Escott with Hawkins, *Good Rockin' Tonight.*

221: "I got an ol' boy down here that can beat a damn piano up": Interview with Carl Perkins, 1993.

221: Account of "Your True Love" recording from interview with Carl Perkins, 1993.

221–222: Account of "Matchbox"'s origin and session from interview with Carl Perkins, 1993.

222: Blind Lemon Jefferson, a towering figure as a blues guitarist: DeCurtis and Henke, *The Rolling Stone Album Guide.*

223–225: Account of session and reflections from interview with Carl Perkins, 1993.

225: Elvis walked into the studio: Ibid.

225: "They had glamorized what was there": Ibid.

226: "We're sort of in the same business": Ibid.

226–227: Account of session from interview with Carl Perkins, 1993.

227: "We may never have these people together again": From Colin Escott's liner notes for *The Million Dollar Quartet* album, RCA, 1990.

227: Johnny Cash had dropped by: Cash's participation in the Million Dollar Quartet session is in dispute. Cash, in an interview from 1994, said he was there for the entire session, but was too far off mic to be heard ("RCA's been trying to write me out of that story," Cash told me); Carl, in an interview in 1993 and a follow-up in 1994, stood by the long-held account that Cash left before the tape rolled.

227: Sam called the *Press-Scimitar*'s Robert Johnson: Escott with Hawkins, *Good Rockin' Tonight.*

227–230: Account of Million Dollar Quartet session, with song selection and the artists' repartee is taken directly from *The Million Dollar Quartet* album, RCA, 1990.

229: "Elvis was affected by Wilson": Interview with Carl Perkins, 1993.

230: Before the tape rolled, Elvis had talked: Ibid.

230: "We shouldn't have been booked in there": Interview with Scotty Moore, 1994.

231–232: Carl enjoyed recording other writers' songs: Interview with Carl Perkins, 1993.

234: "I should have been drug out onto Union Avenue": Ibid.

234–235: "a swingy blues": *Billboard,* February 16, 1957.

235: "Both sides should grab off plenty": Ibid.

235: "youthful sounding": Ibid.

235–236: (his publishing contract gave him the right . . .): Carl's publishing contract is among the papers filed in his lawsuit against Sam Phillips in Chancery Court of Shelby County, 1977.

236: He wasn't making $1,000 a day anymore: Interview with Carl Perkins, 1993.

236–239: Account of being on the road with Jerry Lee and reflections from interview with Carl Perkins, 1993.

239: Cash continuing to inspire Clayton: Interviews with Carl Perkins, 1993; Johnny Cash, 1994.

239: Even Cash was fair game: Ibid.

239: Carl felt their conduct reflected poorly on everyone: Interview with Carl Perkins, 1993.

239–240: Cash would shrug off the more destructive episodes: Interview with Johnny Cash, 1994.

240: Carl . . . would start slugging it out with Clayton: Interviews with Carl Perkins, 1993; Johnny Cash, 1994; Ed Cisco, 1994.

240: Jay had not been himself: Ibid.

240: Cash would purchase his own box of St. Joseph's: Interviews with Carl Perkins, 1993; Johnny Cash, 1994.

240–241: Cash had been introduced to amphetamines: Johnny Cash, *Man in Black.*

241: "West Coast turnaround": Interviews with Carl Perkins, 1993; Johnny Cash, 1994.

241–243: Writing and recording of "That's Right": Ibid.

244–245: Elvis came by the studio: Interview with Carl Perkins, 1993.

245: "Man, I want to stay home": Ibid.

246–248: Carl and Cash helped effect a startling transformation: Interviews with Carl Perkins, 1990, 1993; Johnny Cash, 1994.

248–250: A case in point: Interview with Carl Perkins, 1993.

250–251: After a late July appearance on Steve Allen's television show: Escott with Hawkins, *Good Rockin' Tonight.*

251: Carl's and Jerry Lee's paths crossed again: Interview with Carl Perkins, 1993.

252: "Glad All Over" was the beginning of the end: Ibid.

252: Law offered Carl and Cash recording deals: Escott with Hawkins, *Good Rockin' Tonight;* interviews with Carl Perkins, 1993; Johnny Cash, 1994.

252–253: The two men drove all over Memphis: Interview with Carl Perkins, 1993.

253: "I had given [Carl and Johnny] a lot of time": Escott with Hawkins, *Good Rockin' Tonight.*

253: Cash has a more complex answer: Interview with Johnny Cash, 1994.

▶ RESTLESS, 1958–1980

261: Quonset Hut: Interview with Owen Bradley, 1994.

261: "give me another 'Shoes' ": Interview with Carl Perkins, 1993.

262: it was only partly Carl's song: Interviews with Carl Perkins, 1993; Martha Perkins Bain, 1994.

263: "I had to do four songs in three hours": Interview with Carl Perkins, 1993.

263: "[Don Law] was a wonderful man": Ibid.

265: "The Gibson had a much better sound for what [Carl] was doing": Roland Jones quoted by Colin Escott in "Nashville Calling," a summary of Carl Perkins's Columbia years published in the booklet accompanying *The Classic Carl Perkins* five-CD boxed set, Bear Family Records.

265: "I'd be up at the old James Robinson Hotel": Interview with Mel Tillis, 1994.

265–266: "We'd leave the studio to drive back to Jackson": Interview with Ed Cisco, 1994.

267: the manufacture of hundreds of pairs of pointed-toe suede shoes: Interviews with Carl Perkins, 1993; Ed Cisco, 1994.

267: he gave serious thought to backing out of his Columbia deal: Interview with Carl Perkins, 1993.

267–268: A new decade was ushered in with a federal inquiry: Miller, *The Rolling Stone Illustrated History of Rock & Roll.*

270: In 1957 Roy Orbison fulfilled his pledge to marry Claudette: Escott with Hawkins, *Good Rockin' Tonight.*

271: Roy and Carl remained close: Interviews with Carl Perkins, 1993; Valda Perkins, 1994; Stan Perkins, 1993.

272–274: In the fall of 1958 . . . Carl suffered a blow: Interviews with Carl Perkins, 1993; Valda Perkins, 1994; Martha Perkins Bain, 1994; Ed Cisco, 1994.

274: One of Jay's first visitors: Interview with Johnny Cash, 1994.

274–276: In mid-October . . . : Interviews with Carl Perkins, 1993; Valda Perkins, 1994; Martha Perkins Bain, 1994; Ed Cisco, 1994.

276: Johnny Cash organized a benefit concert: Interviews with Carl Perkins, 1993; Johnny Cash, 1994; Ed Cisco, 1994.

276–277: Various news blurbs: "Ranch Party," October 11, 1958; *Billboard,* June 1, 1959; *Billboard,* August 17, 1959.

277: "only when I got hungry": Interview with Carl Perkins, 1993.

277: Fluke Holland left the band: Interviews with Carl Perkins, 1993; Johnny Cash, 1994.

277: Mann had a top-30 hit: Escott with Hawkins, *Good Rockin' Tonight.*

277–278: Holland decided to leave the music business: Interviews with Carl Perkins, 1993; Johnny Cash, 1994; W.S. Holland interviewed by Bill Way on "Area Code 901," WBBJ-TV, Jackson, Tennessee, January 12, 1993.

278: Carl began drinking at home: Interviews with Carl Perkins, 1993; Valda Perkins, 1994; Martha Perkins Bain, 1994.

278: "I was never afraid of him.": Interview with Valda Perkins, 1994.

278–279: Stan . . . feared his father's wrath: Interviews with Carl Perkins, 1993; Valda Perkins, 1994; Stan Perkins, 1994.

279: Carl would disappear: Interviews with Carl Perkins, 1994; Valda Perkins, 1993.

279: "I'd get mad": Interview with Carl Perkins, 1993.

279: Every day he visited Jay's grave: Ibid.

281–282: Carl visited Jim Denny: Interviews with Carl Perkins, 1993; Valda Perkins, 1994; Bill Denny, 1994.

282: "studied, pretty well written, and well constructed": Interview with Carl Perkins, 1994.

282: recorded under the name C.D. Cedar: Interviews with Carl Perkins, 1993; Valda Perkins, 1994; Bill Denny, 1994.

282–283: Les Paul: Interviews with Carl Perkins, 1993; Les Paul, 1994; John Denny, 1994.

283: "Carl was in the back room": Interview with Les Paul, 1994.

283: Jim Denny was also responsible: Interviews with Carl Perkins, 1993; Valda Perkins, 1994; Bill Denny, 1994.

283: "You get paid half": Interview with Carl Perkins, 1993.

284: When Denny checked with BMI: Ibid.

284: "The music industry to me": Interview with Bill Denny, 1994.

285: he was still Clayton: Interview with Carl Perkins, 1993.

285–286: Clayton had taken to singing: Ibid.

286: Patsy Cline: Interviews with Carl Perkins, 1993; Owen Bradley, 1994.

286: two-week package tour: Interview with Carl Perkins, 1993; essay for Patsy Cline boxed set, MCA Records, 1992.

286–287: "You better watch that boy": Interview with Carl Perkins, 1993.

287: Cline brought her mother to see Carl's show: Interview with Carl Perkins, 1993.

287: teased Carl about his singing: Ibid.

288: "Perkins! Whose song is that?": Ibid.

288: He gave the unfinished song to Mel Tillis: Interviews with Carl Perkins, 1993; Mel Tillis, 1994.

288: To Owen Bradley the "So Wrong" session stands out: Interview with Owen Bradley, 1994.

288–289: "I never worked with a greater lady": Interview with Carl Perkins, 1993.

289: "It wasn't something I'd rush to see again": Interview with Carl Perkins, 1993.

289–292: Clayton's behavior had taken an ugly turn: Ibid.

292–293: Carl signed a two-year deal with Decca: Interviews with Carl Perkins, 1993; Owen Bradley, 1994; Bill Denny, 1994.

293: duet album with Brenda Lee: Interview with Owen Bradley, 1994.

294: "Carl was having a problem with alcohol": Interview with Bill Denny, 1994.

294: "I always felt badly about Carl not making it": Interview with Harold Bradley, 1994.

294: "Carl would leave it all up to me": Interview with Owen Bradley, 1994.

295: "Carl is unique": Interview with Johnny Cash, 1994.

295: "You'll never stop playing music": Interview with Valda Perkins, 1994.

295: The English rock fans embraced Carl: Bill Millar, essay, "The Decca Years," published in booklet accompanying *The Classic Carl Perkins* five-CD boxed set, Bear Family Records.

295: "Them boys could use haircuts": Interview with Stan Perkins, 1993.

295–296: Carl Harrison: *Guitar Player.*

296: "You don't know just how happy": from booklet accompanying *The Classic Carl Perkins* five-CD boxed set, Bear Family Records.

297: Prison had changed Chuck Berry: Interview with Carl Perkins, 1993.

297–299: Account of recording session with Beatles: Interview with Carl Perkins, 1993.

298: Beatles recorded five takes of "Matchbox": Lewisohn, *The Beatles Recording Sessions.*

298: "I'll Be Back" in sixteen takes: Ibid.

299: blades . . . tore through Carl's hand: Interview with Carl Perkins, 1993.

300: "My spirit left my body": Ibid.

300–301: Account of Carl's injury, surgery, and rehabilitation from interviews with Carl Perkins, 1993; Valda Perkins, 1994.

301: Carl's left foot was nearly severed: Interview with Carl Perkins, 1993.

301–302: visited by Johnny Cash: Interviews with Carl Perkins, 1993; Valda Perkins, 1994; Johnny Cash, 1994.

301–302: "Biscuits! Meat! Eggs!": Interview with Valda Perkins, 1994.

303: They could and did try to support each other in getting straight: Interviews with Carl Perkins, 1993; Johnny Cash, 1994.

303: "I picked up some wisdom from that book": Interview with Carl Perkins, 1993.

303–304: In a generous portrait: *Rolling Stone*, December 7, 1968.

304: Signed with Dollie: Interviews with Carl Perkins, 1993; Bill Denny, 1994; John Denny, 1994.

304: Plagued by poor distribution: Interview with Bill Denny, 1994.

305: "The simplicity in Carl's music came through": Interview with John Denny, 1994.

305–306: a sixty-six-acre farm near Clarksburg, Tennessee: Interviews with Carl Perkins, 1993; Ed Cisco, 1994.

306: "Well, you don't know what this means to me": Interview with Carl Perkins, 1993.

306: "For one time in my mama and daddy's life": Ibid.

306–308: Cash was over the edge: Interviews with Carl Perkins, 1993; Johnny Cash, 1994.

308: Carl was keeping up by drinking beer: Interview with Carl Perkins, 1993.

308: "We knew what Carl was feeling": Interview with Harold Reid, 1993.

308: "They're crazy": Interview with Jerry Kennedy, 1993.

308: Phil Balsley sitting there in a chair: Interview with Phil Balsley, 1993.

308–309: Snappy Simmons: Interview with Harold Reid, 1993.

309: Carl . . . left town drunk: Interview with Carl Perkins, 1993.

309–310: "John, I can't go out there": Interviews with Carl Perkins, 1993; Johnny Cash, 1994.

310: "four or five of me in the mirror": Interview with Carl Perkins, 1993.

312: he began developing a taste for screwdrivers: Ibid.

312: "We know the story": Interview with Harold Reid, 1993.

312: "He was standing way down there": Interview with Johnny Cash, 1994.

313–315: Writing of "Daddy Sang Bass": Interviews with Carl Perkins, 1993; Johnny Cash, 1994.

315: He was re-signed to the label by Larry Butler: Interview with Bill Denny, 1994.

316: "My guitar playing on 'Restless' ": Interview with Carl Perkins, 1993.

317–318: Account of writing "Champaign, Illinois" with Bob Dylan from interviews with Carl Perkins, 1993; Bob Dylan, 1994.

318: "I could've done it before I started playing folk music": Interview with Bob Dylan, 1994.

319: "To me [Carl] looked like he was in his prime": Ibid.

319: "He really stood for freedom": Ibid.

320: Peter Guralnick praised Carl: *Rolling Stone*, 1970.

320–321: In late 1968, Carl had accompanied the Cash troupe on a tour of the Far East: Interviews with Carl Perkins, 1993; Johnny Cash, 1994.

321–322: Details of Carl Perkins Day from interviews with Carl Perkins, 1993; Valda Perkins, 1994; *The Jackson Sun*, February 3, 1969.

321–322: "I had a brilliant little boy in my class": Interviews with Carl Perkins, 1993; Valda Perkins, 1994.

322: "She bent down": Interview with Carl Perkins, 1993.

323: "I can remember gettin' with Carl": Interview with Jerry Kennedy, 1993.

323: "was the closest stuff to Memphis that Carl had experienced": Interview with Harold Bradley, 1993.

325: "my kind of country.": Interviews with Carl Perkins, 1993; Jerry Kennedy, 1993.

326: "We took time to cut it right": Interview with Carl Perkins, 1993.

326: "They were the best we had done on three labels": Interview with Harold Bradley, 1993.

326: "E.P. Express" was breaking on the country chart: Interviews with Carl Perkins, 1993; Jerry Kennedy, 1993.

326: "There wasn't any need in us sittin' ": Interview with Carl Perkins, 1993.

326: Bill Denny sold Cedarwood: Interview with Bill Denny, 1994.

327: "Time's run out for Perkins": *Melody Maker*, March 25, 1978.

328: "creating an industry with his songs": Interview with Bill Denny, 1994.

328–329: "He lived the life of a hobo": Interview with Carl Perkins, 1993.

329: "He was not threatening me": Ibid.

329–330: Airport scene reconstructed through interviews with Carl Perkins, 1993; Johnny Cash, 1994.

330: "I just got in a frozen state of mind": Interview with Carl Perkins, 1993.

330: Greg . . . and Stan . . . found the body: Interviews with Greg and Stan Perkins, 1993; Carl Perkins, 1993; Valda Perkins, 1994.

330–331: Carl went so far as to hire a private detective: Interviews with Carl Perkins, 1993; Valda Perkins, 1994.

331: "The bullet hole in his T-shirt": Interview with Carl Perkins, 1993.

331: "I felt there would be a tragedy": Interview with Valda Perkins, 1994.

331: Cash offered to come off the road: Interviews with Carl Perkins, 1993; Johnny Cash, 1994.

332–333: Account of Buck Perkins's demise from interviews with Carl Perkins, 1993; Valda Perkins, 1994.

334: "There's an old saying": Interview with Carl Perkins, 1993.

334: "I stayed out there": Ibid.

335: Cash's brother Tommy was having personal problems: Interviews with Carl Perkins, 1993; Johnny Cash, 1994.

335–336: 'I had it in mind that we'd be just buddies and partners": Interview with Johnny Cash, 1994.

336–337: Background on Stan and Greg Perkins from interviews with the principals, 1993.

337: "I just knew music was in them boys' blood": Interview with Carl Perkins, 1993.

337–338: "You want your children to grow up decent": Interview with Greg Perkins, 1993.

338: "When we first started out": Interview with Stan Perkins, 1993.

338–339: "I knew the talent in my dad": Interview with Greg Perkins, 1993.

339: "Man, them boys know where I'm goin' ": Interview with Carl Perkins, 1993.

339: "if a man lives long enough": Interview with Carl Perkins, 1990.

340, 342–345: Account of *Carl Perkins, Plaintiff v. Samuel C. Phillips, Defendant*, taken from documents filed in Chancery Court of Shelby County, and from interviews with Carl Perkins, 1993; Valda Perkins, 1994; Stan Chernau, 1994.

340–342: Account of confrontation between Sam Phillips and Carl Perkins referred to in November 1977 response from interview with Carl Perkins, 1993.

343: "The allegations you're making": Interviews with Carl Perkins, 1993; Stan Chernau, 1994.

343: "I sure like the last way you said that": Ibid.

344: Stanley Chernau . . . threatened yet another lawsuit: Ibid.

345: "Daddy, did you hear about Elvis?": Interviews with Carl Perkins, 1993; Greg and Stan Perkins, 1993.

345–346: Carl had made a trip to Graceland: Interview with Carl Perkins, 1993.

▶HOME, 1981–PRESENT

349–352: Account of formation of Exchange Club Carl Perkins Center for the Prevention of Child Abuse: Interviews with Carl Perkins, 1993; Jim Bailey, 1993, 1994; Pam Nash, 1993; Valda Perkins, 1994.

351: Most of the Center's children are under twelve years of age: Interviews with Carl Perkins, 1993; Pam Nash, 1993.

351: "Are you tellin' me": Interview with Carl Perkins, 1993.

351: The first telethon: Interviews with Carl Perkins, 1993; Pam Nash, 1993.

352: The first $64,000: Interview with Pam Nash, 1993.

352: The building is erected: Interview with Carl Perkins, 1994.

353–354: Carl had mixed feelings about Twitty: Interview with Carl Perkins, 1993.

354: Stilts's introduction to Carl: Interview with Ken Stilts, 1993.

354: "Carl recognized that this was unique": Ibid.

354–355: "Carl called me Mama": Interview with Naomi Judd, 1994.

356: "a lovefest": Interview with Johnny Cash, 1994.

356: "One of the best weeks of my life": Interview with Carl Perkins, 1993.

357: "There's two or three times I could've killed Jerry Lee": Ibid.

357–358: "On the planet Earth": Interview with Marty Stuart, 1994.

358: he arranged to interview Carl: Ibid.

358: "Carl's timeless": Ibid.

358–359: "This box has got some songs in it": Ibid.; interview with Carl Perkins, 1993.

360: a dispute between Moman and the parent company's New York executives: Interview with Carl Perkins, 1993.

360: "You're the man": Ibid.

361: "So much sadness": Ibid.

361: "I'd heard his name": Ibid.

362–363: Conversation with Roy Orbison at Hall of Fame induction: Interview with Carl Perkins, 1993.

363: "He walked in and saw the house": *The Jackson Sun,* October 26, 1987.

363–364: Reunion with Charlie: Interview with Carl Perkins, 1993.

364–365: Final show with Roy Orbison: Interview with Carl Perkins, 1993.

366: Mother and daughter used him as a sounding board: Interview with Naomi Judd, 1994.

368: With Stilts funding demo sessions: Interviews with Carl Perkins, 1993; Ken Stilts, 1993.

368: "I didn't think it was in the groove": Interview with Ken Stilts, 1993.

368: Carl asked out of his management deal: Interviews with Carl Perkins, 1993; Ken Stilts, 1994.

368: "as fine a guy": Interview with Carl Perkins, 1993.

369: "Carl is such a sentimental person": Interview with Ken Stilts, 1993.

369–371: Account of writing "Silver and Gold": Interview with Carl Perkins, 1993.

371: The deal had been negotiated by Stan Vincent: Interview with Stan Vincent, 1993.

372: "Carl would come in occasionally": Ibid.

372: "I was in the control booth": Interview with Greg Perkins, 1993.

373: "at times Carl's color didn't look quite right": Interview with Valda Perkins, 1994.

373: made an appointment with Dr. Larry Carruth: Interview with Carl Perkins, 1993.

374: "Carl might not be alive": Interview with Dr. James Netterville, 1993.

374: "Somebody as famous as Carl": Ibid.

374: "Drinking and smoking are the main causes": Ibid.

374: a standard regimen: Interview with Dr. William Permenter, 1993.

375: "I knew you were going to ask that": Interviews with Dr. William Permenter, 1993; Carl Perkins, 1993.

375: side effects of radiation: Interviews with Dr. William Permenter, 1993; Dr. James Netterville, 1993.

375–376: "My throat was afire": Interview with Carl Perkins, 1993.

376: the love of his family: Ibid.

376–377: "Dad would come down to the studio": Interview with Stan Perkins, 1993.

377: "I sent him some books": Interview with Naomi Judd, 1994.

377: Valda put on the best face she could: Interview with Valda Perkins, 1994.

378: "Carl was very emotional": Interview with Dr. James Netterville, 1993.

379: During seven and a half weeks of radiation: Interviews with Carl Perkins, 1993; Valda Perkins, 1994; Dr. William Permenter, 1993.

379–380: City of Hope telethon: Interviews with Carl Perkins, 1993; Pam Nash, 1993.

380: "When I had cancer": Interview with Carl Perkins, 1993.

381: Wynonna's request: Interview with Naomi Judd, 1994.

381: "Carl taps into the deepest levels": Ibid.

381: Stan Vincent organized a reception: Interview with Stan Vincent, 1993.

381–382: It was Bob Dylan: Interviews with Carl Perkins, 1993; Stan Vincent, 1993; Bob Dylan, 1994.

382: "It was kinda like something you give somebody": Interview with Bob Dylan, 1994.

382: "Carl looked good": Ibid.

383–384: Elvis Presley tribute show reconstructed from interviews with Carl Perkins, 1993; Stan Perkins, 1993; Valda Perkins, 1994; Pam Nash, 1993.

384: Carl put in another yeoman effort: Interview with Pam Nash, 1993.

385: "It was what I call firin' rockabilly music": Interview with Carl Perkins, 1993.

385: "[The doctor] said": Interview with Carl Perkins, 1993; *The Jackson Sun*, June 18, 1993.

388: "Why would a woman like you": This final scene was witnessed by the author at the conclusion of his twelve-plus hours of interviews with Valda Perkins in the spring of 1994.

INDEX

SONG PERMISSIONS AND CREDITS